The People Factor is Now Regarded as the Most Important Driver of Business Success

Managers and leaders have been faced with significant challenges as a consequence of the Global Financial Crisis (GFC), the full ramifications of which are still yet to be played out. It is contended that this crisis will leave an indelible foot print, including a more strategic and authentic focus on people, who are a real source of sustainable profits.

The people factor is now regarded as the most important driver of business success, yet according to surveys of CEOs, it is one of the least effectively managed corporate functions, with many HR functions typically disparate. Employees and workers now come in all shapes and sizes - one size doesn't fit all! With this increased complexity there is a need to adopt more sophisticated approaches to managing human capital and developing workforce strategies which are closely aligned with business strategies (often there is a disconnect between the two). This people management challenge is not simply a HR issue. It is a business strategy issue where Company Directors, CEOs, CFOs and Executives will inevitably become involved.

This book is a must read for executives, managers, leaders and HR professionals seeking to maximize the flexibility and commitment of their workforce, while at the same time, attracting, developing and retaining valuable skills. It offers some contemporary and innovative human capital models, including the measurement and reporting of human capital. It is sprinkled with case studies, balancing the practical with the latest empirical research.

About this Book

For directors, senior managers and even HR professionals, coming to grips with the volume of research and information on organisation and people management is daunting. Colin Beames takes complex, emergent and critical subjects and presents them in a way that is readily grasped by the reader. This book is timely, given the aftermath of the Global Financial Crisis, which has caused discontinuities to our previous thinking. It provides both frameworks for directors and CEOs, and detail for executives, each trying to understand and answer questions of how best to manage the entity's human capital. Colin's book illustrates how contemporary thinking can be applied to provide practical people solutions for this difficult task.

Richard de Lautour, Regional Director, Finance & Administration, Flight Safety Foundation

I always know I am going to get great value from a book when the author has the integrity to include extensive referencing, bibliography, index and each chapter starts with key points.

This work by the Australian author, organisational consultant, thought leader and originally engineer, covers the substantive issues senior HR [illegible] grapple with in trying to improve their organisations

- *Workplace trends and the future workplace*
- *Workforce segmentation*
- *Corporate governance and risk management*
- *Developing, acquiring and disposing of human capital*
- *Engagement and retention*
- *Psychological contract*
- *Measuring and reporting on human capital.*

As HR professionals we are currently either wading or drowning though the immediate effects of the Global Financial Crisis or contemplating what might be our people direction in the period following. Beames' approach to human capital and workforce segmentation will provide hearty food for thought and an appetite to once again engage in those senior management discussions about the best way forward and the place human capital plays in organisational success.

The ever present need to effectively measure and report on the "people factor" and the depth of material on the psychological contract were highlights for me. Beames' engineering and management background means his approach will also be welcomed by the more operationally focused members of our management teams.

A valuable addition to my library of practical, evidence based Australian texts.

Reviewed by Michael Craner for HR Monthly, General Manager Learning & Organisational Development, Boral Ltd

Transforming Organisational Human Capital

Emerging Stronger from the GFC and Beyond

3rd Edition

Colin Beames

3rd Edition

Typeset by BookPOD

Cover Design by Andrew Tesdorpf

Cover photograph: iStock Photo

Printed and bound in Australia by BookPOD

ISBN: 978-0-9806442-2-7 (paperback)

ISBN: 978-0-9872815-2-4 (e-book)

Contents

Introduction

ACKNOWLEDGEMENTS

Relationships are fundamentally important, both in personal life, business and the workplace. It is through relationships that we experience the full aspects of life, grow and develop. One of the key paradigms underpinning this book and the approach to building sustainable organisations is relational. More specifically, the Workplace Relationship Development Indicator (WRDI®) – the employee engagement and retention tool that I have developed and commercialised, is based on a relationship (or psychological contract) model. From the perspective of employees, the employment relationship is for many, the closest, longest-lasting and most enduring relationship of their lives, aside from marriage or equivalent.

Relationships have constituted an integral part of my journey in writing this book, with many people assisting me along the way. The concepts and ideas that are incorporated in it have been formed, honed and prioritised from a range of sources – academics, researchers, writers, consultants/licensees, clients, friends, associates, colleagues and various others. Authors and academics who have been particularly influential include: Frank Crowther, Bert Cunnington, David Guest, Douglas T. Hall, David Limerick, David Lepak, Denise Rousseau and Scott Snell.

There are a number of people whom I would like to acknowledge and thank for their contribution, assistance, and encouragement. They are in alphabetical order: Georgina Beames, Mark Bloodworth, Jim Bowden, Geoff Cheong, Ray Cooksey, John Cooksey, Stephen Cox, Richard de Lautour, Dan Evans, Lyndall Garrett, David Little, Peter Macqueen, Peter McClenaghan, Chris Patty, Geoff Smith, Warren Smith, Sebastian Salicru, Tony Swords, Michelle Tan, Peter Tan, Pamela Wakefield-Semmens, David Willcox and Mike Webb. Other people to thank include my network of WRDI® licensees (i.e., consultants who have been accredited in their use of the WRDI® tool), clients and prospective clients.

In particular, there are two people deserving of special mention concerning their assistance. Firstly Adam Lowe who is a remarkable young person with wisdom and maturity that belies his age. Adam is the embodiment of the new age employee. He has an unusual but complimentary combination of skills and knowledge which include, amongst other things, IT expertise and qualifications in psychology and in ministry. Adam has assisted with web site development, programming, technical issues and general advice in the integration of business models with IT functionality. I am grateful that I can count Adam as a respected and trusted colleague, advisor and friend.

Secondly and ultimately, the person deserving of the most thanks is my wife Jan, who has supported me in every possible way during my journey. The term "soul mate" is often a much abused one, but in Jan's case, one which is deeply applicable. She has been a "true believer", living through the evolution, development and commercialistion phases of the intellectual property that I have developed. She has been able to effectively deal with the uncertainty of it all, accepting of my limitations, cajoling me when warranted, encouraging me when I was down, and helping me deal with the frustrations and disappointments, all without knowing or having any guarantees of the ultimate outcome. I could not have done this without her support.

ABOUT THIS BOOK

I.1 THE IMPACT OF THE GLOBAL FINANCIAL CRISIS (GFC)

An indelible footprint

Leaders and managers have been confronted with many challenges as a consequence of the Global Financial Crisis (GFC), the longer term effects of which are still yet to be played out. Like any crisis, the GFC has provided a catalyst for breaking ingrained structures and behaviours. It is contended that the GFC has left, and will continue to leave, an indelible foot print including:

- The end of "short termism" and quick get rich schemes that do not generate sustainable profits
- Consolidation (i.e., belt tightening), with a greater emphasis on long-term value creation and sustainability, given lower growth rates
- A higher level of conservatism, with an increased focus on assessing and mitigating risk, and more stringent corporate governance
- Greater transparency and increased shareholder activism
- An overhaul of compensation systems to align executives' pays with sustainable profits, including the removal of obscene bonuses
- A more strategic and authentic focus on people, who are a real source of sustainable profits.

> Note: An alternative term for the Global Financial Crisis is the Giant Financial Correction given the unsustainable growth rates that were experienced over the preceding years.

From the frying pan into the fire!

Whilst many organisations have acted with restraint, others in an environment of uncertainty, fear and panic, have acted impulsively with uncoordinated responses that have conceivably made things worse. You may well recognise these examples of such non-strategic workforce decisions below.

- A knee jerk "slash and burn" reaction to labour cost cutting, according to some arbitrary percentage decrease in head count where the cuts are spread evenly throughout the organisation, has resulted in the wrong people being retrenched. Those in more critical, specialist or core roles should have been retained where possible.

- Outsourcing indiscriminately (e.g., customer facing roles), has resulted in the loss of relationship capital (i.e., between the organisation and its clients), and the loss of critical skills, intellectual property and control, all of which has resulted in a remoteness from the "coal face".
- *Ad hoc* removal of employee benefits (e.g., chopping flexible work practices) at a time when organisations are seeking to "do more with less", which have been counterproductive.
- A blanket approach to employing new recruits on short-term contract arrangements, which is less likely to have attracted talent or maximised their retention, bearing in mind that the skills shortage will still be ongoing.
- A recruitment freeze which has resulted in a neglect of critical roles, or a drop in performance through the redeployment of unsuitable people into vacant roles.
- A "peanut butter" approach to salary cuts (i.e., spread evenly which constitutes a failure to differentiate), which has encouraged key talent and high performers to look elsewhere.

> Note: Critical or core roles typically require the acquisition of unique knowledge of the business, so people in these roles are not easily replaced. Most probably there has been substantial earlier investment in the training and development of people in these roles. Hence the loss of people in these roles has much more significant cost implications compared to people in other roles.

The dangers of downsizing, and in particular the adverse secondary impacts which include increased turnover in subsequent years, are dealt with in Chapter 5 of this book. Suffice to say, those organisations that have recently downsized may well be sitting on a "ticking time bomb" regarding retention of their key talent down the track.

For those organisations that have exercised restraint and have consulted with their workers concerning medium term sacrifices (e.g., reduced working hours, salary freezes, compulsory leave, extra effort, etc.), the question is to what extent working conditions will revert back to the *status quo* or business as usual, or whether the new norm of restraint has now become the established order.

1.2 SUMMARY OF OVERALL WORKPLACE TRENDS AND THEIR IMPACT

> Note: These trends and their impacts are dealt with more comprehensively in Chapter 1.

Employment landscape and workplace trends

Apart from the impacts of the GFC, there are also a number of factors that will shape the workplace of the future. Demographic, organisational, individual, market, environmental and social trends will all add to the complexities of workforce management, posing significant challenges for executives in the workplace of the future. Whilst one is cautious about predicting this future, it is likely that the workplace will be generally characterised by increasing volatility and uncertainty, which has implications for organisations as to how to best manage their workforce.

Overall, there is likely to be an ongoing shortage of talent and skills, and an excess of labour. However this supply and demand equation (i.e., the influence of labour market forces), will vary across industry sectors and geographical locations, both globally and locally. Power shift fluctuations between employers and various categories of employees (depending on the skills and value that they add), will be a defining characteristic of the workplace of the future.

Summary of the impacts on organisations and employees

Organisations will still "want to have their cake and eat it" by building a workforce that is flexible, accessible, skilled, aligned, committed, efficiently deployed and retained. They will shift, or attempt to shift, even more of the risk (i.e., maximize workforce flexibility), across to employees/workers through:

- Outsourcing
- Use of contingent workers (e.g., casuals, part-timers, temps, contractors, consultants)
- Offering shorter term employment contracts.

Employees will continue to come in all shapes and sizes (one size won't fit all), and organisations will continue to adopt a variety of employment modes (or psychological contracts) from longer term relational to shorter term transactional modes. A key strategic workforce question is: *What combination of these various employment modes leads to a sustainable competitive advantage for a particular organisation?*

On the other side of the coin, individuals will have to be prepared to invest more in their own training and development, continuously upgrade their skills, as well as self-manage their careers by taking greater control over their own destiny. The latter includes managing transitions and developing the "soft skills" (e.g., resilience and relationship building), to ride out the "white water turbulence".

1.3 LEGITIMACY FOR CHANGE HAS PROVIDED NEW OPPORTUNITIES

Notwithstanding the above impacts, the post GFC economic climate has provided an opportunity for CEOs and executives to draw breath – not only in respect to the people issues, but in every aspect of the business. It has provided them with a legitimacy for change, and possibly the pursuit of new opportunities. For example, these opportunities have involved discarding unsustainable business models, restructuring, outsourcing peripheral or non-core activities, discarding non-profitable products and services, etc. Whatever the case, the impact of the GFC has triggered a rethink of workforce strategies and the management of human capital, consistent with both the short and long term needs of the business.

Thus there have been the challenges posed from the changing external circumstances, as well as the challenges of within and how to best respond, including the capability to do so. Responding appropriately, from a people management perspective, is fundamentally about making the right people choices. These choices or decisions in turn are underpinned by people mindsets. To that end, a fundamental question arises: *Do you view people as an asset to be developed or a cost to be minimized?* We shall explore the answer(s) to this question later on in Chapters 3 and 4.

1.4 SOME KEY WORKFORCE QUESTIONS FOR CONSIDERATION

Against this background, some key workforce questions that you may consider asking about your organisation include the following.

Business and workforce strategies:

- *Are your business and workforce strategies really aligned?*
- *Do you know what is the differentiating capability of your organisation (i.e., that is critical to its success and which separates it from your competitors)?*
- *What are the key competencies of your organisation that continually need to be developed, and which are vital to its sustainability and success?*

- *Do you have the optimum mix of permanents and contingent workers to achieve a competitive advantage through people?*
- *Are you clear about your employment strategies concerning "make" (i.e., develop from within), versus "buy" (i.e., acquire from the market, including outsourcing) decisions?*
- *Do you really know which are your critical roles?*
- *Are your investments in people aligned to their various contributions and value to the organisation?*

Workforce segmentation and Employment Value Propositions (EVPs):

- *Does a "one size fit all" approach apply to your people management policies and practices or have you adopted a more differentiated approach?*
- *What configurations of staffing, training, appraisal and reward practices are appropriate to employees/workers embodied within your various employment modes (i.e., from permanents to contingents)?*
- *What kind of Employment Value Propositions (EVPs) or "deals" (i.e., both the tangibles and intangibles), should you be offering to various segments of your workforce?*
- *Are you delivering on the EVP/"deal" or promise?*

Attraction, engagement and retention:

- *How do your "deals" or EVPs link to employee engagement, performance and retention?*
- *Do you have differentiated attraction, engagement and retention strategies for various segments of your workforce, given that one size doesn't fit all, and if so, what is the model that underpins this differentiated approach?*
- *How does the leadership of your organisation relate to employee engagement and retention?*
- *How should you best measure, diagnose and report on employee engagement and retention risk?*
- *Do you have a model and a defined methodology for comprehensively addressing employee engagement and retention risk over the employment life cycle (i.e., from entry or on-boarding through to exit)?*

Organisational and people capability:

- *Are your executives aware of the trends and complexities that will shape the 21st century workplace, and how best to respond to these trends?*
- *Does your organisation have a Human Capital Strategic Plan – a blueprint which demonstrates how it manages or intends to manage its most vital intangible asset – its people?*
- *Against this background, are you concerned about meeting your organisation's strategic and business objectives?*

If you are unclear as to the answers to any of these key questions then this book will assist you in seeking an appropriate way forward.

1.5 THE APPEAL OF THIS BOOK, WHATEVER YOUR ROLE

Depending upon which one of the categories or roles that you fit into below, this book will appeal to you for the following reasons:

- **Company Director** – corporate governance, risk mitigation and organisational capability to deliver desired business outcomes
- **Chief Executive Officer (CEO)** - workforce strategies, organisational capability, risk mitigation, and the management of human capital including its attraction, performance, engagement, development, and retention
- **Chief Financial Officer (CFO)** – allocation of resources, including investments in human capital initiatives
- **General Manager (GM)** – attraction, performance, development and retention
- **Human Resources Director or Human Resources Manager or Human Resources Professional** – enhancing influence within the organisation, becoming more strategic, providing better human capital metrics and reporting, and improving the integration of disparate HR functions, including their alignment with the business strategy
- **Consultant** – enhancing knowledge and awareness of workplace trends and enhancing knowledge of latest human capital research, models, measures and their application
- **Academic/Researcher** – further developing frameworks and models for understanding and researching workplace trends and their impacts, organisations and their people

- **Investor or Analyst** – a better understanding of human capital and its impact on company performance
- **Interested Observer** – making sense of the characteristics and dynamics of the contemporary workplace and what the future may hold
- **Employee/Worker** – gaining some insight into the workplace of the future, what this may mean, and possible actions to be taken.

Your level of interest in the various chapters of this book may vary depending upon your role and orientation. Notwithstanding, you will have a reference book on key contemporary workplace themes, issues and concepts. In the case of Company Directors, CEOs, and executives, you will have a framework of understanding, a basis for asking the right questions concerning the management of human capital in your organisation, and an approach to providing answers to these questions. Whatever the case, it is hoped that this book will assist in deepening your understanding and provide you with some clarity concerning the complexities of the 21st century workplace, and the effective management of human capital.

1.6 KEY ASSUMPTIONS THAT UNDERPIN THIS BOOK

The inspiration and motivation for this book has been drawn from the following assumptions, which are based on the writings and comments of others (including academics and thought leaders), together with my own research and observations.

Emerging employment landscape and workplace trends will result in greater people management complexity

- We are at the beginning of an unprecedented shift in the workforce age distribution, driven by the disproportionate size of the baby boomer generation, increased life expectancy and declining birth rates. This shift, combined with the need for increased skills and higher education levels, is creating and will continue to create, a skills and talent shortage.

- Notwithstanding this skills shortage and the extent and depth of the GFC, we will experience an oversupply of labour (i.e., lower skilled workers), at least in the medium term.
- As in the case of our natural resources (e.g., water, energy, oil), there is a greater need to conserve our people (in particular key talent) resources (i.e., to do more with less, eliminate some activities, and find new ways of doing other activities more efficiently).
- Apart from the talent and skills shortage, there are other emerging trends in the employment landscape and workplace, with often competing demands between employers and employees/workers, all of which will add to the complexity of workforce or people management in the 21st century workplace.
- Dealing adequately with this complexity calls for the adoption of new mindsets, more differentiated and sophisticated people management strategies, with better models, measures and methodologies now required to shore up organisations' competitive positions.

The importance of human capital: The largest driver of organisational performance

- There is now a great deal of evidence that the contribution of people is the largest driver of organisational performance (CIPD, 2003). Human capital costs comprise between 30-80% of the cost base of organisations, depending upon the business sector or industry. The management of human capital is now emerging as a powerful management concept which is creeping up the corporate agenda.

> Note: The cost of the HR function is typically around 0.3% of the total operating costs of an organisation so the leveraging potential of HR is enormous.

- Global warming and the impact of the GFC aside, the next decade and beyond will be very much about the management of human capital, with human capabilities determining winners and losers in tomorrow's global markets.
- Employees now come in all shapes and sizes, with a variety of employer/employee relationships (e.g., permanents, part-time, casuals, contractors, consultants). Getting the composition of the workforce right in order to maximize flexibility (i.e., minimise risk), whilst at the same time maximizing worker commitment and attracting, developing and retaining valuable skills, is fundamental to sustaining a competitive advantage.

The management of human capital is a shared responsibility amongst leaders

- These people management challenges are strategic ones, and not solely the domain of HR. As such, they must inevitably concern Directors, CEOs, CFOs and executives. The management of human capital is a shared responsibility across all leaders.
- Human assets are less well understood and less well managed compared to other assets of the business, with HR one of the least effectively managed corporate function, according to CEO surveys (Hall, 2008). There is a need to educate executives on the evidence that links people management practices with the "bottom line".
- Whilst other business processes and components have moved forward via innovations and paradigm shifts (such as procurement, marketing, supply chain management, accounting and quality assurance), there hasn't been anything modestly comparable in advancements concerning the management of human capital.
- Integration multiplies business value but HR functions (including various HR programs), are typically disparate, with "black holes" often existing between key activities such as recruitment, learning and development, engagement and retention, some of which are often "out of synch" with the business strategy.
- CEOs are under pressure to demonstrate to board members and shareholders how they are managing their human capital, and that they have the organisational capability to deliver business success. To that end, the development of a Human Capital Strategic Plan (i.e., similar to what exists for other assets of the business), represents a comprehensive and integrated platform for moving beyond this human capital stagnation.
- In a paradoxical way, having to focus on and address these workforce management challenges may help organisations to unlock the potential and surface those hidden aspects of their workforce that may be impeding business growth and/or profitability.

One size doesn't fit all: Workforce segmentation is fundamental to effective workforce strategies, measurement, reporting and management

> Note: Refer to the skills' based workforce segmentation model in the coloured pages of this Introduction Chapter.

- Just as a marketer segments their products and clients, so the same principles of segmentation should be applied to the workforce - not every role, including the people occupying those roles, are equal!
- Therefore one size doesn't fit all in terms of people management policies and practices. Given the complexities of workforce management in the contemporary workplace, organisations will increasingly need to adopt more differentiated and sophisticated employment or people management policies and practices.

> Note: Some people management policies and practices will be universally applicable across an organisation (e.g., grievances, bullying, drugs and alcohol).

- Typically organisations segment their workforce on a hierarchical, job level or salary basis. However this hierarchical model is inadequate for identifying critical roles if salary is the sole criteria. Salary levels are typically more determined by market forces, and the need to preserve internal relativities, and not so much by their importance to the business. The skills' based workforce segmentation model referred to earlier dictates vastly different attraction, engagement and retention strategies for people who may be paid similar salaries, yet occupy roles with different levels and combinations of unique and valuable skills (i.e., belong to different skills' based workforce segments or quadrants).
- Skills are the new currency! A skills' based workforce segmentation model offers a sound rationale for determining "buy" versus "make" employee decisions, including labour outsourcing. It also provides a basis for formulating differentiated HR policies and practices, recruitment and selection methodologies, levels of investment in people, and relationships/psychological contracts, with various workforce segments.

Engagement – A much confused and abused term!

- The term "engagement" is a much abused one, meaning totally different things to different people, including survey providers. Engagement is a diffuse concept, variously defined, and not a recognised academic construct. Furthermore, it is not a uni-dimensional construct. It typically includes an amalgamation of constructs or variables (e.g., discretionary effort, intention to stay, commitment, job satisfaction), some of which are not sufficiently closely related to combine into an index.
- The territory of engagement is plagued with "pop psychology", superficial abstractions and opinions. Many of the popular engagement surveys are not underpinned by solid empirical research, and therefore only

offer a partial or piecemeal solution to addressing both performance and retention issues.

- Engagement indices are a blunt measure - intuitively appealing to managers and executives for the purpose of making comparisons, but psychometrically flawed! Some engagement measures (whatever definition is adopted), and retention prediction measures (i.e., employees' intention to stay), should never be combined. Thus there is a need to move beyond engagement indices. Performance and retention drivers are not sufficiently closely related such that they can be combined and reduced down to, and understood, in terms of a single number or index.

> Note: How hard employees work is only weakly related to their intention to stay (or leave). By combining measures of discretionary effort and intentions to stay/leave into a single index, the interpretation of what this index means becomes problematic.

The psychological contract provides a more comprehensive framework for addressing employee engagement and retention

- Retention represents the highest return on investment (ROI) of any HR initiative. However most companies continue to struggle with retention because they rely on salary increases and bonuses to prevent turnover. It is more often the case that the intangibles (e.g., career development, leadership, recognition) rather than the tangibles (e.g., pay) are the key triggers for turnover.

- Engagement (whatever definition is adopted), and retention, can be more comprehensively addressed through a relationship (i.e., psychological contract) approach. Relationships are fundamentally important, be they in personal life or in the workplace, with the psychological representing the "essence" of the employer/employee relationship.

- In today's turbulent workplace where change is ongoing (e.g., downsizing, restructuring, new programs, etc.), the willingness of employees to accept change (and hence the success of change initiatives and even organisational survival), will depend on maintaining healthy and productive employer/employee relationships.

- The psychological contract underpins a strategic basis for structuring, measuring, diagnosing and aligning differentiated Employment Value Propositions (EVPs) or "deals", with various workforce segments within an organisation, over the employment life cycle. Thus it combines the concept of "the deal" or the EVP, the delivery of the "deal", and links all of this to employee engagement and retention.

- The psychological contract is a pervasive and useful concept that directly impacts on the various ways that organisations can build human capital. It has implications for organisations and individuals across a range of people management policies and practices, and organisational development initiatives (e.g., recruitment, on-boarding, performance enhancement, careers, succession planning, retention, remuneration, learning and development, leadership, exit interviews, etc.).
- The psychological contract binds organisations and individuals together, and it is consistent with the concept of the "new deal" between employers and employees. The concept is flexible to accommodate a variety of "new deals" and relationships (from shorter term transactional through to longer term relational), and it serves as a basis for healthy dialogue to discuss and reconcile the continually changing needs of both parties.

> Note: The psychological contract arguably represents the "hottest" topic in organisational psychology research, having been reported as "possibly the most emergent area for organisational research in the current landscape" (Del Campo, 2007, p. 43). It is predicted to become the next "big thing" in the HR arena.

The need for a HR makeover

- HR is an emerging discipline, with the two somewhat unrelated arms of administrative HR and strategic HR. Many HR functions are in transition from an administration department to a strategic partner, with HR not yet geared up to provide the appropriate level of insight.
- HR is sometimes disempowered, lacking in influence, process driven rather than strategic, non-commercial, preoccupied with costs rather than outcomes, and unable to argue a successful business case.
- Some HR professionals are unduly influenced by fads and popularism, looking for quick fixes and simplistic solutions, with little by way of a Return On Investment (ROI) or rigorous evaluation of various HR initiatives undertaken. HR innovations have followed patterns more akin to fashion rather than to rational strategic logic. HR professionals need and want to become more evidenced based, with their role shifting from tactical to more strategic.
- HR functions are typically disparate, with HR often locked into rigid budgets and reactive spending (e.g., making a hire to fill a vacancy,

increasing compensation to stave off a threatened departure, or to deliver process improvements).

- Some HR practitioners have muddled beliefs, often flailing around, out of step with the fundamentals of the business. There are often some serious disconnects between HR Departments and line management.

> Note: For example, investing in recognition programs as a retention strategy is a waste of resources if there are more fundamental issues with a loss of management trust/leadership, poor person-job fit, failure to deliver on the "deal", etc. It's akin to treating a melanoma with a band-aid!

- Some HR professionals know little about research. There is a significant gap between the empirical research and some customs and practices concerning people management, performance and retention. Like other leaders, some HR executives hold flawed and incomplete beliefs. They fall prey to second-rate evidence, logic and advice, all of which produce suspect practices, which in the end, can damage performance and people.

> Note: It is also the case that many academics and researchers have little idea of, or interest in, the real world of business, including how managers think, what they need, and the successful application of empirical research into practical solutions.

The need for better people measurement and reporting

- HR professionals need to become more critical consumers of human capital tools. They are typically not trained in measurement, and are therefore susceptible to being duped by the questionable claims of suppliers of products and services where "spin" predominates over substance.

> Note: It is not necessarily HR's fault that they are not trained in measurement. Rather it is a systemic failure of educational institutions and professional bodies to identify the emerging needs of organisations in terms of better people measurement.

- You can't manage what you don't measure! Senior executives are data needy and data hungry, and concerned with measuring and managing risk (including people risk). However the quality of reporting on human assets lags well behind that of other assets of the business. There is a need for valid and reliable human capital measures. Without proper measurement, politics fills the gap.

- HR has a key role to play at the interface and alignment between business strategies and workforce strategies. A new mindset needs to be developed towards the HR role and its positioning, given the importance of people to business success.

> Note: There are a number of paradoxes emerging in HR. For example, there has been a trend towards organisations appointing executives/managers in senior HR roles who don't come with a background in HR. To what extent this reflects a lack of talent of those with a HR background, or a dismissiveness of the value of HR by business leaders, is a debatable point. Whatever the case, this result is a self-fulfilling prophecy. Such appointments would be extremely unlikely in most other key business functions.
>
> It is interesting to note that there is a gender imbalance in HR with many people being female (estimate between two thirds to three quarters). Given that women occupy somewhere between 10-15% of senior roles (i.e., the "glass ceiling syndrome"), it may be the case that the HR role is one that is more accessible to them, or perceived as a softer target. Perhaps men are discouraged from choosing this (HR) career path, because of perceived limitations of further promotional opportunities.

- HR possibly constitutes the most diverse array of functions of any part of the business, with different skill sets required for learning and development versus talent acquisition, versus compensation, etc. Hence the challenge of not only integrating this diversity, but then linking workforce strategies in these various specialities with the business strategy.

1.7 THE EDUCATION CHALLENGE AND A "3 M" FRAMEWORK

No silver bullet solution

The birth of this book has been germinating and evolving for some time, and like all such emergent activities, takes on a life of its own. Apart from the altruistic perspective of creating a better world of work, one of the key aims of this book is to educate directors, executives, general managers, HR professionals and key decision makers in the areas of human capital, strategic people management issues, employee engagement and retention, etc. No executive can now live in ignorance or maintain superficial and outdated attitudes concerning these topics.

This book lays a foundation of background knowledge, concepts, understandings, models and measures from which the impact of the GFC and other emerging trends in the employment landscape can be best addressed (from a micro or organisational perspective). It aims to support senior decision makers seeking to develop deeper workforce insights and more effectively mobilise their human capital. It will set them on route to better internal measurement and reporting and the improved management of one of their most important assets. Whilst it doesn't purport to offer a "silver bullet" solution, it does offer a way forward for organisations seeking to shore up their competitive position and enhance their sustainability.

An innovative "3 M" framework (Mindsets, Models and Measurement)

The book extends beyond simply:

- Addressing changes in workforce demographics, accommodating an ageing workforce, and customising "deals" or EVPs to attract and retain the three main demographic cohorts of Gen Y, Gen X and Baby Boomers (which are somewhat artificially created categories manufactured for simplicity purposes, and which are not homogeneous), although this topic is nevertheless addressed.
- Strengthening the talent pipeline and associated recruitment methodologies, including branding.

As such, it constitutes much more than an *ad hoc* check list of do's and don'ts, which if implemented without an overarching framework of understanding, may be wasteful at best, and counterproductive at worst.

One of the governing principles of this book is the building of a sound human capital foundation. To that end, an innovative "3 M" framework is introduced in this book comprising:

1. Right Mindsets
2. Right Models
3. Right Measures.

> Note: Additionally the WRDI Institute has developed a Methodology (i.e., the fourth "M"), in the application of these people management challenges in the form of a Human Capital Strategic Plan for organisations (refer to Chapter 4).

With respect to the second "M", there are five main models offered:

1. A skills' based workforce segmentation model
2. A human capital model, including the five ways for enhancing human capital
3. A model of capabilities and competencies, from organisational through to individual or job related
4. An employer/employee relational model (i.e., that of the psychological contract)
5. A model for categorising and then reporting the various types of human capital data (i.e., the people data cube).

These models (refer to the coloured pages in this Introduction for diagrams of the five models) are then linked to provide an integrated framework for addressing the management of human capital and the people challenges ahead. An introductory summary is provided below in relation to these models.

I.8 MODEL 1: SKILLS' BASED WORKFORCE SEGMENTATION

As indicated earlier, segmentation is a fundamental concept in marketing, be it the segmentation of products and services or clients. Building on the work of Lepak and Snell (1999, 2002), the WRDI Institute has developed a skills' based workforce segmentation model. This model takes into account two dimensions of skills – both their value and uniqueness to the organisation.

Valuable skills either create lower costs, increased revenue, or innovation (resulting in either lower costs, or increased revenue, or increased increased financial performance including ROI, cash flow etc.).

Unique skills are organisational specific, unlikely to be found in the open market, hard to replace, and hard for competitors to imitate or duplicate.

According to this model, various jobs within an organisation can be classified in four possible employment roles:

1. Criticals
2. Professionals, Skilled and Semi-Skilled
3. Doers
4. Specialists.

This skills' based model is fundamental to managing human capital – it forms the basis of:

- "Make" versus "buy" labour decisions, including outsourcing
- The identification of Critical roles
- Determining levels of investment in people

THE FIVE MODELS UNDERPINNING THIS BOOK

Model 1: The Skills' Based Workforce Segmentation Model

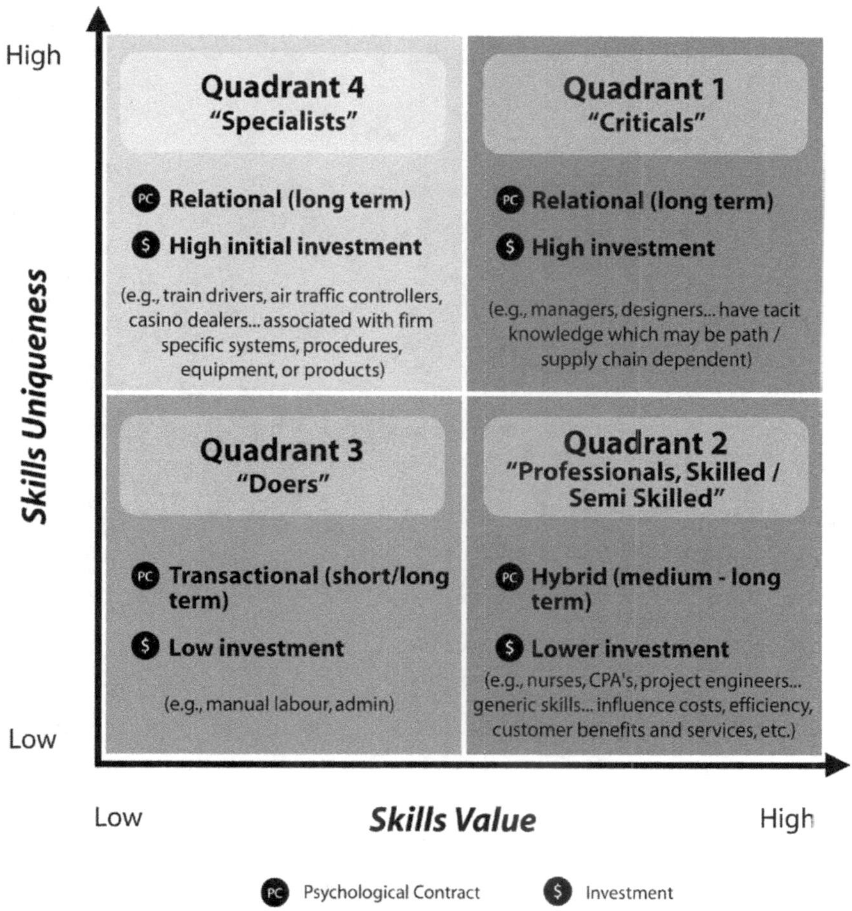

Model 1: Examples of Plotting Roles by Skills Quadrants

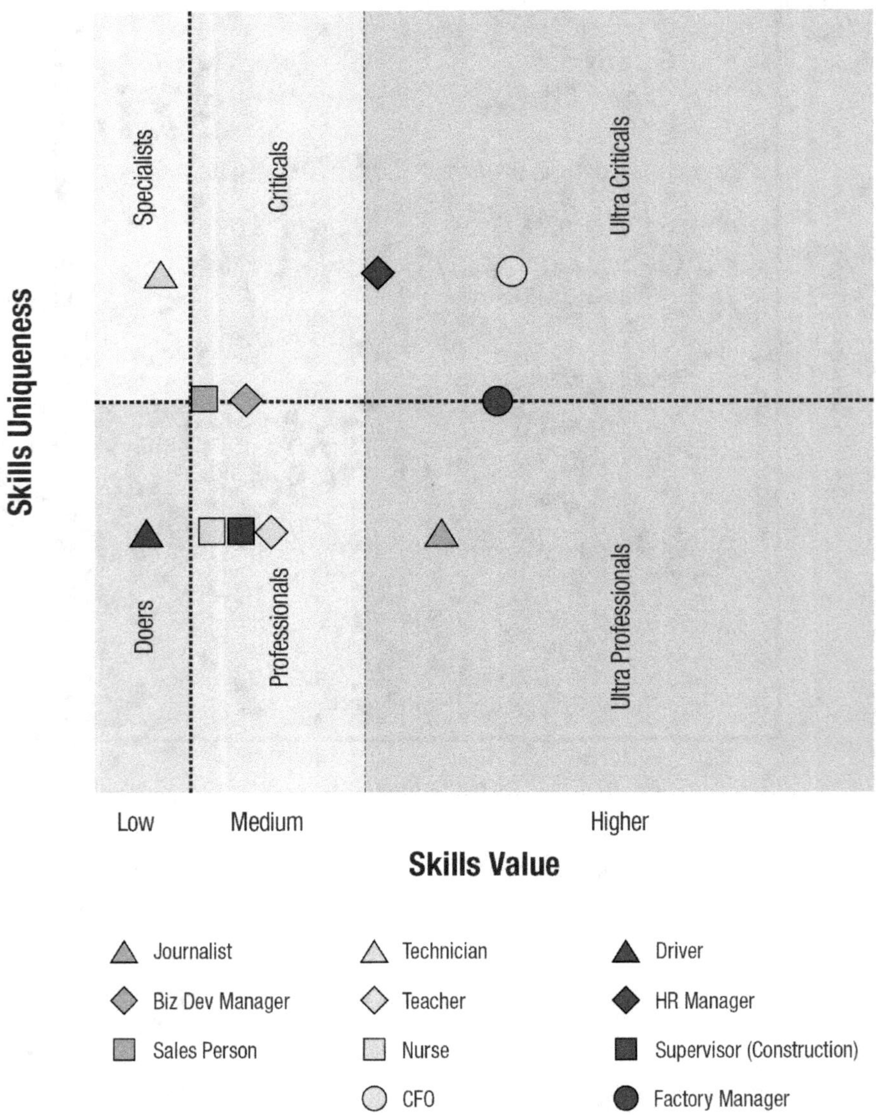

Model 2: Five Ways of Increasing Human Capital

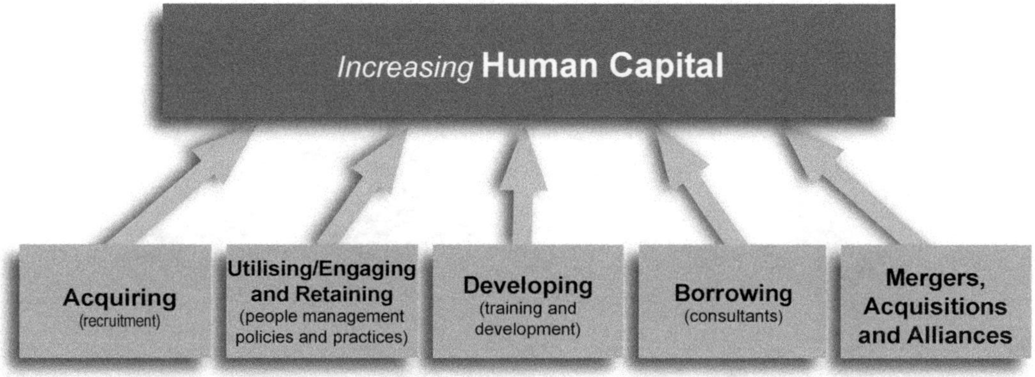

Model 4: The Psychological Contract (PC)

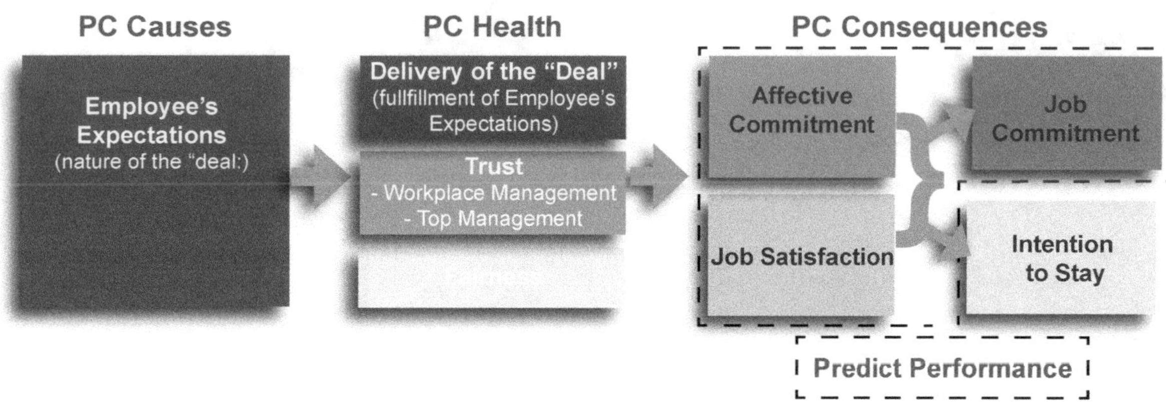

Model 3: A Three Level Model of Capabilities/Competencies

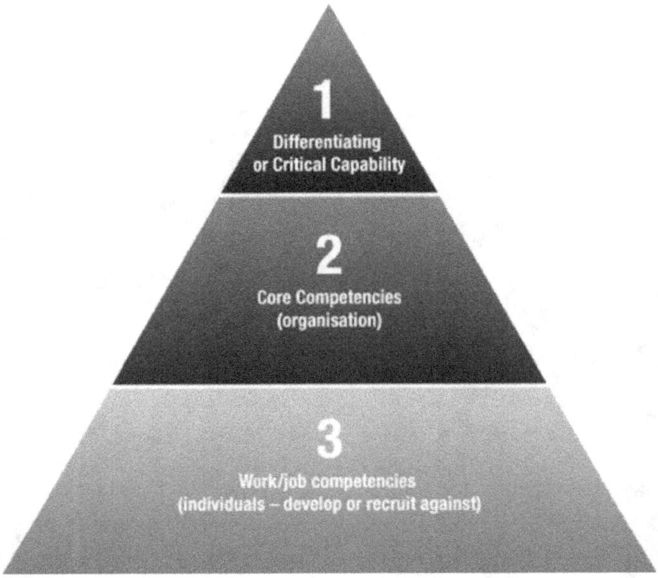

Model 5: The People Data Cube

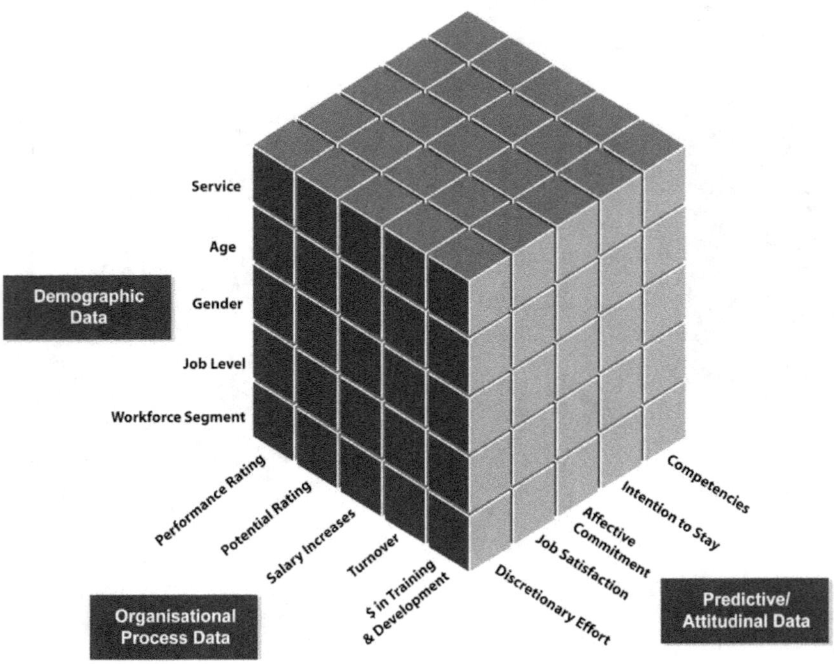

Note: The above People Data Cube Model was developed by the WRDI Institute in conjunction with Australian Survey Research.

- Differentiated HR policies and practices
- Psychological contracts (i.e., employer/employee relationships including EVPs or "deals"), for employees in each of these four skills' quadrant roles, including differentiated engagement and retention strategies
- Reporting of human capital data according to the four workforce segments (refer to Chapter 9 for examples of such reporting).

I.9 MODEL 2: INCREASING HUMAN CAPITAL

Human capital includes the knowledge, skills, experience and initiative possessed by employees. There are five main ways in which an organisation can enhance their stock of human capital, and therefore enhance their performance and sustainability:

1. Acquiring (i.e., selection and recruitment)
2. Utilising engaging and retaining
3. Developing
4. Merger/acquisition
5. Borrowing.

I.10 MODEL 3: CAPABILITIES AND COMPETENCIES: THREE LEVELS

There are three types or levels of capabilities and competencies:

- Differentiating or critical capabilities (of organisations)
- Core competencies (of organisations)
- Work competencies (of individuals and teams).

Differentiating or critical capabilities:

- Differentiate an organisation from its competitors
- Characterise the organisation to their customers (i.e., are the main reason why customers purchase products or services)
- Contribute to success.

Differentiating capabilities (or a single capability which may be the case for many organisations), are vital to the success of an organisation. It is important to identify the drivers of these capabilities, and then to maximise or differentiate that capability. A methodology linking these drivers and core competencies (see below) to the analysis of job roles has been presented in Appendix C.

Core competencies directly relate to the key activities that the organisation undertakes in conducting its business. They are more generalised or spread across the organisation, but they will be incorporated, in part, in various work/job competencies (i.e., for individuals).

Work competencies are those competencies specific to various roles. They can be broadly classified into three areas:

1. Technical/Functional
2. Managerial
3. Behavioural.

1.11 MODEL 4: THE PSYCHOLOGICAL CONTRACT

As indicated in the acknowledgement section of this chapter, relationships are fundamentally important. Think about any relationship and ask yourself the following questions:

- *What are my expectations?*
- *Have my expectations been met?*
- *Do I trust the other party?*
- *Is the relationship fair (or lop sided)?*

If the answer to the above latter three questions is yes, then you are more likely to:

- Be emotionally attached to the relationship/other party
- Be more satisfied in the relationship
- Work harder in the relationship
- Stay or remain in the relationship.

The workplace is no different with the same fundamentals applying. Every relationship has a psychological contract. In the context of the workplace, the psychological contract can be defined as: *the stated and implied set of expectations, obligations, and understandings, operating between workers (a wider term than employees) and their employer.* It defines the essence of the employment relationship and it is a powerful determinant of employee behavior (Schein, 1978).

The psychological contract is not a legal document as such, but it is nevertheless real in the minds of employees and employers. It is a broader concept than an employment agreement or contract, and includes both what has been written, said, unsaid and observed. The content of the psychological contract (i.e., the items which make up the "deal" and upon which employees' expectations are based), comprises the:

- Tangibles (e.g., pay, resources, etc.)
- Intangibles (e.g., support, training, recognition, advancement, etc.).

The combination of these tangibles and intangibles equates to the "deal" or the EVP. Employees then form certain expectations about these tangibles and intangibles, based on what is offered, along with their other initial observations and experiences in the organisation.

A dynamic model of the state of the psychological contract is presented– its' health and consequences. This model links the concept of EVPs or the "deal" and its delivery, as well as trust and fairness, with engagement (whatever definition is adopted), and retention. The meeting of expectations constitutes a vital aspect of any relationship and is fundamental to fostering higher levels of organisational commitment and job satisfaction.

The model is diagnostic whereby psychological contract health factors, in part, predict psychological contract consequences. These consequences are in two stages, with affective commitment (i.e., emotional attachment to the organisation), and job satisfaction predicting in part, job commitment/ discretionary effort and intention to stay. Intention to stay is the main predictor of retention. Actions typically follow on from intentions, but not always, as we will discover in Chapter 6. Affective commitment, job satisfaction and job commitment/discretionary effort are all key drivers of performance. Hence the psychological contract model presented is both a performance and retention model.

> Note: Affective commitment is the extent to which employees are emotionally attached to an organisation. It is a *de facto* measure of person-organisational fit. Job satisfaction is a *de facto* measure of person-job fit.

Various models of engagement include some, but typically not all, of the four psychological contract consequences measures. Some adopt different terminology to describe these measures (e.g., "Stay", "Say" and "Strive"). The incorporation of the measurement of expectations in the psychological contract model constitutes a missing link in various employee engagement models but more of this in Chapter 7.

I.12 MODEL 5: THE PEOPLE DATA CUBE

It is generally acknowledged that measurement drives behaviour and that what gets measured gets managed! The people (human capital) data cube provides a conceptual framework for categorising and reporting on human capital. There are three categories of data:

1. Demographic

2. Organisational process data
3. Predictive data.

The three categories of human capital data form the basis of a practical framework of appropriate workforce measures which otherwise transforms *ad hoc* or disjointed data into a more integrated platform for effective human capital analysis and reporting.

I.13 THE STRUCTURE OF THIS BOOK

In this Introduction Chapter, we introduce the main themes of the book and the key assumptions underpinning it. Then in Chapter 1, we deal with recent changes in the workplace, both for organisations and individuals, in order to provide a relevant background and context to that which follows. In particular we focus on the changing employer/employee relationship, and the "new deal". Also 12 emergent trends in the workplace/employment landscape are identified, including their overall implications for both organisations and individuals. Then in Chapter 2, we indulge in some future predictions concerning the workplace – a rather perilous undertaking given the volatile and uncertain circumstances over the past few years.

In Chapter 3 of the book we introduce the first model - a skills' based workforce segmentation model. It is contended that this model is fundamental to developing appropriate employment strategies and people management policies and practices, including the reporting of human capital data.

Chapter 4 of the book is about education (i.e., developing the right people mindsets). We provide an understanding of human capital, including a model of the five ways of building human capital. We also present a case for why corporate governance and risk management should now be applied to the management of human capital.

Then in Chapter 5, we deal with the third model relating to capabilities and competencies, and thereafter the development, acquisition and disposal of human capital, including downsizing. As a precursor to comprehensively addressing the engagement and retention of human capital, we provide a comprehensive summary of relevant background material - our second educational thrust in Chapter 6. The rationale for this emphasis is:

- The increasing importance of engagement and retention to organisational performance (and even more so in the future)
- The misunderstandings surrounding these topics
- That this is the most important of the five ways of building human capital, because unless the workforce is fundamentally engaged and likely to remain, other human capital initiatives and investments are likely to prove somewhat futile.

In Chapter 7, we offer a fourth model – that of the psychological contract. We explain the concept, present a model of the psychological contract, and explain how the constructs that comprise the psychological contract impact on attraction, performance and retention, including relevant empirical research. The Workplace Relationship Development Indicator (WRDI®) diagnostic engagement and retention tool, based on a model of the psychological contract, is introduced bringing the above research into the applied/practical world.

Then in Chapter 8, we outline the universality of the concept of the psychological contract, including its relevance to the building of human capital. In particular, we address the engagement and retention of human capital, together with the various applications of the psychological contract over the employment life cycle, explaining how it impacts on so many areas of organisational life.

Finally in Chapter 9 we bring it all together in dealing with the measurement and reporting of human capital, including the various measures, psychometric properties, surveys, and utopia in human capital measurement and reporting - workforce analytics. We introduce the fifth model – the people data cube which defines and classifies the three types of human capital data. An example reporting output is provided which integrates the various models and measures into a coherent whole, providing essential workforce intelligence.

For those interested in exploring some related topics further, in the Appendices we provide the following additional information:

- A summary of Erikson's (1969) model of the stages of life, with an emphasis on mid-life (we believe that this is a deeper and more appropriate model to view human development from, rather than the more artificially created Gen Y, Gen X and Baby Boomer approach)
- A summary of changing career perspectives and understandings, including the implications for organisations and individuals.

An explanation of the Skills Segmentation Questionnaire (SSQ) and its application to the analysis and plotting of roles according to the skills' based workforce segmentation model is presented in the coloured pages of this chapter and also in Appendix C.

1.14 A "PRACADEMIC" STYLE

It should come as no surprise to you (given my engineering background), that I am committed to a scientific approach to measurement and reporting. After all, "you can take the boy out of engineering, but not engineering out of the boy"! At times I may be accused of being unduly critical of HR, but what I take for granted in terms of a more rigorous scientific approach – measurement, diagnosis, intervention and evaluation - is not always the norm when applied to people. Often the mindsets and approaches that are adopted towards people are somewhat inconsistent with the mindsets that we adopt to other assets of a business, notwithstanding that human assets have some unique characteristics (refer Chapter 4 for examples).

I have written this book from the perspective of a "pracademic" – practical applications of valid empirical research based approaches, packaged in a way that is hopefully digestible and relatively easily applied. The ideas and strategies are drawn from researchers, authors, our network of accredited consultants, clients and others, as well as my own experience. I suspect that this book will not fully satisfy the academic purists. However often there is a need to compromise (although not unduly so), or balance purity with practicality and outcomes. Reasonably extensive referencing has been provided but readers may seek further references from me should they feel so inclined.

1.15 MORE THAN A SERIES OF CASE STUDIES

I am often amused by the preoccupation with case studies as a magic panacea. Isomorphism (i.e., copying what everyone else does) is rife in the HR domain. What one organisation does, taking into account their particular circumstances, may not necessarily be applicable to another organisation, where their circumstances, both internally and externally, may be different. Without a holistic and deeper framework of understanding, it is conceivable to make matters worse by implementing costly programs which have no effect, because they address the wrong issues or address symptoms rather than causes, or are contradicted by other HR initiatives.

Notwithstanding, numerous case studies and examples are provided throughout the book to illustrate the concepts being presented. The "3 M" approach foreshadowed is applicable to organisations of all sizes, emphasizing employment strategies and practices that will boost performance and retention, and which will position organisations to become true Employers of Choice.

1.16 WHAT'S NOT INCLUDED

It is not possible to explore and cover every topic comprehensively. A detailed treatment of some specific attraction, development and retention initiatives such as recruitment, succession planning, leadership development, remuneration packaging, performance management, recognition programs, career development, including HR systems and IT platforms, etc., are beyond the scope of this book. Others have specialised expertise in these areas. Rather, some broader principles and guidelines are offered, as there is often not one best solution. As is the case for any author, the detailed treatment of various topics in a book, or the lack thereof, will vary according one's own biases.

I.17 SOME TRADITIONAL PEOPLE NOTIONS CHALLENGED AND MYTHS DEBUNKED

This book challenges some traditional people notions, superficial thinking, faulty mindsets, and debunks a number of people or HR myths, e.g.:

- The abuse and confusion surrounding the term "employee engagement"
- Why engagement (whatever definition is adopted) and retention measures should never be combined into a single index
- That the relationship with one's boss, which is purported to be the primary cause of turnover, actually only accounts for around 25-30% of voluntary turnover
- The limitations of segmenting the workforce based on job or salary Levels, and the flawed approaches of many organistions in basing their attraction, engagement and retention strategies on hierarchical segmentation models
- The allure of downsizing in light of the adverse second order consequences that may outweigh the benefits
- Why low turnover rates may not be an indication of organisational health and capability
- The overly simplistic and artificial creation of generational cohorts that are not homogeneous, and the exaggeration of their apparent differences.

The book argues a case for some new ways of thinking to address the people challenges of the 21st century workplace. Please note that I am not a HR person, having come from an engineering background. Being somewhat of an outsider, I can perhaps offer a perspective that is uncontaminated by earlier HR influences or conditioning. This may or may not be perceived as an advantage. Some may be happy with what they have in place regarding employment strategies, engagement and retention, and the measuring and reporting of the same. So be it. This book is more likely to appeal to those others who are committed to breakthrough approaches, continual improvement, innovation and seeking better frameworks of understandings and solutions.

An old university professor of mine once said that very few of us have original ideas. The originality or creativity comes from repackaging other's ideas into a new or enhanced, conceptual approach. I therefore take only moderate kudos in terms of the originality of the concepts presented in this book. However I take a little more credit in integrating or packaging a number of these concepts and ideas (i.e., "3 M" framework), and directing them towards offering practical solutions to a significant contemporary challenge facing many organisations.

Chapter 1

Looking Back and Understanding Emerging Workplace Trends

KEY POINTS

Key questions and issues that we will address in this chapter:

- *What changes have occurred in the workplace over the past couple of decades?*
- *What have been the key drivers of these changes?*
- *What new meanings and trends have emerged?*
- *What is meant by the terms, the "old deal" and the "new deal"?*
- *What have been the implications of these changes for organisations?*
- *What have been the implications of these changes for employees/workers?*

What are the consequences of failing to adequately address these questions/issues or ending up with the wrong answers?

- *All strategies and decisions should be developed and made within a relevant context. A failure to understand and appreciate the recent history of workplace change, and the characteristics and dynamics of the current workplace context, is likely to result in a miss-management of an organisation's key intangible asset – its people.*
- *Furthermore, a failure to come to grips with emerging workplace and employment landscape trends will most likely result in poor people strategies and decision making, resulting in poorer performance and increased turnover.*

1. LOOKING BACK AND UNDERSTANDING EMERGING WORKPLACE TRENDS

1.1 DRIVERS OF RECENT WORKPLACE CHANGE

Over the past two decades, we have witnessed unprecedented change sweeping the workplaces of the western world. A combination of factors has contributed to this revolution including:

- Economic reform, of which the recent GFC is now a significant part
- Technological developments (including improved communications and information systems)
- Globalisation, with the world becoming smaller and more interdependent
- A greater concern for the environment and future generations
- Changing social and cultural values
- Increased customer demands.

In the public sector, the volume and pace of administrative reform pursued by governments has been unrelenting with:

- A demand for improved efficiency in the delivery of quality services
- Increased emphasis on accountability and transparency of transactions
- Increased competition for resources and a demand to do more with less
- Outsourcing, corporatisation, and privatization
- Greater customer focus, analysis of activity costs, and a recognition of community service obligations
- An emphasis on equity, diversity, equal opportunity, etc.

In the private sector, emphasis has shifted more towards short-term profits (which up until the advent of the GFC had been steadily rising), with shareholder demands increasingly being perceived to override employees'/workers' welfare. It's interesting to note that shareholders are less loyal than employees, with the average shareholder tenure (according to Cascio, 2009), being around 12 months, compared to employees of around six years (i.e., average turnover of the Australian workforce is around 15%)! We shall explore this issue of the value of people later in Chapter 4.

The turbulent business environment has become more decentralised and information driven, with ever increasing diversity. Organisations now need to be lean, fast and flexible in order to survive and remain competitive (apart from the universities and the churches, very few organisations have stood the test of time). In so doing, they have had to continually redefine themselves through cost cutting, restructuring, re-engineering, divestments, acquisitions, etc. They have become more demanding of higher levels of employees'/workers' performance in responding to increased customer demands, changing markets, products and technology.

> Note: The term "employee" used throughout this book, predominantly refers to insiders (i.e., permanents, part-timers), whereas the term "worker" refers more to outsiders or contingents (i.e., those who are self-employed, contractors, casuals, temps, part-timers, etc.), although it sometimes refers as well to employees in some instances, because it seems more appropriate to use that term. Sometimes I have used the combined term of employee/worker to refer to both categories – insiders and outsiders.

1.2 NEW MEANINGS IN THE WORKPLACE

New workplace meanings have emerged from the turbulence of the past two decades, some of which have been referred to later in the "new deal". These include the following:

- The traditional notions of employment and careers have changed, as have the characteristics of organisations, the workplace, and the needs of individuals
- Some concepts such as "job security" are fading and have been replaced by the notion of "employability"
- The term "management" has acquired a new significance, with an increased emphasis on strategic considerations, co-ordination, integration, facilitation and support, with a reduced emphasis on authoritarianism and control
- Traditional boundaries between organisations and customers have become blurred (e.g., formation of alliances), with both employees/workers and organisations now coming in many shapes and sizes
- Work restructuring and more flexible arrangements, including the delocalisation of work, has given many employees/workers the task of managing their own work
- Widespread changes in education levels (with an increased emphasis on professionalism), and work related values such as autonomy and responsibility, have also emerged with restructuring.

Work and careers have now become more of a series of employers and learning opportunities, rather than a life-long relationship with one company until death (retirement) do us part!

1.3 ORGANISATIONAL TRENDS

We shall separate these trends or changes into two broad categories:

1. Changes to how organisations are operating
2. Changes in people management practices.

Trends in terms of how organisations are operating include:

- Flatter hierarchies with the outsourcing of non-core activities
- More fluid forms with the formation of alliances, networks, project based teams, team based structures and virtual organisations
- An emphasis on organisational agility and faster response times
- The development of service oriented cultures
- A concern for Corporate Social Responsibility and the triple bottom line beyond a sole focus on short-term profits.

Trends concerning people management practices include:

- An emphasis on competitive advantage in the recruitment and retention of capable and valued employees, and in particular employer branding, talent management, succession planning and workforce planning
- An increased emphasis on leadership and coaching, and the development of "soft skills" (e.g., emotional intelligence), as being seen to be critical to effective leadership, management and performance
- A demand for higher skill levels and experience of people
- A preference for experience of new hires over internal development
- A requirement for managers with deeper knowledge (either industry or subject areas) plus people skills
- The abandonment of the traditional employment relationship (i.e., the paternalistic "old deal"), with greater complexity in managing employer/ employee relations
- The adoption of employment strategies which are designed to share more of the risks with employees/workers (e.g., adoption of shorter-term contracts and recourse to a contingent workforce of contractors, casuals and part-time employees, contractors and consultants).

1.4 CHANGING EMPLOYMENT PRACTICES: SHARING THE RISK

As referred to above, many organisations of all sizes and industries have reviewed their employment strategies in order to remain competitive. Consequently a variety of employment relationships have spawned, generally designed to:

- Maximise the flexibility of the workforce
- Share more of the risk and uncertainty with employees/workers, resulting in reduced job security and less predictability in employment relationships.

In maximising the flexibility of the workforce and minimising risk, the following employment practices have been adopted, with a move towards:

- Fixed-term contracts
- Greater use of casuals
- More flexible work practices, such as part-time, job sharing and telecommuting
- Greater use of contractor/consultant alternatives
- Outsourcing of various activities (typically non-core activities or lower knowledge/lower skill activities).

Opportunities are now more readily able to import knowledge and expertise, including diversification and expansion through the establishment of alliances, virtual organisations, access to consultants and contractors, etc. Notwithstanding this increased flexibility and risk minimisation, organisations are also vitally concerned with:

- Preserving (or attempting to increase or optimise) employees'/workers' commitment and performance
- Developing a positive corporate culture
- Attracting, engaging, developing and retaining valuable people and their skills, including key talent and those in more critical roles.

Organisations now need to "have their cake and eat it" in terms of the flexibility and commitment of their workforce.

> Note: Most studies show that contingent workers are just as committed to the organisation they work for as permanents, and generally they are willing to act in the interests of the organisation. However retention of contingent workers is more problematic as their barriers to exit are lower.

1.5 FURTHER EXAMINATION OF THE CHANGING EMPLOYER/EMPLOYEE RELATIONSHIP

The composition of the workforce

In Australia the composition of the workforce is as follows:

- Approximately 55% of the workforce is employed in traditional 38/40 hour a week, longer-term employment arrangements
- Approximately 25-30% in casual or part-time work
- With the remainder (i.e., 15-20%) in self-employment, contractor or franchise type employment arrangements (CEDA, 2005).

The public sector is estimated to employ around 15% of the workforce and it is estimated that around 15% of the total Australian workforce is currently overseas. There has been a strong downward trend in the percentage of people in full-time permanent jobs, notwithstanding record low unemployment rates up until recent times. The traditional employer/ employee model is progressively being replaced with other arrangements, with the phenomena of labour hire agencies growing.

Externalisation of the workforce

In essence, the more flexible employment practices adopted have created shorter-term arrangements and higher externalisation. In the current climate of business uncertainty and volatility, the use of contingent workers is likely to increase in meeting fluctuating business needs and providing specific skills and expertise. Where employment relations at one time prevailed over labour contracting, the opposite is now increasingly the case. This move towards the externalisation of employees (i.e., workers) reflects the shift by organisations away from a reliance on social exchange considerations, to more of a reliance on economic exchange considerations. The end result is that employees/workers are now taken on as calculated risks. This shift has implications for:

- Employees/workers in managing their careers, investing in their own skills' development and taking greater control over their own destiny
- Organisations in terms of the development and retention of skills to maintain their competitive advantage.

One size doesn't fit all!

Overall, employment relationships have become more diverse, individualised, implicit, deregulated, decentralised and generally more tenuous and transitory. As such, it is clear that a "one size fits all" approach to workforce management will no longer suffice. People management policies and practices have, and will continue to become, increasingly more complex with the:

- Polarisation of skilled and unskilled jobs, and their associated value within the organisation (see later in this chapter)
- Diversity of various demographic groups (i.e., Gen Y, Gen X, Baby Boomers, and those with special needs).

Complexity equates with differentiation. This need for differentiation raises new challenges for management, including:

- Maintaining traditional notions of equity, against the background of labour market forces (i.e., supply and demand for skills) and resolving tensions between permanents and contingents
- Developing better and more sophisticated frameworks and models including new mindsets for rethinking and determining workforce strategies in addressing this complexity.

Consider the following extract from "The Manager of the 21st Century", a report by The Boston Consulting Group (Nicholson & Nairn, 2006) for Innovation & Business Skills Australia, on how the role of Australia's senior managers is likely to change between now and 2020.

> ...Models of flexible working will continue to evolve in response to a diversity of needs of Baby Boomers through to Generation Y. Greater attention will be given to the engagement, performance and retention of people. The focus will be on human optimisation. Managers will find themselves assessed on a new range of metrics. They will require new skills to create more flexible environments and better accommodate the need of their employees, including greater numbers of contractors and part-time workers.

1.6 THE "NEW DEAL"

The "old deal"

Loyalty has been considered essential for survival in the past where belonging and being part of a community was necessary for survival. And so it was the case in the workplace with the paternalistic relationship between employer and employee that existed up until the late 80's - referred to as the "old deal" between employer and employee. This "old deal" was based on the straightforward exchange of job security (and financial security), promotion and advancement, and material rewards, for loyalty and service, with employees prepared to move around (i.e., to locations as required by the employer). It was largely implicit and unquestioned, and assumed homogeneity of employees' requirements.

Whilst the "old deal" provided certainty, stability, and a sense of place and purpose in one's class structure, it may well be argued that it also created a form of blind loyalty and dependence that inhibited performance, initiative, risk taking and willingness to change. To some extent it required the willing sacrifice of the employee's sense of and desire for freedom, to the higher demands of the organisation, with subservience to command and control. When loyalty is demanded however, accountability becomes diffused! As indicated in the beginning of this chapter, the organisational change revolution that began in the 1980s with mergers, acquisitions and downsizing, sent a clear and unforgiving message that organisations could and would only be loyal to individuals while it suited their purposes – only while economic circumstances enabled them to afford it.

Characteristics of the "new deal"

So if the paternalistic "old deal" is dead, what has replaced it? What is the "new deal" employment relationship that has emerged over the past two decades? Essentially the "new deal ":

- Is more exchanged based (i.e., what's in it for the employee/worker as well as what's in it for the organisation), and of shorter-term duration
- Incorporates new employee/worker attitudes and values

- Incorporates clarified mutual expectations, responsibilities, understandings and commitments between organisations and their employees/workers.

More specifically, "new deal" employment relationships typically:

- Are less paternalistic (i.e., more "arms length")
- Are characterised by greater flexibility (including a tolerance for role ambiguity and change), mobility (i.e., of shorter-term duration), openness and self-reliance/autonomy
- Should be built on the basis of adult–adult attitudes and responsibilities, trust and cooperation
- Incorporate a more mature form of commitment (i.e., to the vision, values and goals of the organisation, as opposed to "blind loyalty")
- Incorporate a greater employee/worker involvement and "voice" in what is going on
- Foster the career prospects for higher knowledge/skill and value employees, where "employability" is emphasised rather than job security
- Need to balance short and long term considerations
- Are more performance based, where what counts is the current value that employees/workers contribute
- Emphasise quality working relationships (e.g., teams, customers, suppliers, alliances)
- Incorporate recognition and an understanding of the continually changing needs of both parties.

The Typical "New Deal" Employment Relationship

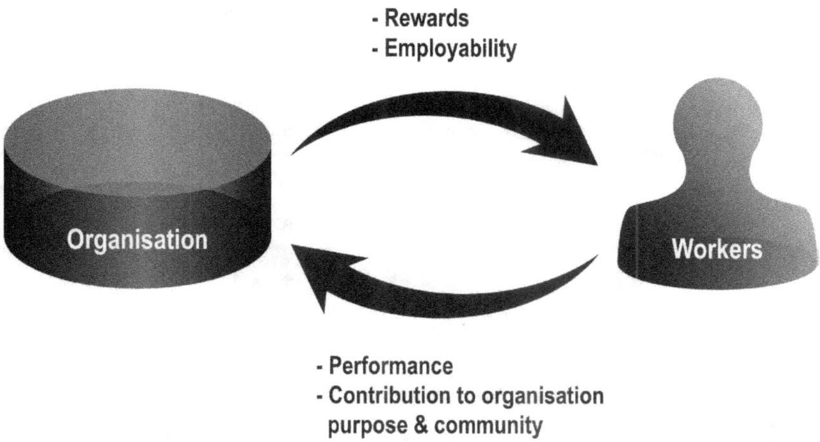

Some organisations have imposed "deals" and ill-thought out attempts to re-harmonise an insecure workforce. However no one "new deal" will provide the ultimate collaborative solution given the:

- Diversity of the nature of industries, organisations and the environments in which they operate
- The value which various levels or groups of employees/workers contribute
- The needs and interests of various demographic groups and individuals.

In summary, the employment agenda spotlight has now shifted to the relationships between management and employees/workers. We now live in the era of employment relations - not industrial relations, where the continually changing needs of both parties need to be addressed.

1.7 "NEW DEAL" IMPLICATIONS

For organisations

Clearly organisations have much more flexibility in terms of how they are able to configure and manage their workforce. As referred to earlier, having a workforce that is accessible, skilled, motivated and efficiently deployed will increasingly be a key differentiator of business performance and financial success. However this increased flexibility may have come at a cost to both parties – employers and employees/workers.

The loss of employees'/workers' job security has weakened their attachment to employers, leading to reduced incentives for employer funded training (apart from key talent). Long-term commitment by employees to the organisation has been replaced by greater attachment to their careers. The conundrum for employers is that by promoting the concept of employability, they have encouraged employees to focus on the market and direct their attention outside the organisation. Employees are therefore continually re-evaluating their existing "deal", the benefits of working for their current employer, and their career progression. This conundrum has been exacerbated in recent times with the growth of search firms and the increasing propensity to "poach" talent.

> Note: There has been a fall in employers' commitment to providing formal training to employees. Employment investment in training as a proportion of payroll stayed at 1.3% while investment in structured training fell from 1.7% to 1.5% between 1996 and 2001/02.

For more mature employees

More mature aged employees, from senior management down to shop floor level, have experienced the legacy from two decades of workplace change (e.g., outsourcing, contracting out, restructuring, downsizing, mergers and acquisitions, etc.). In so doing, some have experienced a sense of loss of organisational identity and affiliation, and have had to come to terms with the:

- Abandonment of traditional employment and career models
- New age of self-determinism
- Need to readjust career aspirations (given limited promotional opportunities with flatter structures)
- Uncertainties and demands of the continuously changing workplace
- Need to upgrade their skills and knowledge to remain marketable
- Need to perform at a consistently high level
- Prejudices against older employees
- Need to balance work and family demands.

For other employees/workers who have become "free agents"

however this background has also served as the catalyst for some employees/workers of all ages (from Gen Y through to Baby Boomers), to become more of "free agents", whose loyalty is predominantly to themselves. They have taken advantage of the autonomy, freedom, flexibility and new career choices that the contemporary workplace has to offer. Their attachment to particular organisations has become more tenuous as they seek "employability" (i.e., development of their knowledge, skills and experience), rather than employment. In short, they have learnt to use the organisation that they are with to achieve their own ends.

1.8 OTHER WORKPLACE AND EMPLOYMENT LANDSCAPE TRENDS

Apart from the "new deal" and its implications, in the beginning of this chapter, we referred to a variety of other workplace and employment landscape trends which have emerged over recent years. They include a mix of individual, demographic, organisational, market, and environmental trends, which we shall now explore in further detail. Thereafter, we shall summarise the overall impacts of these trends on both organisations and individuals.

1.9 THE EMERGENCE OF INDIVIDUALISM

The emergence of the independent employee/worker

Western societies have moved away from their tribal roots. We have moved on from the idea that central benevolent bodies will protect us. In free societies it is the ability to experience and express our individuality that has become one of our most cherished values. Thus people in educated societies have become less disposed to being controlled. In their private lives, they generally:

- Are free voters and consumers
- Decide what to buy and when
- Demand that their needs and wants are satisfied by service providers whom they pay to do so
- Are not controlled outside of work, other than complying with the law of the land
- Want to do and think for themselves
- Are decision makers and self-managers
- Seek to control their own destinies and careers, and not necessarily to have their employer determine either their current or future place in the world.

Of course there are two broad and conflicting problems:

- The individual's need to belong and survive and in so doing, surrender their individuality to the organisation
- On the other hand, the need for them to express their individuality.

It is argued that there has been and will continue to be a shift towards the latter.

The individuation movement

According to Pro Bronson (2005), people have a sense that is more intricate, acute, detailed, vaster and richer than at any other time in history. He contends that people are now seeking to satisfy both their professional and personal lives, demanding something deeper, richer or more substantive in their urge to self-hood. The new individual is asking more from their work life than pay cheques and corporate ladders to ascend. Increasingly they:

- Want rewarding work, and to belong to a worthwhile enterprise that allows for their development and caters to differences
- Want to explore their inner self, to find the thing that drives them, to risk and create
- Are seeking the freedom that allows them to find the mental space to discover spiritual and personal values of significance
- Are less accepting of failure and negative behaviour of those around them.

The "new deal" and the individuation movement

Relationships will only survive whilst the mutual needs of both parties are being accommodated and the benefits outweigh the costs. The challenge for organisations and their managers is how to:

- Motivate employees
- Get them to act with imagination, creativity and responsibility while remaining with the firm, and not leaving for other competing firms or starting up their own businesses
- Exercise control without destroying creativity and performance.

Management has had to respond to this challenge by trying to create systems and processes which allow scope for individuality but retain order and control. At the end of the day, organisations need employees to create value that is retained by the firm.

> Note: A critical task facing managers is to afford staff as much autonomy as possible over how they do their job, and then decide how best to manage that autonomy. Finding the right balance of autonomy and control has become an increasingly complex task with the advent of new forms of information and communications technology. This technology has created greater opportunities for both greater autonomy and increased monitoring of performance.

Summary: What employees/workers want

We have referred to the "new deal" and the changing values, expectations and needs of individuals. Within the context of the workplace, we have summarised what employees/workers want:

- To know more about what is happening in the organisation
- To understand why managers have made decisions
- To contribute their own ideas and to participate in the decision-making process
- To feel valued and personally recognised for their contribution to the success of the organisation
- Greater autonomy in decision making
- Take increased control over their destiny, including greater responsibility for their career development
- Find deeper meaning and purpose in their efforts and contribution, including an alignment in values for the organisations that they work for
- More flexible work arrangements (including the balancing of work and family demands and career needs and aspirations).

Overall, employees/workers are demanding more flexibility and life time choices. The "casualisation of the workforce", or the flexible work practices which employers introduced over the past decade or so to cut or minimise labour costs, have now "come back to bite". Coupled with technological advancements (i.e., access to the web, emails, etc.), employees/workers are now demanding the flexibility to work when and where they want.

Organisations slow to recognise?

It is argued that some organisations haven't yet recognised this individuation movement. They are too focused on the institution's performance, and aren't always up to the task of the care and development of individuals. Managers don't always know what's on the minds of their people. It is not necessarily appreciated that employees/workers have changed as much as the organisations that depend on them. We have referred in the next section to the need for managers to treat people as individuals, to connect better with them, and to understand their needs, even if they are not always in a position to satisfy those needs.

1.10 DEMOGRAPHIC TRENDS

An ageing population

We are in the throws of experiencing an age wave – an unprecedented shift in the age distribution of the population. Global population has put its brakes on hard with declining fertility rates in both the developed (1.7 children apiece) and under developed countries (2.9 children apiece). In Australia, the age of women giving birth has risen from 26.5 in 1979 to 29.7 in 1999, with increased workforce participation of women being the main reason.

Mortality is also declining as we experience a longevity boom. Life expectancy in Australia in 1975 was 73 years of age, and by 2000, had reached 80 years and climbing, with advances in health practices and medicine. In each of the last 40 year blocks, life expectancy has risen by 10 years. People are now living longer with all the milestones of life shifting upwards. Age 60 is now regarded by many as the new 50. Approximately 30% of the workforce is sandwiched between obligations to children and aging parents. In the coming decades, four generation families will most likely become the norm.

> Note: Around the year 1900, the life expectancy was 47 years.
>
> The average age of the Australian workforce is now 42 years.

Some age predictions

Growth predictions in the Australian labour force for the period 2002 – 2012, in the 45+ years age bracket is 85%, compared with the under 45 years age bracket of 23% growth over the same period. Baby boomers will represent the predominant demographic group. The percentage of employees/ workers 55 years or over will double in the next 5-10 years, with between two-thrids to three-quarters of today's employees/workers planning to work part-time in their retirement. Some will need to work for financial reasons (particularly in the aftermath of the GFC). Questions arise as to:

- *At what age are employees/workers no longer productive?*
- *At what age do employees/workers stop learning?*

New perspectives on ageing: the pattern of predictability is broken

The pattern of life cycle predictability has been broken with:

- More people are delaying marrying or having children
- Job tenure of women having increased, as they are less likely to quit or have children*

- Rapid growth in the older population and rapid shrinking of the younger population
- The correlation between work and age breaking down, with people no longer "acting their age"
- More people divorcing and starting second families.

*This may explain why turnover rates have remained relatively stable over the past decade, as the reduced turnover of younger women has probably have been offset by increased turnover of Gen Y, although the latter has been somewhat exaggerated.

Lifestyle diversity

The workforce has become much diverse in terms of age, gender, ethnicity, level of education, family status and personal ambition. An employee/ worker at almost any age can be in any life-stage. They may be unattached and highly mobile, raising young children, putting kids through college, empty nesting, looking after older parents, etc. Their life plans are no longer linear and predictable, differing in how they integrate work and other pursuits into their lives. Some people want different patterns of time-off for specific recreational or educational pursuits, work-life balance with partners, etc.

1.11 WORKFORCE DIVERSITY AND THREE GENERATIONS

Generational boundaries artificial

The workforce has become more multi-generational in terms of age. Unfamiliar managerial challenges are emerging, associated with all age cohorts in the evolving workforce mix, all with different wants and needs. We shall focus on three age and career cohorts – Gen Y, Gen X and Baby Boomers. These generational boundaries are somewhat arbitrary, having been artificially created for the sake of simplicity, with the generational differences often exaggerated. Furthermore, these generational groups are not homogeneous (refer to Baby Boomers later). One should therefore be careful to avoid stereotypes, and assume that perceived generational characteristics apply to particular individuals. Notwithstanding, people learn, work, interrelate and even think as a consequence of the culture, dominant events, technology and educational methods of their formative years. Therefore it is useful for employers to understand the generational mix of their workforce and how different cohorts are more likely to behave and interact.

Gen Y (born from 1981)

Most Gen Y employees are not amenable to accepting organisational practices and decisions that are not advantageous to them and their careers. They:

- Are demanding substitutes for job security that include competitive rewards, opportunities for learning and career progression and being treated with respect
- Value a more collegiate workplace and democratic participation
- Work more to live (i.e., require flexible work practices), as opposed to the reverse, so work may not necessarily be as important in their lives.

Of all of the cohorts, they appear to be unhappiest in their jobs and less satisfied (Dytchwald, Erikson & Morison, 2006), possibly because they are still finding their place in the world. Contrary to popular notions, statistically, it would appear that younger employees "job hop" not too much than their counterparts did 20 years ago.

Gen X (born from 1965 to 1980)

Like Gen Y, Gen X seeks:

- More immediate and competitive rewards (both extrinsic and intrinsic)
- Job challenge, opportunities for learning and skill development, career development, support, autonomy and equitable treatment.

More flexible work practices are important to some (e.g., those with family responsibilities), but not to others.

Baby boomers and more mature aged employees/workers (born from 1946 to 1964)

Older employees/workers have different motivations for working with some:

- Needing to work for financial reasons
- Simply enjoying working and are not yet ready to retire
- Wanting to give something back, to make a difference or make a meaningful contribution (i.e., leave a legacy).

Research indicates that around one third of older employees/workers wish to keep on working beyond the eligible retirement age, one third are looking to work part-time (not necessarily in the roles to which they are currently engaged), and another third are seeking to stop work altogether.

However this is a changing mix with the aftermath of the GFC and the erosion of superannuation provisions.

Flexibility is a key theme in supporting their retention, including options around work schedules and location. Most research converges on the conclusion that work content that provides intrinsic challenge and satisfaction for older employees/workers may be the core element in any successful strategy for dealing with such career concerns as plateauing and the downsized organisation. Increasingly, mature aged employees/workers are interested in pursuing worthwhile projects, developing new goals and interests, which signal their entering a period of new beginnings.

Thus, we are witnessing a new shape to the careers of older employees/ workers. For businesses competing for skills, there is a clear value in retaining capable and experienced staff for longer, and in smoothing management transitions. Furthermore, as Boomers represent a very large group of customers, companies may also benefit from ensuring the profile of their front line staff broadly aligns with their customer base.

Generational differences overcooked?

As alluded to earlier, generational differences may well be over emphasized. It is contended that we have much more in common than we have differences, whatever our age. For example, most people are looking to:

- Do meaningful work and make a contribution
- Work with an organisation that they can identify with
- Work for a supportive boss and with a supportive team
- Be recognized for their efforts
- Be provided with adequate resources
- Have open communication with their employer concerning workload, performance targets and other matters that are likely to affect them.

Hudson research (Levy, Carroll, Francoeur & Logue, 2006) on the perceived differences between Gen Y and Gen X concluded the following:

> Both crave gentle direction and pat on the back feedback from sensitive but strong leaders who seek to engage their staff. This study debunks popular theories that Gen X and Y are different and require different management approaches to allow them to flourish.

Nevertheless, one should be careful in assuming that various groups are seeking the same benefits for the same reasons. For example, on the subject of flexible work practices, the three age cohorts all want flexible work practices but for different reasons:

- Young people want time to explore things outside of work (e.g., travel)
- Mid-career employees/workers want time for family and community
- Mature aged employees/workers want to pursue other interests outside work (e.g., recreation, volunteering, travel, etc.).

Finally, a word of caution on the tendency towards stereotyping individuals according to perceived generational differences. There is a danger of:

- Blaming turnover on generational differences rather than looking within at the true causes
- Assuming to know the desires and aspirations of individuals based on what demographic group they may belong to (i.e., there is a need to drill down to understand these desires and aspirations to an individual level).

The clear conclusion from all of the above is that there is a need to treat people as individuals – to better connect with them, to identify their wants and needs, and where it suits both parties; to address and try to meet those needs. Furthermore, a more sophisticated analysis of and approach to workforce strategies is required rather than simply just appealing to perceived generational differences.

1.12 WORKFORCE DIVERSITY: OTHER GROUPS AND THEIR NEEDS

Single adults without dependent children (SAWDC's)

SAWDC's (i.e., men and women who are not currently in a long-term relationship and who do not have children under 18yrs), comprise almost a third of the workforce (Parker, 1996). They may be separated, divorced or widowed. There is some adverse stereotyping about singles, with assumptions about marriage and parenting having ebbed and flowed over time. The current trend is towards postponing marriage and family.

A potential exists for SAWDC's to have an over investment in work. It is not necessary to have a spouse or children to experience the relentless "tug of war" between having and doing good work, and living a good life outside of work. Over commitment in one area invariably takes its toll on the other. Non-work needs and responsibilities are significant for SAWDC's, with the need for them to maintain an adequate life outside of work. Maintenance activities such as social responsibilities which can't be delegated may demand more in time. There is a need to experience that one's entire self-identity is not solely dependent upon either work or family.

The "sandwich generation"

Reference has been made earlier to the "sandwich generation" with around 30% of the workforce sandwiched between caring for children as well as elderly parents. For many women (and also many men) with children, flexible work practices are very important.

Women, work and families: balancing demands

Growth in female employees/workers will have doubled in the last 50 years from 22% in 1960 to an estimated 44% in 2011 (IBIS). Women have accounted for 75% of all new jobs in low paying occupations from 1985 to 2001, which directly correlates with an increase in part-time positions and flexible work hours. The increase in female workforce participation means that most women with family responsibilities are employed. Single breadwinner households have dropped from 51% of couples with children in 1981 to 31% in 2000. For many people, these changes have significantly increased the tensions and pressures between competing responsibilities of work and family.

Women returning to the workforce may be late starters. For some women who combine maternity with career, their psychological investment in their career may be less because they are not as dependent upon work as their source of self esteem. Typically women generally place greater importance on workplace issues such as respect, recognition, work-family balance and co-worker relations.

> Note: Many men take on equal responsibility or more with their partners in sharing the domestic and parental load.

Career plateauing and an aging workforce

Career plateauing occurs when there is a disjunction between organisational structure and development, and the career aspirations of individuals. As we have discussed, the hierarchical career is too rigid to survive in the competitive world. Even in those industries which have returned to prosperity, the conventional career has been unable to re-establish itself. Major plateauing problems associated with an ageing workforce include the areas of promotion and succession planning. Promotions usually end before retirement for most people. Individuals may question the value of their lives and have regrets when they realise that their career has plateaued.

There are two types of plateauing:

1. Structural plateauing, which stems from lack of opportunity in the organisation

2. Content plateauing, which occurs when the job holds no further challenges.

Structural plateauing happens to nearly everyone sooner or later caused by factors outside of one's control (e.g., limitations with the size and structure of the organisation and hence opportunities). Content plateauing can lead to diminished performance unless counteracted by further training, project or committee involvement, mentoring, and other interventions, including forming work teams.

Plateauing is associated with the feeling that work has no momentum. The most common type of symptom is passivity, with an individual who doesn't care, shows no initiative, and who is withdrawn.

There is a cost of plateauing to the organisation through a loss of morale and drop in job performance. For the employee, this may lead to company hopping, sacrificing hard earned credits and taking on unknown risks. Alternatively, the employee may seek fulfillment outside of work. Many organisations are reluctant to deal pro-actively with those employees who have hit the wall! Some employees are unprepared for it or unwilling to accept it. Being plateaued does not need to equate with failure.

1.13 ORGANISATIONS BECOMING MORE DEMANDING

As mentioned earlier, organisations have become more selective in terms of their people needs, with a:

- Preference for experience of new hires over internal development
- A requirement for managers with deeper knowledge (either industry or subject areas) plus people skills.

Some are seeking the impossible - to recruit people with 20+ years experience, with an extensive array of skills, who are still in their 30's! Competition in the private sector, combined with cash constraints in the public sector, have each contributed to the intensification of work, which has meant increased pressure, stress and longer hours of work. Organisations have become more demanding in terms of their performance requirements, with the need to "do more with less", respond to increasing customer demands, and to otherwise maintain or gain a competitive advantage (see later in this chapter).

Employees/workers now need to be able to continually perform. Past "brownie points" don't count for much if current performance deteriorates. Many employees/workers are now working longer and harder, under pressure both at work and at home, having to juggle responsibilities. Employees/workers will more than ever before, share a sense of risk and vulnerability.

1.14 POLARISATION OF SKILLS AND WIDENING INEQUALITIES

Economic and workplace change has also been associated with deepening inequality of income, opportunity and security. Low quality jobs have been on the rise over the past two decades, with most of the job gains having been achieved in low paid, part-time and casual work, in low skilled occupations. In particular, the workplace has been transformed by an increasingly large proportion of part-time roles, with Australia having the largest proportion of temporary employees of any OECD country.

Labour markets have thus divided into the "haves" and the "have nots". Those employees with good skills, superior information about opportunities, and an overall high level of marketability, have found that their job prospects have been enhanced. Conversely, those who lack skills and are less marketable will now find their employment prospects deteriorating. Those with power and resources are able to exercise a greater number of choices, whilst those with limited or no bargaining power have increasingly fewer choices.

Skilled jobs require higher levels of reasoning ability, coupled with specialised knowledge and skills acquired through previous education or work experience. Unskilled jobs require little or no prior knowledge or experience and depend primarily on general work behaviours such as attendance, compliance and getting along with others. Whatever technical knowledge is required may be "brittle" (i.e., not necessarily transferable to other roles or organisations).

This growing divide is primarily a result of technology, automating many simple or repetitive and moderately complex tasks and processes, and either eliminating semi or unskilled jobs, or turning semi skilled jobs into unskilled jobs. These semi or unskilled jobs are less valuable as a source of development opportunities because they do not require employees/ workers to perform tasks where they can develop skills and capabilities associated with more highly skilled work. On the other side of the coin, new technologies and business practices have made many jobs more interesting and rewarding.

Both the skilled and unskilled labour markets have their own set of challenges. Organisations employing skilled and unskilled labour need to understand the strategic and tactical issues affecting two almost different staffing environments. Refer to Chapter 3 concerning the skills' based workforce segmentation model for a more extensive discussion of this challenge. Overall, there is likely to be more growth in skilled jobs, with the gap between the two widening as skilled jobs become increasingly more demanding and complex (i.e., shortage of talent and an excess of labour).

1.15 THE KNOWLEDGE ECONOMY AND MORE DEMANDING CONSUMERS

The shift to knowledge-intensive industries highlights the importance and scarcity of well-trained talent. As we continue to move further towards a knowledge based economy, consumers have also become more demanding, more sophisticated and more fickle, with less loyalty to particular suppliers/ providers. Their demands include:

- Improved customer service (e.g., 24/7 service), with the era of a 9 to 5 day at the office coming to a close, and with technology enabling employees and customers to be continuously accessible
- More choices and a greater preparedness to shop around (consumerism is alive and well)
- Better quality products.

Low cost competition is becoming a more precarious game. Those that want to succeed in the long-term will need to compete on product and service quality, design and efficiency of delivery, rather than on cost and price alone. This means being responsive to customer demands and innovation in both product and service development, in order to keep ahead of the game. Increasing competition, continual advances in technology and changing consumer tastes, also means that organisations must be prepared for change and be able to constantly adapt and reorganize.

In a world of increasingly sophisticated supply chains, outsourcing, off-shoring, cross-border operations, growing numbers of joint ventures and collaborations (all of which depend on relationships between people), it's difficult to think of an organisation where human capital and people management are not of critical importance.

1.16 GLOBALISATION OF LABOUR MARKETS

The economic rise of China and India, coupled with the growth in off-shoring, has changed the labour supply landscape. The world has become smaller – one where executives will increasingly face global labour markets and complex environments generated by off-shoring and other multi-country strategies. This increasing integration of global markets is opening up vast new talent sources. For many companies and governments, global labour and talent strategies will become as important as global sourcing and manufacturing strategies. Ongoing shifts in labour and talent will be far more profound than the widely observed migration of jobs to low-wage countries. Already we are seeing unprecedented migration in Europe with Polish guest workers and border restrictions down. There is some anecdotal evidence of a "reverse brain drain" (i.e., from richer countries to developing countries), with green card professionals exiting the USA.

Furthermore, organisations have historically located labour near production resources in order to keep transportation costs low. They have also located near customers so they could frequently communicate with each other. However the advent of a more knowledge-based economy, coupled with increasingly advanced information technology, has relaxed the importance of placing employees in certain specific geographical locations. These changes have allowed much greater use of distributed workforces, as well as off-shoring jobs to other countries. For example, in the mining industry, we are now seeing the advent of driverless trucks, with the possibility of some mining operational staff being located in head office or coastal environments, as opposed to remote, harsher mine locations.

1.17 GLOBAL WARMING AND INTERGENERATIONAL EQUITY

Of course one of the biggest unknowns is the impact of global warming on business. Coupled with the emerging social need of concerns for future generations and sustainability (e.g., Corporate Social Responsibility, triple bottom line reporting), global warming will shake up the nature and availability of work. The winners will be new technologies and clean industries, whilst the losers are likely to include the agricultural, transport and energy intensive industries. One of the consequences of global warming will be the implementation of more flexible work practices, with people working more from home and commuting less. Advancements in technology in the form of holograms and the creation of virtual offices will make this more feasible.

1.18 OVERALL IMPLICATIONS AND CHALLENGES FOR ORGANISATIONS

Implications and challenges for organisations include:

- The need for their workforce to be flexible and to adapt in a volatile environment
- Greater workforce diversity with organisations having to reckon more with the needs of various demographic groups (e.g., Gen Y, Gen X and Baby Boomers, Sandwich Generation, etc.)
- Structuring and managing a variety of employer/worker relationships in an increasingly complex workplace, consistent with the needs of the business
- Fostering of citizenship commitment amongst employees/workers and a sense of community
- Maintaining organisational coherence and some semblance of internal equity, given the polarisation between skilled and unskilled jobs, and the different workforce strategies applicable to these two groups (e.g., reward mechanisms, flexible work practices, etc.)
- Building commitment in new ways and enhancing performance (i.e., doing more with less) and retention (particularly for those in more critical roles)
- Maintaining trust with their workforce, against a background of uncertainty, rapid change, greater demands and flatter structures (i.e., "walking the talk" with organisational rhetoric)

- Greater vulnerability in terms of the labour market (i.e., not just competing locally), with opportunities to import labour
- Greater demands on managers, employees/workers, some of whom need to be accessible 24/7 given customer service standards are constantly increasing
- Accommodation of a variety of needs of their employees/workers and connecting better with individuals
- Providing for changing work/career needs of people over the employment life cycle, and assisting/supporting employees in their career development, ongoing education and transitions
- Continuously competing for talent (i.e., attraction, development and retention of talent), with "poaching" of talent on the increase (with the growth of search firms)
- Balancing autonomy with control, particularly with flexible work practices and managing a remote workforce
- Responding to increased community sensitivities concerning the environmental and social impacts of their business activities.

1.19 OVERALL IMPLICATIONS AND CHALLENGES FOR INDIVIDUALS

Implications and challenges for individuals include the need to:

- Cope with and adapt to change, including handling transitions
- Develop "soft skills", including relationship building, greater self-reliance and resilience
- Balance work and family demands
- Add value and perform consistently well
- Take charge of their own career, and self-manage it through different stages and cycles
- Commit to ongoing learning and invest in their on-going training and skill development.

1.20 SUMMARY OF 12 TRENDS IMPACTING ON THE WORKPLACE

Based on the previous discussion, trends that are shaping the current workplace and which will continue to shape the workplace of future have been summarised under the following headings below.

Demographic trends (2):

- Ageing workforce
- Greater workforce diversity

Organisational trends (4):

- Demanding more by way of higher people performance and technical skills
- Developing more fluid forms
- Maintaining flexibility and shifting more of the risk with the growth of the contingent workforce
- Polarisation of skilled versus unskilled roles with a focus on the development of talent

Individual trends (2):

- Move towards individualism
- Concerns with juggling work and home responsibilities, maintaining high levels of performance and managing their careers

Market trends (3):

- Continuing shift to the knowledge economy
- Consumers demanding more
- Globalisation of labour markets

Environmental and social trends (1):

- Global warming and intergenerational equity

We shall now take into account some of these trends in looking at the workplace of the future in the following chapter.

Chapter 2

The Workplace of the Future

KEY POINTS

Key questions and issues that we will address in this chapter:

- *What are some of the key people issues that will characterise or define the workplace of the future?*
- *What should organisations be considering now to best prepare themselves for the future?*

What are the consequences of failing to adequately address these questions/issues or ending up with the wrong answers?

- *Without insight into the future and the associated shaping of human capital strategies and practices, organisations run the risk of being left in the "white water turbulence" - hardly a recipe for building organisational sustainability*
- *People decisions that are made in the current business climate should also have one eye to the future otherwise they may go against the tide, resulting in a costly subsequent correction.*

2. THE WORKPLACE OF THE FUTURE

2.1 INTRODUCTION

We have said that people are a core intangible asset and largest driver of business success. This being the case, we shall now spend some time in focusing on the workplace of the future and the associated people challenges and issues. At the end of Chapter 1 we summarised the implications of recent workplace changes and challenges ahead for organisations and employees/ workers. We shall now pick up on some of these issues and challenges, whilst also turning our attention to some newer issues and challenges that are currently incubating. To that end, we have selected the following topics to explore, on the basis that they are most likely to characterize or define the workplace of the future:

- The legacy of the GFC
- The continued rise of market influences and its' impact
- The (possible) death of employment
- The optimization of human resources (including talent), risk mitigation and better human capital measurement systems
- The new role of managers
- A new perspective on careers
- The proliferation of flexible work practices, including working from home
- The lack of investment in training and the potential for a vicious cycle of skill deterioration
- Retention of later Baby Boomers and earlier Gen X
- Confronting the anti-age bias.

However one needs to be very careful in making predictions concerning the future. The financial experts and economists are proof that anybody can get it wrong in light of their failure to predict the GFC.

2.2 THE LEGACY OF THE GLOBAL FINANCIAL CRISIS (GFC)

The GFC – A spiritual crisis?

Some would argue that the GFC is actually a spiritual crisis! They would see it as the manifestation of unsustainable and rampant capitalism as evidenced by an amoral culture of short-term self-interest, greed, irresponsible risk-taking, profit maximisation, emphasis on shareholder value, isolationist thinking and a profligate disregard for long-term consequences.

There is a growing recognition that we are more than economic beings, with a shift in focus towards quality of life and less on consumption. The sacred cow of the shareholder has been questioned, with the growing demands of stakeholders on business, and a renewed emphasis on value to customers, suppliers and employees. If nothing else, the GFC and associated financial meltdown has revealed that traditional company valuations in some instances are meaningless, because they have been to short-term based.

Shift in emphasis from shareholders back to employees/ workers

In a stock market which has been preoccupied with short term profits, this fixation will diminish in significance as stakeholders take a longer term and more sustainable perspective. Investors will come to realize that it is the less tangible and constantly evolving people factors that are increasingly the drivers of value and the developers of competitive capacity. Consistent with this insight, it is likely there will be a greater attention paid to the interests of employees/workers, whereas in recent times, the shareholder has been king.

> Note: Refer to Chapter 5 concerning the dangers of downsizing and the adverse secondary people and financial impacts.

Authenticity is now in!

Every crash reveals unethical behaviour which in turn causes regulatory response. One of the impacts of the GFC has been the investor angst and community outrage concerning the payment of obscene bonuses to some executives. People are now no longer in the mood to tolerate hypocrisy, lack of transparency and actions that promote blatant self-interest. The recent debate over proposed legislation to limit some of the extravagant remuneration practices of the past is clear evidence of the winds of change. Coupled with the rise in individualism, and the search for meaning and purpose (and dare I say it truth), the pendulum is shifting back in favour of authenticity, integrity, transparency and "substance" over "spin". People will, more than ever, be attracted to those companies which articulate values that support a sense of mission and higher purpose. To that end, employees/

workers will, even more so, require that their leaders "walk the talk". In the post GFC era, leaders will therefore have to earn authority. This will mean better connecting with their people, adopting a more collaborative style, and motivating them through enthusiasm, energy, excitement, etc. The hope is that more enlightened approaches to managing people will be adopted. Irrespective of their status, one universal should prevail – that of treating all employees/workers with honesty and respect.

2.3 THE CONTINUED RISE OF MARKET INFLUENCES ANDTHEIR IMPACTS

The rise of the influence of the market in employment relationships is a fundamental development which will continue to generate profound changes. Power in negotiation depends entirely on one thing – options or choices. Those options in turn are dependent on the relative pull of supply and demand. Notwithstanding the current post GFC recession that the western world has recently experienced, the pundits are still predicting a longer term skills shortage, and labour supply problem in some areas. The likely severity and extent of this shortage is a matter of conjecture.

Power shifts and fluctuations between employers and employees/ workers will vary across industries, roles and geographical locations. The "old deal" or the traditional lifetime employment relationship was like a marriage. The new relationship is more like a lifetime of divorces and remarriages - a series of close relationships governed by the expectation that they need to work but may not last. However neither party knows when the relationship is likely to end, as either side can end it unilaterally when it so desires. Refer later in Chapter 7 to the open ended nature of the psychological contract. As such there is a need for both parties to constantly renegotiate their commitments, with pressures of the labour market an important force in shaping the nature of the relationship.

> Note: Organisations will need to be more effective in psychological contract renegotiations and in minimising the risks of psychological contract violation. The psychological contracting model should be used to ensure that the relationship is one of exchange and not coercion.

With the growth in search firms and poaching of talent on the increase, mass poaching may become a more viable substitute for acquiring companies in the future. Growth is more likely to occur through outsourcing, alliances and joint ventures, rather than through expensive takeovers. Remuneration practices will continue to reshape the norms of fairness as they shatter the old pay schedules based on internal equity. High flying subordinates may earn more than their managers, with seniority having less to do with pay. Skills that are valued and are in short supply will be rewarded, with the market continuing to usher in new perceptions of fairness.

2.4 THE DEATH OF EMPLOYMENT?

The changing nature of work

The combination of three factors: economics, technology and demographics, will change the nature of work to become more projects based. More people will be multi-employed. They will use specialised services to market themselves for individual and *ad hoc* projects. Collaborative working will become much more important. There is likely to be a proliferation of "virtual" companies without conventional business premises.

The rise of the contingent workforce has a ceiling

Thus we will continue to see a decline in the employee society but not its extinction. This decline will eventually bottom out as it is virtually impossible to manage all employees through explicit contracts. Contracts struck in the market for many positions cannot define the employment relationship. Some skills are unique to the employer and developed on-the-job, with the tasks interdependent with others, or with systems in the organisation. Performance becomes difficult to monitor accurately, all of which makes contracts imperfect at best. Another consideration is the transactional cost in such contingent arrangements. The rise of the contingent workforce will therefore have an upper limit.

> Note: Relatively little effort has been invested in extracting the best out of the contingent workforce, with many companies having no defined policies and procedures concerning the same. Some are unaware of the numbers of their contractors, consultants, casuals, etc, often with a variety of commercial arrangements applying within organisations.

Managers and contracts: Unlikely bed fellows

The nature of the work that most managers perform does not lend itself to market-based relationships and contracts. In managerial jobs, so much work involves discretion, making it virtually impossible to set explicit performance standards in advance. Managerial work is much more suited to open-ended relationships, in which the obligations can be adjusted, performance can be observed, and rewards allocated accordingly as situations change. Some level of mutual commitment and trust to facilitate changing needs is inevitable, as is the need to develop some unique skills inside the organisation.

However the pressure from markets and the need to change organisations mean that truly open-ended long term relationships are largely dead. Organisations will be continually faced with the pressure to shed obsolete skills, and this coupled with the problem of skill poaching by other employers, makes it difficult to achieve a balance between maintaining flexibility, trust and commitment.

From another perspective, managers are not professionals. Their work is not governed by standards inside the organisation or by professional codes, and their success is inextricably linked to the success of their employer. Furthermore the most important rewards for managers are still associated with promotion and career development inside the company hierarchy.

2.5 FOCUS ON HUMAN OPTIMISATION AND PERFORMANCE

A more systemic understanding

The issues of global warming in particular, has ushered in a heightened realisation that everything is inter-related, with the need to develop a more wholistic, systemic perspective and understanding. Nowhere should this be more evident than in the people area. As indicated in the Introduction Chapter of this book, HR is probably the most diverse function of any business unit, with many HR programs and initiatives typically lacking in integration. *Ad hocracy* and "band aid" solutions are on the outer in the workplace of the future. Superficiality needs to be replaced with deeper and more insightful understandings. The "hard yards" involved in thinking through issues cannot be abdicated or avoided.

> An example of the application of more systemic thinking in the workplace of the future lies in the area of executive coaching. We have seen an explosion in the use of executive coaching in the past few years. In the future, coaching may well extend into dealing with the "whole person" (i.e., from coaching to counseling/therapy), rather than just focusing on the workplace. The separation of one's personal life and circumstances, from how one behaves and performs at work, constitutes a significant missing piece of the people jigsaw.

People management policies

Therefore value will be created from more sophisticated and integrated people management practices. Corporate and HR policies will need to be modified and adapted to meet a variety of ever changing needs. Designing and implementing well thought out employment strategies and associated policies and practices, will significantly impact on future success. These strategies and policies will need to address (but are not necessarily limited to), the following topics or issues:

- Career pathing and advancement opportunities
- Career slow down strategies
- Flexible work practices and work-life balance
- Competitive compensation
- Education and support relating to change
- Ongoing training and development opportunities for employees of all ages
- Performance optimisation
- Succession planning
- Provision of other benefits (e.g., intangibles such as family friendly benefits such as child care).

These policies and practices will need to be principle based rather than rule based in order to cater for the continually changing circumstances and needs of both parties – employers and employees/workers. Greater attention will need to be paid to building and maintaining a coherent, shared set of corporate values and culture in a workplace with high numbers of contractors and project-specific part-time employees. Apart from performance optimisation and the attraction, retention and development of the right skills mix, workplace cultures should be developed that allow employees to lead well integrated lives without them experiencing excessive work related stress.

Performance as a core company asset

Most executives recognise that the value of their business depends heavily on the performance of their people. In the public sector, the unprecedented aging of populations across the developed world will call for new levels of efficiency and creativity. Public sector activities will balloon, making productivity gains essential. Of course the private sector will be similarly motivated in order to stay competitive and be able to "do more with less".

The performance of people will be regarded as a core company asset in the workplace of the future. This will be recognized in the creation of a new HR strategic role – that of a Performance Improvement Specialist (or equivalent), which has influence across the gamut of HR and people management practices and initiatives. Value increasingly comes from:

- Boosting the productivity of individual workers

- Greater workforce innovation (e.g., systems, technology)
- Integration of activities (which multiplies value).

The focus will be on human optimisation with a new era in human capital management and measurement approaching.

> Note: In responding to the impact of the GFC, focusing on engagement and retention of employees/workers is important because they can add value to an organisation in a way that deals with the current reality of managing costs in tough times.

Remuneration and performance

Organisations will need to amend their remuneration structures to reward performance based more on outputs rather than inputs. For executives, these outputs will be tied more to the achievement of longer term objectives (i.e., outputs that contribute to sustainability). Performance standards that encourage shorter term risk taking and expediency will be discouraged. There will be a greater need to match job structures, management approaches and rewards, and career advancement systems, with different skill sets (hence the importance of the skills' based workforce segmentation model presented in Chapter 3).

Managing talent: Building commitment in new ways

With talent emerging as a core asset, remuneration and reward structures must be re-configured to optimise their utilisation and retention. Once key talent is on board, faster career progression is the most effective way to put higher performers on a different compensation trajectory without disrupting overall pay structures. In continuously competing for talent, organisations will need to create "win-win" outcomes, utilising approaches to management that are advantageous to both them and their employees, and that also lead to higher levels of performance.

However achieving such outcomes is easier said than done. Organisations are:

- Less able to rely on the loyalty of their employees as a retention strategy, although trust and leadership are critical in building commitment
- More limited in what they are able to offer talent concerning long-term guarantees and stability.

The traditional motivators of job security or longer term promotional opportunities no longer carry the same importance. Even if hypothetically these "carrots" were able to be guaranteed, many employees are less inclined to wait for such opportunities – they want it now! However on the positive side, organisations are more than ever before able to offer talent exciting job challenges and opportunities to enhance their employability. A key challenge for CEOs will be to satisfy the career development needs of talent, including the creation of internal mobility and succession plans to retain them, consistent with the needs of the business.

People measurement and reporting

We commented earlier in this book on the lack of a more scientific approach to the measurement of people, and that the quality of reporting on human assets lags well behind that of other assets of the business. In the workplace of the future, management will go from art to science. Bigger more complex companies will demand new tools to run them – statistical control tools. Long gone will be the days of "gut instinct". Tomorrow's business leaders will increasingly adopt algorithmic decision-making technologies and use highly sophisticated software to run their organisations. Managers will find themselves assessed on a new range of metrics. Refer to Chapter 9 for an example of human capital reporting.

2.6 THE NEW ROLE OF MANAGERS

People management and other new management competencies

Increasingly, people management will be treated as a core operational process, rather than a support function. People management and other new management competencies emerging in the workplace of the future include:

- Managing a variety of relationships with insiders (i.e., permanents, part-timers) and outsiders (i.e., contingents)
- Basic career counseling
- Managing flexible work practices
- Drawing up contracts, procuring and managing contractors (where activities have been outsourced)
- Negotiating performance specifications and cresting incentives for performance
- Monitoring compliance.

The cult of the CEO

The cult of the CEO (a simplistic and convenient perspective where the CEO's impact on an organisation's success is accorded more weight than it deserves), is likely to be replaced by an increased focus on the team supporting them. Depth of expertise in an industry or functional area will become a more defining requirement for senior executives rather than generalist skills.

Organisational structures

Workplaces of the future will be characterised by a reduced need for centralised structures, a move to decentralised communities, with organisations more defined by markets. The traditional work of management will be done less by managers. It will be pushed out more to the periphery and embedded in systems via technology. Decision making will be more peer-based, with power based on competence, and less on authority vested in organisational structures.

2.7 FOCUS ON CAREERS

> Note: Refer to Appendix B for a further discussion on careers in the contemporary workplace.

Careers will grow longer

Careers will grow longer in the workplace of the future, which potentially opens up exciting opportunities for new career choices. The concept of retirement will change, with a phased withdrawal rather than a definitive cut-off. Adults will seek and require ongoing education. Long standing HR practices which have invested more heavily in youth and pushed out older workers may have to be adjusted. People will need to talk openly about their career aspirations or concerns without fear of reprisals.

Career management practices in organisations will need to take more explicit account of the increasing likelihood that individuals will not simply progress upward through an organisational hierarchy during their careers. Alternate career paths that involve multiple definitions of success and multiple career trajectories must be encouraged and rewarded. Thus, work cultures that accommodate a variety of career patterns will need to be created, which include:

- Moving up the corporate ladder
- Remaining stationary
- Scaling down.

The reality is that most people would prefer to stay where they are provided their career development needs are being met

> Note. Retirement is an outdated precedent that originated in the late 19th century in the Prussian army for the few that survived to 65 years. It is a relatively new concept in human evolution.

Career transition difficulties

However changing careers in the future may prove more difficult for the following reasons:

- Employees need to keep their functional skills at the "cutting edge" and enhance their value and employability in the market, as opposed to broadening their skills
- Attachment to an occupation or profession seems to be stronger than that to an employer
- Employers may be reluctant to invest in and provide training for redeployment, particularly if the required skills are available in the market
- The increased demands by employers for deeper skills and higher performance requirements (performance would typically be lower during the career transition stage whilst new skills are being acquired)
- The move towards single purpose employers.

Whilst larger companies may purport to offer multiple career paths and opportunities, this may well prove to be illusory.

2.8 INVESTMENT IN TRAINING AND THE POTENTIAL FOR A VICIOUS CYCLE OF SKILL DETERIORATION

The willingness of employers to invest

We referred in Chapter 1 to the decline in investment by employers in training. How much training an employer is willing to pay for depends upon a number of factors:

- How hard it is to get new recruits of the required skills, and then to retain those skills, including the need to continually upgrade them
- The Return on Investment (ROI) of such training, with employers having reservations concerning the diminishing returns in so doing, particularly with poaching of talent on the increase
- The extent to which the necessary or required skills are unique to the organisation (refer to Chapter 3 for a further discussion).

Irrespective of whether or not organisations underwrite the cost of training, they will continually need to find ways to combine work and learning, making it possible to support training. The use of computer based training will continue to flourish because training can be delivered at minimal cost (once training programs are developed), when employees/workers are free, or at times that are more convenient in terms of not interrupting work schedules. Furthermore, mentoring and on-the-job training will take greater precedence over the attendance and associated cost of external courses for both economic and time investment reasons.

Vicious cycle of skill deterioration

There is a potential for a vicious cycle of skill deterioration, with employers reluctant to invest in training and development, and more and more outside hiring is done to fill skills shortages. With concerns about the extent to which employees are prepared to invest in their own skill development, there is potential for employee development to decline. This in turn will have a domino effect of a worsening of the skills shortage over the medium to longer term. Reduction in training investment has the potential to create a vicious cycle of skills shortages that leads to even more outside hiring.

Role of education providers and government

Education systems require infrastructure (e.g., supportive education systems for training professionals such as doctors, lawyers, engineers and also for providing apprenticeships), that are independent of employers. Much of this infrastructure is imposed by governments. Amongst other things, this infrastructure helps deal with the problems of employee development, retention and commitment.

Government will become even more of a major player in regulating the labour market in the future. Apart from providing the above infrastructure, its role includes/will include providing information, facilitating/providing remedial training programs, and facilitating/providing transition programs (e.g., for those people exiting "dirty" industries that are under threat from greenhouse gas emissions).

Notwithstanding the declining investment in training by industry, more work-based education and efforts to integrate school and work will be required. The downside for industry in pushing off the development of entry level skills for some professions onto applicants, is that control over their supply and quality is relinquished. It is difficult to get employees to make investments in activities which are not valued by the outside market, or to invest in skills which are truly unique to particular organisations.

2.9 THE PROLIFERATION OF FLEXIBLE WORK PRACTICES AND WORKING FROM HOME

Workforce flexibility: A defining characteristic

Workplace flexibility will be a defining characteristic in the future. In the Australian workplace, flexibility is becoming a "must do", with flexible work arrangements now being included in workplace awards and agreements. There is a growing recognition of the desire of all employed people, regardless of marital or parental status, to achieve a healthier and more satisfying balance of their roles and responsibilities. In Chapter 1 we referred to the evolution of flexible work practices. What started off as a cost cutting measure is now being demanded by employees/workers as they seek to tailor their working day to meet their personal requirements. As a result, we are seeing more flexibility in the workplace in terms of career paths, starting and finishing times, length of the working week, and the location of the workplace.

Furthermore, the allure of home working for employees/workers is becoming greater given the stress, downtime and rising costs associated with commuting. The green credentials of companies can be enhanced by using home working to discourage unnecessary travel. These factors add up to an exodus from the traditional workplace.

> Note: The emphasis for employees/workers should be less about work–life balance and more about work-life integration. The term "work-life balance" implies that work isn't part of life! It implies an exclusivity and inherent conflict between work and other life domains which is not necessarily the case.

Langford and Parkes (2008) found that work-life balance doesn't significantly contribute to employee engagement, although it might be more important in terms of attraction. However it is important for some women and men who bear burden of domestic responsibilities. These researchers found that nearly three-quarters of an Australian sample of 16,000 employees were satisfied with their work-life balance.

The challenge for organisations in accommodating flexible work practices

Organisations will need to embrace the concept of virtual work-spaces and provide managers and their employees/workers with the necessary training and technology needed to work anywhere. In the coming decades, the ability to provide flexible job structures and workplace conditions will be critical to attracting and retaining a demographically diverse talent pool. Accommodating flexible work practices will require:

- Different methods of communication, as individuals and functions operate from an increasing number of different locations
- More sophisticated work monitoring approaches to account for diverse combinations of weeks, days and hours worked
- Education of managers, with a number of studies showing a gap between the rhetoric of promotion of flexible work practices and their implementation, with managers regarded as the major stumbling block.

> Note: Electronic monitoring is eliminating one of the biggest obstacles to working from home – employers' fears that workers will slacken off. This includes taking photos of computer screens at random, counting key strokes or mouse clicks, and watching workers through video cameras.

Presence based communications and web applications are minimising some of the issues as to how people work together from different locations and time zones. Developments in technology will make the virtual workplace a reality. The next generation network will change the way we live and work. The development of 3D hologram technology will create a virtual (office) presence, which has the look and feel of being in the same room together with the other person (or people).

Meeting these challenges will require new ways of thinking about the nature of the workplace. Overall, models of flexible working will continue to evolve in response to a diversity of needs of Generation Y through to Baby Boomers.

> Note: Flexible work practices constitute a defensive retention strategy for minimising "Personal" reasons for leaving, as well as combating the "Pull" effect (refer to Chapter 6).

The impacts of flexible work practices on organisations and their employees/workers

Given such new work scenarios, some interesting questions arise, the answers to which at this stage are yet unknown:

- *How will people interact?*
- *Will they feel the loss of the human factor (i.e., the "real thing" of direct face-to-face contact)?*
- *Will organisations miss out on some of the innovation, problem solving, creativity and inspiration that often happens in informal face-to-face discussions (e.g., over a coffee, a chat in the corridor, etc.)?*
- *Will employees identify in the same way with their organisations as they currently do?*
- *How will employees cope with the blurring of boundaries between work and home?*
- *Will employees have the self-discipline and self-reliance to operate in a more solo or isolated work modes?*
- *Will employees be able to reclaim personal and family time?*
- *What level and kind of control should organisations exercise over employees/workers concerning when, where and what they do to produce value?*

Some employees/workers will have more freedom to shape the way they want to live, but will also have the freedom to do poor quality work and to cheat. Others will not be allowed to cling to traditional patterns of employment, and will be required to be more flexible with regard to organisational needs (e.g., work non-traditional shifts, be on call). A big challenge for people will be just running their own lives.

Organisations will have more flexibility but could abuse that flexibility by exploiting outsiders. Conversely, they will have to compete for employees/workers who will become more footloose and less inclined to work for an organisation that does not allow individuals to tailor the working day to meet their personal requirements. Flexible arrangements may blur into unauthorised "deals", or reflect forms of favouritism that are more likely to be made with the immediate boss, as opposed to the HR Manager. Organisations will more than ever, need to understand what jobs are, the time taken to do them, and what it means to integrate corporate needs with employee motivation, talent and the pursuit of individual fulfillment. Another challenge for organisations will be on managing geographically dispersed teams, maintaining relationships of trust and creating team spirit.

> Note: Work systems in which work is not organised around groups have higher employee turnover (Buch, 1992). Some would argue of the need to bind organisations and people together through social relationships at the workplace – that nothing can replace direct human contact. They would advocate that commitment is developed through a combination of work organisation arrangements and the tight network of relationships.

2.10 CONFRONTING THE ANTIAGE BIAS

Prejudices against mature aged workers

In the past decade or so, the workers most at risk (i.e., of being unemployed), have been more mature workers. Downsizing and delayering, has targeted jobs and positions held by mature workers. The shedding of the more expensive proportion of the headcount has represented a "quick economic fix" when times get tough. Mature workers have appealed as being more attractive to deploy, and as such have borne the brunt of workplace restructuring. This approach to downsizing is referred to as RAPE (Retired Aged Personnel Early). Furthermore, early retirement programs have been invoked and targeted at older employees.

Some would argue that the prejudice against older workers has been entrenched, institutionalised, planned and sanctioned at the highest levels of corporations. It is somewhat ironic that many CEOs and senior executives, deemed fit to run their corporations, are in the same age bracket as those whom their organisations have either been retrenching, or have otherwise denied employment opportunities to. The above prejudices are exacerbated with those involved in recruiting new placements. In the case of external recruiters working for recruitment services firms, they are typically aged in their late 20's to early 30's. Many of them may have little understanding of the issues surrounding the employment of mature workers. In short, there is a fundamental disconnect between many recruiters and mature aged applicants.

The value of mature aged workers

More mature workers are often deemed as being unfit for faster pace jobs, unsuitable for retraining and too expensive to keep on the payroll. Many employers do not expect to recoup the benefits of investing in more mature workers. There is a perception that you can't teach "an old dog new tricks!" Others would argue that mature aged workers add value to organisations which may easily be overlooked or not appreciated (e.g., flexibility, citizenship, experience, consistency, responsibility, wisdom, maturity and mobility).

Older employees generally have lower turnover and absenteeism rates, are generally higher in job satisfaction, and more committed to organisations than younger workers. They still indicate a strong interest in learning and growing, and are suitable for leadership, training, mentoring and coaching roles because of their experience (Dytchwald, Erikson & Morison, 2006). Few generalisable conclusions can be drawn about employee age and work performance (Farr & Ringseis, 2002).

Mature age: Examples of achievements

There are many examples of older people achieving their greatest feats and accomplishments later in life, sometimes against a background of perceived previous failure. Names like Winston Churchill and Nelson Mandella come to mind. These are figures who provide salient illustrations of the genuine qualities of leadership, statesmanship, vision and controlled energy bequeathed by age and experience. Henry Ford's creativity bubbled to the surface at 53 years of age when he invented the mass production line. Creativity, initiative and achievement are not age dependant!

An attitudinal sea change is required

What appears inescapable is that there will be a greater reliance on the employment of mature workers in the longer term, given an ageing population. This will be a necessity for productivity, future competitiveness and survival, otherwise there simply won't be enough workers to go around. This 55+ year old group, which currently comprises around 10% of the workforce, is estimated to double in representation (i.e., to 20%) over the next five to ten years. However there's still a long way to go in so far as changing the thinking towards older workers. A mindshift towards more inclusive corporate cultures for older workers will need to be adopted. Otherwise, if the age bias continues, there is a danger of class distinction between young and old, with mature workers being predominantly limited to more basic work with lower pay, compared to younger workers. It is therefore pointless to ask older workers to stay on if they cannot find appropriate work which meets their extrinsic and intrinsic needs. Even if they accept such work offers, they are likely to become disgruntled and less productive employees

Consequently an attitudinal sea change will be required towards older workers, and recruitment agencies and Human Resource Managers will be on the frontline. Towards that end, there is some evidence to suggest that social and business attitudes are capable of being turned around relatively quickly. For example, in the 1980's and early 90's, people who changed careers in mid-life were regarded with some degree of suspicion as being unstable. Those that returned to tertiary studies, as part of their career change transition, were viewed as taking up tertiary places which were the domain of younger people. In a decade or so, the concept of life-long learning has become the norm. Career changers are now seen to offer a greater breadth of experience and able to adapt more readily to the continually changing demands of the contemporary workplace.

As indicated earlier, the milestones of life are shifting upwards with increased longevity. Whilst we have an ageing workforce, we need to create an ageless workforce, where workers are valued – and employed – for their skills, and not judged or penalised because of their date of birth. Confronting the anti-age bias will be fundamental to the effective assimilation and acceptance of older workers. Policies and practices of hiring and retiring must be adjusted, and an environment that clearly welcomes and values older workers must be created. For example, this may include:

- Promotion of older worker role models
- Subsidies for organisations to provide training for older workers
- Education to breakdown perceived myths and challenge stereotypes
- Encouragement of phased retirement
- Education of employers to understand the changing demographics.

In addition to the above, copious research, both in Australia and internationally, has shown a crucial link between mature age workforce participation and flexible work practices that is becoming the strategic centrepiece. Older workers value autonomy – they want ownership over their working week.

> Note: Current employment models where a person retires at their most senior position and leaves the organisation, completely lack flexibility and are a result of widespread ageism in the workplace. Leadership models also suffer from a similar inflexibility with companies assuming they should continue to be led by their oldest employees. There is a need to alter our fundamental assumptions about work and retirement and the transition between the two.

The challenge of managing the mature aged workforce

Managers will be required to manage a generation of older workers who will not retire in the traditional manner. A key challenge for corporations will be creating an environment which enables older workers to remain motivated, engaged and productive longer – whilst at the same time, developing and retaining younger workers in an increasingly competitive job market. Higher numbers of older workers pose a number of executive and management challenges:

- *How are roles to be redefined to suit older workers?*
- *How should they be paid relative to younger employees?*
- *What obligations do older workers have to refresh their skills and to learn new products, approaches and techniques?*
- *How do younger executives learn to manage their own predecessors?*

2.11 RETENTION OF LATER BABY BOOMERS AND EARLIER GEN X

Commitment and retention of those in the early to mid 40's (i.e., mid career workers – a mix of later Baby Boomers and early Gen X), will assume greater importance. They are required for productivity today and will be required for retention tomorrow. The period of early to mid 40's is one where people often re-evaluate their lifestyle and career, termed by some as a "mid-life crisis". The recognition of ageing triggers the quest for change. It includes taking stock of one's accomplishments, seldom with complete satisfaction. Compromises may have been made at work and home, with some feeling that life and career decisions may have painted them into a corner.

> A man in the mid-life period examines every component of the career structure built up to date, knocks it all down and starts all over again (Levinson, 1977).

This period of life can vary in intensity for different people - some becoming increasingly resigned and disillusioned. Others disrupt their lives through divorce, career change and relocation, all in search of a new start or direction. At this stage of their career, employees are ripe for change and renewal, yet few businesses recognise or take advantage of this.

The most severe period of worker shortage and brain drain may well be when most Baby Boomers (mid-career workers today), will reach their sixties. To retain tomorrow, they must be engaged today! Once people have made retirement plans that don't include the organisations for which they are currently working, then it becomes difficult to change their minds. Refer to Chapter 6 on the dynamic process of leaving, and the need to take charge of this earlier in the process rather than later.

Unfortunately, many are tracked into specific functions or organisational units from which they fear to stray, with their managers loath to lose them. Organisations will need to seek non-traditional candidates from within for openings, and a willingness to release employees from elsewhere. A mid-career change is becoming a sign of success in adapting, and not a failure to thrive in one's original occupation.

Chapter 3

Workforce Segmentation - Determining Employment Strategies

KEY POINTS

Key questions and issues that we will address in this chapter:

- *How to segment your workforce based on skills*
- *Why a skills' based workforce segmentation model is superior to more traditional forms of workforce segmentation (e.g., those based on hierarchy, job or salary level)*
- *Why traditional forms of job evaluation have exceeded their use by date*
- *Why workforce segmentation based on skills underpins the management, measurement and reporting of human capital (including its attraction, engagement, development and retention)*
- *How workforce segmentation based on skills is fundamental to achieving alignment between business and workforce strategies*
- *How the skills' based workforce segmentation model forms the basis for labour outsourcing, "buy" (i.e., ready made from the market), versus "make" (i.e., develop in-house) employee decisions*
- *How to configure the composition of your workforce in order to maximize flexibility, minimize risk, maximize commitment and develop and retain skills*
- *How the skills' based workforce segmentation model forms the basis for determining levels of investment in people*
- *How to identify which are the really critical roles in your organisation (which is not always obvious)*
- *How your HR policies and practices should vary according to different workforce segments, based on the skills segmentation model*
- *How the cost of turnover varies according to different workforce segments, based on the skills segmentation model*
- *Why the skills' based workforce segmentation model is fundamental to workforce strategic planning.*

What are the consequences of failing to adequately address these questions/issues or ending up with the wrong answers?

- *The wrong segmentation model applied to your workforce will result in the wrong people strategies, confusion, ad hoc and inconsistent people decisions, increased turnover, operational inefficiencies and poorer performance, inefficient use of resources and lack of workforce flexibility*
- *A number of case studies in this chapter and throughout this book illustrate the application of wrong workforce segmentation approaches.*

3. WORKFORCE SEGMENTATION – DETERMINING EMPLOYMENT STRATEGIES

3.1 WORKFORCE SEGMENTATION: WHERE IT ALL STARTS

Many organisations now use a variety of employment modes to allocate work, including the simultaneous use of internalised (e.g., permanents) and externalized employment (e.g., contractors, labour hire) modes. As we have identified in Chapter 1, organisations are increasingly depending upon external workers (such as temps, contract workers, consultants, etc.), compared to the use of internal full-time employees, part-timers and casuals. As has been stated previously, having a workforce that is accessible, skilled, motivated and efficiently deployed will increasingly be a key differentiator of business performance and financial success.

Clearly a "one size fits all" approach to people management is no longer appropriate in dealing with the complexity of the 21st Century workplace. Not everyone is equal! Not all employees possess knowledge and skills of equal strategic importance. Just as a marketer segments or stratifies their clients according to their value, the same principles should apply to segmenting the workforce (or more specifically workforce roles/jobs). Making choices about the importance of roles is essential to developing an effective workforce strategy. The choice of segmentation model is therefore fundamental to developing a rational and consistent approach for addressing the people management challenges ahead. It should underpin your organisation's human capital strategy and its implementation. More specifically, it should form the basis for answering the questions posed at the beginning of this chapter and determining:

- Differentiated approaches to attraction, engagement and retention, and the building of human capital
- The reporting of human capital data.

3.2 IDENTIFYING POCKETS OF ORGANISATIONAL DISTRESS

A workforce segmentation scheme invariably enables the clinical identification of pockets of organisational distress, including disengagement, dissatisfaction and retention risk. Targeted interventions can then be applied to address deficits, thus resulting in an efficient and effective use of resources. Without such a scheme, these pockets of distress may not even be identified.

Our Experience with Workforce Segmentation: Examples of Pockets of Distress

Our experience in working with many organisations (including surveying their employees), is that invariably there are issues that emerge in one workforce segment (which may lie anywhere in the organisation from higher up down to lower levels, or within particular business units or sections), that are not necessarily pervasive throughout the rest of the organisation. A few examples of the variety of pockets of organisational distress that we have encountered include issues:

- Between the CEO and the executive team which resulted in a number of executives being at high risk of leaving
- For front-line staff who were not being recognized for their contribution, lacking in sufficient decision making authority, and not having received adequate training, all of which contributed to lower levels of commitment, satisfaction and a higher risk of leaving
- At a middle management level where a lack of communication from above, combined with a silo mentality in the organisation, contributed to lower commitment and dissatisfaction
- With professional IT staff in specialised technical roles who didn't receive adequate training and were consequently dissatisfied and at high risk of leaving
- Within a particular Business Unit where there was a lack of trust between the manager and his direct reports, resulting in dissatisfaction.

An effective workforce segment approach enables such issues to be clearly identified, with targeted interventions implemented to address deficits.

3.3 HOW TO BEST SEGMENT THE WORKFORCE

Building on the ideas and concepts of Lepak and Snell (1999, 2002), the WRDI Institute has developed a skills' based workforce segmentation model, which takes into account both the value and uniqueness of skills, for a particular role, to the organisation. Value and uniqueness are ubiquitous dimensions that differentiate most, if not all, human capital. After all, skills are the new currency, so it makes good sense to think about the workforce through the lens of a skills' perspective.

This skills' based workforce segmentation model (refer to the Introduction Chapter of this book and the models on the coloured pages), offers a strategic and comprehensive framework for underpinning people policies and practices, and managing the complexities of the contemporary workforce. It comprises four different categories of employee roles (or segments), as follows:

- **Quadrant 1: "Criticals"** – higher skills value and higher skills uniqueness
- **Quadrant 2: "Professionals, Skilled and Semi-skilled"** – higher skills value and moderate to lower skills uniqueness
- **Quadrant 3: "Doers"** – lower skills value and lower skills uniqueness
- **Quadrant 4: "Specialists"** – lower skills value and higher skills uniqueness.

Examples of various jobs which fit within each of these quadrants are provided later in this chapter. This model also proposes differing levels of investment and a variety of psychological contracts (from relational to transactional), for the various skills quadrants. For a more extensive explanation of the various types of psychological contracts (i.e., relational, transactional, hybrid), refer to Chapter 7.

> Note: In this adapted skills' based workforce segmentation model (i.e., from Lepak and Snell), the definition of unique skills is a more absolute concept, rather than being relative to particular organisations.

3.4 ABOUT VALUABLE SKILLS

Valuable skills are those skills which improve the efficiency and effectiveness of the organisation, exploit market opportunities, and/or neutralise potential threats. Valuable skills either create:

- Lower costs (e.g., boosting the productivity of employees/workers)
- Increased revenue (e.g., through marketing and pricing strategies which optimize net revenue)
- Greater innovation (e.g., higher quality, enhanced service offerings, improved efficiency, increased benefits to customers, etc.)

These valuable skills may be demonstrated in a number of ways, e.g.:

- Strategically

- Technologically
- Financially
- Operationally
- Organisationally.

3.5 ABOUT UNIQUE SKILLS

Unique skills are rare and specialised, or organisational specific. These skills:

- Are idiosyncratic - unlikely to be found, or only rarely available, in the open market
- Are difficult to replace
- Are difficult for competitors to imitate or duplicate
- Need to be nurtured over time, given that they are not developed and acquired overnight
- Are not transferable, and as such, organisations are required to invest in their acquisition, including education, training and development.

Uniqueness has two dimensions:

1. **Specific or concentrated uniqueness** - which is a function of the availability of skills in the market, together with the degree of specialisation of those skills. This is reflected in the intensity and duration of training required to operate or maintain specialised equipment or in-house systems (e.g., IT systems), acquire knowledge of unique procedures or processes, acquire specific product knowledge, etc.
2. **Generalised uniqueness** - which is tacit knowledge about the organisation and its environment, including the supply chain (e.g., organisational systems, processes and procedures, products, markets, competitors, customers, suppliers, etc.).

Often tacit knowledge is acquired *in situ* (e.g., months or years of experience with the organisation, number of unique projects, etc.). Some organisations are pursuing a policy of non-reliance on specialized skills (refer to Chapter 6 on retention strategies), and the associated training investment, by choosing off-the-shelf products (e.g., IT software). The skills required for operating and maintaining these products are more readily available in the market. Notwithstanding, employees' knowledge and skills sets are becoming increasingly more defined and industry/organisation specific (i.e., unique), not to mention the ongoing requirement for constant skill renewal and updating. The uniqueness of an organisation's skills can be a critical element for their gaining a competitive advantage.

3.6 EXAMPLES OF TYPICAL JOBS IN EACH OF THE FOUR SKILLS QUADRANTS

Examples of jobs and their classification into various skills quadrants have been provided below. However depending upon the nature and circumstances of the business, its products and services, and the markets that it services, these examples may not necessarily be accurate for particular organisations. Some jobs have been mentioned in more than one skills quadrant.

Quadrant 1: "Criticals" (higher skills value, higher skills uniqueness roles)

Examples of Jobs - Higher Value, Higher Generalised Uniqueness

- Senior managers, executives (e.g., regional managers, divisional managers, area managers, business unit managers, senior administrators, production and distribution managers, marketing managers)
- Business development managers and key specialists (e.g., strategic and business planners, general counsel, purchasing managers)
- Designers/innovators (e.g., product and services developers, researchers, fashion designers, programmers, architects, graphic designers)
- Miscellaneous (e.g., winemakers, judges)

Examples of Jobs - Higher Value, Higher Specific Uniqueness

- Sales persons (where more extensive product or services provision training is required and where the product and services are of a more sophisticated nature, e.g., medical drug sales)
- Highly specialised professionals with very rare skills in particular areas (e.g., scientists, consultants, technicians, lawyers, doctors, etc.)

Quadrant 2: "Professionals, Skilled and Semi Skilled" (higher skills value, lower skills uniqueness roles)

Examples of Jobs:

- Professional services (e.g., lawyers, engineers, accountants, consultants, trainers, opticians, dentists, journalists, writers, teachers, vets)
- Health professionals (e.g., nurses, doctors, psychologists, social workers, physiotherapists, dieticians)
- Trades persons (e.g., electricians, plumbers, mechanics, chefs, technicians, builders, inspectors, laboratory personnel)
- Sales persons, where minimal product or services provision training is required, and where the products and services are of a less sophisticated nature (e.g., real estate, cars, financial services, insurance)
- Pilots
- Lower level managers/supervisors (e.g., smaller store/branch managers)

> Note: High potentials from this quadrant should be identified for possible promotion into quadrant 1. Where the skills relating to the above jobs are unrelated to the core competencies of the organisation, these roles may be more likely to be contracted out.

Quadrant 3: "Doers" (lower skills value, lower skills uniqueness roles)

Examples of Jobs:

- Manual workers (e.g., labourers, security personnel, cleaners, production workers, drivers, machinists)
- Administrators and support roles (e.g., clerks, receptionists, cashiers)
- Customer service roles (e.g., call centre operators, waiters, inspectors, nursing aids, day care workers)

> Note: High potentials from this quadrant should be identified for possible promotion into quadrant 2.

Quadrant 4: "Specialists" (lower skills value, higher skills uniqueness roles)

Examples of Jobs:

- Plant and equipment operators or maintenance personnel (e.g., train drivers, programmers, inspectors, instructors)

- Services (e.g., casino dealers, technical customer service support, air traffic controllers, police, armed forces)

Does your Organisation have any Specialist/Quadrant 4 Roles?

Many organisations may not necessarily have Specialist roles in quadrant 4.

A strong indication of whether a role lies in quadrant 4 is if your organisation has developed its own training program for new recruits, and invests in this training because there are little or no other options available for employees to acquire these skills (i.e., these skills are not available in the market). Typically this training will occur over a minimum three month period up to a number of years (e.g., casino dealers, train drivers, police roles or armed forces roles).

Whilst the availability of labour with certain skill sets may be tight, this does not mean that the skills are unique, and that associated roles reside in skills quadrant 4.

An example of role classification by the skills' based workforce segmentation model is provided on the coloured pages in the Introduction Chapter and also in this chapter for a SME in the resources sector.

3.7 GETTING IT WRONG: MISS-CLASSIFYING ROLES AND MISS-ALIGNING WORKFORCE AND BUSINESS STRATEGIES

Miss-classifying roles

It can often be the case that a critical role (i.e., quadrant 1) is not recognised or identified as such within an organisation. The fall out as a consequence of miss-classifying roles can adversely impact business outcomes, as illustrated in the following case studies.

Case Study: Global Mining Company – Mine Planners in Open Cut Coal Mines

One of the core capabilities of a mining company in a large open cut mine is the effective integration of various activities within that mine; from mine development, drilling and blasting, loading and hauling, processing, etc. There is a high level of complexity involved in the operation considering the volumes of material that are typically being shifted (particularly on a 24/7 operating cycle), the need to blend raw product from various pits, the geographical spread of those pits (sometimes over a distance of around 70 km), the movement of heavy equipment throughout the mine, the dewatering of those pits, etc.

A global mining company that we were consulting to recently was experiencing shortages with mine planners. To fill the gap, they employed contract planners (who were relatively inexperienced), and also used junior mining engineers in planning roles for an interim period, as part of their career development progression. The overall result of these decisions was that mine planning capability was compromised with frequent planning errors and poor decision making.

Coupled with a high demand for product and a lack of previous investment in mine development (i.e., lack of overburden removal), the resultant impact on production efficiency was significant. There were more frequent interruptions to mining operations due to continuously changing plans, less efficient operations (e.g., smaller shots being fired, more frequent movement of equipment with resultant downtime), and hand-to-mouth or short-term decisions that were not in the best interests of longer term economical mine development.

Essentially, this company had failed to recognize the importance of the mine planning role, and its relevance to the successful integration of various mining activities and efficiency in a high pressure operating environment.

Case Study: High Turnover of Support and Administrators in a Global Recruitment Company

We were called in to examine causes of high turnover in the Australian office of a global recruitment company. Staff were surveyed with the reporting of the findings according to four workforce segments as follows:

- Senior executives, business unit managers
- Team leaders
- Recruitment consultants
- Support and administration.

The "hot spot" in this organisation (from our survey findings) was at the support and administration level, where it also transpired that staff turnover of 32% was being experienced. The other segments of the organisation indicated much lower retention risk. Specifically the survey data indicated lower levels of job satisfaction for support and administration staff and a high risk of them leaving. It emerged that this company was miss-representing the role by effectively selling it as a quadrant 2 role (Professional), when in fact it was a quadrant 3 role (Doer). The company was recruiting graduates for administration roles, overselling these roles, and then not being able to deliver on the promise (i.e., the "deal"), in terms of adequate job challenge.

Our recommended interventions included the following:

- Modification to the selection and recruitment procedures to include a percentage of support and administration people who were not graduates, and who were comfortable to remain in such a role, at least in the medium term
- Insertion of an intermediate role (associate) between a support/ administration and recruitment consultant role, such that a graduate could articulate more easily and progressively up the ladder (previously the step-up from support/administration to recruitment consultant was a large one).

These interventions did not result in any direct cost increase to the company, yet they had a dramatic impact in more than halving turnover for this workforce segment.

Case Study: Global IT Company, Key Management and Technical Role

A global IT company was experiencing high turnover among their 40 technical professional staff, and we were called in to investigate. Our survey findings confirmed that a number of these people were at high risk of leaving. The company was in imminent danger of losing even more people!

More specifically, the survey findings revealed lower levels of workplace trust (i.e., with their immediate manager), a lack of adequate training for the job and lower levels of top management trust (i.e., psychological contract health factor deficits). The psychological contract consequences were low levels of affective commitment, job satisfaction and intention to stay.

This was a case of a company failing to adequately invest in the initial training of its people. These employees were in fact in Specialist (i.e., quadrant 4) roles, as the company had developed unique software programs which took some time to learn. However they were being treated as Professionals (i.e., quadrant 2 roles), by the company which was expecting them to be competent. The low trust in management (by these floundering employees who had been thrown in at the "deep end"), was partly a result of management failing to honour its promise of providing adequate training.

Misalignment of business and workforce strategies

Are your business and workforce strategies aligned? Before you jump in and answer this question in the affirmative, the answer may not necessarily be obvious. The symptoms of this misalignment often become accepted as the norm, or their root cause is not always appreciated or identified. These symptoms may manifest in higher turnover, poorer performance, difficulties in attracting suitable people, etc. Often it is necessary to "kick the tyres" to fully identify the extent of such misalignment. Only by spending time at the "coal face" can the effects of inappropriate HR policies and practices, and their adverse impact on operational efficiencies, be more clearly recognised and appreciated.

Case Study: Mining Company – Housing Policies, Recruitment and Retention

Continuing on from the previous case study with a global mining company, we were working on a consulting project concerning supervisor effectiveness. As indicated above, this company was under extreme pressure to maximize production output to meet clients' demands.

However the company had entered into an Enterprise Bargaining Agreement (EBA) whereby they were required to provide housing, or subsidise the same, for permanent blue collar employees. The locations in which the company was operating were experiencing acute housing shortages. Whilst the rationale for the company having entered into the EBA was to "buy" industrial peace, it was hamstrung in its recruitment practices by:

- Being unable to appoint permanents, and therefore having to rely on temporaries who were at high risk of leaving if they subsequently had a permanent job offer from another mining company
- Having to rely on contractors who came at a premium cost
- Recruiting inexperienced people (who did have local accommodation, but in whom some initial investment in training and development was required), which also jeopardized safety and production performance in the shorter term.

Furthermore this company had adopted a "one size fits all" philosophy to the provision of limited housing resources. It didn't differentiate higher skilled workers (e.g., mechanics, fitters, electricians) from lower skilled roles (truck drivers). The former category of workers were more critical to the operation and in shorter supply, so their attraction and retention (including the provision of housing), should have been a priority compared to the lower skill roles.

3.8 THE IMPORTANCE OF THE SEGMENT/ROLE TO THE BUSINESS

Notwithstanding the importance of Criticals (i.e., quadrant 1 employees) to business success, other segments (and roles within those segments) may be crucial. For example, in professional services, knowledge workers will be an important group, whereas in an industry where costs and services differentiate competitors, skilled and lower skilled/knowledge workers (e.g., customer service) may be crucial. Furthermore the importance of a particular workforce segment may vary over time, depending upon the history and positioning of the business.

For a start up business, top management (i.e., quadrant 1 - Criticals) is obviously vital to success. Other examples include the following:

- Store managers in an expanding retail business
- Research and development scientists for a drug supply company seeking to expand its product line and generate fresh revenue streams by developing new drugs, which would be important to organisational sustainability, particularly if that company was at the more mature stage of its existing product cycle.

Case Study: Fast Growing ICT Company

We undertook an employee survey for a BRW Top 100 fast growing company in the ICT sector. This company was experiencing difficulties in attracting programmers at a stage in its development where programmers were absolutely vital to business success. More specifically, the company was developing new software to meet client requirements. For this company, these programmers were Criticals (i.e., in quadrant 1).

However the company had made no distinction between the HR policies and people practices for programmers compared to other employees in the organisation. The following initiatives were implemented to shore up programming capacity:

- Sign on bonuses offered to new programmer recruits
- Productivity bonus offered to existing programmers for extended work hours whilst client demands were high
- Salary increases for programmers to pay them in the top 1/3rd of the market, whereas other employees in various quadrants were paid at around average market rates.

3.9 SIMILARITIES AND DIFFERENCES: TRADITIONAL WORKFORCE SEGMENTATION APPROACHES AND JOB EVALUATION MODELS COMPARED WITH THE SKILLS' BASED MODEL

Most organisations segment their workforce on a job/salary level basis, using a job evaluation model and methodology that evaluates jobs typically on the basis of:

- Know-how (both depth and breadth)

- Problem solving
- Accountability (which is related to budget or $ considerations).

Job evaluation is undertaken for the primary purpose of determining salary levels, both for internal relativity and external competitiveness.

There is some degree of overlap (relatively small), in job evaluation models and the skills' based workforce segmentation model. For example:

- Both approaches take into account the impact or influence of the role (although in the case of the skills' based model, it is the impact of these skills on the provision of the organisation's products and services to clients)
- The level of know-how (i.e., skills) in job evaluation includes an aspect of integrative and tacit knowledge (and therefore generalized uniqueness according to the skills' based model).

However other aspects of skills uniqueness in relation to the specific or concentrated unique skills and the associated investments in training and development are not taken into account in job evaluation.

Furthermore the value of skills in relation to both the business strategy and the creation of customer benefits are typically not addressed in job evaluation models. In other words, some jobs will be more important in executing the business strategy than others at a particular period in the life cycle of the organisation. Compared to the typical job evaluation models, the skills' based workforce segmentation model and associated role analysis has a more business strategy and external client or customer focus (refer to Appendix C for a further explanation).

Whether organisations use typical job evaluation approaches or not, inevitably they segment their workforce based on salary levels or job organisational levels (i.e., a hierarchical segmentation model). Their attraction, engagement, development and retention strategies, and reporting of human capital is also based on the same segmentation model. It is contended that this approach is flawed for a whole host of reasons as elaborated upon later in this chapter.

However to illustrate or contrast the differences in the skills' based segmentation model versus the job/salary level or hierarchical segmentation model, it is possible that a job or role in quadrant 2 may be paid at the same rate as a job in quadrant 4. Under the skills' based workforce segmentation model, different acquisition, engagement and retention strategies would apply to the two jobs or roles; whereas the hierarchical model would treat them equally. Examples of how EVPs vary for roles by skills quadrant are provided in Chapter 7.

An Example of Role Classification

BUSINESS UNIT (BU)	QUADRANT 1 Criticals	QUADRANT 2 Professionals, Skilled & Semi Skilled	QUADRANT 3 Doers	QUADRANT 4 Specialists
Raw Materials	▪ BU Manager ▪ Sales Manager ▪ Quarry and Sand Pit Managers ▪ Geologist	▪ Engineers ▪ Technical ▪ Supervisors, Foremen ▪ Maintenance ▪ Sales ▪ Transport	▪ Clerical and Administration ▪ Equipment Operators ▪ Labourers ▪ Drivers	
Concrete	▪ BU Manager ▪ Sales Manager ▪ Operations Manager	▪ Plant Managers ▪ Technical ▪ Maintenance ▪ Transport	▪ Clerical and Administration ▪ Labourers ▪ Equipment Operators	
Asphalt and Contracting	▪ BU Manager ▪ Operations Manager ▪ Chief Estimator ▪ Plant Managers	▪ Engineers ▪ Estimators ▪ Technical ▪ Supervisors, Foremen ▪ Maintenance ▪ Sales ▪ Transport	▪ Clerical and Administration ▪ Equipment Operators ▪ Labourers ▪ Drivers	
Services	▪ Engineering Services Manager	▪ Engineers		
Management and Corporate Services	▪ CEO ▪ CFO ▪ Manager, IT Services ▪ Manager, HR ▪ Manager, Property and Assets ▪ OH & S Manager ▪ Credit Manager ▪ Comms / PR ▪ Business Analyst	▪ HR Professionals ▪ Accountants	▪ Clerical and Administration	▪ IT Programming & Maintenance

Note. BU = Business Unit Manager.

HR Policies and Practices by Skills' Based Workforce Segment/Quadrant

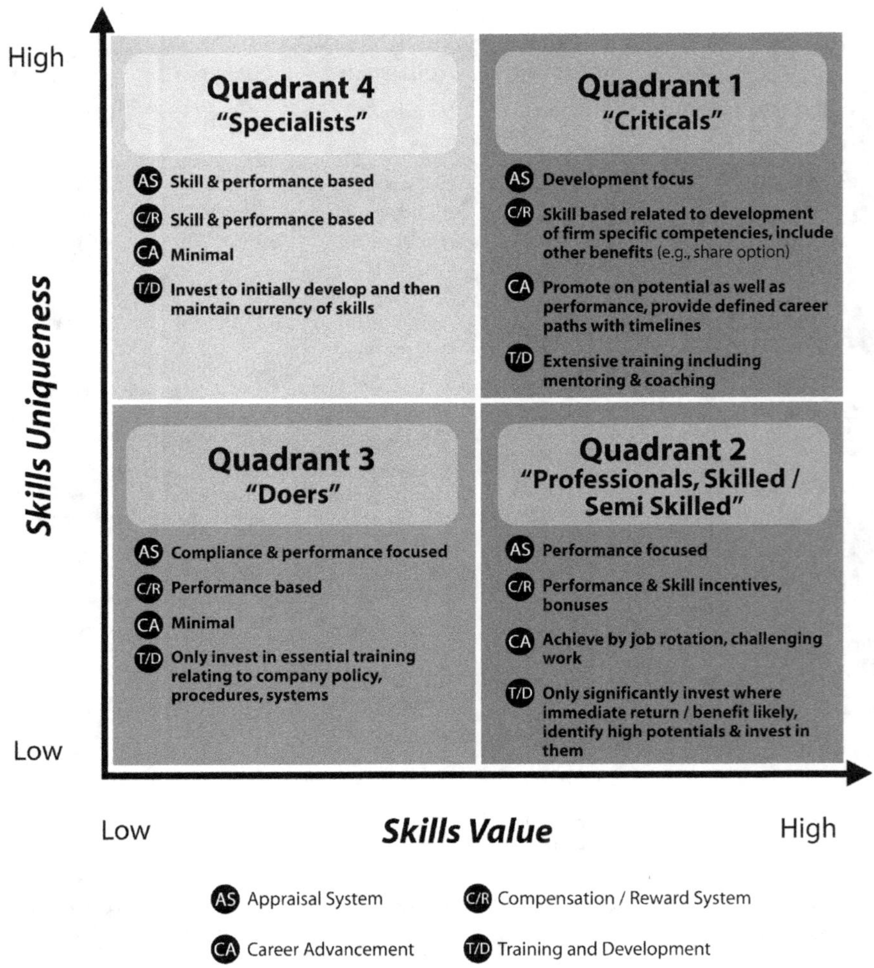

3.10 A FAILURE TO DIFFERENTIATE ROLES AND THE ADVERSE CONSEQUENCES OF NOT HAVING A WORKFORCE STRATEGY

> In significantly upgrading our workforce, we identified our strategic positions first, and then address the talent issues. (Paul Newton-Syms, Sr. HR VP, Roche Pharmaceuticals)
>
> We must significantly change our workforce to meet significant competitive challenges Sony faces. To do this we must identify the strategic positions first and then assess the talent in those positions. (Roy White, Sr. HR VP, Sony Europe)

Recruitment Strategies by Skills' Based Workforce Segment/Quadrant

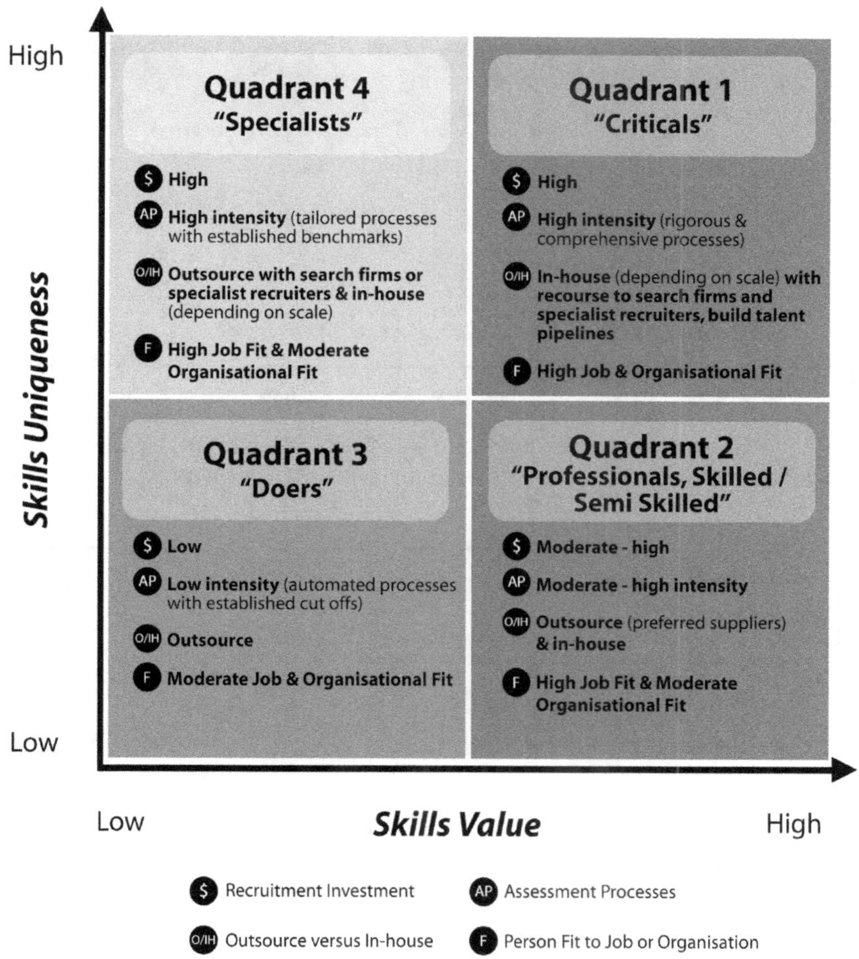

Jobs and roles can differ dramatically in the extent to which they contribute strategically and add value. As we shall see in Chapter 5, whilst many organisations have developed, or may have developed bundles of HR policies and practices, very few have developed and documented a human capital strategy. As indicated previously, at the core of such strategy is a focus on workforce differentiation— making choices about the importance of roles to the business.

A failure to adequately differentiate roles and/or to simply apply bundles of HR policies and practices on a "one size fits all" basis is a recipe for mediocrity. Such a lack of insight is likely to result in muddled, inconsistent and poor people decisions, the consequences of which could include:

- A waste of resources (e.g., could include paying the wrong people too much and the right people too little)
- Locking in low performers by over delivering, and pushing out high performers by under delivering on expectations
- Operational inefficiencies and poorer performance through having inexperienced people in important roles
- Lack of labour flexibility
- Increased turnover.

Do You Really have a Workforce Strategy?

Are You Differentiating Your Workforce Sufficiently?

The following is a brief questionnaire which acts as a prompt for you to answer the question as to whether you are differentiating your workforce sufficiently and whether you really do have a workforce strategy.

Complete the following questions about various roles/jobs in your organisation:

1. **Most positions are paid at the market midpoint.**

   T__ F__

2. **Recruitment for all roles has the same assessment process.**

   T__ F__

3. **The Employment Value Proposition (EVP) is the same for all roles.**

   T__ F__

4. **A "one size fits all" approach applies to the application of all of our people management policies and practices to various roles.**

   T__ F__

5. **Turnover is only reported for the workforce as a whole.**
   T__ F__

6. **The workforce is only segmented on an organizational level or job/salary level basis.**

   T__ F__

7. **Our performance management system/forms are the same for all roles**

   T__ F__

8. **There is no defined methodology for identifying Critical roles**

   T__ F__

9. **There is no defined methodology for determining which roles are outsourced or considered for potential outsourcing**

   T__ F__

10. **There is little recognition or appreciation of the relative importance of various roles to the business strategy and outcomes.**

    T__ F__

If you answered False to all of these questions, then you are likely to have developed a workforce/human capital strategy. However this may not necessarily be in the form of a documented plan.

If you answered True to only one or two of these questions, then you are well on the way to developing a workforce/human capital strategy.

If you answered True to three or more of these questions, you are unlikely to be differentiating your workforce roles sufficiently. As such, it is very unlikely that you have developed a comprehensive and effective workforce or human capital strategy (i.e., you may have bundles of HR policies and conducting workforce planning and talent management but this is very different from having such a strategy). Consequently you are unlikely to be making optimal people management decisions.

3.11 WORKFORCE DIFFERENTIATION - FURTHER LIMITATIONS OF TRADITIONAL JOB EVALUATION MODELS

> The conventional approach to job evaluation is static, inflexible and primarily focused on internal equity. There is a need to move away from conventional approaches to determining job importance and job-worth to a model which focuses on future value creation, strategic job worth and competitive advantage. (Becker, Huselid & Beatty, 2009)

Traditional job evaluation models are incapable of answering the above questions regarding job importance in relation to future value creation, competitive advantage, etc. As Beatty, Huselid and Becker (2009) contend, this conventional approach looks both internally and to history for its definition of value. Its deficiencies include the following:

- It is static
- It is inflexible

- It is primarily focused on internal equity at the expense of strategic capabilities, value creation, and market competitiveness or relativities.

Accordingly this approach may not necessarily reflect the true value of the contribution of the role to business success.

Beatty *et al* maintain that over time, organisations lose focus on the importance of a job or position, and bureaucracy takes over. HR processes and systems tend to become standardized, with firms focusing on process improvement at the expense of strategic value. The consequences are that workforce strategy becomes more homogenous and disconnected from business strategy.

Compounding the above limitations, and as mentioned earlier, many organisations then segment their roles, and hence their workforce, based on salary levels. However salary levels:

- Don't indicate true relativities between roles in so far as their impact on business outcomes (i.e., value creation, competitive advantage)
- Shouldn't serve as the basis for determining HR policies and practices, and specifically attraction, engagement and retention strategies.

Furthermore and as indicated above, one of the aims of job evaluation is to determine internal salary relativities. However we have seen with the advent of tighter labour markets, that internal remuneration relativities have been over ridden. Market forces (i.e., supply and demand for skills) have become much more influential in determining remuneration levels and challenging traditional notions of equity. The compensation for jobs is being increasingly shaped by the market wage for those jobs outside of the organisation, and not by how it fits into the hierarchy of an internal compensation system. Consequently, internal management practices are being redrafted by the growing power and influence of the labour market.

Taking into account all of the above, what is required is a more dynamic or fluid approach to the evaluation of jobs, based on future value creation, strategic job worth and competitive advantage. Organisations therefore need to develop a new basis for appreciating the importance of job roles to the business – particularly the identification of critical roles and the relativities between such roles. The workforce segmentation and job analysis methodology linked to the business strategy foreshadowed in Appendix C goes some way towards achieving this objective. Additionally a three step approach to quickly enhancing business performance is outlined in Appendix C, based on a focus on critical roles.

3.12 WHY THE SKILLS' BASED WORKFORCE SEGMENTATION MODEL IS A FUNDAMENTAL AND PERVASIVE HUMAN CAPITAL CONCEPT

One of the purposes of the skills' based workforce segmentation model is to develop a deeper insight and level of understanding of:

- The types of skills (according to the two dimensions of value and uniqueness) relative to various roles
- The importance of skills to the organisation (relative to the customers which they service, the business strategy, competitors and their availability in the market).

This understanding then forms the basis of differentiated employment strategies relative to the acquisition, utilisation and retention of those various types of skills, all of which is vital to organisational competitiveness and survival. This model is fundamental to workforce planning in terms of rethinking outsourcing and investment decisions.

We shall now examine how this skills' based segmentation model is applied to determining employment strategies, including outsourcing, and "make" versus "buy" employee decisions. Then later on in this chapter, we shall examine how this model forms the basis for attraction, engagement, development and retention of human capital, and the associated measurement and reporting of the same. More specifically, we shall outline approaches to the following based on this model:

- HR policies and practices
- Recruitment
- Careers and career development
- Turnover implications and costs
- The measurement and reporting of human capital data.

3.13 "BUY" VERSUS "MAKE" DECISIONS: INTERNALISING VERSUS EXTERNALISING EMPLOYMENT

As with other capital investments, the management of human capital can be broken down into "make" or "buy" decisions. Organisations may internalise employment and build the employee skill base through training and development initiatives, or externalise employment by outsourcing certain functions to market-based agents.

Internalising employment

Internalisation of employment is appropriate when it allows organisations to more effectively monitor employees' performance and ensure that their skills are deployed correctly and efficiently. Organisations develop resources internally when investments in employee skills are justified in terms of future productivity or customer benefits. For example, with an internalised labour force, investment in the training and development of people will vary depending on whether the required skills can be acquired from the market (i.e., most likely skills of a more generic nature), as opposed to developing from within (i.e., likely to be of a more unique nature). The cost of training needs to be justified against the benefits of organisational competitiveness (i.e., whether these benefits can be recovered in the market place through improved performance).

Externalising Employment

Replacing permanent workers with contingent ones (i.e., externalisation), has been part of the effort to squeeze out the fixed costs of employment and increase flexibility. This in turn has redistributed job instability from the permanent to the temporary workforce. However within this simplistic "make" or "buy" decision, there are a growing number of subtle variations (i.e., employees come in all shapes and sizes), making the effective management of employment somewhat complicated.

According to IBIS (2008), 20% of the revenue of businesses (non-core activities) was outsourced (450 billion) in Australia in 2005. IBIS contends that outsourcing creates growth in most industries. The shedding of non-core functions reduces complexity and increases focus, lightness and flexibility. It frees up management and resources to grow the core business.

The advantages and disadvantages of an internalised and externalized labour force are summarized in the table below.

Internalised Employment	
Advantages	**Disadvantages**
■ Greater stability and predictability of the organisation's stock of skills and capabilities ■ Better co-ordination and control ■ Enhanced socialisation ■ Lower transaction costs.	■ Increased managerial and bureaucratic costs stemming from administering the employment relationship, including staff expenses, training, benefits, etc. ■ Constraints on the organisation's ability to adapt to environmental changes.
Externalised Employment	
■ Reduced overheads and administration costs ■ Flexibility to balance workforce requirements to meet fluctuating demands ■ More discretion in the number and types of workers used ■ Access to vendor innovations while focusing on the development of core capabilities.	■ The organisation's continued reliance may mitigate the development of core skills and capabilities, critical for long term organisation performance.

3.14 TO OUTSOURCE OR NOT TO OUTSOURCE?

Outsourcing based on skills value and skills uniqueness

Skills that are of lower value and uniqueness (i.e., more generic), and available to multiple organisations, may not justify the costs of internal development. Typically employers rely on the external market to provide these skills. Individuals are expected to make their own investments in acquiring generic (transferable) skills. For these people (e.g., Doers in quadrant 3 roles), work tends to be standardised with little discretion. They are more likely to be prime candidates for outsourcing, or reductions in numbers through the application of information and communications technology. This is why we are seeing a proliferation of outsourcing of various lower level services and administration functions across a range of industries.

Developing skills from within: Succession Planning

As referred to earlier, employees who possess both valuable and unique skills are critical or core knowledge employees, who serve as a source of competitive advantage. The intellectual capital and corporate memory of the organisation resides in these core workers (i.e., Criticals). They are likely to be central to innovation and knowledge generation.

Therefore outsourcing these kinds of skills may jeopardize the competitive advantage of the organisation by eroding its stock of core skills. This is one of the reasons why we are seeing an increased emphasis on succession planning and talent management. It is also a reason why a blanket approach to transferring job instability from a permanent workforce to contractors or temporaries, whilst maximising flexibility, is unlikely to be of longer term benefit to the organisation in the case of more critical roles. From an employee perspective, those in contract or temporary roles are more likely to "jump ship" if offered permanent roles or better jobs, because of low barriers to exit. Retention of core workers promotes organisational stability, as well as continuity and learning, and the longer-term relationship complements the development and assimilation of shared values and beliefs.

Because unique skills have to be developed internally, there is a disproportionally higher level of investment in the training and development of people in roles with unique skills (i.e., quadrants 1 and 4). Furthermore because organisation specific skills (i.e., unique skills) are non-transferable, internal development will less likely result in a capital loss, because the value of these skills is less with any other organisation. Employee turnover rates are typically lower for people in such roles.

Case Study: Outsourcing Core Skills in a Statutory Authority

We recently undertook a consulting assignment for a statutory authority which was responsible for a diverse range of activities, including the design and construction of infrastructure. Because architects and engineers were in short supply, this authority had elected to outsource most roles within the infrastructure business unit, including the Business Unit Manager. In so doing, it was able to offer a more competitive package to attract suitable experienced staff, not being restricted by salary policies. However the organisation had become vulnerable in terms of its longer term capability (i.e., retention and building of its knowledge and corporate memory). It was doing little to nurture skills from within, and the Business Unit Manager was approaching retirement.

Core competencies of an organisation and investment in skills

As we will see in Chapter 5, the core competencies of an organisation relate directly to the key activities which that organisation undertakes in conducting its business. For example, in the case of a manufacturing and sales company, these core competencies would include: design, manufacturing, marketing and distribution of its various products. Now even though some of the above competencies may be classed as valuable but not particularly unique, this should not necessarily preclude or deter an organisation from investing in the ongoing maintenance and development of these competencies (subject to ROI type considerations), in order to maintain or enhance its competitive advantage. Investment in the further development of these competencies may result in higher levels of efficiencies and effectiveness in conducting the business.

3.15 OTHER OUTSOURCING CONSIDERATIONS: ENVIRONMENTAL AND ORGANISATIONAL

The skills' based workforce segmentation employment model offers a "broad brush" approach for organisations to think more deeply about their employment strategies, and in particular, "make" versus "buy" employment strategies. Outsourcing is more likely to occur in quadrant 3, "Doers", and also to some extent quadrant 2, "Professionals, Skilled and Semi-Skilled". However a range of other environmental, organisational, demographic and career factors are also likely to influence the "make" versus "buy" decision. These are elaborated upon below.

1. **Size of the organisation**
   The size of the organisation may mean that there are insufficient economies of scale to contract out. Alternatively, in a small organisation, there may not be sufficient work load to justify a full-time employee, in which case the role may be contracted out.

2. **Complexity of organisational systems**
   Organisations that have less developed internalized employment systems and less organisation-specific training are more likely to use temps and contractors for quadrant 2 and 3 roles (i.e., contract out).

3. **Nature of customer relations and customer interfacing roles**
   The nature of an organisation's relationships with its clients should reflect, to a certain extent, the relationships that the organisation has with its employees. For example, if an organisation is involved in one-off transactions (either products or services) with no repeat business, and these products and services are of a relatively unsophisticated nature, then the sales activity may be contracted out (i.e., quadrant 3 workers). However where an organisation seeks a longer term relationships with their customers, then the relationships with their customer facing employees should be similar (i.e., relational psychological contract), where cultural norms which support good customer relations are developed. Employee attitudes are a central determinant of customer attitudes. Outsourcing the things that create the company's culture or the engagement that employees feel with the company is dangerous.

> **Outsourcing Client Relationships a No No!**
>
> We have seen examples recently where some of the banks, having outsourced their call centre activities to a contract provider, have then subsequently brought back these activities in-house. The reason for this is to maintain closer contact with their customers at the "coal face". A workforce of intractable mercenaries in a seductive land constitutes a poor cocktail for engaging and retaining people and customers.

Notwithstanding, there may be scenarios (e.g., outbound call centres where there is a specific campaign or new product or services launch, where only product knowledge of a basic nature is required, and customers are relatively unsophisticated), where contractors may be used (refer continuity of work below). Under such circumstances, it may be the case that the training of contracted individuals undertaking the work is provided by the organisation that is providing the products and services (i.e., which has entered into arrangements with the contracting organisation), and that organisation then monitors the quality of the contractor's services.

Miss-match of Relationships between Supplier/Client and Employer/ Employee Relationships: High Turnover in the Recruitment Industry

Many recruitment companies experience high staff turnover (e.g., up to 50% turnover compared to an average of around 25% for sales based and professional services organisations). This is somewhat ironic, given that often recruitment companies act as advisors to their clients on how to retain their staff.

Fundamentally the reason for this high turnover is that whilst recruitment companies espouse their aspiration to build long term relations with their clients, they reward their consultants primarily on short term results (i.e., high commission base from successful placements). This practice encourages short-term or transactional thinking. Thus there is a "disconnect" between the nature of the service provider/client relationship and the employer/consultant relationship of the service provider.

This is another example of workforce and business strategies being miss-aligned.

4. **Continuity of work**
   If work is of a more intermittent, cyclical or project based nature, then such work is more likely to be contracted out, especially if minimal training is required (e.g., the construction industry). In a high growth phase, contracting out may provide an immediate boost to productivity to cope with demand. Even with work that requires more sophisticated skills, where that work is of an intermittent or more specialised nature (e.g., legal or accounting advice or services), then such work may also be contracted out (e.g., quadrant 2).

5. **Supply of labour and contractors**
   If there is a shortage of supply of labour, then roles may be contracted out. However there may be risk in contracting out if there are few suppliers available in the market, as an unhealthy dependency on the contractor(s) may develop.

6. **Industrial issues**
   Contracting out may pose risks of industrial disputes, souring of relationships with unions and employee groups, potentially leading to strikes and interruption to business. In such circumstances, the longer term gains of outsourcing therefore need to be weighed up against the shorter term pain.

3.16 MAKING EMPLOYMENT STRATEGY DECISIONS: HR'S OPPORTUNITY

We have presented a framework from which employment strategy decisions can best be made. Unfortunately decisions relating to the use of contractors, consultants and outsourcing are often made on an *ad hoc* basis with virtually no HR input whatsoever. These decisions are not driven by HR, but by finance or general management. As indicated in Chapter 4, the new role of HR is to focus on the intersection between business and workforce strategies. The employment strategy framework presented provid HR professionals with the means to do so. Being intimately involved in determining employment strategy decisions, including internalising and externalising the labour force, offers HR a significant opportunity to meaningfully contribute towards their organisation's total human capital efforts.

3.17 HR POLICIES AND PRACTICES AND THE SKILLS' BASED WORKFORCE SEGMENTATION MODEL

We have stated previously that the skills' based workforce segmentation model should form the basis of differentiating roles and the attraction, engagement, development and retention of human capital. To that end, HR policies and practices will vary for each workforce segment/quadrant, consistent with the nature of the psychological contract for that segment/ quadrant. These HR policies and practices have been summarised under the following key topics:

- Appraisal systems (i.e., utilising/engaging and retaining human capital)
- Compensation/reward system (i.e., utilising/engaging and retaining human capital)
- Training and development (i.e., developing human capital)
- Career development (i.e., developing human capital).

Refer to the diagram entitled HR Policies and Practices by Skills' Based Workforce Segment/Quadrant on the coloured pages in this chapter, which summarises the above HR policies, and how they typically vary between the quadrants. For a further explanation of the psychological contract, refer to chapter 7.

3.18 RECRUITMENT AND THE SKILLS' BASED WORKFORCE SEGMENTATION MODEL

A variety of Employment Value Propositions (EVPs)/"deals"

As we shall see in Chapter 5, there is no single EVP or "deal" for all employees in an organisation. Different "deals"/psychological contracts will apply to each of the four skills quadrants. What may be offered to those in critical roles (quadrant 1), compared to those general or front-line workers (quadrant 3), will be like "chalk and cheese". For profiling of typical "deals" (i.e., mix of tangibles and intangibles), in each of the four quadrants, refer to Chapter 7.

Because there are differentiated "deals" for each of the four segments, it follows that there will be differentiated engagement and retention strategies as foreshadowed in the previous section. For example, career development is an important retention driver for those in critical roles, which organisations may seek to satisfy through talent development and succession plans. However the same organisation may need to rely on developing a more supportive work environment or flexible work practices as a retention driver for Doers. Notwithstanding, there are some universals including healthy psychological contracts, good person-organisational fit and good person-job fit, all of which are likely to result in higher performance levels and retention rates, as we shall see in Chapter 6.

Recruitment strategies will vary

Recruitment strategies will vary for each workforce segment/quadrant. These strategies have been summarised in the diagram entitled Recruitment Strategies by Skills Quadrants on the coloured pages in this chapter, according to the following four criteria:

- Investment in recruitment
- Decision to outsource versus the need for in-house recruitment capability
- Intensity of assessment processes
- Emphasis on person – organisation fit and person - job fit.

3.19 CAREER CONSIDERATIONS AND THE SKILLS' BASED WORKFORCE SEGMENTATION MODEL

Schein (1990) has developed the concept of Career Anchors. These are a combination of perceived areas of competence, motives and values that are of such paramount importance to an individual that they would be unlikely to give them up. Career Anchors are underlying themes that knowingly or often unwittingly influence the decisions that people make about their paths, as their career evolves. They represent the person's real self (i.e., define their self-concept) and their orientation towards work.

According to Schein, most people see themselves in one of the following eight categories.

- Technical/Functional Competence
- General Managerial Competence
- Autonomy/Independence
- Security/Stability

- Entrepreneurial/Creativity
- Service/Dedication to a Cause
- Pure Challenge
- Lifestyle.

Please note the following about these Career Anchors:

- They apply over a variety of occupations
- They describe the person and not the job
- There is a need to match the individual's career anchors with the characteristics of the job, otherwise this will result in a miss-match of job and career interests which will in turn be reflected in lower levels of job satisfaction, which is a key predictor of turnover.

Different skills quadrants are more likely to be associated with some specific career anchors more than others (see diagram).

Career Anchors and Workforce Segmentation/Quadrant

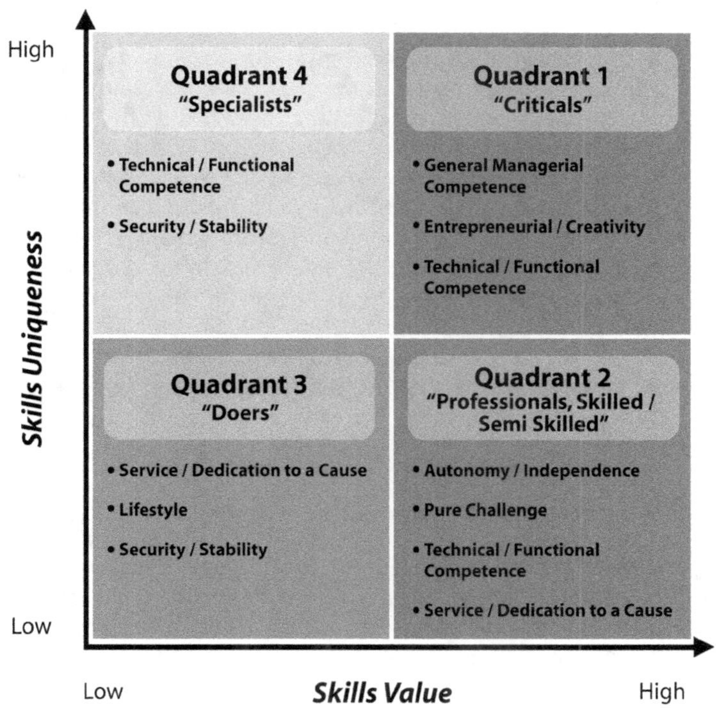

Note: For further information, refer E. H. Schein, 1990. Career anchors: Discovering your real values. Josey-Bass/Pfeiffer: San Francisco.

Examples of miss-matching career anchors and career aspirations referred to above are provided in the two following case studies.

Case Study: High Turnover in a Call Centre

We were recently called in to investigate high turnover in a call centre. The call centre employed a high percentage of tertiary students who regarded the job as a shorter term "means to an end", rather than a longer term career path. As such, the career anchors of the students didn't match the requirements or demands of the role (i.e., lack of job challenge and limited career paths).

It was recommended that the company recruit less numbers of students and focus on middle aged female employees. It was anticipated that the latter were more likely to remain in the role in the longer term, as they didn't have particularly ambitious career aspirations, given that many also had family responsibilities (i.e., lifestyle considerations and job security/stability more important to this group).

Case Study: Higher Retention Risk for Store Managers in the Fashion Retail Industry

We recently undertook a survey consulting assignment for a national retail fashion chain with well over 100 stores. Store managers were female, typically in their mid 20's, and had worked their way up the company, having started off in casual sales roles in their late teenage years. Whilst their psychological contracts were healthy (i.e., the company was delivering on the "deal", there were relatively high levels of trust with senior management, etc.), and they liked working for the company (i.e., relatively high levels of affective commitment), the survey findings indicated that some of these managers were at higher risk of leaving compared to the rest of the population.

The explanation for this was that those managers (i.e., of higher risk of leaving), harboured other career ambitions outside of the fashion industry, with some of them having completed tertiary studies along the way. Whilst the company had people friendly practices and had developed a positive culture, there was a miss-match in so far as some of the career aspirations of the managers and what was on offer or available from the company.

Horizontal versus vertical careers and turnover

Some occupations (e.g., quadrant 2 crafts, technicians and some professions), can be described as having more horizontal career paths. Individuals tend to move across organisations, particularly for project work (e.g., the construction industry), not necessarily advancing up a vertical hierarchy within those organisations. Employees initially invest in their own training, or training takes place in the market (e.g., apprenticeships), with employees less likely to be committed to careers at individual organisations. Typically turnover tends to be higher in these occupations.

Conversely, Specialists in quadrant 4 may become trapped in their jobs and careers, given that there may be few opportunities for their advancement in their respective organisations, and little scope for the use of their skills in other jobs and careers (i.e., unique skills with a lower transferability of those skills).

Knowledge workers and turnover

Knowledge workers, particularly those in quadrant 2, typically have higher mobility, exhibiting the following characteristics:

- They need to apply highly structured technical knowledge to ambiguous client demands
- They work in an autonomous fashion, with fluid leadership structures
- They are normally ambitious and upwardly mobile, and their key focus is on the development of their careers.

The retention and employability dilemma faced by organisations employing knowledge workers is that:

- They want to have up-to-date skills that make them desirable to employers
- Yet employers are wary of offering development that makes them too attractive to the competition.

Career development and training strategies

Career development and training strategies will vary between segments, commensurate with the necessity to maintain and develop relevant skills, as illustrated in the following diagram.

Career Development Strategies by Workforce Segment/ Quadrant

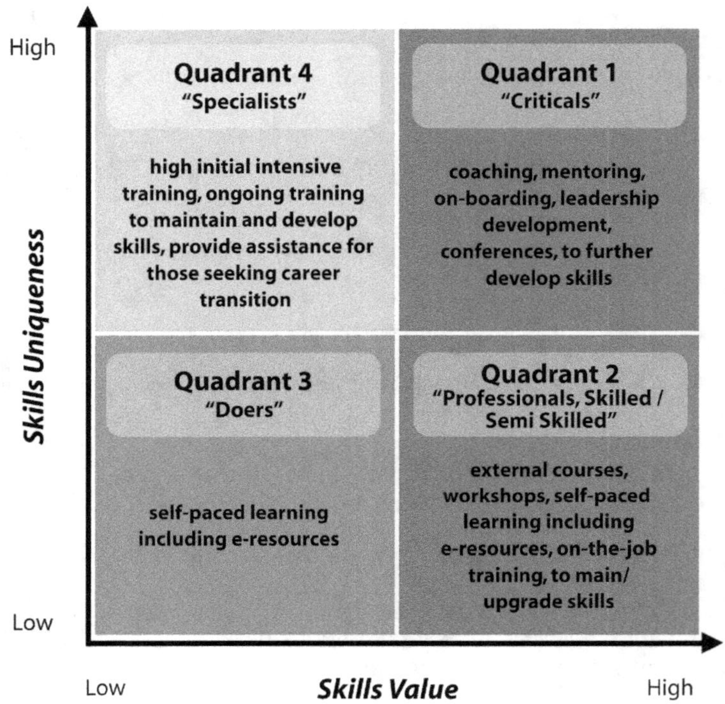

3.20 THE COST OF TURNOVER AND THE SKILLS' BASED WORKFORCE SEGMENTATION MODEL

As we shall see in Chapter 6, the cost of turnover varies as a multiple of the salary of the job in question, from 0.5 to 2.5 (Cascio, 1995). This multiple will vary according to the skills quadrant, and is typically as per the diagram below. However these turnover multiples are an indicative guide only, and may vary according to particular organisational circumstances. For example, the cost of training those people entering the armed forces (Specialists who would be in quadrant 4), is likely to be such that the multiple of 1-1.5 is grossly understated, given the extensive initial training required.

The costs of leaving are higher if the investments in training and developing employees are organisation specific (i.e., unique skills in quadrants 1 and 4), because of the necessity to reinvest in the training and development of replacements. However as we have referred to earlier, the flip side is that people with these unique skills are typically less likely to leave because their skills are less transferable.

Cost of Turnover (Multiple by the Salary of the Job) by Workforce Segment/Quadrant

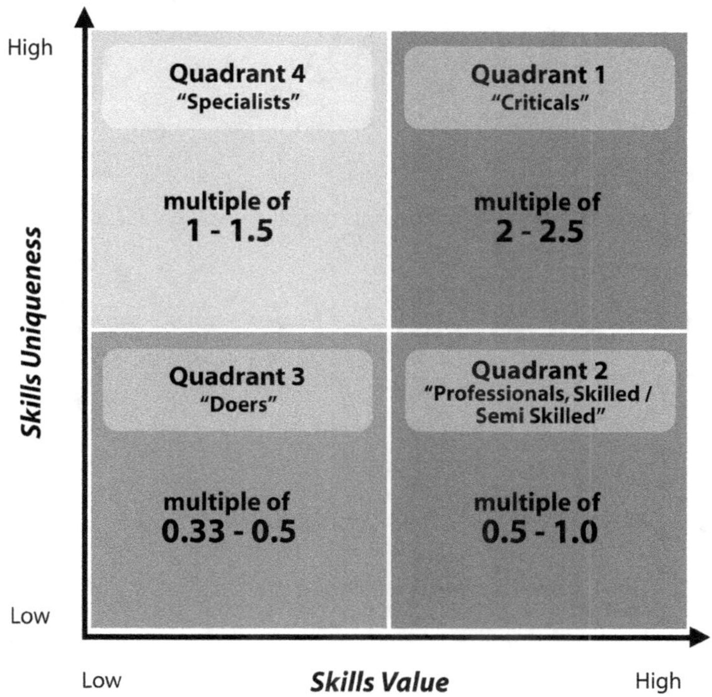

Reporting turnover by workforce segment/quadrant

Reporting on groups of employees, according to the skills' based segmentation model, inevitably provides some deeper workforce insights. A different picture might emerge for a more fine grained assessment of turnover (i.e., by skills quadrant) compared to an overall turnover rate for the organisation.

> **A More "Fine Grained" Reporting of Turnover by Segment**
>
> The implications of a 20% turnover of lower performing employees in skills quadrant 3 (i.e., Doers), and a 2% turnover of employees in skills quadrant 1 (i.e., Criticals), would most likely be a cause of celebration, even if the overall staff turnover rate for the organisation was higher than industry average.
>
> For examples of this reporting, refer to Chapter 9.

3.21 OTHER WORKFORCE SEGMENTATION OPTIONS

Beyond the skills' based workforce segmentation model, there is a need to look at sub-segments within the four skills quadrants. The key variables in this expanded segmentation of the workforce may include, amongst other things:

- Age
- Length of time in the job
- Length of time in the organisation
- Location
- Business unit
- Job level
- Function
- Team membership
- Performance and/or potential rating, etc.

Age and generational differences

Age and generational cohort is an important workforce sub-segment. The issues and needs of different cohort groups (e.g., Gen Y, Gen X, Baby Boomers), has been previously elaborated upon in Chapter 1. Suffice to say, it is important for organisations to understand the engagement and retention risk profiles of these various cohorts.

For example, with the ageing workforce and the imminent retirement of Baby Boomers, it is important to have a retention risk versus age profile, particularly for Criticals. If the average age of Criticals is say 55 years, and the retention risk profile looks unfavourable, then this scenario would represent a significant workforce risk and cause for concern.

Experience

Age is also important, because apart from it being an indication of turnover risk, it:

- Is also an indication of experience (refer to the definition of human capital in Chapter 4 which includes experience)
- May be relevant to the age of the client or customer base to which the organisation is supplying goods and services.

Ideally these respective ages (i.e., of workforce and customers) should be reasonably closely matched to ensure an identification with, and a better understanding of, customer needs.

Length of time in the job and with the organisation is another important sub-segment as it constitutes an approximate indication of experience (refer to the definition of human capital in Chapter 4 which includes experience).

Organisational structure and "hot spots"

as indicated earlier, segmentation and reporting by business unit, location, job level, team, etc., may well uncover pockets of organisational distress, which are not necessarily pervasive throughout the wider organisation. This reporting will in turn provide a basis for targeted interventions, making the most efficient use of resources, to address perceived deficits.

High performers and high potentials – Retention risk

Segmentation by performance and/or potential ratings enables discernment as to whether higher or lower performers are at greater risk of leaving. In the case of the latter, this would be welcomed, whereas in the case of the former, it would constitute a significant workforce risk and cause for immediate remedial action. Typically lower performers are more likely to leave compared to higher performers, for reasons elaborated upon in Chapter 6.

> Note: In undertaking employee surveys to measure the performance or potential – retention risk profile, these ratings can be back-end coded after surveys have been completed. However participant names are required for this to be achieved with confidentiality guaranteed. When administered through a third party, the survey is confidential (with undertakings provided that no individual will be able to be identified, and that only group reporting in numbers of 10 or more will be fed back to the organisation).

3.22 BRINGING IT ALL TOGETHER: ANALYSING AND PLOTTING ROLES AND PROFILING EMPLOYMENT VALUE PROPOSITIONS (EVPs)

Plotting roles according to the skills' based model

The WRDI Institute has developed a 49 item questionnaire called the Skills Segmentation Questionnaire (SSQ) that enables roles to be analysed, classified and plotted according to the four quadrant skills' based workforce segmentation model. The design and scoring of this questionnaire takes into account the:

- Skills relative to the role – both valuable and unique

- Impact of those skills on the provision of products and services that the organisation provides to its clients.

There is flexibility in the questionnaire for customisation to accommodate each organisation's unique characteristics, business strategy and priorities. This means that (assuming the customisation option is applied) the same role may plot a little differently for different organisations, because of their different circumstances. Refer to Appendix C for a further explanation and the coloured pages in the Introduction Chapter for example plots for various roles.

Profiling Employment Value Propositions (EVPs)

The WRDI Institute has also developed the Employment Value Proposition (EVP) Profiler tool. This tool allows organisations to profile (i.e., plot) the EVP for each role (refer examples in the coloured pages in Chapter 7). It also includes provision to record details relating to each of the items comprising the EVP. This EVP profile can also serve as a Realistic Job Preview (RJP), for new recruits as a means of "vaccinating" their expectations (i.e., to ensure that these expectations are realistic). It can also be used as a post recruitment expectations delivery check to determine whether the EVP or the "deal" has been delivered.

Thus the combination of these two tools provides a unique foundation or reference point for each role in an organisation, and for the many activities that may follow associated with those respective roles, including for example:

- Recruitment (e.g., framing the EVP/"deal", selection of methodology and process for recruitment, Realistic Job Preview, etc.)
- Employee engagement and retention (e.g., HR policies including performance management, career development, investment, etc.)
- Reporting of human capital data.

Chapter 4

About Human Capital, Corporate Governance and Risk Management

KEY POINTS

Key questions and issues that we will address in this chapter:

- *What is meant by the term "human capital"?*
- *Why human capital is growing in importance*
- *What are the five ways organisations can build human capital?*
- *How does human capital differ from other forms of capital?*
- *What is meant by the term "Human Capital Management" and how does this differ from Human Resources Management?*
- *Who is responsible for managing human capital?*
- *Why and how HR needs to step up to the plate in managing human capital*
- *How different mindsets apply to people compared to other assets and aspects of life experiences*
- *Should people be viewed as a cost or an asset?*
- *How does the management of human capital link to corporate governance?*
- *How should the concept of risk management be applied to the workforce?*
- *Why developing a Human Capital Strategic Plan is fundamental to the effective management of human capital*

What are the consequences of failing to adequately answer these questions/issues or ending up with the wrong answers?

- *Human capital is the most important driver of business success, but faulty mindsets (or understandings) will result in poor people decisions and confusion, impacting adversely on that success*
- *There is now much greater complexity in the workforce with employees coming in all shapes and sizes, hence the need to move beyond some of the simplistic thinking of yesteryear*
- *Corporate governance and risk management are becoming increasingly more important in the aftermath of the GFC, and a failure to adopt and apply these concepts to the workforce may ultimately have adverse consequences for directors, CEOs and their executives*

4. ABOUT HUMAN CAPITAL, CORPORATE GOVERNANCE AND RISK MANAGEMENT

4.1 THE EMERGENCE OF HUMAN CAPITAL AS A KEY ASSET

> As companies around the world transform themselves for competition that is based on information, their ability to exploit intangible assets has become far more decisive than their ability to invest in and manage physical assets (Kaplan & Norton, 1996).

Intangible assets have now overtaken physical assets

It has been argued that the next decade and beyond will be very much about addressing emerging trends in the workplace and employment landscape, and the consequent people management challenges ahead. Human capabilities will largely determine winners and losers in tomorrow's global markets. To that end, an understanding and appreciation of human capital, and its importance to organisations, is considered to be an essential precursor to effectively addressing these people management challenges.

This importance is illustrated by the following brief history of corporations. In the 19th and early 20th centuries, the key assets most firms competed with were physical assets. Most of the top firms owed their success to ownership of natural physical assets, including minerals, oil and land. As the 20th century progressed, the physical assets shifted from natural resources to plant and equipment, and financial assets. The latter became more important as determinants of competitive advantage. By the late 20th century, the terms of competition changed quite dramatically, with dominant physical assets and financial assets no longer determining success.

The revolution in information technology, globalisation and knowledge management has driven a new organisational order. Many of the today's top firms in the world by market capitalisation began quite recently, with little or no physical or financial assets (e.g., Microsoft, Cisco, Intel, AOL and Wal-Mart). The vast majority of these firms depend on the following intangible assets (which are human capital centred), for their competitive advantage:

- Superior human assets for their advantage (e.g., research scientists, code writers, distribution experts, product innovators)
- Knowledge assets (patents, brands, know-how, experience)
- Network/social assets (e.g., relationships with suppliers, distributors, customers, alliance partnerships, educational institutions and reputation).

In a modern, networked, and knowledge-based business environment, intangible assets (such as skills, reputations and relationships), generate the highest value. They represent the largest contributor to overall market value for many organisations. Business value has been trending towards the intangibles for some time. Tayloristic task management has given way to knowledge management, the latter seeking to be cost efficient by developing an organisation's people assets, unlike the former, which views labour as a cost to be minimised.

The knowledge economy however, requires a considerably higher level of human development than the industrial economy. The conversion of the labour force into knowledge workers demands a significant expansion in investment in education, training, research and development – the major formal generating activities. In 1999, management guru Peter Drucker estimated that knowledge workers already comprised two-fifths of the US workforce. It is now likely to be higher than that 40% of some ten years ago.

Human capital therefore has economic value to organisations, directly impacting upon organisational productivity and profitability. High performing organisations are continually seeking ways to extract the most value from their human assets. Given the widely held premise that people provide organisations with an important source of sustainable competitive advantage, maximising business performance through people is now the aim of the game!

Human capital – Now the largest driver of organisational performance

As stated earlier, there is now a great deal of evidence that the contribution of people is the largest driver of organisational performance (CIPD, 2003). The management of human capital is emerging as a powerful management philosophy and creeping up the corporate agenda. The importance of human capital is being reflected in boards, investors and analysts placing pressure on financial executives to show how human capital is being managed within their companies.

Human capital has now become very much part of today's business language, and is at last being recognised as a critical corporate asset in today's economy. Increasingly, human capital management will form a central part of corporate strategy, alongside financial planning, plant utilisation, marketing strategy and other board level priorities.

Human assets less understood and less well managed

Human assets are generally less well understood and less well managed compared to other areas of the business. The value of physical assets, such as buildings, plant and equipment, is easily established, can be shown on the balance sheet, and can also be monitored over time. However the value of human capital is not so easy to define. Putting a value against people's potential, capabilities and contribution is not without its difficulties, even though it is generally recognised that this intangible asset forms a significant component of the intangible asset base of an organisation. Whilst other business processes and components have moved forward via innovations and paradigm shifts (such as procurement, marketing, supply chain management, accounting and quality assurance), there hasn't been anything modestly comparable in advancements in human capital management, workforce relations and people management practices.

4.2 WHAT IS HUMAN CAPITAL?

Human Capital = Knowledge + Skills + Experience + Initiative

Human capital includes the knowledge, skills, experience and initiative possessed by employees. Employees add value to an organisation to the extent that they will perform future services. Some of this value is added directly by transforming, developing and delivering the organisation's products and services, but much of it is less tangible. Examples of how this added value may manifest include:

- Developing effective strategy
- Solving problems
- Innovation
- Building quality customer relations
- Coordinating the work of departments
- Exercising judgment in novel situations, etc.

More recently the term "Human Capital" has been applied to selection, training, compensation and human resource (HR) management practices in general (Cascio, 1991).

4.3 THE FIVE WAYS ORGANISATIONS CAN BUILD HUMAN CAPITAL

There are five main ways in which an organisation can enhance and effectively utilise their stock of human capital. Refer to the Introduction Chapter of this book, and to the diagram of this model in the coloured pages.

1. **Through the individuals that are hired**
   By distinguishing between skill and ability levels with new hires, organisations can easily justify this more rigorous approach to acquisition by recouping their additional initial investment through higher performance and productivity, and less training.

2. **Through utilising/engaging and retaining existing employees**
   Organisations that have effective HR people management policies and practices can create motivating environments, maximise the utilisation of the human capital at their disposal, and just as importantly, retain that human capital.

3. **Through training and development of existing employees**
   Organisations that invest in skill development expect increased employee productivity and performance to offset such training costs.

4. **Through merger and/or acquisition**
   Organisations may acquire or merge with other organisations, or form alliances with them.

5. **Through borrowing/renting**
   Organisations may acquire temporary access to human capital though outsourcing (i.e., contracting out, temporary employees, consultants, etc.).

> Note: Borrowing or renting doesn't significantly contribute to long term gain.

4.4 PEOPLE – A COST OR AN ASSET?

There are predominantly two competing views of people in relation to a business:

- A cost to be minimized in order to stay in business
- An asset which can be used more effectively to sustain the business.

Let us assume the latter for the moment. If people are to be regarded as an asset, then without wishing to denigrate their humanity, the question arises: How then does human capital differ from other forms of capital? Like any other (physical) asset, human capital needs to be acquired, maintained, developed and ultimately disposed of. For example, acquisition equates to selection and recruitment. Disposal equates to voluntary or involuntary resignation (retrenchment, sacking, or retirement). However human capital differs from other forms of capital in three key aspects.

1. **Human capital is transferable**
Human capital commands a price in the market. It is valuable to other organisations, and most importantly, it is transferable or mobile. This transferability constitutes a critical difference between human capital and physical capital. The essential characteristic of human freedom makes it difficult to capture the value of investments in human capability as a property right of the investor or an institution. Therefore organisations do not actually "own" human capital – it is embodied in their employees, who are free (within limits), to move from one organisation to another. Even if they stay with an organisation, employees' contributions also depend upon their willingness to perform. Therefore the control costs, or the costs of retaining and motivating employees (such as reward systems), should also be considered human capital investments.

2. **Human capital value depends on performance or contribution**
Unlike other forms of capital, people cannot be mechanically manipulated or fine tuned to work at capacity. Human capital has ideas of its own. Human capital becomes economically valuable when manifested in performance or contribution. The value of human capital therefore depends upon the demands placed upon employees, and the willingness of those employees to respond to those demands.
However since organisations invest in employees, but do not actually own their human capital, they must devise methods for ensuing that individuals act in the organisation's interest. To that end, organisations need to develop high levels of employee (affective) commitment. This form of commitment and loyalty should be to both the hearts (i.e., where organisations are able to capture the imagination of their employees and harness their energy) and minds (i.e., to the vision, values and goals of the organisation) of employees.

3. **Human capital is active**
Human capital differs from other forms of capital in that it is the only capital that is dynamic or active – it is the force (Fitz-enz, 2002). It is the one thing that can look three or five years ahead. It can drive the change in redesigning systems. Without human capital, nothing can happen in organisations.

In summary, human capital is a precious intangible and dynamic asset, lying somewhere in the spectrum between a leased or rented asset and an owned asset. However not everyone is equal, as we have discovered in Chapter 3 (refer the skills' based workforce segmentation model), so some forms of human capital are more valuable than other forms.

4.5 WHAT IS HUMAN CAPITAL MANAGEMENT (HCM)?

Human Capital Management (HCM) is a business philosophy focused on attracting, engaging, developing, retaining, measuring, managing and leveraging an organisation's employee asset base (refer previous section on building human capital). One of the underlying assumptions behind HCM is that the value of employees increases over time through:

- Improved productivity, as employees become more familiar with their work environment and job functions
- Increased skills and knowledge levels (including tacit knowledge)
- Strengthened relationships, both internally (i.e., within the organisation), and with external organisations (from customers to partners) and improved satisfaction.

While the management of human capital should be an enterprise-wide strategy, nowhere are its benefits more apparent than in customer-facing functions. The ability to maximise skills and experience in the sales and marketing functions has a direct impact on top-line revenue. Customer service – whether through a call centre or in the field – directly impacts client satisfaction, customer retention and the customer life cycle. High levels of service are important since the number of completely satisfied customers is one of the few predictors of long-term profitability (Jones & Sasser, 1995). This is one of the reasons why sales people in certain industries (e.g., ICT), appear to be paid disproportionally higher salaries compared to other staff (e.g., program engineers).

4.6 HOW HUMAN CAPITAL APPRECIATES

Rodgers and Howlett (2002) liken employee acquisition and value to that of customers. Just as the costs of acquiring new customers are high (when sales resources are deployed and execution of marketing campaigns are factored in), the costs are also high of bringing new employees on board. Over time, these costs drop significantly as customers become better acquainted with the organisation, its products and services. The value generated by customers increases over time – they cost less to service as they become more familiar with the way the organisation operates.

Likewise, the value equation for employees increases over time. Employees typically become more productive as they settle into organisations, acquiring skills and knowledge that are deployed to the organisation's benefit. Similarly business relationships with suppliers or alliance partners become more profitable over time. The flip side to attrition is to understand the value derived from retaining employees.

The Cost/Value Equation of Employees over Time

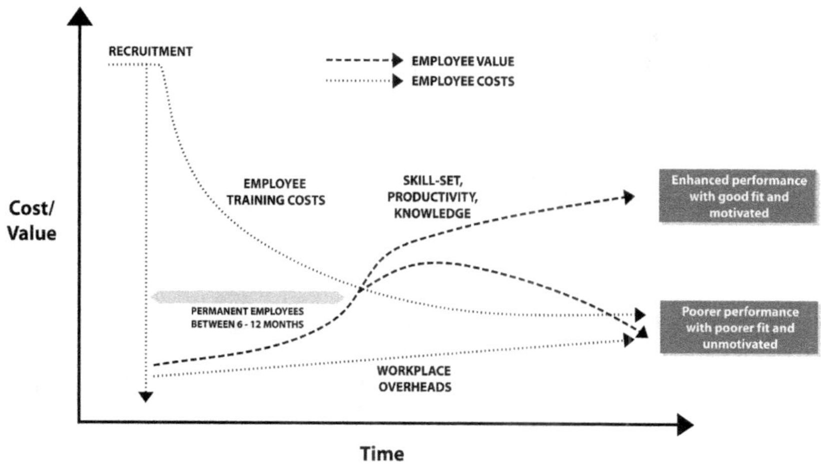

Note: The above diagram has been adapted from Webster Buchanan Research (2002).

Increasingly, skilled people will become a more precious resource, and accordingly there is a strong case for treating them much more as an asset rather than a cost. Whilst the replacement period is more difficult to predict in the case of human capital, good maintenance extends the life of capital. Human capital maintenance includes a wide range of systems, services and initiatives that help to engage, develop and preserve human capital. This argument is strengthened when taking into account the previous contention that the value of people appreciates over time (e.g., like a building or house). This is the reverse of the approach to some other assets (e.g., a motor vehicle, plant and equipment), which are typically depreciated and lose value.

4.7 HOW DOES HUMAN CAPITAL MANAGEMENT (HCM) DIFFER FROM HUMAN RESOURCES MANAGEMENT (HRM)?

The difference between HCM and HRM is the former's emphasis on the value of people and what they produce, rather than a focus on HR itself. This book is concerned with the former (i.e., HCM as opposed to HRM). The management of human capital is an approach to people management that treats it as a high-level strategic issue, and seeks systematically to analyse, measure and evaluate how people policies and practices create value. A HCM approach implies that a realistic business strategy must be informed by human capital data (i.e., takes into account the capacity of all resources available, including human ones).

HCM therefore lies at the intersection and alignment between business and workforce strategies. Amongst other things, it includes the fit between the demand for and supply of human capabilities. At an organisatonal level, the contribution of human capital is contingent on the supply and relevance of employees' skills and competencies to the business needs of the organisation. It is also contingent upon the activation, motivation, development and retention of those skills. To that end, workforce strategies "in synch" with the business needs, combined with the use of good HR policies and practices, form the foundation for HCM.

4.8 INVESTMENTS IN HUMAN CAPITAL

Treating people as costs

The earlier discussion aside about whether people should be viewed as an asset or a cost, and despite the term "human capital", many companies have traditionally treated people as a commodity or economic number (i.e., cost). Furthermore the often repeated mantra that "people are our most important asset" is hardly reflected in traditional current accounting systems that treat people as costs, and not assets. Little is known about what investments companies make in their people to back up such a declaration.

Company accounts record the costs associated with people, but not the benefits they bring. Reasons for these accounting methods include, amongst other things:

- An inability to depreciate investments in people, because of their transferability/mobility
- A focus on maximising short term profits
- The longer line of sight or time delay between investments in people and the resulting benefits that accrue
- The perceived "grey" link between non-financial people measures and the "bottom line".

The treatment of all people related expenditures (including those associated with employee development) as expenses, creates an external force from financial markets that promotes under-investment in creating human capital (Bassi, McGraw & McMurrer, 2003). The challenge for executives and directors is to break free from a management perspective that is unduly influenced by short-term factors (i.e., shareholder pressures to maximise short-term profitability). To that end, the impact of the GFC has most probably assisted in developing a longer-term and more sustainable perspective. Whilst not disputing the need for belt tightening in tough economic times, there is compelling evidence that retrenchments in downturns typically end up destroying shareholder value in the not-too-distant future (Cascio, Young & Morris, 1997).

Competing investment options and difficulties justifying a ROI

Organisations must continually make choices among competing options in determining where to invest their resources. Budgets must be divided among all the factors of production that are deemed necessary for an organisation to be effective – buildings, plant and equipment, technology, R & D and people (including salaries, benefits and development). Investments in people (either through hiring certain individuals "on the market" or developing them in-house), or via human resource management, carry both out-of-pocket and opportunity costs. They are justified only if they produce future returns via increased productivity or profitability.

Since organisations are likely to undertake additional investments up to the point at which the marginal cost equals the marginal return, the value of human capital investments depends on the contribution of employees to an organisation. With investment predicated on a rate of return, the return on people investments should be identical to returns on other factors of production.

However as mentioned earlier, one of the difficulties in investing in people is demonstrating the return on such investments. Unlike other types of investments (e.g., R & D which leads to new revenue streams associated with new products, advertising campaigns which lead to increased sales, etc.), the effects of investments in developing and managing people are much more difficult to isolate. The returns are not always immediate and the investment is therefore harder to justify. The problem with an ROI approach is that even when done correctly, it does not provide the insight for improving future outcomes (Bassi et al, 2003).

> Note: Refer Chapter 6.9 relating to a landmark study by Patterson, West, Lathom and Nickell (1997) on the link between good people management practices and the bottom line.

4.9 HUMAN CAPITAL MANAGEMENT AND TALENT

HCM tends to be practiced most rigorously in the assessment of small concentrations of individuals who are seen as highly talented and critical to the organisation's future. It is in these people where the corporate memory resides. They are more likely to facilitate organisational success. For example:

- They are often the people charged with winning market share, attracting investors or new clients, securing large contracts and having the technical and operational know how to complete large projects
- They are the innovators of new business ideas
- They make it possible for organisations to deal with today's rapidly changing and uncertain business environment
- They produce and manage the intangible assets that are the primary way companies in a wide array of industries create value.

This is the reason why there has recently been an increased focus on their retention (Lavelle, 2003; Lee, Mitchell, Sablynski, Burton & Holton, 2004; Sturman, Trevor, Boudreau & Gerhart, 2003). It is why we have witnessed an increasing emphasis on succession planning and talent management and development programs in many organisations. The war for talent is a recurring theme. Since management must continue to develop and execute value-creating initiatives, talent is becoming more critical to corporate performance. Specific needs for talent are now more unpredictable, and companies must develop talent more rapidly than ever.

The higher the potential for employees' contributions in an organisation, the more likely it is that the organisation will invest in human capital (via human resource management activities), and that these investments will lead to higher individual productivity and organisation performance. McKinsey's research (Axelrod, Handfield-Jones & Welsh, 2001) found that companies doing the best job of managing their talent deliver far better results for shareholders. Companies scoring in the top quintile of talent-management practices outperformed their industry's mean return to shareholders by a remarkable 22 percentage points.

4.10 NEW RESPONSIBILITIES IN HUMAN CAPITAL MANAGEMENT (HCM)

Responsibility for human capital management (HCM)

HCM is not just a HR issue – it goes right to the heart of organisational performance and survival. It requires a mandate and commitment from the CEO, and thereafter, a coordinated approach between executives, senior management and HR. HCM is now being seen as a shared responsibility by all the leaders of an organisation. The CEO and executives must take responsibility for HCM – visibly and collectively. This is not a function that can be managed with a siloed approach, where HCM can be siphoned off to the HR Department or a particular business unit or function.

The CFO's role

The role of CFO is one of chief resource allocator – helping direct the organisation's resources to the most productive investments. However many CFOs are in a predicament – unable to apply ordinary financial discipline to managing what is often their company's largest investment. On average, companies spend 36% of their revenues on human capital expenses, yet very few understand the ROI on these investments (CFO Research Services, 2003). Typically the evaluation of investments in people management initiatives is lacking. Furthermore in this vast area of spending, it is perceived that there are few tools or methodologies in place to help guide meaningful decision making. As indicated earlier, organisations know little about the returns they get for their considerable investments in people.

The new role of HR

HR is finding itself under intense pressure to deliver value to organisations. The human capital perspective provides a new rationale for the role of the HR function. From this perspective, HR is no longer viewed as a cost centre, but rather as an asset provider, and a resource for developing and protecting human capital. The HR role is expanding into two main streams:

1. The traditional Human Resources Management System (e.g., policy, managing employee related data, pay roll, assisting in areas such as recruitment and benefits, arbitrating in employees' disputes, etc.)
2. The Human Capital Management System that provides high value and strategic people management intelligence (i.e., the acquisition, development, performance and retention of employees, and the associated measurement and leveraging of employees).

In this second role, HR is a strategic partner and tactical advisor to line management:

- Focusing on the integration of HR policies and practices, and the intersection and alignment of workforce and business strategies
- Overseeing the redesign of the processes of employee recruitment, development, administration, performance and retention
- Focusing on balancing labour supply and demand*
- Ensuring the supply of skills and talent to meet the business and strategic goals*
- Building and monitoring performance metrics.

> Note: The above activities marked * relate to workforce planning but the Human Capital Management perspective being promoted in this book (including the other above activities), extends well beyond workforce planning.

In the new millennium, people management takes centre stage, with people at the heart of the business model. Reference has been made in the Introduction Chapter of this book for the need of a HR makeover. Deficiencies in HR are dealt with in greater detail later on in this chapter. These deficiencies will need to be addressed for HR to be effective in this new strategic human capital role.

Collaboration between the CFO and HR roles

HR management practices constitute investments in human capital. However the HR function has traditionally been regarded as a non¬strategic cost centre. Furthermore relationships between the finance and HR functions have traditionally ranged from hostile to cordial. Now there is evidence emerging that the CFO's view of human capital is evolving, with many coming to see HCM as a source of value add and competitive advantage. The changing business and employment landscape now makes it necessary for these two areas (i.e., CFO and HR), to come together in new and more collaborative ways.

The role of managers

Reference has been made in Chapter 2 to the redefined role of managers in managing a variety of relationships with various groups of employees - a core management responsibility in the 21st century workplace. Managers play an integral part in the performance, development and retention of their employees. Each manager should understand how they can best participate in and contribute to the flow of people, and the development of experience and skills across the enterprise. HR and line management also need to partner with each other in overseeing the development of policies and systems, and their effective implementation. Saying that employee engagement and retention is the responsibility of HR makes as much sense as saying that profitability is the responsibility of the finance department!

4.11 MANY ORGANISATIONS UNPREPARED

It is contended that many organisations are unprepared to address the people management challenges of the future as evidenced by three examples of HR practices described below: retention, recruitment and branding.

Retention approaches *ad hoc*

Whilst there has been an abundance of rhetoric around the talent and skills shortages in recent times, this interest has not yet translated into any comprehensive or deeper strategic commitment to managing human capital. For example, a recent employee retention survey of 282 firms in seven major industry sectors by TMP (2005) to gain market knowledge and insights into employee retention methodologies within Australian business, confirmed that most firms have adopted an *ad hoc* approach to managing retention. Of the companies surveyed, despite the tight labour market experienced up until the GFC:

- 60% said they spend less than $50,000 per year on retention, while 54% had an annual spend of more than $100,000 on recruitment costs
- Two out of three companies didn't have a formal retention program
- 84% of respondents said they have someone responsible for recruitment, with less than half (40%) having an equivalent person for retention
- 89% of respondents had a formal induction program, with only one in two employers tracking new employees' progress in the early stages of employment
- Less than 30% of information on new hires, for those companies which did track their progress, reached senior managers.

The survey report concluded that:

- The reality is that the immediate needs of finding people to fill current vacancies in the business significantly outweighs the pressure an organisation feels to retain their people
- The level of commitment around practices such as formal 30/60 and 90 day interviews appears lacking, and most companies have not yet commenced any affirmative action to look at this
- Despite many (79%) respondents rating employee retention as a high priority and the majority (93%) predicting that it will become a more pressing issue, there is a significant gap between the annual spend on recruitment advertising and internal/external recruitment costs, and the amount invested on retention.

Recruitment practices are poorly defined

At the acquisition or front-end of the employment life cycle, a recent survey revealed poorly defined recruitment practices in most Australian enterprises (Chandler McLeod, 2008). Only 60% had a documented recruitment plan, and of these, less than one third linked in any way to organisational strategy. This study concluded that companies often treat recruitment as a reflexive distress purchase, made without regard to broad organisational requirements. Fewer than half of the respondents considered their recruitment function to be strategic, and less than one third had an EVP articulating their appeal to potential recruits. The link between a sound recruitment strategy and employee engagement/alignment and retention would appear to be poorly understood.

Branding: Is the rhetoric being matched by the substance?

given the recent competitive market for attracting labour (and in particular talent), branding has become one of the latest HR buzz words. Whilst not disputing the importance of branding, evidence would suggest that there has been a tendency to oversell both the roles and the merits of organisations. The emphasis has been on getting people through the door, and then worrying about the downstream consequences later. For example, Lisa Pryor's book entitled "The Pin Striped Prison" (2008) contrasts the gap between the appeal and the reality of professional services firms.

The promise held out in the brand campaign should align with reality. Good employment branding leads to partially qualified candidates, and enhances the probability of a good match between what the applicant expects of the job and organisation, and what is actually delivered. Recent research by Chandler and McLeod (2007) has highlighted the fact that many organisations are failing to meet employees' expectations.

Unless the rhetoric is matched by the substance, such practices only lead to downstream turnover and/or performance problems. We know from our many case studies and a statistical analysis of our data, that unmet expectations leads to a lowering of employee commitment and job satisfaction, reduced effort and lower performance, and a higher risk of turnover. Refer to Chapter 7 for further information and discussion on this matter.

4.12 HOW MINDSETS TOWARDS PEOPLE ARE DIFFERENT: SIX HYPOTHETICAL SCENARIOS

Notwithstanding the differences alluded to previously between human assets and other assets of the business, the mindsets towards managing people differ significantly from those mindsets typically adopted to managing other assets of the business. The following six scenarios relating to retention and engagement illustrate this point.

Scenario 1: After sales service on your $30,000 new motor vehicle purchase

Key Question: *Would you be acting negligently if you ignored the 1,500km after sales service check on your new motor vehicle purchase?*

Presumably you would want to make sure that your new vehicle was working as intended and that there were no "teething problems". Yet few organisations adopt the same principle when applied to their investment in people. Take the case of a new senior manager, which may be of the same order of investment as the new motor vehicle purchase, and possibly even of much higher value. Few organisations provide on-boarding to assist in new employee adaptation, or measure engagement, fit and retention risk of new recruits, despite the fact that they are the highest "at risk" group in terms of turnover!

In the business world, it is quite common for suppliers of products and services to survey their customers after new purchases to check that customer expectations have been met. Yet very few organisations check to confirm that they are delivering on their promise or the EVP or the "deal". Few organisations go to the trouble of evaluating the effectiveness of their selection and recruitment processes (including outsourcing), by measuring the fit of new recruits to both the organisation and to the job, and the risk of that person leaving the organisation.

Scenario 2: House insurance

Key Question: *If you failed to insure and protect your physical assets (e.g., house), would you be considered negligent?*

The answer to the question is obviously in the affirmative. Yet the concept of risk management when applied to people, and in particular, retention of an organisation's most vital intangible asset – its key talent - is somewhat lacking! Whilst many organisations use engagement surveys, most of these tools are "blunt instruments" in so far as measuring and reporting separately on retention risk. They fail to provide a comprehensive approach to measuring and diagnosing all of the key drivers of retention, and their survey models are often ignorant of the empirical research concerning turnover and retention. Refer to Chapter 6 for further information on engagement and retention.

Scenario 3: The bleeding patient

You are a doctor and a patient has just been admitted to the emergency ward of the hospital at which you are working. This patient is bleeding profusely.

Key Question: *Would you attempt to stop the haemorrhaging first or give a blood transfusion?*

For many companies, their method of addressing turnover (i.e., the bleeding) has been to focus on recruitment. This is a reactive or tactical HR initiative rather than a strategic one, equivalent to a blood transfusion in the above analogy. These companies have invested, and are continuing to invest, in enhancing their recruitment methodologies by "beefing up" their capability at the front-end of the employment life cycle (e.g., building talent pipelines). Whilst this may well be an appropriate strategy, it only offers a piecemeal rather than a holistic solution to addressing the talent shortage.

The responsibility for retention represents a "black hole" in many organisations. The structure of HR Departments (with associated budgets), is often segmented in ways that doesn't offer overarching approaches or responsibilities. Budget funds are allocated on a reactive (e.g., recruitment), rather than a proactive basis. Proactive HR expenditure, such as a decision to use say 20% of the recruitment budget and apply this to retention strategies (which in turn will reduce the need for recruitment and associated expenditure), becomes a much more difficult decision. Often this more discretionary expenditure is invested in *ad hoc* interventions without an overall strategic framework in place. The end result is that recruitment departments may well end up continuing to recruit more staff to fill ever-increasing vacancies – a "finger in the dyke" solution based on urgency rather than importance.

Apart from the above HR structural difficulties, the territory of engagement and retention is plagued with "pop" psychology, superficial abstractions, opinions and prejudices, many of which are perpetuated. For example, local management is often purported to be the single cause of turnover (refer to Chapter 6 for a further elaboration of this point). Informal theories that managers choose to emphasise are self-serving and harmful such as turnover being largely beyond the control of the organisation. This also partly explains the relative absence of strategies for fighting turnover. Some managers would prefer to look for an external solution (i.e., recruitment), rather than look within, to determine and address the causes of voluntary turnover. They would prefer to attach blame for turnover on people, the economy or on perceived generational differences. Retention represents the highest ROI of any HR initiative, yet many companies fail to adopt a strategic approach with relevant risk measures in place to proactively address employee retention.

Scenario 4: The ill patient

Again, you are a doctor and a new patient has come to you suffering from an illness.

Key Question: *Whilst interviewing this patient is important for you to obtain an indication of their symptoms and their severity, would you would also want to carry out some tests to measure and diagnose the cause of their illness?*

Yet in many instances in organisations, few HR professionals would be aware of the right measures to diagnose key drivers of retention* and performance. Many know little about research. Alternatively, no measurements are undertaken, or the preferred methodology in addressing retention is by focus groups or exit interviews. Neither of these options provide the objective and quantified data against established norms or benchmarks, or offer a diagnosis that enables targeted interventions that have predictable outcomes to be applied, to address any deficits.

**Empirical studies (e.g., Griffeth, Hom & Gaertner, 2000), confirm that affective commitment and job satisfaction are the two key predictors of intention to stay, which in turn is the main predictor of turnover/retention. These findings are also confirmed by the WRDI Institute survey data (i.e., the WRDI® survey) and analysis.*

Scenario 5: Marriage counselling

You have been married a number of years and of late, there have been some irritants in the relationship or a desire for some changes to be made.

Key Question: *Rather than go separate ways, given the time and energy invested in the relationship to date, would you not decide to work proactively in addressing your respective expectations, needs and concerns (including seeking third party advice from a counsellor)?*

We know that divorce is much more expensive than marriage. Relationships need to be worked on and nourished. However many companies accept turnover as a *fait accompli* - simply "the cost of doing business". There are no formal mechanisms in place to discuss the continually changing needs of both parties – apart from maybe the annual performance review, where there are other agendas (e.g., performance based pay), which can often cloud such discussions.

Scenario 6: A cholesterol test

You decide to have a regular cholesterol test. Your regular doctor is off sick so you go to another doctor. However the test he or she gives to you is different to that which your regular doctor gives.

Key Question: *Would you expect doctors to adopt the same standardized test, definition and reporting of cholesterol?*

The analogy here relates to the term "engagement" which is a much abused one. Given that there is no uniform definition as to what this term means, this raises the question as to which definition is best. Like cholesterol, engagement is not a unitary construct, so it shouldn't be reported as a single index. For example, your doctor doesn't combine your different types of cholesterol into a single index or number. Whilst it may be intuitively appealing for managers to be able to make comparisons based on a single number, this approach is psychometrically flawed. There is a need to unpack engagement indexes to provide a more "fine grained" explanation and interpretation of performance related indicators and retention risk indicators (refer to Chapter 6).

4.13 WHY KNOWLEDGE AND EXPERTISE IN MANAGING PEOPLE IS DEFICIENT

Bearing in mind the previous hypothetical scenarios, some key questions arise:

- *Why does our approach to people differ from that which we would normally apply to our tangible or physical assets, or our health/well-being?*
- *Why are investments in people viewed differently to other investments?*

- *Why isn't the same risk management approach and rigour applied to an organisation's key intangible asset (i.e., its people), as that which applies to other assets of the business?*
- *Why does the standard of measurement and reporting on people lag well behind that of other assets of the business?*

We shall now focus on providing some answers to these questions.

Human assets are different

Obviously part of the answers to the above questions is that human assets have some unique characteristics compared to other assets of the business as explained earlier in this chapter. Notwithstanding the above, it is suggested that there are five other main reasons which provide some insight towards answering the above people mindset questions.

Reason 1: Expendability and treating people as costs

Historically there has been a "revolving door" mindset towards people with the labour supply and demand equation working in favour of employers. This tendency to treat human assets as a cost or commodity has created a mindset of "expendability", which is perhaps exacerbated by our throw-away oriented society. Such a mindset assumes that human assets can be readily replaced (and in particular those in critical roles), with only the direct costs of replacement being reflected in the profit and loss statement, and with no other adverse impacts on the business. This mindset leads to short term thinking concerning investments in people. If only for internal purposes, expenditure on people was treated as a capital item, then mindsets towards such costs would change dramatically. This revolving door mindset towards people is less relevant now in the era of talent and skills shortages.

> Note: There is a perception that employees are apt to leave organisations after large investments have been made in developing them. Whilst this may well be the case for some individuals (probably more so with graduate recruits after their completion of an initial training and development program), the typical root cause of employee turnover is not the investment made in employees. In fact, avoidable or dysfunctional turnover is more likely to be caused by the absence of human capital infrastructure and associated investments.

Reason 2: HR lack of influence and in need of a makeover

Former CEO guru, Jack Welch, notes in his book entitled Winning (2005), that the role of HR Director should rank as the second most important role (after the CEO) in any organisation, alongside the role of CFO. He asks the question: *"If you managed a basketball team, would you listen to the team accountant or the director of playing personnel?"* Welch laments the fact that very few organisations treat HR Directors on an equal footing to CFOs.

The current reality is that some in HR are often disempowered, under resourced, lack influence, process driven, non-strategic, out of touch with commercial realities, lacking in the ability to argue a compelling business case with evidenced based approaches, seduced by hype, preoccupied with costs rather than outcomes and benefits, and continually under threat of having to justify their existence as a cost centre.

HR functions are diverse, with different skill sets required for learning and development versus talent acquisition, versus compensation, etc. HR possibly constitutes the most diverse array of functions of any part of the business. Hence the challenge of not only integrating this diversity, but then linking workforce strategies with the business strategy. However as referred to earlier, the structure of HR Departments (with associated budgets), is often segmented in ways which don't foster overarching approaches or responsibilities (e.g., recruitment departments have no retention budget and bear no responsibility for turnover, yet retention starts with recruitment).

In defence of HR, they are often caught as the "meat in the sandwich". Line management often have some misunderstandings concerning the nature of HR's role, with the former failing to take responsibility for managing their people, sometimes ignoring HR's advice, expecting HR to fix their people issues, and then blaming HR when things go wrong. In short, there is often a serious disconnect between line management and HR departments.

As mentioned earlier, HR is still evolving or emerging from the personnel and administration function of 30 years ago, and is still relatively immature. As in the case of accounting, where there are the two streams of financial and management accounting, HR is diverging into the two somewhat unrelated streams of strategic HR and administrative HR. However unlike accounting which is regulated by tax legislation, apart from selected areas (e.g., OH & S, equal opportunity, unfair dismissal, IR), HR is not a regulated profession.

Another difference between HR and other professionals is that of identity, whereby other occupational groups such as lawyers, doctors and engineers have a more clearly defined career path and professional identity. However HR professionals come from different paths into the profession. The result of all of this is a significant variation in knowledge and capability across the HR profession.

Reason 3: HR is not trained in measurement

HR is typically not trained in measurement and psychometrics, and as such, they are not critical consumers of HR products and services. They often lack the skills and knowledge to ask the right questions in assessing and comparing various tools. To put it bluntly, some people in HR would have difficulty discerning between a questionnaire that appears in a popular magazine, from that of a psychometrically validated tool based on empirical research. Furthermore HR often uses the wrong reasons to justify their choice of tools (e.g., global benchmarks which means very little if the tool is missing some of the key measures or measuring the wrong things).

Consequently the marketing prowess and "spin" of some providers of tools triumphs over substance.

In the era of skills shortages and the need to do more with less, measuring, diagnosing and reporting on key drivers of performance and retention (with surgical precision), is essential for people investment decisions, investment tracking, continuous improvement monitoring and managing risk. The same level of rigour that applies to the measurement and reporting of financial processes should be applied to people. Imagine the outcry if accountants were not trained in financial measurement and reporting. Without the right data, executives have an inadequate basis for informed decision making in managing their most vital intangible asset. The phrase that people are our greatest asset becomes empty rhetoric!

Furthermore HR has the reputation of being influenced more by fads, popularism and *ad hocracy.* There is often little by way of evaluation of the effectiveness of initiatives and interventions, or a ROI analysis. Yet paradoxically, one way that HR could enhance their status and influence is to provide better quality metrics and risk reporting, given that executives are both data hungry and data needy. Refer to Chapter 9 for further details on human capital measurement and reporting.

Notwithstanding the above lack of emphasis on measurement and rigour in HR, it should be noted that the measurement of people is not as precise as perhaps some other areas of business. There are many variables that impact on performance and retention, so it's a case of balancing the number of things measured with their relative impact or importance. In other words, the measurement of people is not an exact science, but this doesn't excuse the lack of scientific principles and methodologies being applied to optimise the accuracy or precision of the measurement. Bear in mind that it could also be claimed that the reporting of annual profits of companies can be inconsistent and open to interpretation. For example, assets may well have been run down through constrained expenditure on maintenance in order to boost profitability in the short-term.

Reason 4: Ignorance at the top of the "bottom line" impacts of good people practices

There is a lack of understanding of the linkage between people management practices, key human capital measures and the "bottom line" at top management, extending through to Directors. According to Philpott (2003), Chief Economist at the Chartered Institute of Personnel and Development (CIPD), improving the awareness and implementation of good people management practices is the missing x-factor in improving the U.K.'s productivity performance. A CIPD survey, Voices from the Boardroom (2002), showed that only 13 of the 48 board members interviewed about their views on HR were aware of the evidence that links people management practices with improved "bottom line" performance.

Reason 5: HR lacking in an evidenced based approach

HR practitioners typically know little about research. Practitioner journals cover very little of the most robust research related to human resources management. A disconnect clearly exists between those who practice HR and those who research HR topics. Many HR practitioners have muddled or incorrect beliefs. Research has previously identified a number of clear scientific findings that are not obvious to practitioners. Specifically, Rynes, Colbert and Brown (2002) surveyed nearly 1,000 HR vice presidents, directors and managers to identify which of 35 well-documented research findings HR practitioners widely disbelieve. Their results showed widespread disagreement or lack of knowledge, with more than 50% of practitioners actively disagreeing with or not knowing about key research findings concerning testing and performance. The gap between science and practice is so persistent and pervasive that some have despaired of its ever being narrowed.

> Note: The failure to implement research-supported practices has been observed in nearly every field where there is separation between those who conduct research, and those who are in a position to implement research findings (Rynes, Colbert & Brown, 2002).

HR is often flailing around, out of step with the fundamentals of the business. It is behind the "eight ball" at a critical time. HR needs to move away from personal preference and unsystematic experience towards that based on the best scientific evidence. Isomorphism is often rife in organisations where HR practitioners are looking for innovations from people like themselves and in organisations like their own, which means that the adoption of new practices seems to occur from judgement based more on intuition or implicit knowledge.

Summary including HR's dilemma

In summary, the HR profession needs to adopt a more pragmatic approach to supporting business profitability. It needs to focus on more evidenced based approaches – after all, its numbers that really matter in the boardroom. Until HR measures the effectiveness of its programs, managers and HR professionals will be unable to distinguish between a fad and a valid program. There has been an over reliance on qualitative, perception based HR results, with a shift required to more hard edged business language requiring quantitative, performance measurement. HR and its evaluation may be an imperfect science but it is better than no science at all. The same criticisms of imprecision could be levelled at marketing, IT, economics, etc., but it does not prevent these disciplines presenting their potentially less than perfect measures of strategies, practices and actions against targets.

An organisation's work force is the last frontier of competitive advantage – getting the most out of people. HR has a pivotal role that links people, performance, productivity and profit. However there is a troubling gulf between the needs of the business and the ability of HR to respond, the implications of which are dissatisfied stakeholders and lack of integration between the HR and business agendas. The role of the HR generalist is at the cross roads. On one hand, HR needs employees with cross-functional, service focused skills in order to become a true partner of the business. On the other hand, there is a need for specialist providers with deep knowledge and expertise in particular service areas, and to design, implement and run HR policies and processes in those areas, consistent with the strategic and operational needs of the business. In their shift to a more strategic role, HR has a clear requirement to demonstrate rigour in what they do, and to show value to their organisations. They are under pressure to assist in achieving high levels of employee motivation and performance.

4.14 HUMAN CAPITAL, CORPORATE GOVERNANCE AND THE RESPONSIBILITIES OF DIRECTORS

Governance provides the rules for decision making and accountability, of setting levels and measurement of performance against objectives, and providing the structure and the compliance requirements, ranging from mandatory to discretionary. Recent regulatory efforts to deter corporate malfeasance and provide investors with more transparent information have significantly raised the corporate governance bar. However these new regulations establish only minimum standards of conduct. The explosion of community expectations, legislation and standards has triggered a seismic shift in the demands for greater governance, compliance and risk management.

Companies must go well beyond new regulatory requirements to effectively manage corporate governance risk. Focusing on legal obligations in isolation represents a minimalist and narrow approach. Directors are now acutely aware of corporate governance risk. As alluded to earlier in the Introduction Chapter, one of the impacts of the GFC has been an increased emphasis on corporate governance, risk assessment and mitigation.

The role of employees has not previously been treated as a central concern of corporate governance. However the role between a firm and its employees would seem to be a central, if not a defining feature, of the firm itself. There is a gap, and as such, it is argued that when divergence occurs between rhetoric, systems and practice, then there is a failure of governance.

A dichotomy exists between those organisations that operate from a low commitment, low cost and marginal role of employee voice, to those that operate from a high commitment, high value and employee democratic approach. Evidence of the latter approach points towards improved corporate performance. Organisations may chose to adopt the former approach to gain market share through a strategy of cost reduction. However employees are a key to long-term sustainable operations as they are a vital stakeholder and vital contributors to profit.

Effective governance implies that organisations recognise the impact of stakeholders on organisational success and the corresponding responsibilities that they have to the community of stakeholders – both internal and external. Organisations depend upon and provide substance to a wide variety of stakeholders, and to not recognise the contribution of employees is a failure of governance.

In support of the above, it has been argued that HCM is now a critical priority for organisations. This is Board level material which Directors must inevitably get involved in. Whilst there are no specific legal obligations requiring the reporting of human capital, given its emerging importance, Boards, CEOs and CFOs need to come to grips with how human capital is being managed within their organisations. They have a responsibility to ensure:

- Appropriate and integrated human capital and workforce management strategies and associated reporting are in place
- That the organisational capability exists to achieve the desired business outcomes.

Whilst Directors have been faced with many recent challenges, including Corporate Governance Guidelines, changes to OH & S and IR Legislation, and Corporate Social Responsibility, the effective management of their organisation's human capital represents one of their next most significant challenges.

4.15 ABOUT RISK MANAGEMENT AND HUMAN CAPITAL

The purpose of risk management is to identify potential events that may impact on an entity, quantify the impact and likelihood of occurrence, and then manage the risk in accordance with the organisation's risk appetite. Risk management includes putting in place appropriate risk management procedures and controls. It deals with issues that are both mandatory and non-mandatory. If the risk management process is flawed, a company will suffer in the competitive market place.

The concept of "risk management" is well accepted in the legal world, and often applies to physical assets, the environment, the area of IT, etc. It has been previously applied to the workforce in the area of Occupational

Health and Safety, largely as a result of legislative requirements. The type, scope, and frequency of both internal and external risks facing companies today has increased significantly. To meet business objectives, business leaders must now address new and different forms of business risks. One of these emerging risks applies to an organisation's key intangible asset – its workforce.

4.16 RISK MANAGEMENT TOWARDS PEOPLE HAS BEEN MISSING

Boards and management would be negligent if they failed to protect their physical assets (e.g., appropriate security measures, insurance, etc.), yet the protection of human capital assets has been largely ignored or left to chance. If management was as poor at identifying and reporting on any of the other major resources at their command, their stakeholders would express immediate concern. Some of the primary reasons for the failure to report on human capital have been alluded to earlier, and have been summarised below:

- The lack of valid and reliable measures (i.e., objective, fact-based metrics), which has been a source of considerable frustration for those seeking to manage this vital asset
- The lack of "clout" or influence by HR Departments, which have traditionally been viewed as a non-strategic cost centre, not commercially oriented and struggling to convince management of the value that they may be adding
- A lack of understanding of the linkage between people management practices, key human capital measures and the "bottom line"
- A previous buoyant economic environment where times have been good and supply has exceeded demand.

4.17 WHY WORKFORCE RISK MANAGEMENT SHOULD BE APPLIED NOW

We live in a dynamic environment. There are at least four critical reasons why workforce risk management should now be placed squarely on the corporate governance and risk management agenda:

1. The emerging importance of human capital
2. Emerging trends in the employment landscape, including the talent and skills shortage
3. The need to maximise workforce performance and productivity to remain competitive (i.e., "do more with less")

4. The development of better measures, enabling the identification, quantification, diagnosis and control of workforce risk.

Furthermore whilst forming part of an expanded corporate governance approach, workforce risk management provides an opportunity for utilizing risk as a competitive advantage in the market place.

4.18 THE NEED FOR A FRESH START: DEVELOPING A HUMAN CAPITAL STRATEGIC PLAN

Consistent with an increased focus on managing risk, corporate governance, and people, and taking into account what occurs with other assets and operations of the business, the development of a Human Capital Strategic Plan constitutes an essential blue print document for any organisation in building a sustainable workforce. It has been argued that organisations need to:

- Report on their human capital strategy – to explain their approach to the acquisition, development, management and performance of human capital
- Then provide evidence how current people management practices regarding acquisition, development, motivation and retention, are effecting organisational and business performance.

However very few organisations have such a documented human capital strategy (i.e., a Human Capital Strategic Plan). Such a plan constitutes the "blue print" for how an organisation manages (or intends to manage), their human capital. Amongst other things, it should include a summary of actions taken or proposed to be taken to acquire, retain, develop, motivate and deploy human capital in the service of an organisation's mission.

What should be included in a Human Capital Strategic Plan?

The WRDI Institute has developed a Human Capital Strategic Plan package that incorporates and integrates five key human capital concepts and models:

- The five ways to build human capital
- The three types of capabilities/competencies from organisational through to individual
- Segmentation of the workforce and differentiation of roles according to a skills' based model (i.e., according to skills value and skills uniqueness)
- Profiling EVP for defining job roles, based on the concept of the Psychological Contract

- The three types of Human Capital Data and reporting of this data in a compelling format (refer later in Chapter 9).

This package provides concepts and value on an entirely different plane:

- Going past traditional quantitative workforce planning (see below) to provide a strategic, actionable view to the future
- Providing the necessary workforce intelligence, derived from making more sense of HR data (both current and proposed), thus leading to more informed decision making and better outcomes
- Providing the strategy, step-by-step methodology, and powerful tools to deliver the necessary insight to more effectively manage an organisation's most vital intangible asset, and otherwise best execute the strategy and mission of the organisation, from a people perspective.

> Note: The Basic Version of this Package is able to be purchased and downloaded from the WRDI Institute web site (www.wrdi-institute.com). The Advanced Version of the Package includes the Skills Segmentation Questionnaire and plotting tool (SSQ).

How does the development of a Human Capital Strategic Plan differ from workforce planning?

Typically workforce planning is about primarily filling roles. It is tactically focused on head counts and time lines. As such, it neglects to consider the wider strategic workforce questions raised earlier in this chapter and neglects to differentiate roles (and in particular the identification of Critical roles), according to a rigorous methodology. There is a need to move beyond workforce planning to a more strategic and comprehensive workforce/talent management approach. Those who can effectively translate their business strategy into an actionable human capital strategy can drive a new kind of competitive advantage—one extremely difficult for others to imitate.

Chapter 5

How to Develop, Acquire and Dispose of Human Capital

KEY POINTS

Key questions and issues that we will address in this chapter:

Development of Human Capital:

- *A framework for developing human capital*
- *What are differentiating capabilities, core competences and work competencies*
- *How to develop differentiating capabilities and core competencies by identifying their key drivers*

Acquisition of Human Capital:

- *A framework for acquiring human capital*
- *What is employment branding?*
- *How does branding link to the EVP or the "deal"?*
- *What comprises the EVP or the "deal"?*
- *How should EVPs be developed?*
- *How should EVPs link to employee engagement and retention?*
- *How can EVPs be profiled?*

Disposal of Human Capital:

- *Why downsizing is the method of last resort to reduce labour costs*
- *How to effectively dispose of human capital*

What are the consequences of failing to adequately address these questions/issues or ending up with the wrong answers?

- *Waste or inefficient use of resources due to a lack of strategic focus*
- *Ad hoc or lack of integration of people management policies and practices*
- *Lack of organisation capability to deliver desired business outcomes*
- *Failure to clarify the EVP may lead to misunderstandings, disappointment, frustration and lowered performance and higher retention risk down the road*
- *Ineffective disposal of human capital can have longer term adverse organisational consequences, with survivor syndrome and increased turnover down the track.*

5. HOW TO DEVELOP, ACQUIRE AND DISPOSE OF HUMAN CAPITAL

> Note: As indicated in the Introduction Chapter of this book, it is only intended to outline some of the fundamental concepts, and not provide a detailed treatise of these topics.

5.1 TYPES OF CAPABILITIES AND COMPETENCIES

Firstly we will address the development of human capital. There are three types or three levels of capabilities and competencies:

- Differentiating capabilities (of organisations)
- Core competencies (of organisations)
- Work competencies (of individuals and teams).

We shall now discuss each of these types of capabilities/competencies in turn. Refer to model 3 in the coloured pages of the Introduction Chapter.

5.2 DIFFERENTIATING CAPABILITIES (OF ORGANISATIONS)

Every organisation operates in a unique competitive situation. In order to achieve its goals, each organisation must develop and build capabilities that are critical to strategic intent. Such capabilities:

- Differentiate an organisation from its competitors
- Characterise the organisation to their customers
- Contribute to success.

Differentiating capabilities (or a single capability which may be the case for each organisation), are therefore vital to the success of an organisation, in that they constitute a key source of sustainable competitive advantage. They are one of the main reasons why customers purchase products or services from one organisation versus another. These capabilities are typically unable to be reflected in individual or work level competencies. They reside more within various groups of people and the processes and systems that are in place across the organisation, rather than within a particular individual or group.

Consequently these differentiating capabilities are more difficult to measure, and typically such measures need to be developed for various specific organisational circumstances.

It is important to identify the drivers of these capabilities, and then to maximise and differentiate that capability. The following are examples of differentiating capabilities and their drivers for various types of organisations.

Global IT Provider:

- Differentiating capability: Skill to rapidly assemble global expert teams
- Key skills value elements or drivers: Organisational capability.

International Bank:

- Differentiating capability: Provide exceptional service at low cost
- Key skills value elements or drivers: Organisational capability, customer satisfaction and costs.

Consultancy Firm:

- Differentiating capability: Ability to learn (knowledge management), productise new ideas and offerings
- Key skills value elements or drivers: Organisational capability and innovation.

Coal Mining Company (high customer demand):

- Differentiating capability: Integration of activities (e.g., from mine planning, to operations and processing, through to transport and loading onto ship) to provide a range of products to meet customer requirements
- Key skills value elements or drivers: productivity, costs and quality and customer satisfaction.

5.3 CORE COMPETENCIES (OF THE ORGANISATION)

Core competencies directly relate to the key activities that the organisation undertakes in conducting its business. They are more generalised or spread across the organisation. Some of these core competencies will be more important than others, depending upon the circumstances of the firm, as illustrated below:

- Productivity, costs and quality combined with reputation (including managing risk), would be more important to a nuclear power generating company that is under pressure to meet high customer demands;
- Innovation would be more important to a drug company looking to develop new products (e.g., R & D scientists);

- Revenue and customer satisfaction combined with reputation, would be more important to a recruitment company trying to increase sales in a tight market.

Further examples of core competencies and differentiating competencies are provided below for two organisations - a concrete and quarrying company, and a water supply authority.

Example 1: Acme Contracting

Acme Contracting operates a number of quarries, sand pits, concrete plants and asphalt plants, providing various raw and processed materials to its customers. The core competencies of the organisation include the following:

- Marketing, sales and distribution of raw materials, concrete and asphalt
- Planning, design and establishment of raw materials (i.e., quarries and sand pits) operations
- Production of raw materials for concrete, asphalt and road paving to meet specifications and client requirements, and otherwise comply with environmental constraints
- Production and delivery of pre-mix concrete and asphalt to meet specifications and customer requirements.

Acme's differentiating capabilities are:

- Integration of activities to optimize the product/sales mix
- Sourcing, approval and development of new raw material deposits, and concrete and asphalt plant locations.

Example 2: XYZ Water Supply Authority

XYZ Water Authority operates a number of dams and pipeline facilities to supply water to farmers in the ABC region of Australia. The core competencies of the organisation include the following:

- Planning of water supply requirements and distribution
- Maintenance of dam storage facilities
- Design and maintenance of efficient water distribution systems and pipelines
- Drafting of water supply contracts, negotiations with consumers (farmers), and developing quality relationships with the same
- Financial planning and control concerning the costs, revenues and capital works associated with water storage and distribution.

XYZ's differentiating capability is:

- Balancing investment in storage and distribution, and water distribution efficiency
- Achieving equality of water supply to consumers, at a competitive cost.

5.4 WORK COMPETENCIES (OF INDIVIDUALS OR TEAMS)

Work competencies are those competencies specific to various roles and can be broadly classified into three areas:

- Technical/Functional *
- Managerial
- Behavioural.

Note: *Examples of functional competencies include activities relating to marketing, sales, PR, legal, financial, HR, etc., whereas technical functions have a more scientific or engineering orientation.

For many roles in the organisation, work competencies will include only some of the core competencies referred to in the previous section. For example, the marketing people may not require highly developed technical competencies compared to the manufacturing or production people.

Competency profiling enables a comparison of an individual's existing skills and competencies with the requirements of the job. It provides a basis for a targeted approach to addressing development needs. Refer to Chapter 9 for a further discussion on measuring competencies.

Note: Refer to Appendix C for a conceptual approach to workforce segmentation and job/role analysis that links core competencies with job roles, including three steps to quickly increasing business performance.

5.5 DEVELOPING CORE AND WORK COMPETENCIES

These competencies can either be:

- Recruited against, if they are available in the market, along with the appropriate levels of experience and knowledge required for the role
- Otherwise developed from within (refer to Chapter 3 for further information on "make" versus "buy" employment strategies).

If the core and work competencies are more unique to the organisation (i.e., its systems, plant, equipment, processes), then these competencies need to be developed from within, by a combination of internal training programs, experience in the role, coaching and mentoring, etc.

Managerial/leadership and behavioural competencies (i.e., "soft skills") may be developed through various means including:

- Stretch jobs
- Coaching and mentoring
- As well as specific training and development courses.

As a precursor to developing core and work competencies, if there are issues concerning employee engagement and retention, then these should be addressed in the first instance. For example:

- There is little point in investing in a leadership development program for senior executives if those executives are at high risk of leaving the organisation because of dysfunctional organisational factors
- Investments in developing or enhancing core competencies are likely to prove futile if the wrong people are in the wrong job, due to defective recruitment and selection practices.

We shall now turn our attention to the acquisition of human capital.

Case Study: Proposed Leadership Development Program for At Risk Executives

A professional services organisation was about to undertake an expensive leadership development program for its key executives. However knowing that all was not well with some of the senior executives, the CEO was convinced to run a WRDI® engagement and retention risk survey first.

Sure enough this survey revealed that 3 of the 6 senior executives were at moderate to high risk of leaving because of issues with the CEO. It would have been a waste of resources in developing people who were about to "fly the coup"! A more important priority was to address and resolve the issues between these 3 executives and the CEO prior to further HR initiatives and investment. The Board was briefed on these findings.

Individual reports were generated for the executives and the CEO, and each was debriefed on their report findings. A workshop was then developed and facilitated by an external consultant to work through the issues of concern. The CEO was also provided with ongoing coaching.

5.6 WHAT IS THE EMPLOYMENT BRAND?

The organisation's brand – the face that it presents to the external world, including its appeal to the specific people it wants to find and keep - is an important factor in attraction, engagement and retention of people. The employment brand includes, amongst other things, the organisation's:

- Values
- Culture
- Management/leadership capability
- Challenges that it faces and its proposed direction in addressing those challenges
- Success/performance
- Industry leader status.

Organisational culture consists of both **objective** and **subjective** components. Objective aspects consist of the tangible artifacts of an organisation (e.g., office decor, types of company cars, etc.). Subjective culture includes the shared goals, roles, norms, ideologies, and values held by the organisation and its members. It is manifest in shared facets of organisational life such as the organisation's:

- Identification of corporate heroes
- Leadership style
- Visible structures and processes
- Espoused values, strategies, goals and philosophies
- Shared tacit assumptions
- Decision-making practices
- Feelings of "family" among workers
- Degree of encouragement and mentoring from management to subordinates
- Other characteristics of the employees and their relationships.

5.7 WHAT IS THE PURPOSE OF BRANDING?

A corporate personality

Many organisations have concluded that they need to create a corporate personality, or an identity that employees as well as customers will recognise and relate to. Brand is intended to capture the essence of the company:

- What it is
- What it stands for
- What it would be like to work within it.

The purpose of a brand is to efficiently bring employers (buyers) and sellers (employees) together, to establish an enduring relationship. The organisation espouses to have something that is unique and relevant. This distinguishes that organisation from its competitors, and is sufficiently appealing to attract a significant number of people, with certain preferences, who can relatively easily locate an organisation that uniquely caters to these preferences.

> Unless organisations are genuinely able to define their own unique brand and Employment Value Proposition(s), the market will pull them down, not only by pulling out key employees, but also by shaping the attitudes and behaviour of those who remain (Capelli, 1999).

Brands should not be all things to all people

Most brands don't have universal appeal, nor should they, otherwise their message is compromised. Brand awareness is typically tailored to a particular audience, not to be all things to all people. Organisations must understand their unique value - why some people want to work for them and why others don't. Brand should convey two messages:

- The unique benefit of the corporate environment
- The type of person who is likely to thrive in that environment.

Brands have inherent value. By attracting the right candidates, the organisation doesn't need to pay top dollar, because it is supplying value in other ways.

For employees, brand reduces risk. They are better placed to make decisions as to whether the corporate offering is consistent with their values, personalities, interests and preferences. The great hope offered by an effective employer branding strategy is that many of today's HR challenges – those revolving around fit, engagement and retention – can be partially solved long before they arise.

5.8 BRANDING AND EVPS

Fashioning a compelling platform

Emphasis on branding and EVPs has transformed recruitment from purchasing to marketing. Organisations now need to fashion a compelling platform that clearly establishes:

- Who they are (the brand)
- What they offer (the EVP)
- What they expect from employees.

This platform establishes the initial set of practices to ensure that the organisation employs people who are more likely to be aligned with both the organisation (i.e., person–organisational fit), and the job (i.e., person-job fit). It should outline the positive benefits for employees of buying into the relationship with that employer. The focus should be on attracting those people who have the motivation, skills, knowledge, experience and competencies (refer to the definition of human capital in the Introduction Chapter and Chapter 4), to perform well, given the strategy, goals and practices of the organisation, and the nature of the role.

One brand but many EVPs

Whilst there is one brand (i.e., a constant), there are numerous EVPs within an organisation consistent with the variety of jobs or roles within that organisation. Thus the EVP relates to the specifics of the job, including its terms and conditions, or the "deal" – both the tangibles and the intangibles. The intent of the EVP/"deal" is for the employer to define the content of the psychological contract with prospective employees, so as to help in recruiting and ultimately retaining those employees.

5.9 WHAT COMPRISES EVPS OR "DEALS"?

As stated, the EVP/"deal" includes a mix of tangibles and intangibles. Tangibles include such things as:

- Pay
- Training and development
- Resources to do the job, etc.

Intangibles include such things as:

- Management support

- Career development
- Recognition, etc.

Reference has been made above to the content of the psychological contract in relation to EVPs/"deals". That which comprises the psychological contract (i.e., the items comprising a mix of tangibles and intangibles), and the different types of psychological contracts, are explained in Chapter 7.

5.10 WHAT ATTRACTS PEOPLE IS NOT IDENTICAL TO THAT WHICH RETAINS THEM

The reasons for getting married are not necessarily the same reasons for staying married! What attracts people to an organisation is somewhat different to what causes them to stay or leave. People typically join companies more because of organisational factors, including for example:

- An organisation that they can identify with
- Favourable career prospects
- A competitive salary.

Leadership issues are not so significant given that candidates usually know little about their supervisor, manager or top management when they begin a new job. Nor are relationships with others significant at the time of job acceptance, given that the newcomer has not yet had the opportunity to establish them.

However once in the job, the intangibles assume much greater significance in their impact on affective commitment and job satisfaction (and hence retention) compared to the tangibles. These intangibles include local workplace and top management leadership, fair treatment, job challenge, recognition, autonomy, a supportive work environment, etc. (refer to Chapter 7 for a further discussion).

5.11 THE PROCESS OF DEVELOPING EVPS/"DEALS"

The sequence for determining EVPs/"deals"

The sequence for determining EVPs or "deals" should be as follows:

- Firstly, analyse the role according to the skills' based workforce segmentation model (refer to Chapter 3)
- Secondly develop and profile the EVP based on which skills quadrant the role fits into (refer to Chapter 7 for examples of EVPs by the four skills quadrants)

- Thirdly, modify if necessary, to suit various demographic groups (i.e., to satisfy the needs of the multi-generational and diverse workforce), organisational considerations and needs, and environmental factors (see below).

Ideally this process is best undertaken with a focus group discussion comprising representatives from HR, line management and the recruitment consultant. Aspects of both the job and work setting should be diagnosed, consistent with the principles and guidelines outlined herein. The challenge is to balance trade-offs between benefits and costs, both direct and indirect, across those items comprising the EVP/"deal", and optimise performance and retention. Input from accounting professionals may be required to evaluate and assess the EVP/"deal".

Customising the EVP/"deal"

The extent to which an organisation is prepared to customise the EVP/"deal" will depend upon:

- Internal considerations (e.g., the skills quadrant where the role belongs, the performance level required of the individual in the role, current needs of the organisation, the business strategy, etc.)
- External labour supply factors relating to the difficulty in replacing an individual in their role should they decide to leave.

If recruiting for a particular role in a tight labour market, then this may require a sweetening of the "deal" as an attraction and retention strategy. In some instances, the "deal" may be best sweetened with dollars (i.e., enhanced remuneration package which may include a sign on bonus). Alternatively in other instances, it may be sweetened through offering more by way of intangibles (e.g., training, development, attendance at conferences, flexible work practices, housing and accommodation), which is more likely to be the case for skills quadrants 1 and 4 roles. As indicated earlier, market forces will be disruptive of internal remuneration relativities, challenging traditional notions of equity.

It's not all about $

Creating competitive EVPs/"deals" for various workforce segments is vital to engagement and retention. Whilst an organisation may be unable to offer a highly competitive salary (e.g., government agency constrained by award or policy requirements), it may be able to offer great career growth prospects as a substitute. The EVP/"deal" should include, amongst other things, a system that contains a mix of both extrinsic and intrinsic rewards and benefits that the workforce will value and respond to. A portfolio of benefits may be offered to present applicants with more choices that reflect the values and motivations of different employee types (refer to Chapter 1 on the preferences of various demographic groups).

5.12 EVPS/"DEALS" AND DIFFERENT JOB ROLES

Notwithstanding the skills' based workforce segmentation approach, and the different EVPs/"deals" associated with those segments, different job roles also require different EVPs / "deals" (i.e., different mixes of tangibles and intangibles). For example:

- Senior managers require job challenge and the stimulation of career development opportunities
- Salespeople typically require recognition
- Professionals value the opportunity to develop technical skills, autonomy in decision making, sufficient resources to do the job
- Workers in lower knowledge jobs value a supportive work environment (i.e., being part of the team), with some not as concerned about career development or progression.

5.13 EVPS/"DEALS" AND ORGANISATIONAL SIZE

The ability to define, develop and deliver competitive EVPs/"deals" - is critical for both large and small organisations. Smaller organisations may offer more opportunity to satisfy a desire for:

- Meaning and impact
- Excitement, challenge and responsibility
- Flexibility and diversity.

Small companies may also offer equity ownership in a business where a few talented executives can drive up the share price. However large companies need not be too defensive, as they possess natural advantages of their own, including the:

- Magnitude of the impact
- Depth (the resources to take risks)
- Capital (resources to support big decisions)
- Variety of experiences with multiple career paths and opportunities.

5.14 LINKING EVPS/"DEALS" TO THE BUSINESS STRATEGY

In Chapter 7 we explore how different EVPs/"deals" should be designed to fit with the business strategy. We discuss how the nature of the EVP/"deal" can significantly impact on the commitment and retention of employees, and hence the performance and business success of the organisation. We also discuss how incongruent EVPs/"deals" can lead to excessive turnover, including examples of the same.

5.15 EVPS/"DEALS" AND DEMOGRAPHIC CONSIDERATIONS

There are a number of populations that comprise the diverse workforce, each with different needs and preferences. We have summarized these preferences in Chapter 1. As indicated, despite the emphasis on these differences, which are to some extent exaggerated, these populations have much more in common than they have differences.

5.16 PROFILING EVPS/"DEALS"

Ideally the EVP/"deal" should be documented and presented in the form of a profile quantifying what is being offered by the organisation, across the items which typically comprise the psychological contract. This profile can be combined with a written statement, providing candidates with a clear picture as to what their employment situation will be like (i.e., a Realistic Job Preview). Refer to Chapter 7 for samples of typical EVPs or "deals" for various skills' based workforce segments or skills quadrants. These profiles also form a basis for subsequently determining whether the "deal" or the promise has been delivered.

> Note: Refer to Chapter 3 regarding the EVP Profiling tool which has been developed by the WRDI Institute.

5.17 EMPLOYERS OF CHOICE (EOC) AND BRANDING

> Note: For a further discussion on Employer of Choice and the psychological contract, refer to Chapter 8.

The term "Employer of Choice" (EOC) is a much abused one, meaning different things to different people. Some organisations are delusional about their EOC status claims. An organisation can't have a good external employment brand without having a good internal one. There has to be integrity, with the rhetoric matched to the substance (i.e., internal reality of the organisation), for the reasons set out below, and also elaborated upon in the following section.

Increasingly employers are relying on their current employees to help recruit others. Employee referrals are becoming a more popular path/ method of recruitment. Their use, including the payment of referral fees, is likely to impact even more significantly on turnover in the future. If one person leaves an organisation, then they may encourage others from their network to leave. However employee referral schemes are hardly likely to be effective if many employees are disengaged and dissatisfied.

5.18 ARE EMPLOYERS DELIVERING ON THEIR EVPS OR THE PROMISE?

Job advertisements that exaggerate the virtues of the role and/or the employing organisation, tend to be the rule rather than the exception in today's aggressive recruitment market. Unfortunately in these cases, the rhetoric of what is reportedly on offer never matches the substance of what is ultimately available and delivered! Put simply, the promise isn't being honoured. Furthermore such unsophisticated attempts to attract top talent are likely to be counterproductive. Frustration and disappointment for the selected applicant, shortly after they commence their new job, is likely to lead to:

- Reduced job satisfaction
- Reduced commitment
- Higher turnover.

Reference has been made previously in Chapter 4 to the failure of many organisations to deliver on the promise.

5.19 EVPS AND REALISTIC JOB PREVIEWS (RJPS)

It is important to develop an accurate, realistic view of the job as this will:

- Enhance the development of a more complete and accurate knowledge of the job and work setting
- Ensure greater role clarity, with more accurate job expectations
- Improve the efficiency of recruitment and selection
- Increase new employees' adaptation and job survival (retention), guarding against the possibility of unrealistic, or a miss-match of, expectations.

EVPs and Realistic Job Previews (RJPs) are closely related concepts. RJPs clarify expectations of both parties, their intent being to manage/ vaccinate prospective employees' expectations. These expectations can be thought about in the context of the "deal" (i.e., both the tangibles and intangibles). The greater the matching of mutual expectations, the greater is the probability of higher alignment and performance, and reduced turnover.

> RJP research has shown that accurate and realistic job information during recruitment and selection is associated with positive work outcomes (e.g., low attrition rates, high job satisfaction, low voluntary turnover, high work performance), (Meglino, Ravlin, & deNisi, 2000; Phillips, 1998).
>
> A review of 11 field studies of over 4,500 participants in a variety of organisations (military, service, educational and manufacturing), has confirmed that recruiters or employers not using realisitic job previews, had in excess of 25% higher turnover on average (Reilly, Brown, Blood & Malatesta, 1981).

5.20 SUMMARY: RECRUITMENT STAGES AND THE RELEVANCE OF THE EVP

The process of selection and recruitment can be conceived in a number of stages as outlined below, with the concept of the EVP prevalent in a number of these stages.

Recruitment Stage	Activities
Employment branding	Newspaper advertorial Web site Industry review
Determining the job specification*	Writing the job description Determining the EVP for the role (varies according to skills quadrant) Writing the advertisement
Sourcing candidates (varies according to the skills quadrant)	Job boards Newspapers Industry list servers and online journals Government Gazette Referrals through current employees
Shortlisting candidates	Screen all applicants Initial phone interviews with potential candidates Face to face behavioural and competency based interviews with further qualified potential candidates

Interviewing preferred candidates#	Includes a Realistic Job Preview (RJP) Reporting on candidates
Reference checking of candidates	Conduct detailed reference checks on preferred candidates Criminal history check on preferred candidates
Testing/assessment of Candidates	Psychometric testing on preferred candidates (varies according to skills quadrant)
Offer and acceptance	Negotiate with selected candidate Notify unsuccessful candidates
Post placement^	On-boarding or 3 monthly review regarding satisfaction, fit and performance

The EVP has application at the above stages:

*Profiling the EVP for the role

#Measuring the candidate's expectations and matching with the EVP for the role

^Post Recruitment Expectations Delivery Check matching whether the new employee's expectations against the EVP have been met.

We shall now turn our attention to the opposite end of the spectrum - severing the relationship or the disposal of human capital.

5.21 THE DOWNSIDE OF DOWNSIZING: THE METHOD OF LAST RESORT!

So far we have focused on the various ways of enhancing human capital. However in the aftermath of the GFC and associated volatility, many organisations have reviewed their operations and sought to cut costs in response to declining revenues. Direct labour costs can represent anything between 30% (e.g., mining) up to 80% (e.g., professional services) of the cost base of an organisation. The allure of downsizing labour is its potential to quickly yield substantial savings in people costs. However this allure may represent "fools gold". Managers have a responsibility to run their organisations as efficiently as possible, but they need to be sure about future savings. Downsizing (labour) should only be considered as the method of last resort for a whole range of reasons, as set out below:

1. Severance costs can be very significant (e.g., one month's notice plus up to say three to four weeks for each year of service). The direct severance costs for a senior executive may easily run well into a six figure sum.

2. Those companies that downsize can typically experience voluntary turnover rates of 50% greater (i.e., for survivors), than those that don't in the year following the downsizing (Trevor & Nyberg, 2008). As we will see in Chapter 6, the cost of turnover, particularly for knowledge based businesses, can be very substantial.

> Note: The above findings were based on a recent study of 206 Fortune 500 companies.

3. It is much easier to shut a project down compared to restarting it.

4. There is a danger of litigation from disgruntled ex-employees.

5. There is evidence that quality suffers with poor labour relations (Bridgestone/Firestone), when brute force is used (Krueger & Mas, 2002).

6. Firms that downsize fail to improve their ROA (return on assets) until year two after downsizing (Cascio, 2002).

7. Downsizing often begets downsizing, with two thirds of firms that layoff employees in a year, do so the following year (U.S. Department of Labor, 1995).

8. The loss of significant chunks of the organisation's memory (knowledge firms, those that rely on creativity and innovation are more at risk, e.g., biotechnology, pharmaceuticals, software).

9. The drop in morale of survivors (Appelbaum, Everard & Hung, 1999).

10. More than half the companies that downsize (56%) end up hiring replacements, with the associated cost tag (Cascio, 2002).

11. Survivor syndrome in the form of an immobilized workforce that is risk averse and self-absorbed, doesn't constitute a sound people platform for responding to the dynamics and challenges of the contemporary workplace, and otherwise avoiding further difficulties down the road.

In respect of the latter point, stress related medical disorders for those laid off are prevalent to the same extent as those for survivors – the risks are equal for both groups (Cascio, 2002). However those who resign voluntarily are at lesser health risk, presumably because they have acted out of their own choice (as opposed to the choice dictated by their previous employer), and feel more empowered accordingly.

> Note: Downsizing is a broad term that includes any number of combinations of a reduction in an organisation's use of assets, be they financial, physical, human (layoffs) or information (Cascio, 2002). However within the context of this chapter, we are referring predominantly to people downsizing.

5.22 ALTERNATIVES TO DOWNSIZING

As indicated in the Introduction Chapter, the GFC provided an opportunity to review all aspects of the business, and therefore provided a legitimacy for change, which may have included any of the following:

- Selling off assets that were of poorer fit
- Replacing unsustainable business models, with associated restructuring and possible downsizing*
- Reviewing the way work was done and continuing to innovate
- Reviewing employment strategies, including identification of critical roles, "make" versus "buy" employment decisions, outsourcing, etc.

*Downsizing under such circumstances constitutes part of a strategic restructuring, rather than simply cost cutting. This may mean a change in the skills mix required for the organisation, with the simultaneous outplacement and recruitment of people if redeployment doesn't represent a viable solution. Under such circumstances, the organisation gets a workforce that is more competitive, and employees get more interesting and challenging jobs with restructuring.

Other considerations before downsizing (i.e., cutting costs before cutting people), include the following:

- Redeploy employees who are satisfactory performers
- Cut temporary staff and contractors (i.e., reduce the contingent workforce)
- Reduce or eliminate over time
- Offer voluntary retirements
- Offer voluntary redundancies with the proviso that if the redundancy is not accepted by the employer, there will be no stigma attached to individual applicants
- Implement salary cuts or salary restrictions

- Eliminate or reduce bonuses
- Implement hiring restrictions
- Reduce work hours and offer flexible work practices
- Implement work sharing (i.e., share the pain)
- Implement mandatory holidays, or voluntary days without pay
- Bring holidays forward
- Offer unpaid or partly paid sabbaticals
- Get rid of poorer performers, which may include holding mid-term reviews.

If employees can't be provided with more pay, then as a substitute, they may be compensated with more power (e.g., autonomy), or other intangibles (e.g., career development activities). The element of choice is a key to the success of the above initiatives, where people feel more in control and are therefore likely to be more engaged.

5.23 WHEN DOWNSIZING IS UNAVOIDABLE: WHAT TO DO, WHAT NOT TO DO

What to do:

- Stick to the espoused values, mission, guiding principles of the organisation
- Tell the truth with the CEO getting out on the front foot and clearly explaining both the short-term and longer-term goals – exercising sound leadership is vital
- Cut with surgical precision, removing the "fat" and not the "lean muscle"
- Focus on the stars and mission critical people to ensure their retention
- Involve employees in decisions as far as is practical
- Ensure procedural fairness, whereby people have the right of appeal (including recourse to an ombudsman or equivalent), and can have their grievances heard
- Ensure distributive fairness (i.e., fair outcomes), where people get fair severance pay
- Develop a communication plan and ensure a consistent communication message prevails down through the organisation
- Train managers to communicate the message consistently and effectively

- Tell survivors how departing employees are being treated
- Allow people to stay on for up to four weeks rather than march them out the door immediately

> Note: This provides an opportunity to say good bye and providing there is procedural justice, the risk of sabotage is likely to be low.

- Conduct post mortems - survivors will want to know whether there is a new business strategy, and why they should stay
- Conduct a risk assessment a few months after the event - the organisation should want to know the levels of trust, commitment, job satisfaction and retention risk of survivors, particularly those in critical roles
- Practice open book management and enhance the business literacy of employees by educating them on the profit and loss performance of the business
- As far as possible maintain goodwill.

What not to do:

- Don't adopt the "peanut butter" approach - one that spreads the cuts (which are typically around 10%), evenly across the organisation (i.e., by department or business unit)
- Don't implement a blanket salary freeze, as it may restrict correcting any salary inequities or rewarding outstanding performance
- Don't implement a blanket recruitment freeze as it may result in positions being left vacant, or filled with unsuitable internal candidates, or opportunities foregone to recruit outstanding external candidates
- Don't implement uniform pay cuts, as such actions are less likely to retain top performers
- Be very careful about removing employee benefits such as flexible work practices, as in a climate where people may be required to do more with less, removal of such benefits may be counterproductive.

> Note: It may be appropriate to implement a total head count freeze, which still allows some flexibility in recruitment.

Case Study: Global ICT Firm and Premature Ejaculation!

A global ICT firm made an announcement in mid November 2008 of its intention to layoff in excess of 15% of its workforce worldwide over the next 12 months, within the context of a "restructure". There was no specific details provided as to the business units or locations that would be more affected, or on what basis these layoffs would be made (presumably because this had not been thought through in any detail at the time of the announcement).

One can only assume that the prime motivation for this announcement was for the benefit of shareholders (i.e., to maintain the share price). However from the employees' perspective, you can image the concern and drop off in morale of the staff. They were not told of their fate until four to five months into 2009 (a delay of around six months since the initial announcement). Such premature communication would hardly encourage innovation, improvements to work methods, etc., during this period.

As indicated in the Introduction, shareholders are less loyal than employees.

Case Study 2: Global ICT Firm and Punitive Cost Cutting

IBM recently announced it had cut tea and coffee from the office budget worldwide to cut costs. The company had already flagged its intention to cut 10,000 jobs from its global workforce. It declined to say what these savings would amount to. One would have thought that there was enough nervousness out in the current business climate without restoring to eliminating basic amenities. In terms of preserving goodwill, this punitive cost cutting would seem to have sent all the wrong messages.

Chapter 6

About Engagement and Retention: Everything You Ever Wanted to Know

KEY POINTS

Key questions and issues that we will address in this chapter:

Retention of Human Capital:

- *What is the cost of turnover?*
- *What are the six key factors influencing turnover?*
- *What are the two key drivers of employees' intention to stay/leave?*
- *What are the three types of reasons people leave organisations?*
- *What is meant by selective retention and why is it important?*
- *What is the link between performance and retention?*
- *How to re-recruit your existing workforce*
- *How to retain human capital*

Engagement of Human Capital:

- *What is meant by the term "Employee Engagement"?*
- *What are the four "holy grail" workforce measures?*
- *Why are Engagement Indices a blunt measure?*
- *How to engage human capital*

What are the consequences of failing to adequately address these questions/issues or ending up with the wrong answers?

- *Unless the workforce is fundamentally engaged and retained, then investments in other human capital initiatives are likely to prove relatively futile*
- *It is important to separate predictors of performance from predictors of retention - engaged employees can still leave, and disengaged people can still stay*
- *You may be sitting on a "ticking time bomb", about to lose valuable people by relying on an Engagement Index and not separately measuring retention risk*

6. ABOUT ENGAGEMENT AND RETENTION

6.1 RETENTION IS A STRATEGIC ISSUE

> A recent study found 80% of CEO's surveyed, rated recruiting and retaining skilled employees as the No 1 challenge for business in Australia (Australian Human Resources Institute and Council for Economic Development of Australia, 2004).
>
> Attraction and retention - the biggest challenges post - 2000. There is a war for talent and it will intensify! The average executive will work in 5 companies. (The War for Talent, The McKinsey Quarterly, 1998)
>
> Retention represents the highest ROI of any HR initiative (Sullivan, 2004).

The success of organisations in the future will increasingly depend upon them having a stable and productive workforce of skilled employees. Retention of those more highly skilled employees should therefore constitute a core business strategy. Irrespective of what strategies organisations may adopt to manage their workforce, stopping or preventing the "bleeding" (i.e., retention), particularly for people in critical roles, must rank as one of the top priorities.

However understanding turnover and retention, and what lies within the control of organisations, has proven to be a "grey area". Limitations of previous methodologies for understanding and addressing turnover (e.g., focus groups, exit interviews), has contributed to this impression. Furthermore as indicated earlier, the responsibility for retention represents a "black hole" in many organisations, with disconnects between various HR activities, including recruitment and retention. Typically *ad hoc* approaches have been adopted without a deeper framework of understanding of the causes, best practices and approaches that work. For example:

- Provision of gym memberships or dog walking services for employees (i.e., superficial corporate benefits), is hardly likely to impact positively on retention if there is a failure to attend to significant issues of concern that are more relevant to daily on the job experiences (e.g., lack of autonomy, unfair work loads)

- "Stop gap" pay measures and bonuses may provide "breathing room" to address critical issues, but they are not a long-term "fix", as they do not address the underlying intangible issues (e.g., ineffective leadership, lack of recognition)

- A focus on recognition or reward programs is likely to be ineffective if there are deeper concerns with trust in management, poor-person job fit, or if the EVP/"deal" hasn't been delivered.

Retention is ultimately a reflection of how an organisation manages its relationships (or psychological contracts) with its people, and as such, it should be treated as a strategic issue. It is a multifaceted phenomena - there is no "silver bullet" solution (although some people look for simple solutions to more complex problems). Superficial initiatives or patchwork solutions are therefore unlikely to succeed in addressing such problems of a deeper or more systemic nature.

Notwithstanding, there may or may not be a "quick fix" solution. Case study examples have been provided in Chapter 3 which did in fact provide some quick fix solutions at minimal or no cost (e.g., restructuring, changes in recruitment approaches). On the other hand, the rebuilding of relationships takes time and energy, particularly if they are severely distressed from past actions and events. Trust takes time to build but it can be destroyed in a second.

Furthermore a "shotgun" approach to turnover where all employees are dealt with as one large mass is also unlikely to work. Typically within organisations (as we have and will see in the various case study examples in this book) there will be pockets of turnover, either within a particular workforce segment, or at a particular layer, or within a business unit or a demographic group. A "one size fits all" approach is not only likely to miss the mark, but will most likely result in interventions which are unnecessary, may be counter-productive, and otherwise wasteful of resources.

6.2 THE COST OF TURNOVER (DIRECT AND INDIRECT)

Estimates of turnover costs vary, e.g.:

- The U.S. Department of Labor estimates that it costs a company one-third of a new hire's annual salary to replace an employee

- The typical cost of voluntary turnover ranges from 0.5 to 2.5 times the annual salary of the job in question (Cascio, 1991)

- The Saratoga Institute Turnover Costing Model (Davidson & Fitz-enz, 1997) estimates that turnover costs are between one to two times an employee's annual salary and benefits.

- Mercer Delta (2006) estimates the cost of turnover, particularly for knowledge based businesses, can be very substantial - up to 10 times the salary of the job in question in the case of CEOs.

> Note: Refer to the skills' based workforce segmentation model in Chapter 3 and the cost of turnover multiple estimated for roles in the various skills' quadrants.

The Saratoga Institute model includes both direct and indirect costs, with the three major categories of direct costs being:

- The cost of termination (including any pay-out arrangements)
- The cost of hiring (including advertising expenses, recruitment consultant's fees, etc)
- The cost of the new hire (only 60 % as effective in the first three months compared to an experienced employee), with this last category being by far the most expensive.

The direct replacement costs comprise only a small portion of the total cost of turnover. Indirect or less visible costs (which are not immediately apparent in an organisation's financial reporting), and which constitute up to 80% of the total cost of turnover, include:

- Lost customers or damaged customer relations
- The additional marketing and sales expenditures needed to win replacement customers
- The loss of intellectual capital and corporate memory
- Lost opportunities (particularly in the development of new technologies and products)
- A decrease in the "bench strength" required for effective succession planning
- An advantage to competitors from the knowledge acquisition of their new recruit's ex-employer
- Decreased morale and increased stress among remaining employees (i.e., the vicious cycle as under staffed or inexperienced staff take on too much work and responsibility)
- The negative effect on an organisation's reputation.

The loss of high performers costs more than money - it dilutes the ability to perform. Recent research indicates that turnover rates are negatively associated with business unit and organisational success (Glebbeek & Bax, 2004; Kacmar, Andrews, Rooy, Steilberg & Cerrone, 2006; Shaw, Gupta & Delery, 2005).

There is also strong evidence to show that increased employee loyalty and retention has a positive impact on customer satisfaction and retention (Reichheld, 1996). Small improvements in the rate of employee retention, and in turn customer retention, lifts profitability. A firm's ability to retain its key employees is in turn a fundamental determinant of a number of important outcomes, according to Heskett, Jones, Loveman, Sasser and Schelesinger (1994), such as:

- Customer satisfaction
- Sales per employee
- Market capitalisation.

Companies that have formal employee retention plans in place have 2 year retention rates that are 17% better than at average companies, and turnover costs that are 31% lower (Hackett Best Practices Study, 2002).

The Turnover Cost Iceberg - Visible and Invisible Costs

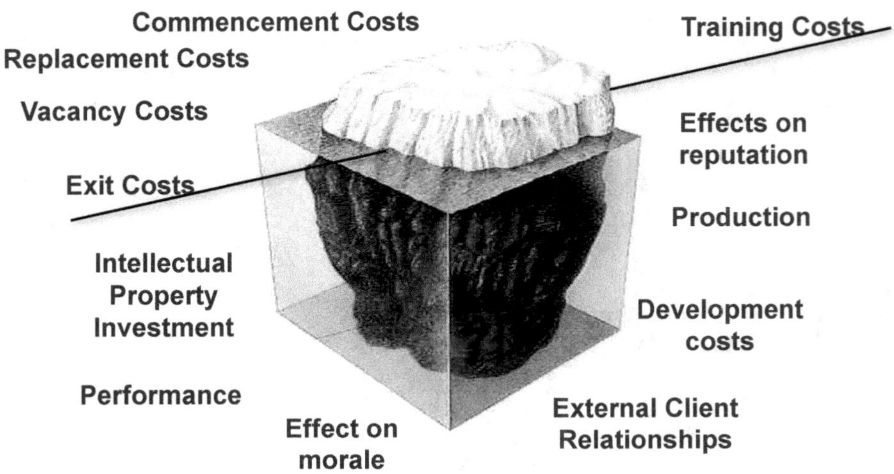

6.3 DIVORCE IS MORE EXPENSIVE THAN MARRIAGE: THE BUSINESS CASE FOR RETENTION OF TALENT

The business case for proactively addressing turnover

Consider the economic or business case for addressing retention proactively, based on the following scenario.

A turnover cost example for talent in an organisation

Assume the following about this organisation:

- A workforce of 1000 employees
- 5% are key talent (i.e., 50 people)
- Current talent turnover of 15% (i.e., 7.5 people leave annually)
- Average total salary package for key talent is 200k
- A multiple factor of 2.5 times the salary package.

> The total cost of talent turnover is approximately $3.75m per annum (i.e., 7.5 x 200 x 2.5).
>
> For one senior executive on a salary package of 200k per annum, assuming a turnover multiple of 2.5, this equates to a total cost of 500k if that individual leaves.
>
> Note: Even if a lesser turnover multiple is adopted (i.e., lower than 2.5 times the salary in question), the cost of turnover is nevertheless very significant.

Whatever the business scenario, this simple "back of the envelope" cost benefit analysis will convince most executives that efforts to improve retention can have significant payoffs. Divorce is more expensive then marriage! Proactively addressing retention and reducing turnover can deliver lasting bottom line benefits to an organisation.

6.4 THE UPSIDE OF TURNOVER

Notwithstanding the cost implications of turnover, some turnover in an organisation may be desirable, as it allows:

- The infusion of new ideas and perspectives from newcomers (i.e., refreshes the "gene pool")
- The creation of opportunities for advancement and promotion for existing staff
- Improved organisational effectiveness and morale through the departure of poor performers
- An opportunity to change the culture for the better.

Refer later in this chapter for further information on selective retention.

6.5 THE SIX KEY FACTORS ASSOCIATED WITH TURNOVER

Research findings have confirmed that the six most significant factors generally associated with higher voluntary turnover are:

- **Job satisfaction** - those with lower job satisfaction are more likely to leave (Irvine & Evans, 1995; Tett & Meyer, 1993; Griffeth, Hom & Gaertner, 2000)

- **Emotional attachment (affective commitment) or identification with the organisation** - those with lower affective commitment are more likely to leave (Tett & Meyer, 1993; Griffeth, Hom & Gaertner, 2000)
- **Tenure of workers with their employer** - those who have been with their employer a lesser time are more likely to leave
- **Job level** - those in lower knowledge or lower skill jobs or jobs with flatter career paths are more likely to leave
- **Employment opportunities** - where unemployment rates are low, turnover is higher (see next section)
- **Age** - younger workers are more likely to leave, being less concerned with stability, and still carving out a niche for themselves in the world (i.e., Generation Y).

Of the above factors, job satisfaction and affective commitment are more controllable by the organisation. The other factors are due to environmental and human issues which are mainly outside the direct control of the organisation. For example, in periods of low unemployment, turnover rises (see graph below) because people perceive that they have more choices and that there is less risk in changing jobs.

As unemployment rises, turnover falls

Turnover generally rises during economic expansions and falls during recession, in an inverse relationship to the unemployment rate.

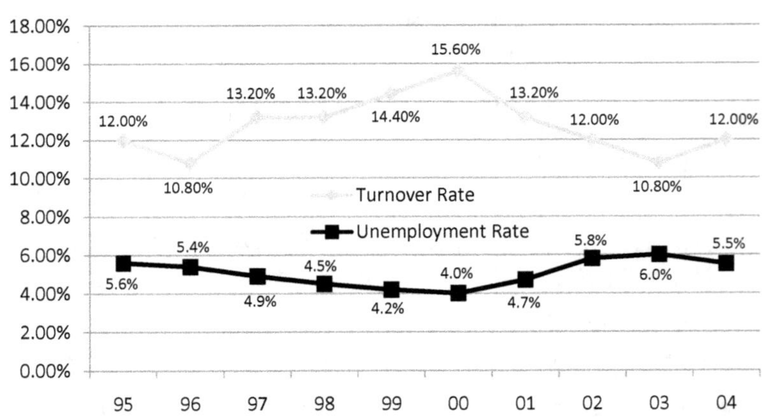

Source: Turnover rates from the Bureau of National Affairs Inc.; unemployment rates from the Bureau of Labor Statistics

People are most likely to divorce within the first few years of marriage. Similarly, in the case of organisations, new recruits (i.e., those with shortest tenure) are the highest "at risk" group in terms of turnover. In terms of age, it may be essential that the organisation employs younger people in lower level jobs (e.g., check out positions in supermarkets with lower salaries), as there may be no other realistic employee alternatives available at a comparable cost.

6.6 TWO KEY DRIVERS OF INTENTION TO STAY (AND HENCE RETENTION)

Affective Commitment and Job Satisfaction Drive Intention to Stay

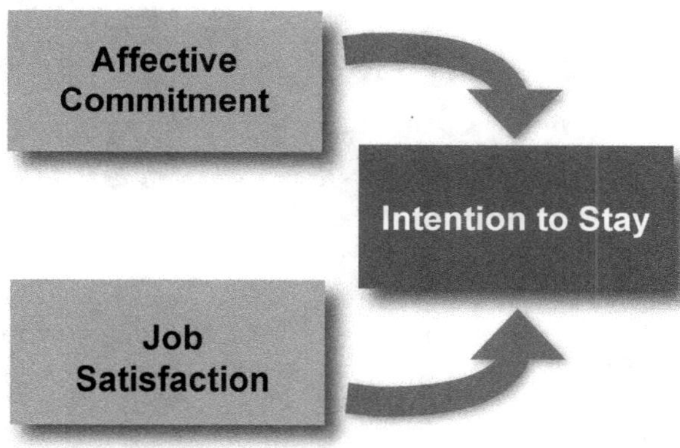

As referred to earlier, affective commitment and job satisfaction are the two key predictors of intention to stay, which is the main predictor of retention or turnover. In simple terms, if a person:

- Identifies more emotionally with an organisation (i.e., indicates higher levels of affective commitment)
- Is more satisfied in their job
- Their intention to stay with the organisation is likely to be strengthened
- Turnover is likely to be lower (i.e., they are less likely to leave).

Our findings concerning the relationship between these three variables are provided below.

Correlations: Affective Commitment and Job Satisfaction Predicting Intention to Stay (and Retention)

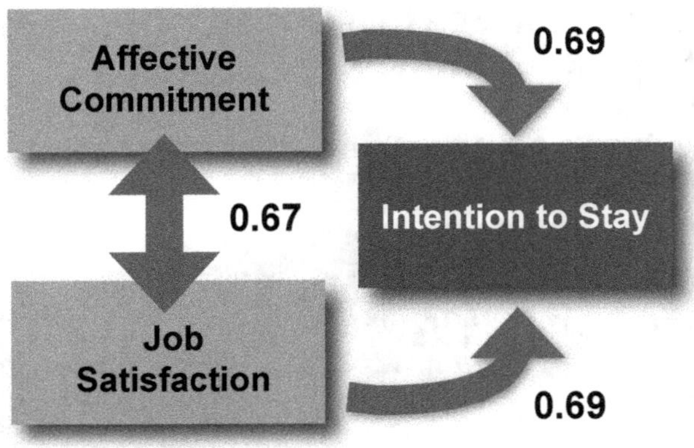

Note: A correlation or r of < 0.4 is considered to be low, an r > 0.4 to < 0.5 is considered to be medium, and an r > 0.5 is considered to be high.

6.7 PERSON – ORGANISATIONAL FIT (AFFECTIVE COMMITMENT) AND PERSON – JOB FIT (JOB SATISFACTION)

Affective commitment is a *de facto* measure of person – organisational fit and likewise job satisfaction is a *de facto* measure of person – job fit. It is possible for a person to have a good fit to an organisation, and poor fit to the job, or vice versa. However the correlation between affective commitment and job satisfaction is also high (r = 0.67), which means that on average those who have a higher level of emotional attachment or commitment (or fit) to an organisation, are more likely to be satisfied with (or have a better fit to) their job.

> Note: Fit to the organisation (i.e., affective commitment) may be more important than fit to the job (i.e., job satisfaction), from both the employer's and employee's perspective. There may be redeployment opportunities within the organisation to achieve a better person job fit if this is lacking, providing the employee is a reasonable performer. Also higher levels of affective commitment provide increased employee resilience to future job changes caused by organisational restructuring, including downsizing.

Understanding the determinants of job satisfaction and affective commitment within an organisation is therefore critical to reducing the high cost of turnover in the workforce, and just as importantly, to managing a psychologically healthy workforce. Antecedents of affective commitment and job satisfaction (and hence intention to stay and then retention) are nested into:

- Corporate wide influences
- Local or workplace influences
- Individual issues.

It is here that the concept of the psychological contract is so useful. It provides an approach to optimizing affective commitment and job satisfaction, and therefore intention to stay, which in turn enhances retention. The psychological contract is elaborated upon in Chapters 7 and 8.

6.8 SUMMARY OF KEY RESEARCH: AFFECTIVE COMITMENT, JOB SATISFACTION AND PERFORMANCE

The relationship between job satisfaction and performance is a controversial one. The old notion that satisfaction and performance are unrelated has now been replaced with the new finding that the true mean correlation between satisfaction and performance is 0.3 (Judge, Thoresen, Bono, & Patton, 2001). Furthermore the link between good people management practices and the bottom line is demonstrated in a landmark U.K. study of 67 firms ranging from 60-1000 employees by Patterson, West, Lawthom, and Nickell (1997), which found that (see diagram below):

- The management of people had a greater effect on a business's performance than competitive strategy, quality focus, manufacturing technology and investment in R & D put together
- Job satisfaction and organisational commitment accounted for a 10% profitability and 23% productivity difference between companies.

Job Satisfaction, Organisational (Affective) Commitment and the "Bottom Line"

Findings from a recent UK study involving 67 organisations:

"Job satisfaction and organisational commitment accounted for a 10% profitability and 23% productivity difference between companies"

(Patterson, West, Lawthom & Nickell, 1997)

> Note: The term organisational commitment used in this study equates closely to affective commitment.

The above findings are also consistent with those of other researchers. Meyer, Paunonen, Gellatly, Goffin and Jackson (1989) found that higher levels of affective commitment were linked to enhanced employee performance. Our own findings have confirmed that those who are aligned (i.e., those who are more satisfied in the job and indicating higher levels of affective commitment), have an overall performance rating of approximately 20% more compared to those who are misaligned.

> Note: These performance rating findings have been established by "back end" coding WRDI® survey participants' performance ratings after they have completed the survey.

Apart from providing some buffer against the need for recruiting replacement or additional labour, addressing retention pro-actively will most likely simultaneously enhance productivity and otherwise return lasting organisational benefits (i.e., by doing more with less).

6.9 WHY SELECTIVE RETENTION IS IMPORTANT: CATEGORISING "STAYERS" AND "LEAVERS"

> The organisations that will thrive in the new reality are those with employees who have the option to leave but choose to stay. Those that fail will be populated by employees who are there only because they are afraid to go elsewhere. (Noer, 1997)

Notwithstanding the cost of turnover, what is also important is retaining and engaging the "right" people. Retention doesn't automatically deliver stellar performance or discretionary effort towards business critical goals. Who stays is just as important as who goes! Sticking around might mean stuck in the mud! Two critical questions arise:

- *Does a desire to stay with an employer signal engagement with the organisation?*
- *Are employees, who do not wish to leave, motivated to perform, or are they purely motivated to attend?*

Commitment is not only about staying but it is also about buying into the vision of the company. In fact what employees do while they are with organisations is just as important, if not more important, than how long they stay. It may be the case that an organisation is retaining a workforce which is disengaged and dissatisfied (i.e., the "walking wounded"), which is hardly a basis to move forward in meeting the challenges of the contemporary dynamic business environment.

Types of "Stayers" and "Leavers": Various patterns of Affective Commitment, Job Satisfaction and Intention to Stay

The diagram below contrasts two types of "Stayers" (i.e., those employees who indicate a high Intention to Stay with the organisation). The "In Love and Satisfied" employee on the left indicates high levels of affective commitment and job satisfaction, whereas the employee on the right ("Locked In") indicates the opposite. There are significant implications for both the individual and the organisation with these contrasting profiles. The Stayer on the left is more likely to perform better on average than the one on the right.

STAYERS

"In Love & Satisfied" **"Locked In"**

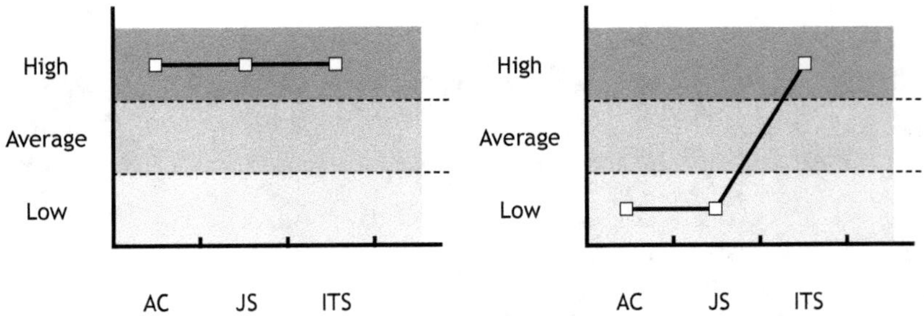

AC: Affective Commitment JS: Job Satisfaction ITS: Intention to Stay

More specifically, for the two Stayers in the above examples, the:

- "In love and satisfied" (high job satisfaction and affective commitment), is unlikely to leave the organisation, at least in the medium term
- "Locked in" (low job satisfaction and affective commitment) is also unlikely to leave, possibly:
  - seeing too few opportunities outside the organisation
  - feeling that they have too much to lose by leaving
  - being unprepared to take risks with their job or career
  - otherwise feeling that work is not such an important part of their life.

A "locked in" employee should consider seeking career counselling and advice, as it is likely that the quality of their work life and enjoyment of life in general, is being adversely affected. Most likely they need to either:

- Re-invent themselves
- Change their job, career or employer.

What is important in the case of the "locked in" employee on the right is being able to diagnose whether their profile is due to:

1. Dysfunctional factors concerning the organisation, workplace or job (e.g., either unmet expectations, low trust, or injustice), which are dampening their levels of affective commitment and/or job satisfaction
2. Poor person "fit" to both the job (job satisfaction), and the organisation (affective commitment), which is due to poor selection and recruitment practices
3. Individual characteristics.

Similarly, considering the two Leavers in the diagram below, it is possible to have contrasting profiles.

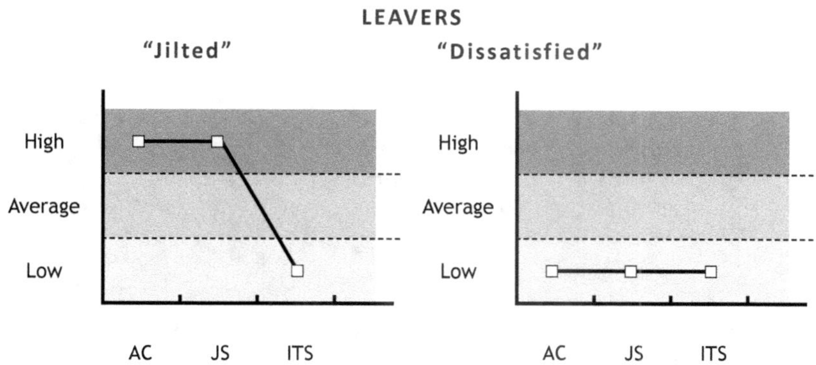

AC: Affective Commitment JS: Job Satisfaction ITS: Intention to Stay

For these two Leavers, the:

- "Jilted" (high to moderate levels of job satisfaction and affective commitment) is possibly:
  - seeing insufficient career opportunities compared with those outside
  - may be leaving for personal reasons unrelated to the organisation
- "Dissatisfied and uncommitted" (low to moderate levels of job satisfaction and affective commitment), is likely to be disenchanted with work life in general, possibly:
  - seeking a career change
  - seeking employment opportunities with another organisation in a different job.

The high performing "Jilted" employee may be open to offers concerning their career development within the organisation, rather than going elsewhere. However a "Dissatisfied and Uncommitted" employee is unlikely to reconsider their intention to leave, nor would it probably be in the best interests of either party for them to stay (i.e., a lost cause for both parties).

Evidence why Engagement Indices are flawed!

It is worth noting that the various profiles above provide further evidence (see later in this chapter) of why Engagement Indices are flawed, and the need to unpack engagement (whatever definition is adopted), and retention risk. For example, if one collapses scores on affective commitment, job satisfaction and intention to stay into a single index, the interpretation of this score becomes problematic. As witnessed in the above examples, it is possible to end up with various combinations of these three scale scores which have the same collapsed score but which have vastly different interpretations. This issue is further discussed later on in this chapter.

> Note: In instances where there is low affective commitment, this may be due to a poor selection and recruitment decision (i.e., lack or person – organisational fit), rather than any other dysfunctional organisational factors. However this lack of fit should not be viewed as a criticism of either party. Organisations have particular characteristics and values in the sense that people have personalities, and as in the case of relationships between people, not everyone is suited to co-existing.

6.10 THE THREE P'S - WHY PEOPLE LEAVE ORGANISATIONS

Whilst there are six key factors which predict those who are more likely to leave an organisation, these factors don't explain the reasons why people do indeed leave. These reasons (i.e., for leaving) may be classified according to one or more of the three P's, viz:

- "Push" effect
- "Pull" effect
- "Personal" reasons.

The "Push" effect

The "Push" effect – unfavourable circumstances which result in the employee seeking alternative employment opportunities – may be due to:

- Dysfunctional organisational, local workplace and/or job factors
- Organisational limitations (e.g., lack of career development opportunities)
- Poor recruitment and selection resulting in a lack of "fit" between the employee and the job and/or the organisation.

Dysfunctional organisational, local workplace and/or job factors may include:

- The employee's expectations not being met (e.g., career development, supportive management, resources, etc.)
- Perceptions of unfair treatment (e.g., inequity)

- A lack of trust between management and the employee, which may be due to poor leadership.

According to Branham (2005), employees' expectations may have been unrealistic, and may well be the number one reason why most employees leave. It is:

- The reason why 4% of employees walk off the job in the first day
- Most certainly the main reason why more than 50% of American workers quit in the first six months
- Probably a key factor in the failure of 40% of new executives to last more than 18 months in their new positions.

Presumably then it makes sense to measure these expectations - both the extent and strength of these expectations and their delivery (refer to Chapter 7 concerning the profiling and measurement of these expectations and their delivery from the employee's perspective).

The "Pull" effect

The "Pull" effect – the attraction of superior external employment opportunities - where employees are seduced away from their existing organisation, may be precipitated by:

- Better terms and conditions of employment (e.g., compensation or rewards, flexible work practices, etc.)
- A better job (e.g., more responsibility and challenge, more favourable career prospects including training and development, more support, etc.)
- A better organisation to join (e.g., more successful, stronger leadership, better person - cultural "fit", etc.).

"Personal" reasons

Personal reasons for leaving may include a desire to change career, wanting to spend time doing other activities, family reasons, health, location and travel difficulties, etc.

> Note: It is possible to quantify numbers of imminent leavers and also to classify their reasons for leaving according to the 3 Ps based on the WRDI® diagnostic tool. Refer to Chapters 7 and 9 for a sample reporting output.

6.11 LEAVING IS A DYNAMIC PROCESS

The leaving decision is complex

Turnover research has demonstrated that an individual's decision to leave is typically not a single, simple stay or go determination. Whilst the decision to stay or go is ultimately a yes and no event, personal reasons aside, that event is the culmination of a series of experiences that attach to, or disengage people from, organisations. This decision involves a series of related cognitive and behavioural considerations before the person actually terminates. It is a complex decision with a variety of factors coming into play.

There may or may not be a discrete causal or trigger event. Such a trigger event or shock is likely to be present in approximately 60% of cases (Lee & Mitchell, 1994) and;

- Could be caused by some dissatisfaction with a work related issue (e.g., downsizing or restructuring)
- May be unrelated to the organisation (e.g., a personal issue such as health or family concern).

The dissolution of a relationship can often correspond to external events (e.g., after holidays, after a move, new baby, etc.).

In the workplace, typically employees engage in a fairly standard cognitive process before deciding to leave one job for another. This dynamic process occurs over time (could be 3 to 6 months or even longer), and unfolds as follows:

- Firstly, the individual begins by having thoughts (i.e., withdrawal cognitions) about leaving the current job and thoughts about searching for a new job
- In turn, these withdrawal thoughts activate other thoughts dealing with career mobility (e.g., likelihood of finding suitable available alternatives)
- If the individual determines that the likelihood is high, thoughts become actions and withdrawal behaviors occur, with the individual beginning an active search, with the intention to quit if he/she finds an appropriate alternative; and
- The final step in this process is leaving the current job.

The decision to leave is therefore not simply a case of an individual waking up one morning, having a sudden rush of blood to the head, and then deciding to immediately resign.

The initial stage is crucial

The pace and focus of leaving differs amongst employees. Some people make quick judgments whilst others take longer to think about it. Many have jobs to go to (approximately 80% of people who resign from their current role have already accepted a new position), while others do not. Nevertheless, the initial stage seems especially crucial in this process and managers need to have an understanding of potential triggers. The deeper the individual is into this (leaving) process, the more chance that they will leave. Notwithstanding, the good news about this dynamic process is that it can be interrupted and turned around.

Whilst intention to stay is the strongest indicator of retention risk (i.e., whether an individual is likely to leave), intentions don't always translate into actions. It's a little like joining a gym or going on a diet – not everyone who indicates such intentions ultimately acts on them. Furthermore it may be the case that the prospective job that the individual had in mind doesn't eventuate, or there could be a change in organisational or personal circumstances that causes them to change their mind. However we do know the relationship between those who say they are going to leave, and those who actually do leave over the ensuing six to twelve months (i.e., the correlation between those who say they are going to leave and those who actually leave is approximately 0.65 - refer to Chapter 7).

6.12 KEY RESEARCH FINDINGS ABOUT REASONS FOR LEAVING

Changing jobs can be disruptive and stressful: most people prefer to stay where they are. Employees are significantly more likely to consider quitting because of shortcomings and obstacles in the current organisation (i.e., "Push" factors), rather than for the presumed attractions of an alternative opportunity (i.e., "Pull" factors). These internal "Push" factors are under the control of the organisation. More often it is a combination of "Push", "Pull" and "Personal" reasons, with "Push" factors acting as the catalyst for people to start seeking other opportunities. It is simplistic and superficial to accept "Pull" factors as the root cause of turnover.

A recent study on reasons for leaving conducted by the CIPD (Recruitment, Retention and Turnover - Annual Survey Report, 2005) - captured 715 responses from UK based organisations across a variety of industries with 40% employing less than 250 workers. The most commonly reported key reason for employee turnover was:

- Promotion outside the organisation (53%)
- Followed by lack of career and development opportunities (42%).

The former reason tends to camouflage the "Push" factors that might otherwise be contributing to the decision to leave. In this study, pay seemed relatively unimportant, and lack of support from line managers came way down the list of factors identified by employers as causing staff to quit.

Simply relying on salary increases and bonuses to prevent turnover will most likely cause organisations to struggle in arresting turnover, although it may be the case that the prevalence of this reason for leaving is underestimated (Rynes, Gerhart & Parks, 2005).

However the data relating to reasons for employees leaving organisations is notoriously difficult to validate because:

- The reasons that people give for leaving are not always reflective of the underlying causes
- People may not necessarily be honest because of issues surrounding confidentiality and them not wanting to "burn their bridges"
- There is no consistent taxonomy for categorising leavers and their reasons for leaving (i.e., the 3 Ps), which renders comparisons between various studies difficult
- Many studies fail to ask the right questions, due in part to a lack of understanding of turnover and no underlying model upon which the questions have been framed.

Notwithstanding, these findings dispel the myth that the main cause of turnover is the relationship between the departing employee and their manager. Our own best estimate of the percentage breakdown of leavers according to the 3 Ps derived from a variety of sources, including our own anecdotal observations, is as follows:

- Approximately 60% due to "Push" factors
- Approximately 20% due to "Pull" factors
- Approximately 20% due to "Personal" reasons.

> Note: These anecdotal observations are based on our survey work and other feedback (i.e., show of hands), from groups at various workshops and speaking engagements which I have conducted.

This estimate indicates that approximately 60% of turnover is under the direct control of organisations, with part of the remaining 40% also able to be influenced by the organisation. For example, if an individual is leaving because of Personal reasons (e.g., family member experiencing an illness), it may be the case that the individual is prepared and willing to stay on, but on the basis of reduced work hours for an interim period. Alternatively if an individual is seeking to change jobs because of "Pull" reasons (e.g., a better job), it may be the case that there are other opportunities within the organisation which that individual can be redeployed to.

6.13 KEY RESEARCH FINDINGS ABOUT TURNOVER

Research by Griffeth, Hom and Gaertner (2000) and others has drawn the following conclusions concerning turnover:

- There is no correlation between cognitive ability and turnover (i.e., more intelligent employees are no more prone to quit than less intelligent employees)
- Women's quit rate is similar to that of men's, with educated women resembling men in turnover rate and pattern (i.e., leave to assume another job rather than abandon the labour force which is a route generally taken by less well educated female leavers)
- High performers are less likely to quit than low performers, but when high performers are not sufficiently rewarded, they leave
- Those who are more conscientious and emotionally stable are less likely to quit
- Structured interviews conducted at the recruitment stage only modestly predict turnover.

Measures that can be adopted to reduce turnover

Some implications of these findings include the following:

- Where collective reward programs replace individual based incentives, their introduction may stimulate greater exits among high performers
- Those individuals with high turnover propensity (i.e., less conscientious and less emotionally stable), can be screened out prior to organisational entry through psychological assessment
- By targeting turnover resistant competencies in the recruitment stage, such as perseverance and resilience, organisations can subsequently reduce the risk of turnover.

6.14 RE-RECRUITING YOUR EXISTING WORKFORCE: FINDING OUT WHY PEOPLE STAY

A defensive strategy

Relationships need to be refreshed, otherwise there is a tendency for them to become stale and disconnected. Like any asset, they need preventative maintenance. In re-recruiting the existing workforce – which constitutes a defensive strategy - there is a need to constantly revisit the question as to: *What motivates employees to stay?* Good communication and feedback systems are integral to effective retention strategies.

Re-recruitment strategies include:

- Surveying the workforce concerning their intentions (i.e., to stay or go)
- Validating what the organisation is doing well in terms of people management policies and practices
- Identifying organisational "hot spots", issues of discontent, etc., and then applying targeted interventions to address perceived deficits
- Facilitating structured and healthy job and career dialogue between employees and their respective managers, that is divorced from performance reviews where other issues may be at stake (e.g., salary negotiations, which might otherwise cloud such discussions).

The regular surveying of employees and associated feedback can provide management with vital:

- Objective
- Quantitative
- Diagnostic information by workforce segment, business unit or demographic group, concerning retention risk and alignment issues.

Often senior managers are isolated from the "coal face". Survey findings provide a reality check with "real time" feedback. Organisations without a re-recruitment strategy are in danger of experiencing a fundamental disconnect with their workforce. Refer to Chapters 7, 8 and 9 for further information on engagement and retention surveys.

Addressing turnover proactively: Prioritising the approach

In addressing turnover proactively:

- Firstly, the focus should be on measures aimed at alleviating "Push" factors – those factors that erode employees' commitment and job satisfaction, and which make them actively consider a move
- Then secondly, combat "Pull" factors (e.g., improving pay and benefits, career development), to diminish the allure of preying competitors
- Minimise "Personal" factors (e.g., provide flexible work practices, flexible career paths – horizontal and vertical).

Above all, there is a need to maintain ongoing dialogue with employees in the dynamic and rapidly changing workplace, to try and meet the continually changing needs of both parties. Such dialogue helps to ensure that all options are explored between the parties prior to a resignation. Retention efforts should include the development of retention competences in leaders and local managers (i.e., building relationship and trust with employees). To that end, the WRDI Institute has developed a guide for managers on how to have constructive career conversations. Refer to the WRDI Institute web site for further details.

> Note: With divorce rates skyrocketing in personal relationships, people often find it easier to walk away from a relationship. As indicated earlier, there are significant costs incurred relating to turnover, both direct and indirect, not to mention the emotional fall-out for all concerned. Often people take for granted what they have until it's too late, and in retrospect, realize that the relationship could have been salvaged.

Other defensive retention strategies

Other defensive retention strategies designed to minimise the impact of turnover include:

- Reducing reliance on specific skills (e.g., purchasing off-the-shelf software – refer to Chapter 3 on unique skills)
- Redesigning jobs
- Multi-skilling to enhance workforce flexibility
- Outsourcing, or contracting out some activities
- Enhancing talent pipelines
- Maximising attraction.

6.15 KEY TALENT RETENTION: DRILLING DOWN TO INDIVIDUALS

We have previously referred to the importance of retaining key talent and those in critical roles, given their impact on business success. For key talent, retention efforts should drill down to an individual level with the aim of minimising involuntary quitting by taking control of, or influencing/interrupting the dynamic leaving process (the earlier the better). As a prevention or risk mitigation strategy, an early warning system is therefore essential to detect "Push", "Pull" and "Personal" factors on the turnover intentions of talent. Then what should follow is a deliberately, highly targeted action.

> Note: The WRDI Institute has developed an early warning system – a methodology to quantify retention risk which can extend down to an individual level. This methodology also extends to reporting on the reasons for leaving. Refer to Chapters 7 and 9 for examples of this reporting output.

Apart from any possible organisational dysfunctional issues (e.g., issues relating to delivery of the "deal", trust and fairness), it may be the case that an individual is looking for a change. Under such circumstances, options at an individual level to address talent retention risk include:

- Redeployment (either in part or in full) to special projects
- Job redesign or change in responsibilities (e.g., reduced work load with greater flexitime)
- Golden handcuffs (stock options, retention bonuses), although over reliance on this mechanism is not recommended for the reasons elaborated upon in Chapter 7
- Career counselling, fresh training and development
- Mentoring
- Career change/redeployment
- Sabbaticals, personal growth leave.

6.16 A DIAGNOSTIC SURVEY APPROACH TO ASSESSING AND ADDRESSING TURNOVER RISK

Past approaches to addressing turnover problematic

As referred to earlier, past approaches to addressing turnover have included exit interviews and focus groups. Exit interviews are analogous to "shutting the stable door after the horse has bolted" (refer to Chapter 8 for further information about exit interviews). Focus groups, whilst useful for collecting anecdotal and qualitative information, lack scientific rigour. Typically there is no underlying model that serves as a basis for understanding how the answers to various questions can best be categorised. Often the right questions aren't even asked, and notwithstanding, uncertainty exists as to whether the questions (and associated answers) relate to causes or effects. In the absence of a model and quantitative data, such answers require a value judgement concerning their importance or relevance. The effectiveness of any subsequent interventions may therefore be problematic.

A pre-emptive approach preferable

From a practical and pre-emptive perspective, it makes sense to deal with the turnover intentions of present employees, rather than deal with turnover on a *post hoc* basis with former employees, by relying on exit interviews. These intentions are best measured by an employee survey, but not any survey! Recent innovations in survey design now provide a scientific approach to proactively address retention risk. These survey tools include specific information on the key drivers of retention, including a measurement and diagnosis of antecedents of these key drivers. Refer to Chapters 7, 8 and 9 for further details.

Such valid and reliable survey findings provide management with vital objective, quantitative and diagnostic information by workforce segment, concerning retention risk issues. These metrics have lifted away the veil of mystique enabling causes of disengagement/misalignment and retention risk to be isolated, e.g.:

- Failure to deliver on the "deal" (either tangibles or intangibles where the promise isn't matched by the reality of the job/organisation)
- Deficits in management trust/leadership
- Perceived injustice or lack of fairness
- Poor employee "fit" (either to the job or the organisation), due to poor recruitment, selection and induction methodologies.

6.17 "ENGAGEMENT": A MUCH CONFUSED TERM!

We shall now turn our attention to a related concept – employee engagement - which is the HR metric of the moment. This popular term "engagement" is a diffuse and controversial concept. It is variously defined, and is not necessarily recognised as an academic construct. Empirical research concerning it is minimal compared to the related areas of commitment, job satisfaction and turnover. Furthermore this fashionable term means completely different things to different survey providers, all of whom are trying to claim the same ground! It is currently a subject of intense debate amongst the Industrial/Organisational psychology profession.

Some survey providers equate engagement with job satisfaction, whilst others equate engagement with emotional (i.e., affective) commitment to their organisation. One well known international survey provider has a model of engagement based on local people management practices, which are reported to predict job satisfaction, without actually measuring the same, whereas another popular international provider completely ignores job satisfaction in their engagement model.

Some providers also include discretionary effort or job commitment in their survey models. Others define engagement as a combination of effort, commitment to the organisation and intention to stay. However the problem with this definition is that it is not a uni-dimensional concept, but rather an amalgamation of constructs and associated measures which are not necessarily all that closely related. There is tremendous variation in the scope and content of this engagement construct.

In short, there are a bewildering variety of definitions and approaches to raising engagement levels. Without a clear definition of what engagement means, and a deeper understanding of what inspires employees to engage, it is difficult for companies to set priorities for engagement initiatives or to bring about substantial and lasting improvements in engagement. We shall address this issue more specifically in Chapter 7.

> Note: I would prefer to dispense with this term "engagement" and focus on performance and retention because, after all, these are two of the key concerns of management. For those interested in more recent empirical literature reviews concerning the term engagement, there is a suite of papers available for download from the following link: http://www3.interscience.wiley.com/journal/120186299/issue

6.18 ENGAGEMENT INDICES A "BLUNT MEASURE": INTUITIVELY APPEALING BUT PSYCHOMETRICALLY FLAWED!

Why Engagement Indices are flawed: More evidence

Many engagement survey providers report an "Engagement Index". Whilst this concept is intuitively appealing for the unsophisticated (i.e., reduces engagement/retention to a single number and purports to provide a basis for making comparisons between and within organisations), an Engagement Index represents a "blunt measure" and constitutes a psychometrically flawed approach. The index is typically compiled from scales, each comprising a number of items*, the result of which is an overall index which is not uni-¬dimensional (i.e., is a composite of measures that are not necessarily closely related).

> Note: *Generally accepted best practice is a minimum of four items per scale.

Predictors of performance and retention should be separated for the following reason. How hard a person works (i.e., their discretionary effort), is only weakly related to their intention to stay (r = .23). This means that on average, a person who is thinking of leaving an organisation is unlikely to "slacken off" to any great extent. If these two measures are added into a composite index, the interpretation of what that index means becomes somewhat problematic. Hence there is a need to "unpack" predictors of performance from predictors of retention and not combine them. This unpacking provides for a more "fine grained" understanding of both performance and retention risk.

> **A Fruit Index analogy: Why Engagement Indices are psychometrically flawed!**
>
> To illustrate the above point, it's like comparing two people, each of whom has say 10 pieces of fruit (i.e., a Fruit Index of 10). One person has 6 bananas, 2 apples and 2 oranges, whilst the other person has 3 bananas, 6 apples and 1 orange. The comparison and interpretation of what 10 pieces of fruit means is unclear. The interpretation of an Engagement Index (which typically includes some key predictors of performance and retention), and associated comparisons, cannot be simply reduced down to and understood in terms of a single number!

6.19 THE FOUR "HOLY GRAIL" WORKFORCE MEASURES

Most engagement survey providers have models which include some, but not necessarily all of the following four (key workforce measures:

- Job satisfaction
- Affective Commitment
- Job Commitment/Discretionary Effort
- Intention to Stay.

These are the four "holy grail" workforce measures. They incorporate an emphasis on alignment or fit (both to the organisation and the job), effort and retention.

The Four "Holy Grail" Workforce Measures

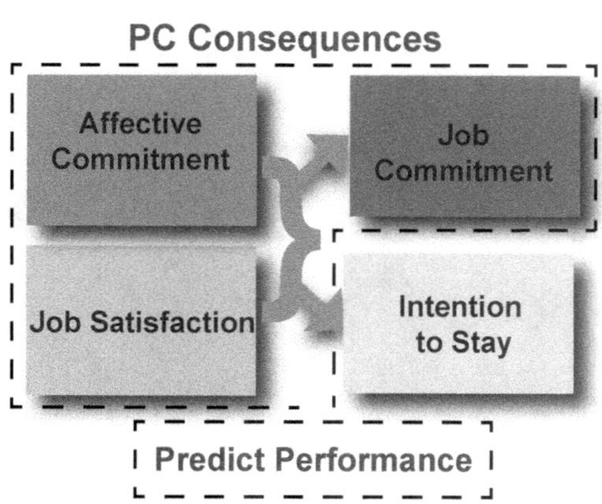

> Note: Performance is also determined by other factors such as an individual's skill, experience, intellect as well as technology and systems.

Correlations: Affective Commitment and Job Satisfaction Predicting Job Commitment/Discretionary Effort

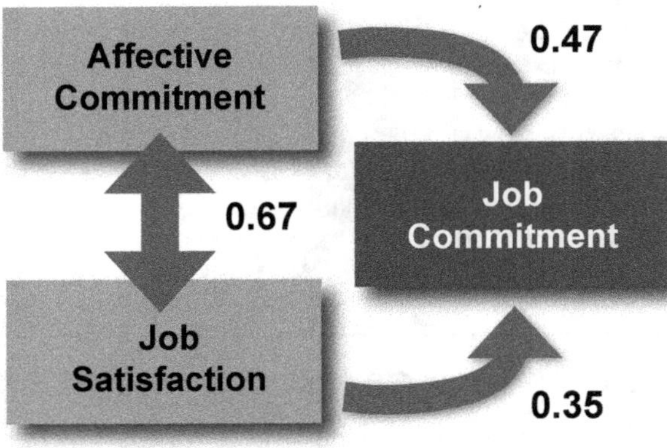

We have seen that affective commitment and job satisfaction are two key predictors of performance along with discretionary effort (i.e., willingness to go beyond the minimum requirements of the job). It seems that more positive emotions at work (i.e., higher levels of affective commitment and job satisfaction), or higher levels of fit, are related to higher performance and also predict higher effort. Higher effort is also determined by other factors such as individual characteristics or personality traits (e.g., conscientiousness), level of interest in the job, demands of the job, etc.

Chapter 7 of this book will explain how to impact positively on these four "holy grail" workforce measures.

Chapter 7

About the Psychological Contract

KEY POINTS

Key questions and issues that we will address in this chapter:

- *What is the psychological contract?*
- *Why is the psychological contract important?*
- *How does the psychological contract link to the business strategy?*
- *What are the various types of psychological contracts and how do these types integrate with the skills' based workforce segmentation model?*
- *What are the elements or items that comprise the content of the psychological contract?*
- *What is the relationship between the content of the psychological contract and the Employment Value Proposition (EVP) or the "deal"?*
- *How does the psychological contract link to employee engagement/ performance and retention?*
- *What research sits behind the psychological contract?*
- *How can the psychological contract be measured?*
- *How can the WRDI® diagnostic tool provide deeper workforce insights?*

What are the consequences of failing to adequately address these questions/issues or ending up with the wrong answers?

- *As in personal life, a failure to appreciate the importance of relationships and attend to them in a systematic way, may result in relationship degradation or disintegration*
- *More specifically, a lack of appreciation of the importance and understanding of the employer/employee relationship (or psychological contract), may well lead to deficiencies in people strategies, confusion, and ad hoc and poor people decisions*
- *Recognising only some of the key drivers of engagement/ performance and retention risk, means that there will be some "black holes" in the measurement and reporting of human capital data*
- *You may not be matching the rhetoric with the promise concerning the delivery of the EVP or the "deal", and damaging your brand as a consequence.*

7. ABOUT THE PSYCHOLOGICAL CONTRACT

7.1 WHAT IS THE PSYCHOLOGICAL CONTRACT?

Every relationship has a psychological contract

Every relationship has a psychological contract, be it in the personal domain or business. Think of a marriage between two people. Notwithstanding the vows which both parties make at the marriage ceremony, as time goes by, both parties develop a mutual understanding and set of expectations concerning their respective obligations, responsibilities, behaviours, etc. Some of these expectations are discussed, whilst others just unfold (e.g., who purchases the food, who does the cooking, who looks after the finances, who does the washing, etc.). The workplace or employer/employee relationship is no different.

The psychological contract in the workplace

In the context of the workplace, the psychological contract can be defined as: **the set of expectations (from the perspective of employees), based on stated or implied promises and understandings, operating between employees and their employer.**

> Note: This definition has been crafted based on the work of various academics and scholars. It has more of an orientation towards Guest's (1998) concept of the psychological contract rather than Rousseau's (1995), for reasons that will be explained later in this chapter.

The psychological contract is not a legal or a written document as such, but it is nevertheless "real" in the minds of employers and employees/workers (like the marriage example above). These employee expectations are formed from a variety of sources, based on what has been:

- Written (e.g., job advertisement, job description, the employment contract, various HR policies, company brochures, etc.)
- Said or unsaid by various parties (e.g., recruiters, HR, managers, work colleagues, etc.)
- Implied
- Observed.

What is implied and observed is often more powerful in influencing employees compared to the written or the stated word. The written employment contract forms a part of the psychological contract, but the latter is a broader concept. For example, some promises or understandings may never be documented (e.g., the promise of future advancement or promotion in the organisation within a specific time frame subject to acceptable performance).

The psychological contract is based on an individual's perception of various promises or understandings, and is to some extent informal, implicit, perceptual and hence somewhat subjective. As indicated above, some elements of it may have been stated or written, and past behaviours and customs and practices in the organisation may have served as a basis for the development of these expectations. Some expectations may be more conscious or prominent than others, with the more unconscious expectations (e.g., long term promotional prospects), only being revealed indirectly over time.

> Note: One might argue that the word "contract" is inappropriate when used in this context, given that it does not satisfy the basic requirements of a contract. Such contract requirements include an explicit and written agreement which both parties have signed. The psychological contract is a more dynamic concept in that it is a more open ended agreement which either party may change arbitrarily and without knowledge or consultation with the other. Refer to the discussion in Chapter 2 concerning this issue.

The "essence" of the employment relationship

The psychological contract defines the "essence" of the employment relationship. It serves to bind individuals and organisations together and regulate their behaviour, making possible the achievement of organisational goals (Robinson, Kraatz & Rousseau, 1994). It is a powerful determinant of the behaviour and attitudes of employees, although it is rarely discussed (Anderson & Schalk, 1998; Schein, 1978).

The content of the psychological contract

The content or elements of the psychological contract include both:

- Tangibles (e.g., monetary rewards, resources)
- Intangibles (e.g., career development, flexible work practices, support).

As referred to in Chapter 5, the content of the psychological contract represents the EVP or the "deal" in terms of this mix of tangibles and intangibles, but more of this later.

7.2 THE PSYCHOLOGICAL CONTRACT: A WAY FORWARD?

Why the psychological contract is important

As indicated in the Introduction Chapter, one of the key assumptions underpinning this book is that relationships are fundamentally important. In the contemporary workplace, where continuous change (e.g., downsizing, restructuring, implementation of new programs or initiatives, etc.) is the norm rather than the exception, the success or acceptance of such change initiatives, and the consequent survival of some organisations, will depend on the quality of their employer/employee relationships.

Employees are much more willing to accept change if their relationship with their employer is healthy (i.e., their employer has largely delivered on the "deal", reasonable levels of trust exist between employees and local as well as top management, and employees perceive that they have been treated fairly). Furthermore the quality of these employer/employee relationships, as we shall see, significantly impacts on both performance and retention.

In summary, it is contended that organisations seeking to maximise the flexibility and commitment of their workforce, and to develop and retain relevant skills, need to structure and manage productive employer/employee relationships with various workforce segments, consistent with their business strategy. Furthermore it is contended that this people management challenge can best be addressed through focusing on the psychological contract.

What leading scholars/researchers/academics say about the importance of the psychological contract

A number of leading scholars, researchers and academics say this about the psychological contract:

> The ability to compete effectively may depend on creating psychological contracts consistent with the expectations of customers, and the flexibility demanded by both technological changes and the marketplace (Rousseau, 1995).
>
> Measurement of the changing psychological contract (although there is no universal agreement on how this should be achieved), may provide a diagnosis of the state of affairs, and be a starting point for interventions in organisations (Anderson & Thomas, 1996; Freeze & Schalk, 1997).
>
> The psychological contract provides a potentially fruitful construct with which to make sense of, and explore, the new employment relationship (Guest, 1998).

> The psychological contract appears to offer a way forward in addressing difficulties in the employment relationship being experienced by many organisations (Herriot & Pemberton, 1995).
> We need a theory to not only describe, but to evaluate, the state of the psychological contract (Guest, 1998).
> There is a need for further development in the measurement of the psychological contract (Anderson & Schalk, 1998).

Murphy (2005) in his keynote address to the Industrial/Organisational (IO) Psychology Conference on the topic of IO Psychology's Greatest Hits and Misses, labels the psychological contract as a "hit" (i.e., topic, area, approach that has been shown particularly strong evidence of progress).

Why the psychological contract is now developing currency

however the significance of the psychological contract in the workplace has not necessarily been appreciated, given that up until recent times, it was relatively stable. Prior to the past 20 years or so, most people were employed in long-term arrangements under the "old deal" of a "job for life". Furthermore employment relationships are rarely assessed or discussed, except perhaps at times of critical incidents (e.g., downsizing, restructuring). However as indicated earlier, since the 1990s, the combination of globalisation and technological change has created a much more turbulent workplace. It is in this context that the psychological contract has come into vogue, becoming highly relevant and acquiring a more prominent status.

As discussed in Chapter 3, getting the composition of their workforce right, and making successful adjustments to structuring and managing a variety of employer/employee relations, has enormous implications for employers. It is fundamental to their achieving a sustained competitive advantage, based on the ability to access and retain a committed and skilled workforce. As Guest (1998) says, there is a need to successfully engage the hearts and minds of the workforce, and it is precisely in this area of communicating with employees/workers that the psychological contract is so important.

A "hot" research topic

> The psychological contract has emerged as a serious topic for analysis by a number of authors and researchers in the management of contemporary employer/worker relationships, capturing the spirit of the times (Guest, 1998).
>
> As an explanatory notion, it has impressively high face validity with employers and employees. Everyone agrees that it exists and most workers appear able to describe the content of their contract (Anderson & Schalk, 1998.

Del Campo (2007) identifies the psychological contract as "possibly the most emergent area for organisational research in the current landscape". As we shall see in Chapter 8, the concept is relevant to many areas of organisational behavior, including:

- Organisational performance
- Retention
- Career development and management
- Organisational transformation and change
- Downsizing and restructuring decisions
- The changing relationship(s) between employers and workers.

Key research findings

The link between distressed or violated psychological contracts, and a lowering of employees' commitment, job satisfaction and higher turnover, has been established by a number of researchers (Guzzo, Noonan & Elron, 1994; Robinson & Morrison, 1995; Robinson & Rousseau, 1994; Schalk, Freeze & Van den Bosch, 1995). Analysis of survey results from Guest and Conway's (1997) study confirm that the psychological contract is a key explanatory variable in contemporary relations, with the state of the psychological contract influencing behavioural outcomes such as motivation at work, organisational citizenship behaviour and intention to leave the organisation. Other research findings relating to the psychological contract are reported later on in this chapter.

Linking engagement and retention to the psychological contract

From another perspective, we have identified that engagement (whatever definition is adopted), and retention are important to business success. We have also identified that levels of engagement and retention are a symptom of a number of underlying causes. A framework of understanding these constructs (including an associated model and diagnosis of those organisational factors contributing to disengagement and turnover), would assist many organisations. It is contended that the concept of the psychological contract provides such a way forward for organisations.

7.3 WHAT ARE THE VARIOUS TYPES OF PSYCHOLOGICAL CONTRACTS?

According to Rousseau (1995), psychological contracts vary within a continuum from "relational" to "transactional", with a shift having occurred towards the latter in recent times. We shall briefly explain what is meant by these terms.

Recent Shift in the Psychological Contract

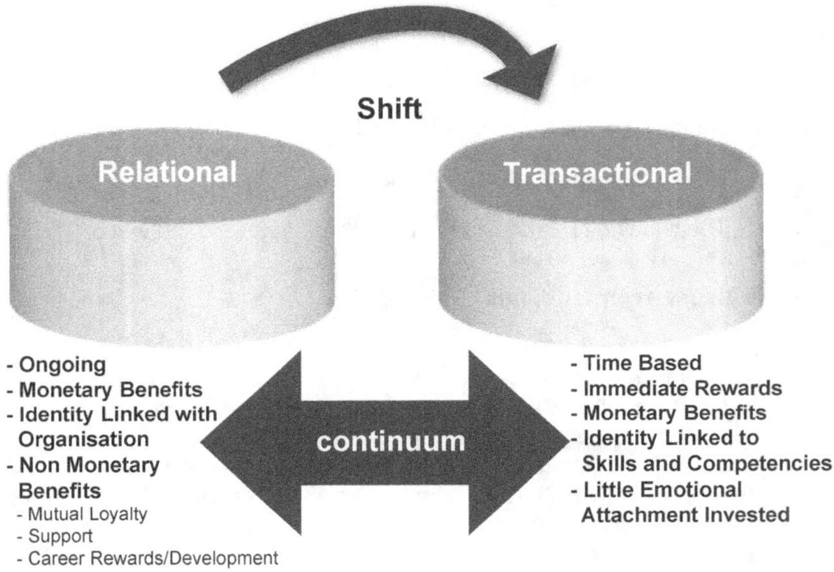

1. **Relational Psychological Contracts**
Relational psychological contracts are more open ended, longer-term arrangements, with a wider range of obligations on the part of both the organisation and its employees. These contracts were very much the norm under the "old deal". The exchange between employer and employee in relational psychological contracts involves monetary (tangibles) as well as non-monetary benefits or intangibles (e.g., mutual loyalty, support, training, career development, etc.). Under such arrangements, employers expect greater flexibility and loyalty from employees, including a commitment to the organisational community and the purpose of the organisation. Employees also come to identify with the organisation through promotion, mentoring and socialisation. There is a higher degree of mutual interdependence.

   Those established organisations competing through distinctive forms of customer service in relatively stable environments, tend to train their employees extensively and foster a service orientation (e.g., insurance, banking and finance industries). These organisations seek a longer-term relationship with their employees (i.e., relational psychological contracts), and hence lower turnover, where cultural norms which support good customer relations are developed.

2. Transactional Psychological Contracts

Transactional psychological contracts are oriented towards economic and performance based considerations, with more finite time frames and clearly defined work roles and responsibilities. An individual's identity involved in such contracts is said to be derived more from their skills and competencies, rather than being closely tied with the organisation. As such, individuals engaged under transactional contracts may be more likely to display lower levels of citizenship behavior (i.e., helping coworkers, contributing to the life of the organisation), and lower levels of collaboration and teamwork. Under transactional contracts, employers are freer to "hire and fire", with lower barriers to both entry and exit. Transactional psychological contracts are more likely to be used for project work.

Examples of transactional contract employees include the following:

- Careerists - those who make their career in an industry but not with a particular organisation (e.g., lawyers, stockbrokers)
- Longer term outsiders - includes casuals (e.g., nurses, cleaners)
- Shorter term outsiders - temporaries including higher skilled (e.g., key specialists, consultants) and lower skilled employees (e.g., fruit pickers, contract labour).

However as Rousseau (1995) points out, whilst the above types of transactional contracts provide for flexibility and minimum training in the short-term (as well as minimising costs and risk), they do not solve critical organisational challenges and problems with such practices. Opportunities down the road are less likely to eventuate given that the learning and development of distinctive strategic competencies may not be captured and retained. To rely solely on transactional contract employees/workers means the possibility of losing organisation specific knowledge and delicate proprietary information to competitors, not to mention jeopardising client relationships.

3. Hybrid Psychological Contracts

Many organisations are opting for a hybrid contract, which incorporates a blending of elements of both (1) and (2) types above. The hybrid contract incorporates shared values and commitments, as well as specified results and time frames. These contracts typically incorporate a component of performance based pay. Examples of hybrid contracts include executives who are employed on say a three year arrangement which includes specific performance requirements to be met, with a percentage of pay that is flexible, depending upon the achievement of those performance requirements.

> Note: There is a fourth type of psychological contract – a transitional contract, which reflects a breakdown or absence of agreement between the parties, as observed in unstable circumstances such as radical change or downsizing in which the commitment between the parties is eroded or does not exist.

7.4 PSYCHOLOGICAL CONTRACTS AND THE BUSINESS STRATEGY

The intersection of business and workforce strategies

We have previously stated that the intersection of business and workforce strategies is a critical focus for HR professionals. It is here that the psychological contract comes into its own (without wanting to diminish its importance in other areas of organisational relevance). Psychological contracts should link to the business strategy, and will vary depending upon the:

- History and positioning of the business (e.g., start up businesses may offer lower job security and resources, but higher job challenge and percentage of pay based on performance – a more transactionally oriented psychological contract)
- Stability of the business and the external environment (e.g., more mature businesses operating in more stable environments may offer longer term job security – a more relationally oriented psychological contract)
- Nature of customer service and relationships (e.g., businesses involved in "one off" customer transactions are more likely to offer high percentage of pay based on performance – a more transactionally oriented psychological contract)
- Value and knowledge contributed by the position (e.g., senior management and key specialists roles are likely to offer higher levels of rewards and career development opportunities – a more relationally oriented psychological contract).

The implications of inappropriate psychological contracts

The type and "health" of the psychological contract can significantly impact on the commitment and retention of employees, and hence the performance and business success of the organisation. Inappropriate psychological contracts (i.e., where workforce strategies don't match business strategies), can lead to excessive turnover.

For example, we referred earlier in Chapter 3 to the example of the recruitment industry which typically experiences high turnover of consultants.

Psychological contracts that excessively emphasise pay, based on short-term performance or results (i.e., numbers of candidates placed), are inconsistent with recruitment company's need to develop longer-term, quality, client relationships. These more transactionally oriented psychological contracts (i.e., based on shorter-term performance targets), encourage recruitment consultants to think and act short-term. If these consultants don't achieve results (either due to their own limitations or downturns in the market), their salary suffers and they may leave to pursue other opportunities.

Alternatively if consultants do achieve more outstanding results (and are rewarded accordingly), then they may also leave to start their own business and compete against their previous employer. Whatever the case, the attachment of the consultant to the recruitment company may have been tenuous and dependent almost entirely on economic factors, with low barriers to entry and exit. The downside for the recruitment company is that their relationship with their clients and reputation potentially suffers as a consequence of recruitment consultant turnover, not to mention the cost of recruiting and training replacement consultants.

Case Study: Global IT firm with high turnover in its sales force

We were undertaking a retention risk assessment consultancy for the sales force of a global IT company. This company sold software licenses for its products and was experiencing around 50% turnover. The reward structure for sales professionals was such that those who achieved high sales revenue figures were rewarded astronomically (i.e., with very high bonuses). The problem was that it typically took around four years to progressively achieve high client sales (i.e., clients would progressively purchase more software licenses and also use existing licenses more extensively over time), before the bonus structure kicked in.

Sales professionals left the company during the four year ramp up period because they weren't prepared to hang around for the "pot of gold at the end of the rainbow." In other words, the progressive nature of the development of the business (longer term revenue generation with clients), did not accord with the "all or nothing" reward structure

7.5 WHAT COMPRISES THE PSYCHOLOGICAL CONTRACT OR THE "DEAL"?

There is no universal agreement by researchers on what elements or items comprise the psychological contract or the "deal". Various methods have been adopted to develop these items, including interview research with:

- Personnel and Human Resource professionals
- Employees and employer representatives.

In the U.K., a number of studies have highlighted a diversity of priorities and preferences. To a certain extent, the elements and lists of psychological contract items appear to be more intuitively derived, or driven by *a priori* hunches or inferences, rather than having been more theoretically based. Also some disparity of opinion exists amongst scholars as to the scope of formation of employees' expectations. The U.K. approach has been to develop a wider definition of what and how these expectations might be formed (which has been reflected in the design of the WRDI® tool). Conversely the US approach is of a narrower perspective, focusing on obligations. In the case of the latter, this means that the psychological contract is not too much different from the written employment agreement.

Taking all of this into account, the following 15 items have been drawn from the literature. They have been grouped, for ease of explanation and consultancy utility, under four broad categories.

1. Rewards/Recognition
    - Competitive salary package
    - High % of pay based on performance
    - Other benefits, both material and non material (e.g., bonuses, shares, travel, vehicle, accommodation, conferences, networking, etc.)
    - Recognition of contribution
2. Security/Safety
    - Short term job security (up to a maximum period of 12 months) versus long term security (longer than 12 months)
    - Safe and physically secure work environment
3. Growth Opportunities
    - Job challenge (e.g., interesting, meaningful and/or challenging work, variety, etc.)
    - Sufficient power and responsibility to do the job
    - Career development (e.g., new skills, knowledge, experience, education, personal development, etc.)
    - Adequate training for the job
    - Promotion or advancement (e.g., increased responsibility, higher level job, lateral or other job moves, etc.)
4. Social/Support
    - Flexible work arrangements (e.g., flexitime, time off, rosters, taking leave, etc.)
    - Supportive management (e.g., personal problems, interest in me, assistance, etc.)

- Supportive work environment (e.g., co-operation from others)
- Adequate resources for doing the job (e.g., people, financial, systems, equipment, technical, expertise, etc.)

These items provide for a comprehensive assessment of the dimensions or content of the psychological contract. However making a complete list of psychological items is impossible. Additional items beyond the 15 items selected are likely to be specific to the organisation or to the individual. For example, several studies on expatriates have shown that certain groups of employees have specific needs (e.g., assistance with re-establishment in their country of origin after a stint overseas), so their psychological contracts may include such additional items. Conversely some of these 15 items may not apply for some psychological contracts (particularly for more transactional psychological contracts), as indicated below.

7.6 INTERPRETING THE "DEAL": DETERMINING THE TYPE OF PSYCHOLOGICAL CONTRACT

The 15 items referred to in the previous section also serve as a basis for determining the nature or type of psychological contract in the continuum from relational to transactional. For example:

- If employees have a more relational type psychological contract with their employer, then they are likely to have at least some moderate expectations on most of the 15 psychological contract items
- If employees have a more transactional type psychological contract, then they may have high expectations on some items (e.g., high % of pay based on performance), but low or nil expectations on other items (e.g., long term job security, training, promotion or advancement).

In summary, these 15 items constitute standardised categories that can then be assessed across persons and settings. There are many types of "deals". It is possible to have all sorts of combinations of different levels or strengths of expectations concerning these items for various roles depending upon organisational and external environmental circumstances.

> Note: In the case of employees engaged under a transactional exchange, this does not preclude the development of a relational contractual orientation (e.g., corporate integration, displays of citizenship commitment). Thus it is possible for organisations to have "their cake and eat it"!

7.7 HOW CAN VARIOUS PSYCHOLOGICAL CONTRACT TYPES BE PROFILED?

Psychological contract types (or the nature of the "deal") can be represented by profiling the extent or strength of employees' expectations, across those 15 items which typically comprise the psychological contract. As referred to earlier in Chapter 3, different skills' based workforce segments have different psychological contract types or "deals". Examples of these types have been plotted on the coloured pages in this chapter, as follows:

- Quadrant 1 – Criticals, Relational Psychological Contract
- Quadrant 2 – Professionals, Skilled, and Semi-Skilled, Hybrid Psychological Contract
- Quadrant 3 – Doers, Transactional Psychological Contract (could be either shorter or longer term)
- Quadrant 4 – Specialists, Relational Psychological Contract.

7.8 THE IMPORTANCE OF THE ITEMS THAT COMPRISE THE "DEAL" AND EMPLOYEES' EXPECTATIONS

Expectations are a powerful influence on employees' attitudes and behaviours. It is important to have clearly defined, well communicated expectations, so both employees and their employer have a common understanding and goal. Unspoken and unrealised expectations in the workplace can lead to job frustration and dissatisfaction, and a lowering of commitment. So let's firstly examine the relevance and implications to both organisations and their employees, of the 15 items that comprise the psychological contract, and upon which basis employees' expectations are formed.

> Note: Statistical analysis conducted by the WRDI Institute indicates that the fulfillment of expectations on each of these 15 items varies in so far as their impact on affective commitment and job satisfaction. The five most influential or important items are all intangibles – job challenge, career development, supportive management, sufficient power and autonomy, and recognition. Refer later in this chapter for a further discussion on their relative importance.

Typical Employment Value Proposition (EVP)/"Deal" Profiles for Q1 (Criticals) & Q2 (Professionals, Skilled / Semi Skilled)

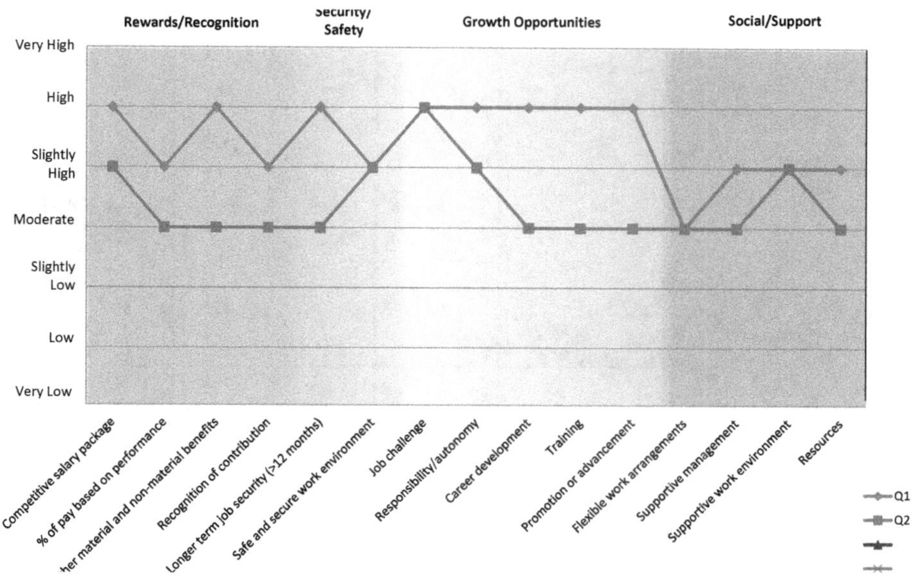

Typical Employment Value Proposition (EVP)/"Deal" Profiles for Q3 (Doers) and Q4 (Specialists)

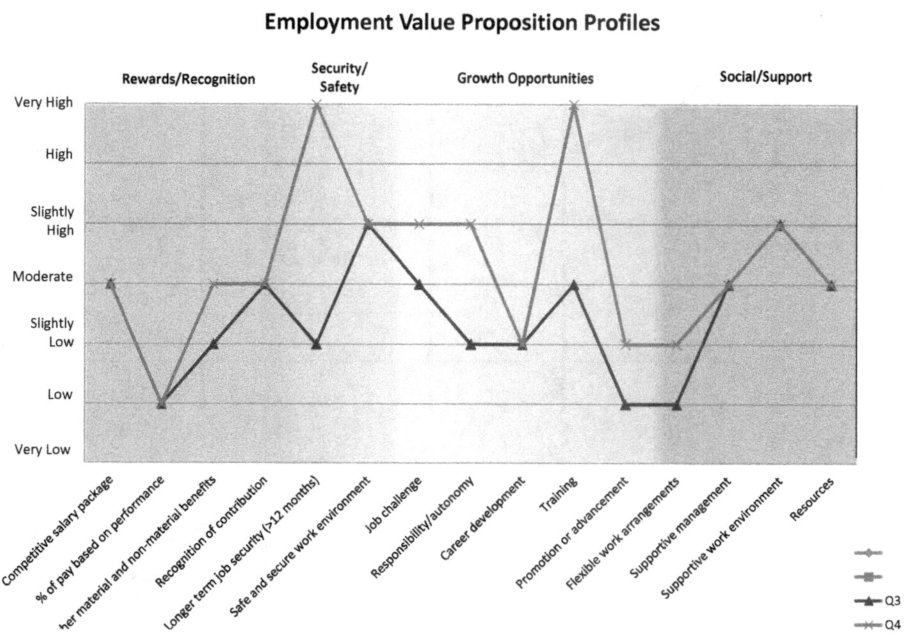

WRDI® Profile A: The Extent of Employees' Expectations

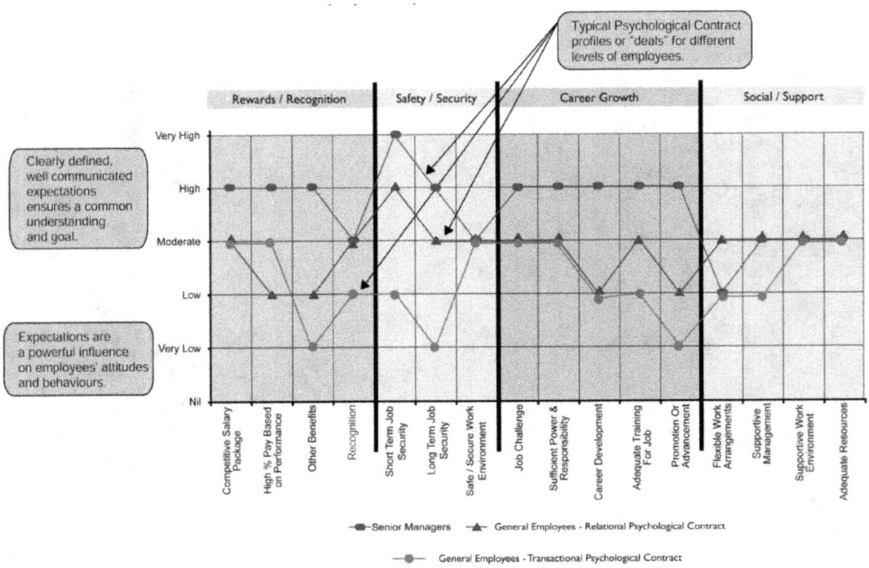

WRDI® Profile B: The Weighted Fulfillment of Employees' Expectations (or Delivery of the "Deal")"

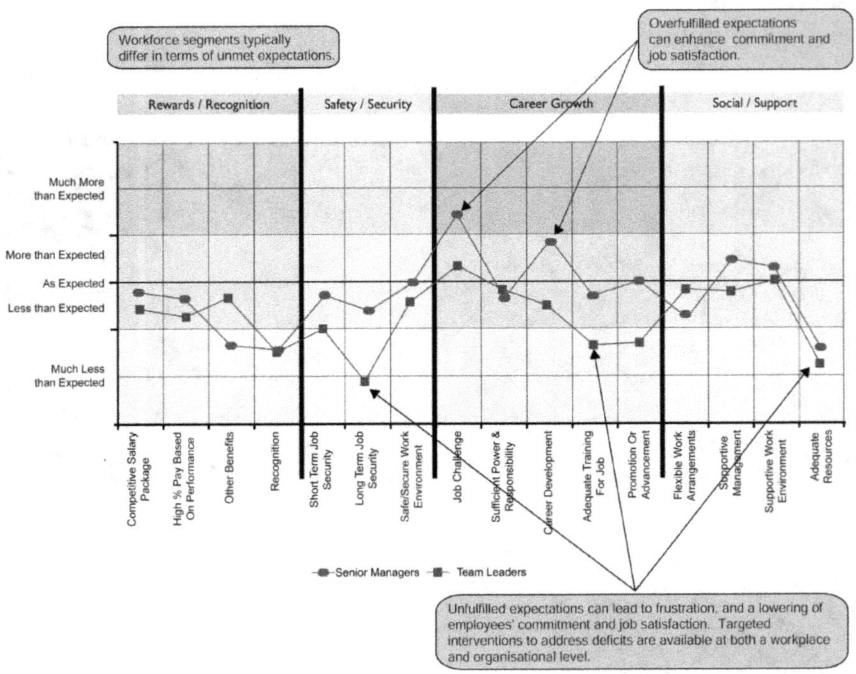

WRDI® Profile C: Psychological Contract Health and Consequences

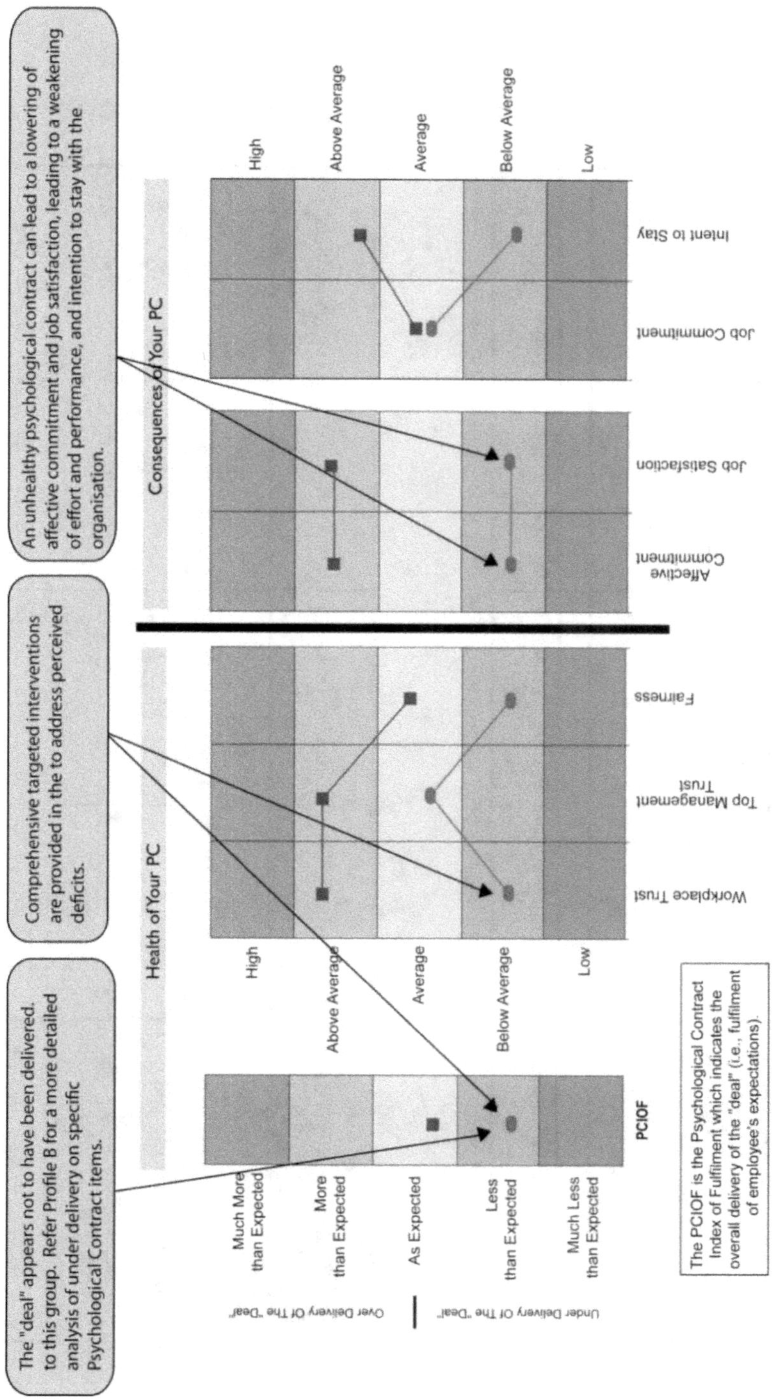

Other WRDI® Reporting Outputs: Retention Risk and Alignment by Skills' Quadrant

Workforce Segment Summary: Employee Numbers by Skills Quadrant

Retention Risk	Q1 Criticals	Q2 Professionals, Skilled	Q3 Doers	Q4 Specialists
Stayers	24	97	98	23
Moderate Risk of Leaving	6	16	25	10
High Risk of Leaving	6	21	10	16

	Q1 Criticals	Q2 Professionals, Skilled	Q3 Doers	Q4 Specialists
Controllable Turnover Risk $	576k	756k	120k	269k

Alignment	Q1 Criticals	Q2 Professionals, Skilled	Q3 Doers	Q4 Specialists
Emotionally Commited and Satisfied	18	81	86	21
Emotionally Commited and Disatisfied	3	20	29	10
Emotionally Uncommited but Satisfied	4	22	11	3
Emotionally Uncommited and Disatisfied	11	11	17	15

1. **Rewards/Recognition**

Pay

Reward systems and employee compensation lie at the heart of the employment relationship. Compensation has direct effects on:

- Job satisfaction
- Attraction and retention
- Performance
- Co-operation
- Flexibility
- Skill development
- Risk taking, etc.

Compensation decisions also have important consequences for individuals, not only in terms of income, but as indicators of their social status and success in life. Compensation is a visible, salient, personal and socially significant signal of the nature of the employment relationship. Messages conveyed by compensation include:

- Values (e.g., productivity, parity, cost containment)
- Performance (e.g., membership versus risk taking, citizenship behaviour versus job achievements)
- Time frames (i.e., short-term returns versus long-term growth)
- Equity (i.e., relative distribution between employees, managers, the organisation and the external labour market).

Pay and recognition combined, are both tools for acknowledging the worth of employees. Pay is also an incentive for motivating future goal achievement. Most employees want comparable compensation and benefits to what their peers in other organisations receive.

Previous focus has been on creating a bullet proof executive compensation schemes at the expense of abdicating those things which are the essence of management. Lucrative retirement plans and service rewards may attract people, but not necessarily motivate them to perform. Such plans may create barriers to leaving through these "golden handcuffs", but they don't encourage people to develop new skills and knowledge, to change their behaviour or embrace organisational change. These plans may create a stability which is counterproductive – limiting promotional and advancement opportunities, limiting opportunities for growth and development, with the result of fewer job openings.

It is therefore important to structure the economics of the relationship in such a way that it doesn't obstruct its seemingly voluntary nature. The relationship needs to be preserved rather than forced or held together purely because of economic considerations. Refer to Chapter 6 on selective retention and retaining the wrong people.

Notwithstanding, different retention needs are required for different scenarios. For project work, it is essential to retain people for the length of the project as a minimum and beyond if there are advantages in carrying over some of these employees to the next project because of their experience, skills, etc. Compensation can play a part in "locking up" employees for a particular period of time, and "unlocking" them at some other time. Practices that bind employees to an organisation, even temporarily, such as employment contracts or "golden handcuffs", will cause them to be more committed to that organisation in the short term by constraining their options. "Golden handcuffs" act as a deterrent to poaching, staving off recruiters, much like burglar alarms do in reducing crime deterrent, persuading criminals that it is easier to rob elsewhere. The provision of stock options buys time, but may exacerbate turnover in the longer term. Cashing in stock options or paying out large bonuses can act as a trigger for turnover. It provides financial security for people to take bigger risks with their careers, or more choices in careers and lifestyle considerations (e.g., reducing work hours, down shifting).

In so far as performance based pay is concerned, this issue is currently the focus of acute attention as a consequence of the fall out effects from the GFC. Firstly it is important to get the balance right between rewards based on individual performance, team performance, and overall company performance. Secondly the focus on short-term versus longer term performance is undergoing, and will continue to undergo, a significant shift towards the latter (i.e., a more sustainable focus). Thirdly different reward structures within an organisation can raise questions of trust, and whether people are acting in the best long-term interests of the organisation, as opposed to their own self-interests.

Other benefits (both financial and non financial)

Some organisations may be unable to compete in terms of straight salary considerations, but they may be able to offer substitutes (e.g., travel, attendance at conferences, accommodation, use of a vehicle, generous superannuation scheme, training and career development, etc.). Or it may simply be that the reputation of the organisation is such that working for it constitutes a "feather in one's cap" (i.e., adds to the substance and credibility of an individual's CV).

Recognition

Recognition is another form of reward. It doesn't replace pay, but it can add to it. Recognition is retro-active (i.e., after the event), and it may be provided in various forms:

- Gift of material possessions
- Experiences (e.g., tickets to a show, overseas trip)
- Favourable comments by management, including performance review ratings
- Being mentioned as part of an employee recognition scheme
- Attendance at conferences.

Several studies show that workers are more committed when the organisation indicates that it respects and appreciates their efforts (Eisenberger, Faolo & David-LaMastro, 1990). This recognition ties in with the concept of reciprocity. People want to feel needed and if they are made to feel so, and that they are making an important and valuable contribution to the organisation, then they are more likely to see themselves attached to that organisation.

2. **Safety/security**

Job security

The provision or otherwise of job security doesn't necessarily impact on performance, but it will impact on retention. Studies have shown that those engaged on shorter-term arrangements typically work just as hard and perform just as well as those on longer-term arrangements. However the attachment of those to the organisation on more shorter term arrangements is tenuous, and if a better offer comes up, then they are more inclined to leave (i.e., lower barriers to exit).

Safety/security

Organisations and their management are becoming increasingly more concerned with safety, particularly now that executives may be liable and subject to a criminal sentence in the event of serious accidents or fatalities. An organisation's reputation for safe work practices, particularly in more dangerous industries, will impact on their Employer of Choice status. Nobody wants to work for an organisation in an environment where they are at risk of being injured, if they can otherwise avoid it. Furthermore we are witnessing an increase in the level of violence in the community and many people are becoming more concerned with their personal safety and security. Therefore safety and personal security considerations play a part in individual's decisions to accept roles and thereafter, remain in those roles.

Note: Some roles are inherently dangerous (e.g., the defence forces).

3. **Career growth**

Job challenge

Job challenge is one of the strongest motivating influences. According to Branham (2005), 11% leave because of boring job duties where there is no challenge. In Chapter 6 we referred to a study by the CIPD (2005) where lack of career and promotional prospects was a strong motivating influence for people to leave, which could be interpreted, in part, as a lack of job challenge. However if the challenge of the job is too high, then it may be stressful. Whilst sign on bonuses may serve to attract talent, people won't stay in the absence of the other key tangibles and intangibles (e.g., challenging work, opportunities for career advancement, etc.).

Sufficient power and decision making (autonomy)

Most employees want a reasonable level of autonomy and decision making authority (refer to the "new deal" in Chapter 1). Studies have shown that employee participation increases the sense of commitment, as does working with greater autonomy (Mathieu & Zajac, 1990). The happy coincidence is that high-performance work systems that require greater commitment from employees also seem to generate it by giving greater participation in decision-making and more autonomy or control over their actions (Dansereau, Graen & Haga, 1975).

However it would be foolish to delegate responsibility to those who are incapable of exercising it (either through lack of training, inexperience, the adverse repercussions of something going amiss, legal compliance, etc.). Thus the appropriate level of delegation in a role will vary depending upon a variety of circumstances.

Career development

As referred to previously, studies show that one of the main reasons why people leave organisations is because of lack of career development opportunities. Many people want opportunities for growth and development and clearly delineated career path alternatives, and the approximate timetable associated with each. Whether organisations are always able to, or want to, provide such opportunities are other questions. As we have seen from Chapter 3, the extent of such willingness will depend upon where the role is positioned within the skills' based segmentation model, the circumstances of the organisation, labour market forces, etc.

Refer to Chapter 8 for a further discussion of careers and the psychological contract, and Appendix B on careers in the contemporary workplace.

Adequate training

Training and development are essential means of improving organisational performance. They are tools to enhance the skills and broaden the career opportunities of individuals, and to improve the effectiveness of services. Studies have shown that training and other investments in employees increases their commitment (Kalleberg & Reve, 1992). The explosion of knowledge and information in recent times has highlighted the need for lifelong learning and ongoing professional development. Knowledge is the only competitive advantage. Organisations need to instil the concepts of continuing knowledge and education, particularly for their higher knowledge workers. Because employees are becoming more sensitive about keeping their skills current, training and development may be an employee benefit that shores up retention, as well as enhancing the skill base of the organisation.

Professionals typically show a higher preference to learn and grow compared to other categories of employees/workers. Providing opportunities for professional development also helps create a balance between organisational and personal aspirations, assuming there are mutual benefits for both parties in so doing. Larger firms hiring graduates and sponsoring internal development tend to have longer average employee tenure. Because these firms are more vertically integrated, have longer lead times for projects, and can afford greater division of labour, they can provide career ladders that facilitate greater internal development. However ultimately training should be more oriented towards implementing the organisation's strategy rather than necessarily benefiting the individual. Some companies have resorted to specific training contracts that require employees to stay for a minimum period after receiving the training and to pay back some portion of the training if they leave within that period.

Training also plays a critical role in helping employees to cope with the rapid pace of change in organisations. Most employees face the prospect of undertaking ongoing training throughout their careers in order to acquire the new skills, or maintain the existing skills, that are demanded by technological and organisational change. Employees need to develop flexible skills that can be readily applied to new tasks or situations, and adapted to meet changing work requirements. Refer to Appendix B on Careers in the Contemporary Workplace for a further discussion on this topic.

Training viewed as an investment (e.g., talent management), also signals a desire to retain and deploy the individual, and their newly acquired skills. This may be in the form of periodic re-skilling, cross-training opportunities, inter-firm experiences, involvement in projects, undertaking development programs, etc. Such training contributes to employees' development, whilst at the same time, facilitating linkages within and between work groups.

Promotion or advancement

Promotion or advancement may not represent the "big attractive carrot" that it once was. People are now less inclined to wait around and be motivated to stay by a longer pay-off or reward in the form of advancement or promotion. There are too many uncertainties in the volatile contemporary workplace, and we live more in the "now era", where what counts is the immediate rather than longer-term, more problematic rewards.

4. Social/support

Flexible work practices

Studies have shown that flexible work practices can improve productivity. Provision of this flexibility will be vitally important for some people (e.g., those with young families, carers, etc), whilst for others, its availability will be relatively inconsequential. In fact the hype around the significance of work-life balance tends to be over rated and miss-placed as discussed in Chapter 2. Notwithstanding, employees want management to recognize that their family and personal time is important.

Forms of flexible work practices include the following:

- Flexible time (hours and shifts, start and finish times, compressed weeks)
- Reduced time (part-time, job sharing, reduced hours or days)
- Flexible place (telecommuting, mobile and off site work).

As indicated in Chapter 1, work has become more about what a person does rather than a place where they go. Increasingly employees will work more from home in the future. However some industries, because of their very nature, are unable to offer flexible work practices, or are unable to cater for home workers (e.g., wholesale/retail trades, construction).

Supportive management

Most employees desire a good working relationship with their manager/supervisor. Whilst somewhat exaggerated, the quality of the relationship between employees and their manager/supervisor is nevertheless a significant factor as to whether they stay or go.

Supportive work environment

Most employees desire a good working relationship with their colleagues. Studies show that employees who have better relations with co-workers are also more committed to their organisations (Rotondi, 1975). The current push towards cross-functional teamwork and projects is a development function that enhances commitment to organisation objectives. It makes interdependence and co-operation among individuals and functions more visible, and otherwise creates a social environment where organisational commitment can be built through relationships, social involvement, and shared values and ideas.

Adequate resources

Employees want "cutting edge" resources in order to be able to perform their jobs properly, effectively and efficiently.

7.9 HOW IS THE PSYCHOLOGICAL CONTRACT FORMED?

Developing the employer/employee relationship: An analogy

like any relationship, the employer/employee relationship develops progressively through a number of phases. An analogy between the forming of a personal relationship and the employer/employee relationship is presented below:

- **Attraction/dating** – the organisation promotes itself, advertises for a position and the applicant submits their resume/CV
- **Going steady** - both parties start to get to know each other better with interviews, testing, reference checking, exchange of other relevant information, etc.
- **Engagement** – the formal offer or invitation
- **Marriage** - acceptance of the offer, organisational entry, publicly recognized union, and a brief period of adjustment (particularly the initial 3-4 months).

Following first impressions, the relationship moves forward, with those impressions consolidated on the basis of observable characteristics and further information. It is important that candidates are moved through these various phases, from one part of the recruitment and selection process to the next, without them uncoupling or disengaging (e.g., maintain intermittent contact, provide debriefs/updates, etc.). The goal is to unite parties into a longer-term relationship. However the relationship is fragile in these early stages, and simple violations of the script or conventions are sufficient to terminate it. In the case of an external recruiter, they represent the organisation, and their attributes and demeanor are generalised to the organisation. Hence their role is critical given that they are the main point of reference in the early stages of the relationship development process.

There are certain things that the organisation can do to facilitate the development of the relationship, including:

- Self-disclosure (e.g., provide information about strategies, markets, products, operations, etc.)
- Responsivity to requests and maintaining ongoing communication
- Relational expression.

The psychological contract evolves over time

We shall now discuss in further detail how the psychological contract develops over time, commencing at around the time of recruitment and job application, be it for an internal applicant (i.e., from an existing position to a new position within the same organisation), or an external applicant. The applicant starts to form certain expectations about the prospective role and the organisation. This information may be initially gathered from various sources such as:

- The web site of the organisation
- The job advertisement
- Press articles
- Company brochures
- What colleagues may have said, etc.

Different people, both external and internal to the organisation, will also have an influence primarily in informational roles. For example, external recruiters may sell certain aspects of the job and the organisation. Then as the application process proceeds with interviews and discussions with various parties (including recruiters, management, etc.), these expectations continue to develop into a rudimentary psychological contract. For new recruits at entry, it is likely that the majority of promises existing between them and their employer are little further developed from those that are set out in their employment contract.

> Note: Research has demonstrated that whilst pre-employment expectations are important, post employment expectations are much more significant in their impact on employees' levels of job satisfaction, affective commitment and retention.

The importance of the initial few months

Once employment commences, the knowledge gained by the new recruit during their initial period of employment, and their socialisation into the organisation, influences the development of their psychological contract. It is during this period that the new recruit, having entered the organisation as somewhat naïve, then starts to make further sense of their new environment, and that their perceptions and expectations develop accordingly. This period of organisational entry is characterised by the new recruit's knowledge acquisition in a number of areas relating to their job and task responsibilities, the work group and the wider organisation. As part of this learning process, the new recruit will elaborate their rudimentary psychological contract that they hold at entry, in line with organisational reality.

Longitudinal research on organisational socialisation has shown that new recruit adjustment occurs most rapidly immediately following organisational entry, reaching relative stability as early as four months into job tenure.

Phases and factors in the development of the psychological contract

Thus there are two phases of expectation development and formation in the development of the psychological contract:

- The "anticipation phase" (expectations developed by employees of their new role prior to organisational entry)
- The "encounter phase" (the initial weeks and months when the newcomer becomes assimilated into the social structure of the organisation).

Also there are two sets of factors operating in forming the psychological contract:

- External messages and social cues (co-workers and work groups) from the organisation
- The individual's internal interpretations, predispositions and constructions.

Both individual and organisational factors will influence what information is available, and what new recruits attend to as they develop their psychological contract. The immediate work group will tend to play a more informal role, but co-workers and supervisors may provide information which allows the new recruit to revise or develop their psychological contract.

Making it real: How employees' expectations are formed

Examples of how employees' expectations are formed (i.e., for the items comprising the psychological contract), based on stated or implied promises or understandings (refer to the definition of the psychological contract at the beginning of this chapter), are summarised below. They include what is stated and implied.

Stated:

- The job advertisement
- What was said during the employee's job position interview, recruitment or selection process
- The letter of engagement
- The job position description
- The employment agreement/contract
- The induction process

- What the employee's boss may have said
- What management may have said to the employee
- Policies, brochures and communications, web site, etc.

Implied:

- What the employee has seen happening with their colleagues
- What colleagues may have said
- How the employer has treated them or other employees
- The past customs and practices of the employer, etc.

7.10 WHO IS RESPONSIBLE FOR MANAGING THE PSYCHOLOGICAL CONTRACT?

The responsibility for managing the psychological contract is spread between senior management, HR and local management. Some items of the psychological contract relate more to wider organisational people management policies and practices, and are more the responsibility of senior management and HR, e.g.:

- Competitive salary package
- High percentage of pay based on performance
- Other benefits, both financial and non financial
- Job security (from short term to long term)
- Job challenge
- Career development.

Other items of the psychological contract relate more to local workplace factors, and are more the responsibility of local management, e.g.:

- Recognition of contribution
- Safe and physically secure work environment
- Sufficient power and responsibility to do the job
- Adequate training for the job
- Promotion or advancement
- Flexible work arrangements
- Supportive management

- Supportive work environment
- Adequate resources to do the job.

The spread of responsibility for managing the above items (i.e., between local management and senior management), will vary between the parties on an organisation by organisation basis.

7.11 HOW DOES THE PSYCHOLOGICAL CONTRACT DIFFER FROM THE SOCIAL CONTRACT?

The psychological contract is different from the social contract. The latter represents employees' expectations based on social norms, customs and practices regarding what organisations should generally provide to their employees. The social contract refers to the "rules of the game" (e.g., right to a decent job, good working conditions, collective bargaining, fair treatment, etc.), although the rules of the game are becoming somewhat blurred with the proliferation of various employment relationships, changing regulations and legislative requirements.

The psychological contract refers to employees' expectations that are of a more specific nature *vis a vis* the social contract. These expectations are based on stated or implied understandings or promises concerning that which is offered by the employer, and not necessarily that which is desired by the employee. What is offered by the employer will vary according to organisational circumstances. Refer to the different types of psychological contracts (from relational versus transactional) earlier in this chapter, and the skills' based workforce segmentation model in Chapter 3.

Employees' expectations based on the social contract may not accord with what some organisations are able to or want to provide, given the contemporary turbulent and unpredictable work environment (e.g., longer-term job security given the trend by organisations to shift the risk of employment uncertainty across to employees). Such social contract expectations don't constitute the psychological contract. Having said that, ideally if organisations were able to satisfy what is desired by employees (and they are more prepared to do this for more critical roles), then this is a win-win outcome for both parties.

7.12 IS THE PSYCHOLOGICAL CONTRACT TWO WAY?

We have been discussing the psychological contract more from the perspective of employees, but relationships are two way. Despite the reciprocal nature of psychological contracts (i.e., the obligations of both employer and employees), the measurement emphasis has been one way (i.e., only focused on what is in the mind of employees). The organisation's expectations of employees might typically include:

- Being productive, organised and meeting performance standards

- Meeting deadlines and being prepared to work flexible hours to achieve the same
- Being concerned for quality of their output
- Working to the best of their abilities
- Flexibility to take on tasks outside of their job description
- Being a good team player
- Developing and improving their skills and competencies
- Not committing fraud or stealing from the company
- Being prepared to speak well of the company
- Showing consideration for others in the company in their actions
- Being polite and courteous to customers, etc.

The performance management and review system would typically examine many of the above organisations' expectations of their employees.

> Note: To a certain extent, the psychological contract consequence measures/scales in the WRDI® model of the psychological contract (refer later in this chapter), partly address employees' obligations to their employer. For example, organisations would expect their employees to be committed to their jobs/exert discretionary effort, and to stay with the organisation at least in the medium term, assuming the organisation has fulfilled its side of the bargain (i.e., delivered on the "deal"), and management has otherwise treated them well.

7.13 IS THE PSYCHOLOGICAL CONTRACT STABLE OVER TIME?

Psychological contracts act as schemas that can be resilient in the face of organisational change and external shocks. Some researchers maintain that psychological contracts tend to be stable because they are rarely assessed. However trigger events such as the GFC, which has caused some discontinuities in our previous thinking, are often the cause for such reassessment. Furthermore as indicated in the beginning of this chapter, psychological contracts are also somewhat dynamic and open-ended with expectations changing as perceptions about the employer's commitment evolve.

Obligations (and expectations) are expected to increase with the trust that develops within maturing relationships. As mutual trust flourishes, so does the extent of the social exchange. Newcomer's perceptions of their employer's obligations may change over time, with some research indicating perceptions of increasing obligations. The longer an employee is with an organisation, the more likely that the obligations which they attribute to their employer will increase. With longer service, the psychological contract is likely to become broader and deeper.

It should be noted that the psychological contract applies to an employee's current job (as opposed to their previous job with the same organisation). However for employees who have been promoted internally into their current job position, or employees with an organisation that has been the subject of a merger, acquisition or new owner, their psychological contracts will be most likely be influenced as a consequence of their history (i.e., previous experiences) with the organisation. What is important is the "deal" (and exchange) between the parties relating to that for which employees are being currently paid by their employer, and their associated performance.

> Note: Measures of test/retest reliability for the WRDI® indicate that the psychological contract is fairly stable over the shorter term (3 months).

7.14 A DYNAMIC AND DIAGNOSTIC MODEL OF THE PSYCHOLOGICAL CONTRACT: ITS HEALTH AND CONSEQUENCES

We will now extend the concept of the "deal" and incorporate it into a dynamic relationship or psychological contract model.

Fundamental questions about any relationship

Think about any relationship you may be involved in and ask yourself the following questions:

- *What are my expectations?*
- *Have these expectations been met?*
- *Do I trust the other party?*
- *Is the arrangement fair?*

These questions relate to the health of the relationship. If the answers to these latter three relationship health questions are positive, then most likely you will be:

- More emotionally attached to the other party
- More satisfied in the relationship
- Prepared to exert more effort in the relationship.

The above attitudes and behaviours are likely outcomes or consequences of the relationship.

Applying the same questions to the employer/employee relationship or psychological contract

The same approach can be applied to the employer/employee relationship, where it is proposed that relationship health factors will in part, predict relationship consequences (i.e., a diagnostic or cause and effect approach). Given the importance of the psychological contract, the development of a dynamic model of the health or state of the psychological contract and its consequences, would appear to represent an important step forward in the structuring and managing of contemporary employer/employee relationships.

To this end, a model of the state of the psychological contract (or employer/employee relationship), is presented in the Introduction Chapter (refer coloured pages). This model is based broadly on Guest's (1998) model of the psychological contract, but also includes a number of enhancements, viz:

- Incorporates a model of turnover, based on empirical studies
- Has a stronger emphasis on performance
- Separates trust at a local level from trust at a top management level
- A more comprehensive array of the tangibles and intangibles that comprise the "deal".

More specifically, this psychological contract model, as applied to employees presented in the Introduction Chapter, includes the:

- Nature and extent employees' expectations (i.e., the "deal")
- "Health" of the psychological contract (i.e., the delivery of the "deal", plus constructs of trust and fairness)
- Consequences of the psychological contract (i.e., the constructs of affective commitment, job satisfaction, commitment to the job/ discretionary effort, and intention to stay with the organisation).

This model is diagnostic, with psychological health factors predicting, in part, psychological contract consequences.

> Note: The Workplace Relationship Development Indicator (WRDI®) engagement and retention diagnostic survey tool has been designed based on this model (refer later in this chapter).

Relevance of the psychological model to latest research: employees' concerns

A recent study by Accenture (2008) identified that employees were concerned about the following issues:

- Increasing work load
- Not getting credit for work
- No clear career path
- Less support to perform their job efficiently
- Lack of support from their immediate supervisor
- Work-life balance
- Too many meetings.

Other than the last item, all of the above items are embedded in the model of the psychological contract, either in the "deal", or the other relationship constructs of fairness and trust.

7.15 HOW THIS MODEL LINKS TO ANTECEDENTS OR KEY DRIVERS OF PERFORMANCE AND RETENTION

Psychological Contract Consequences: Critical (4 "Holy Grail") Workforce Measures

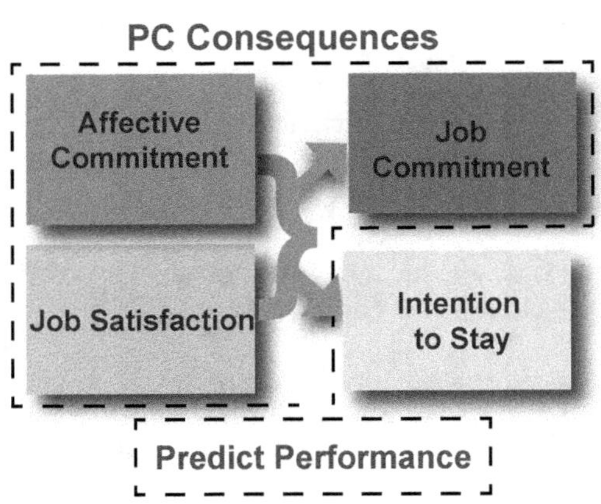

You will see that the consequences of the psychological contract include the four "holy grail" workforce measures in the diagram below. These four measures are key drivers of both performance and retention as previously discussed in Chapter 6. A key question therefore is: *How can affective commitment and job satisfaction be enhanced?*

This is where the concept of the psychological contract is so useful. It provides an overall approach to optimising affective commitment and job satisfaction, job commitment/discretionary effort and intention to stay, which in turn enhances performance and reduces risk of turnover. More specifically (and given that turnover is a symptom of a number of underlying causes), it provides a framework of understanding relating to those people management practices and policies and management behaviours that contribute to performance and turnover. This framework incorporates factors both at a local workplace level and at an organisational wide level. Such a framework therefore enables organisations to systematically enhance performance and retention.

We shall now explore in further detail the constructs that comprise this model, and examine why these constructs are important and relevant to the management of human capital, with a focus on employee engagement and retention.

7.16 DELIVERY OF THE "DEAL"

Fulfillment of employees' expectations or the delivery of the "deal"

Unmet expectations can be a source of frustration – be this in personal relationships, the sporting arena, etc. The workplace is no different. However unmet expectations on some items of the psychological contract are more important than others. The extent of their impact on employees' levels of affective commitment and job satisfaction will vary. According to our findings, the top five most influential items, in order of relative impact or importance, are all intangibles:

- Job challenge (ratio of relative importance = 1)
- Career development (ratio of relative importance = 0.8)
- Supportive management (ratio of relative importance = 0.7)
- Autonomy (ratio of relative importance = 0.7)
- Recognition (ratio of relative importance = 0.65).

> Note. The relative importance of job challenge supports the research linking lack of career development to causes of turnover (refer to Chapter 6).

Tangibles such as pay are down the list which is consistent with other findings.

However contract fulfillment, or the delivery of the "deal", recognises that an employer or contract party can be perceived as keeping some, but not necessarily all, of the contract's terms and conditions. Fulfillment is therefore a matter of degree. Furthermore in some instances, an employer might well provide things to employees beyond that which those employees expected (i.e., over fulfillment of expectations).

A key message and the good news is that deficits in delivery or fulfillment of the intangibles may not cost a lot of money to fix by way of targeted interventions. A number of the case studies presented throughout this book relate to issues with these intangibles.

More about the implications of overfullfilled and underfullfilled expectations

Overfulfilled expectations are generally most likely to result in higher levels of job satisfaction and affective commitment, and similarly the converse applies. However where an employee has unfulfilled expectations, it may be the case that there are other explanations beyond the perceived failure of management to deliver the "deal". These explanations include:

- Some of the expectations of employees being unrealistic or reflecting more their own preferences or predispositions including the social contract, as opposed to what has in fact been offered by their employer
- Circumstances having changed in the job/workplace/organisation, which means that some renegotiation/discussion is required between management and employees (i.e., the "deal" has changed but this change has not been communicated or discussed).

In the case of the latter, where management is unable to deliver on some expectations because of changing internal or external conditions or other constraints, then consideration may be given to the substitution of some other benefit(s) to offset deficits on various item(s). For example, training and development may be offered as a substitute *in lieu* of a pay increase.

The "deal" should be a trade-off

Whilst employers can increase employees' levels of job satisfaction and commitment by promising more (i.e., increase employees' expectations across these 15 items), clearly there needs to be a "trade-off" or balance between what is both realistic and economical, depending on:

- The business strategy of the organisation
- Market forces (i.e., opportunities for employment elsewhere)
- The value and knowledge that various levels or groups of employees contribute to the business/organisation's success (e.g., senior managers receive higher levels of investment in training and development

compared to general or front line workers – refer the skills' based workforce segmentation model in Chapter 3).

Refer to Chapter 5 for a further discussion on the development of EVPs.

Our experience with the delivery of the "deal"

In our experience, organisations typically over deliver on job challenge and under deliver on recognition, adequate training for the job, and the provision of adequate resources. The combination of higher than expected job challenge with lower than expected resources is obviously a symptom of trying to "do more with less", and when combined with lower recognition, can create an unhealthy cocktail.

7.17 TRUST

> Note: An employee may perceive different levels of trust at a local or workplace level with his/her employer (which would predominantly refer to his/her supervisor/manager), compared with the trust at a top management level. The psychological contract model and its application provides for this distinction.

What is trust?

Butler and Cantrell (1984) describe trust as having five dimensions:

- Integrity, honesty and truthfulness
- Competence
- Consistency, reliability, predictability and good judgment
- Loyalty
- Openness and willingness to share information.

How is it trust measured?

Some typical items (in an employee survey), which are used to measure trust include:

- *I am confident that management will stick to assurances given to me in the past.*
- *Management share important information with me.*
- *Management demonstrates good judgment.*

Why is trust important in the workplace?

Working together involves interdependence. People must depend on each other in various ways to accomplish their personal and organisational goals. Trust is necessary for this collaboration at work as it:

- Reduces the transactional costs associated with interpersonal interactions
- Permits organisational flexibility and supports transition (e.g., change and reconfiguration which is paramount in the current business climate given downsizing and other changes that are occurring)
- Reduces uncertainty
- Facilitates a willingness to suspend judgment.

Trust is the social equivalent to air and water! It is a crucial ingredient in the building of productive and sustainable employer/employee relations. Furthermore the trend towards more participative management styles and implementation of work teams, coupled with the rapidly changing business environment, requires greater levels of trust than ever before. The workplace of the future will rely even more so on trust, with work discretion, autonomy, rapid decision making in response to changing demands, and flexible working arrangements (including working from home), becoming more pronounced.

How is trust developed?

Individuals learn about others' intentions through observation of behaviours, and interpretation of perceived motives and intentions. They make judgments about trustworthiness and act upon these judgments. Trust is developed over time, based on experiences in the organisation, and is sustained through:

- Having reciprocal obligations, promises and commitments being continually met

- The confidence that one party will not try to deceive the other party.

Communication is critical

Communication is fundamental to building and sustaining trust. Few things say you're not important more loudly than withholding information that employees want, or need to know. Keeping employees "out of the loop" creates disconnection, alienation and disengagement. In the absence of information, employees fill the void with rumour born of anxiety, and distrust goes up. Like the psychological contract, communication is two-way. An effective two-way communication dialogue between employer and their employees is also a necessary means of giving expression to employees' "voice" – part of the "new deal".

Trust and leadership

Building and maintaining trust is also a key to effective leadership. Employees' perceptions of top management's attitudes and behaviours shape the culture of the organisation. Although good leaders do come in all shapes and sizes, they do have one thing in common – trust. No one wants to work for an organisation where leaders are saying one thing and doing another, and where the stated values are not being lived out (i.e., where the rhetoric isn't matched by the substance and management doesn't "walk the talk"). Employees want to know whether they have hitched their wagon to leaders who have the right vision, strategy, personal character and competence to lead the organisation to where it needs to go.

Trust and psychological contract violation

Trust takes time to build but it can be destroyed over night, either inadvertently or through a deliberate act. Psychological contract violation reflects a single event, or a particular episode within the employment relationship, which impacts adversely on employees. Often inadvertent psychological contract violations occur because of a failure to communicate effectively. However a failure of the employer to deliver on the "deal" may not constitute psychological contract violation as such. This failure wouldn't necessarily reflect a single event, and may well be unintentional, or alternatively may be a consequence of the "deal" having changed through circumstances beyond the control of the organisation.

If trust has been lost, it follows that the first priority is to restore it. Otherwise the consequences are:

- Higher voluntary turnover
- Sub-optimal outcomes from investments in change initiatives or other people management initiatives.

Too many organisations look for the "quick fix", or embrace the latest management fad, without first establishing a climate of trust.

Relevant research findings: Trust and psychological contract violation

Downsizing, if executed poorly, is consistent with the notion of a psychological contract breach, resulting in a lowering of:

- Organisational commitment (Knudsen, Johnson, Martin & Roman, 2003)
- Job satisfaction (Armstrong-Stassen, 2002)
- Trust (Armstrong-Stassen, 2002).

Therefore it is not surprising, given the above findings that a positive relationship exists between downsizing and voluntary turnover (Batt, 2002; Trevor & Nyberg, 2008).

Other research findings have established a link between distressed or violated psychological contracts, and a lowering of employees' commitment, job satisfaction and higher turnover (Guzzo, Noonan & Elron, 1994; Robinson & Morrison, 1995; Robinson & Rousseau, 1994; Schalk, Freeze & Van den Bosch, 1995).

Overall, a loss of trust, particularly through psychological contract violation, has been found to lead to a number of adverse consequences, including:

- Higher turnover (Guzzo, Noonan & Elron, 1994; Robinson & Rousseau, 1994; Schalk, Freeze & Van den Bosch, 1995)
- Lower job satisfaction (Robinson & Rousseau, 1994)
- Lower commitment to the organisation (Guzzo, Noonan & Elron, 1994; Schalk, Freeze & Van den Bosch, 1995).

Our findings

Higher workplace and top management trust predicts higher levels of affective commitment and job satisfaction (and similarly, the converse applies), with a consequent lower risk of turnover.

7.18 FAIRNESS

What is fairness?

There are two elements of fairness in the workplace: procedural and distributive fairness or justice.

Distributive fairness or equity focuses on the nature and level of what individuals and organisations exchange. Distributive justice reflects the outcomes of fairness, and it includes aspects of equity, equality and need.

Procedural fairness or equity focuses on the procedures that are used to decide how various organisational benefits are distributed (i.e., the outcomes). Procedural justice reflects the procedures that resulted in the outcomes. It includes aspects of accuracy, voice and consistency. People want to know that their interests will be taken into account when important decisions are made, and that they are consulted about change. They are more likely to accept the results of decisions, even if they are not entirely satisfied with the outcome (e.g., promotion, pay, etc.), provided procedural fairness has been adhered to.

How is it fairness measured?

Some typical items (in an employee survey), which are used to measure fairness include:

- *My employer has adopted a reasonable approach in discussions/ negotiations with me.*
- *My employer deals with my co-workers on an equal basis.*
- *I am forced to carry an unfair work load.*

Why is fairness important?

Perceived equity or inequity of exchange relationships has been shown by researchers to be critical to many areas of performance, including counter-productive work behaviours, and general levels of organisational citizenship. The rationale for this lies in equity theory, which dictates that individuals strive for a balance between inputs and outcomes. If they feel that outcomes provided by the organisation are inconsistent with the efforts they have put in at work, then they are likely to redress this balance through some regulatory mechanism (e.g., going slow, increased absenteeism). Furthermore where coercion has been used in the formation of psychological contracts, reflecting a lack of fairness, then adverse impacts on employees' commitment are likely to result.

If the principles of procedural and distributive justice are seen to be reasonably met in a downgraded psychological contract (e.g., as a consequence of the impact of the GFC), degradation of the psychological contract *per se* may not necessarily result in negative outcomes.

Fairness in the workplace: traditional notions under challenge

The widespread use of contractors, consultants and temps, each with different pay rates, sets up a group of invidious comparisons. The wage structure of the firm may have little apparent order. It may reflect more the contingent nature of the employment relationship, with clear incentives specifying what outcomes will be rewarded. Traditional notions of internal equity, including greater pay linked to seniority, or to more complex jobs, or to other criteria associated with job evaluation systems, are being challenged in the contemporary workplace. Increasingly market forces (i.e., supply and demand for skills), are becoming more influential in determining salary levels as referred to in Chapter 3. Markets are disconnected from issues of fairness – they are concerned with efficiency.

Fairness and the psychological contract type

If the psychological contract is primarily transactional, then the parties' concerns will probably be centred around whether the outcomes represent a fair exchange. The focus will therefore be concentrated on distributive equity. If on the other hand, the psychological contract is primarily relational, then procedural equity is more likely to be of concern. The parties will pay attention to the fairness of the process, and less to the outcomes.

Relevant research findings

Perceptions of equity have been shown in a number of studies:

- To influence employees' intent to stay (or leave) (Berg, 1991)
- With respect to pay, to influence job satisfaction and organisational commitment, with perceived pay inequity being related to dysfunctional behavior (Makin, Cooper & Cox, 1996)
- To lead to positive organisational attitudes and behaviours, including increased job satisfaction, organisational commitment and organisational citizenship behaviours (Colquitt, Conlon, Wesson, Porter, & Ng, 2001)

- With respect to procedural justice, to have a strong record of predicting favourable employee attitudes towards employers (Cohen-Charash & Spector, 2001; Colquitt, Conlon, Wesson, Porter & Ng, 2001).

Our findings

Higher levels of fairness predict higher levels of affective commitment and job satisfaction (and similarly, the converse applies), with a consequent lower risk of turnover.

7.19 AFFECTIVE COMMITMENT

What is affective commitment?

Affective commitment signals an emotional, non-instrumental attachment to the organisation. It includes employees':

- Loyalty to the organisation
- Regard for the organisation and concern for its future
- Personal investment in the organisation
- Pride in telling others who one works for
- Identification with the organisation, including an acceptance of its goals and values.

This form or conceptualisation of commitment corresponds more with the notion of a relational psychological contract.

How is affective commitment measured?

Some typical items (in an employee survey), which are used to measure affective commitment include:

- *My values match the values of this organisation.*
- *I am proud to tell others about this organisation.*
- *I have a high personal investment in this organisation.*

Why is affective commitment important?

People rarely choose someone to marry purely on the basis of logic. The decision is also partly emotionally based. While prospective employees look carefully at all the logical reasons why they should work for one employer versus another, there is a certain emotional component in their decision. It is contended that there's a certain "chemistry" that acts as a catalyst to influence an individual's decision to accept an employment opportunity, and then to subsequently remain with that particular organisation. The stronger the emotional bonds, the greater the likelihood of the employee really engaging (i.e., performing better) and remaining with the employer for a longer period of time.

A sense of belonging is also important in fulfilling a basic human need. In the early days this was a matter of life and death. Being cast out of a community meant that an individual had to fend for themselves in a dangerous world, and the chances of doing that without community support was slim. Even though most of us live in modern societies, and do not live in a world where our lives are constantly under threat, we still need the support of our communities to survive and prosper. Despite the move towards individuation, the drive to belong continues to play an important part in our lives.

From another perspective, the personal satisfaction of individuals is dependent, to a large extent, upon the degree to which their values find expression in everyday life. Value incompatibility or conflict within or between individuals or groups of individuals (i.e., organisations), is at the root of many personal and interpersonal problems. People will work hard if they believe in the mission of the company, and can identify with its values, aims and activities. They will work even harder if they believe that achieving these values does something for them as well. To be successful, organisations need to integrate as far as possible, the needs and values of the organisation, with those of the individual, so both parties can co-exist in the most productive way. However corporate missions and values have to be motivating, believable and consistently supported for them to be binding. Unsubstantiated value statements about corporate integrity are likely to breed cynicism and disillusionment.

Commitment and commitment

Working for an organisation implies one level of commitment. Belonging to an organisation implies a much deeper level of commitment. It is possible to be structurally committed purely through financial considerations. An emotionally unconnected individual is more likely to be remote and aloof, more likely to pursue their own interests regardless of what the organisation needs or wants, and may be more confrontational or defensive. Notwithstanding, it is also important for both parties that people don't submerge their identity to the organisation, and lose their objectivity and independence. Blind loyalty is not in anybody's interests.

Relevant research findings

Studies show that factors instrumental in predicting higher levels of affective commitment include:

- Two-way communication, decentralisation, and direct participation in decision making
- More discretion, control and other resources for the work
- Confirmed expectations, job challenge and role clarity (Mowday, Porter & Steers, 1982)
- Internal employee development initiatives including promotion from within, clear promotion paths and opportunities for advancement (Shankar & Weitz, 1996).

All of the above factors are incorporated in the design of the WRDI® survey tool.

Higher levels of affective commitment are associated with:

- Lower turnover (see section later on intention to stay)
- Organisational citizenship behavior (O'Reilly & Chatman, 1986)
- Higher levels of performance (Meyer, Paunonen, Gellatly, Goffin & Jackson, 1989).

Our findings

Higher levels of affective commitment strongly predict higher levels of intention to stay, and hence a lower risk of turnover. To a lesser extent, higher levels of affective commitment also predict higher levels of job commitment/discretionary effort. Higher levels of affective commitment also predict higher performance ratings.

7.20 JOB SATISFACTION

What is job satisfaction?

Job satisfaction is an umbrella construct that encompasses both the negative and positive feelings that an individual has about their job or work. It includes employees':

- Fulfillment with their work
- Satisfaction with their work
- Feeling of doing something worthwhile.

How is it job satisfaction measured?

Some typical items (in an employee survey), which are used to measure job satisfaction include:

- *I am satisfied in my job.*
- *I am fulfilled in my job.*

Why is job satisfaction important?

Job satisfaction is frequently used in research as a measure providing some indication of the degree of contentment an individual might feel, or the extent to which their needs and interests are met with their job. As such, it is a significant indicator of the quality of an individual's work life. Job satisfaction is also strongly linked to retention and to a lesser extent to performance.

The job satisfaction and performance relationship

As mentioned earlier in Chapter 6, the relationship between job satisfaction and performance is a somewhat contentious one. In their review of the relationship between job satisfaction and performance, Judge, Thoresen,

Bono & Patton (2001) estimated the association (correlation) to be roughly +.30 as previously stated in Chapter 6. They also reported:

- Considerable differences across occupations with the job satisfaction - performance correlation being more robust in high-complexity jobs
- Measures of job satisfaction display higher correlations than facet measures of job satisfaction.

Despite the variability in the job satisfaction–performance relationship, many of the estimates are certainly large enough to have sizable financial consequences for organisations (Cascio, 1991).

Other relevant research findings

Studies show that higher levels of job satisfaction are also associated with:

- Lower turnover (see later section on intention to stay)
- Lower workplace stress
- Higher levels of pay, good supervisors and interesting work (Makin, Cooper & Cox, 1996)
- Lower levels of absenteeism, although this link is rather weak (Makin, Cooper & Cox, 1996)
- Higher levels of customer satisfaction (Dahlgaard, Kristensen & Kanji, 1998).

Our findings

Job satisfaction strongly predicts intention to stay, and hence a lower risk of turnover. To a lesser extent, higher levels of job satisfaction also predict higher levels of job commitment/ discretionary effort. Higher levels of job satisfaction also predict higher performance ratings.

7.21 JOB COMMITMENT/DISCRETIONARY EFFORT

What is job commitment/discretionary effort?

Job commitment/discretionary effort relates to the extent to which employees invest themselves in their job, and the idea of continuity of action, even in the face of difficulties. It includes their willingness to:

- Expend effort
- Accept responsibility beyond the basic requirements of the job
- Perform to the best of their ability
- Make sacrifices
- Persevere in the face of fluctuating circumstances and feelings.

How is job commitment/discretionary effort measured?

Some typical items (in an employee survey), which are used to measure job commitment/discretionary effort, include:

- *When the situation requires, I am willing to put in extra hours to meet deadlines.*
- *I make a special effort to do a good job.*
- *I persist with tasks in the face of difficulties.*

Why is job commitment/discretionary effort important?

Commitment behaviours should have a quality of sacrifice, sharing and presence aspect to them. Commitment behaviour should exceed the basic requirements of the job and should not necessarily be specifically controlled or rewarded. As such, this preparedness to "go above and beyond the call" should be reflected in enhanced performance. Malcolm Gladwell (2008) in his recent book entitled "Outliers" identifies hard work as one of the key factors critical to an individual's success.

Job commitment/discretionary effort and the psychological contract

Whilst the psychological contract may be articulated in various ways, job commitment/discretionary effort may signal a more instrumental attachment to the organisation. It may be the case that employees are able to invest themselves in their jobs, possibly for the prime reason of remaining employed and drawing an income, but may consider it pointless investing in an organisation that is not fulfilling its obligations (i.e., low affective commitment). Alternatively, they may love their job and the organisation and have few qualms about making sacrifices in their life for the sake of the job. It may also be the case that the demands of the job and the availability of resources are such that individuals have little choice but to devote much of their energies towards doing or executing the job.

Relevant research findings

There is precious little available in the empirical literature on discretionary effort with studies that demonstrate the linkage between discretionary effort and higher performance. The lack of studies should not be taken as an indication that such a linkage doesn't exist, but rather a preoccupation up until now with investigating other forms of commitment – a seemingly glaring omission.

Our findings

Higher levels of job commitment/discretionary effort predict higher performance ratings.

7.22 INTENTION TO STAY

What is intention to stay?

Intention to stay refers to whether an individual intends to remain with the organisation in the medium term (i.e., the next 2 to 3 years). Intention to stay/leave includes employees':

- Willingness to change jobs elsewhere
- Extent of their thinking about leaving the organisation
- Possibility of their leaving the organisation relatively soon
- Extent to which they may be seeking other job prospects.

A higher intention to stay means that employees are less likely to leave the organisation. High levels of intention to stay may reflect a desire to stay, or a perceived lack of choice of alternative employment options. Low levels of intention to stay may mean:

- Some disenchantment with the organisation or the job
- A desire to maintain mobility and enhance employability with either wider or narrower experience
- A desire to change either career or job to something more suitable
- Other personal reasons for leaving (e.g., family, health).

Refer Chapter 6 for a discussion of the 3 P's as to why people leave organisations – "Push", "Pull" or "Personal".

How is intention to stay measured?

Some typical items (in an employee survey), which are used to measure intention to stay include:

- *I often think about leaving this organisation (N).*
- *I intend to leave this organisation in the next 6 months (N).*
- *I regularly seek other job prospects (N).*

> Note: (N) means that the item is negatively worded so it is then reversed scored when calculating and reporting the survey findings.

Why is intention to stay important?

Intention to stay is the strongest predictor or indicator of retention/turnover.

Relevant research findings: Affective commitment, job satisfaction, turnover intent and turnover

The variables of affective commitment, intent to stay and job satisfaction, are found frequently in the commitment and turnover literature. Job satisfaction is also a well known correlate of affective commitment (i.e., they are closely related as confirmed in Chapter 6), which in practical terms means that on average, employees with higher levels of job satisfaction are also likely to indicate higher levels of affective commitment.

Meta-analysis studies by Irvine and Evans (1995) has confirmed a substantial relationship between behavioural intentions (to leave) and turnover (r = .65). Other meta-analysis research has confirmed a substantial relationship between intentions and turnover (Steel & Ovalle, 1984). Tett and Meyer's (1993) meta-analytical study reported high correlations between:

- Affective commitment and turnover intent of -.52 (negative relationship)
- Job satisfaction and turnover intent of -.53 (negative relationship), although this relationship is influenced by the availability of other work (i.e., as mentioned earlier, people don't always act on intentions and in circumstances of low unemployment, turnover rises as previously indicated).

> Note: A correlation or r of < 0.4 is considered to be low, an r > 0.4 to < 0.5 is considered to be medium and an r > 0.5 is considered to be high.

Our findings

Higher levels of intention to stay predict retention. As indicated earlier, healthier psychological contracts (i.e., delivery of the "deal" and higher levels of trust and fairness), predict higher levels of affective commitment and job satisfaction. This is how the psychological contract model provides a basis for positively impacting on affective commitment and job satisfaction.

7.23 BRINGING IT ALL TOGETHER: THE WORKPLACE RELATIONSHIP DEVELOPMENT INDICATOR (WRDI®)

Introduction

The WRDI® – an acronym for Workplace Relationship Development Indicator – is a diagnostic engagement and retention survey which has been broadly based on Guest's (1998) model of the psychological contract (refer to the model in the coloured pages of the Introduction Chapter). It has been developed to meet the emerging employment relationship challenges, and the perceived need to align organisations with their employees.

The WRDI® provides a basis for structuring, measuring, diagnosing and aligning various "deals" and relationships with various workforce segments and demographic groups within an organisation. WRDI® measures include:

- Employees' expectations (including both the tangibles and intangibles) or the EVP or the "deal"
- Key employment relationship factors, including the delivery of the "deal", trust in management and fairness

- Key predictors of performance and retention (i.e., the four "holy grail" workforce measures of affective commitment, job satisfaction, job commitment/discretionary effort and intention to stay).

The WRDI® has both aggregate and individual applications over the employment life cycle.

A general explanation of the WRDI® profiles and reporting outputs

there are three WRDI® graphical profiles produced, linked to the WRDI® model as set out in the diagram below.

WRDI® Model and Profiles

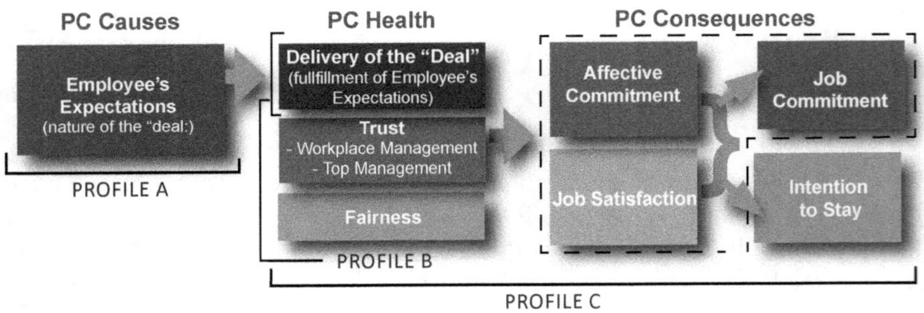

Profile A: Extent of Employees' Expectations (refer sample profile in the coloured pages in this chapter)

- The strength of employees' expectations across the 16 items comprising the psychological contract in the four categories of (1) rewards/ recognition, (2) safety/security, (3) career development, and (4) social/ support

> Note: Short term and long term job security are split into separate items in Profiles A and B.

Profile B: Weighted Fulfillment of Employees' Expectations (refer sample profile in the coloured pages in this chapter)

- The degree of fulfillment of employees' expectations or delivery of the "deal" across the same 16 items and four categories, both over and under fulfillment

Profile C: Psychological Contract – Health and Consequences (refer sample profile in the coloured pages in this chapter)

- The "health" of psychological contracts (i.e., degree of fulfillment of employees' expectations or deliver of the overall "deal", and key relationship factors of trust and fairness)
- The consequences of those psychological contracts (i.e., employees' levels of affective commitment, job satisfaction, job commitment/ discretionary effort, and intention to stay with the organisation).

Other WRDI® reporting outputs: retention risk

Apart from the above profiles, WRDI® reporting outputs include a quantification of retention risk both in terms of the numbers of high risk leavers, as well as a calculation concerning the cost implications for the organisation if nothing is done to address this risk (refer sample reporting output in the coloured pages in this chapter).

> Note: This calculation is based on a patented methodology which takes into account the number of high risk leavers, the relationship between those who say they are intending to leave and those who actually do leave, the percentage of turnover typically under the control of the organisation, the salary of the job in question and the turnover salary multiple of the job depending upon which skills quadrant that it resides in.

The diagnostic capability of the WRDI®

We referred earlier to the psychological contract health factors predicting psychological contract consequences. Accordingly we have presented the correlations below. Please note that we have undertaken a more sophisticated statistical analysis concerning the relationships between these variables. However to avoid complexity, the correlations provide an indication of the strength of these relationships in the simplest form.

> Note: A correlation or r of < 0.4 is considered to be low, an $r > 0.4$ to < 0.5 is considered to be medium, and an $r > 0.5$ is considered to be high.

Psychological Contract Health Factors and Affective Commitment Correlations

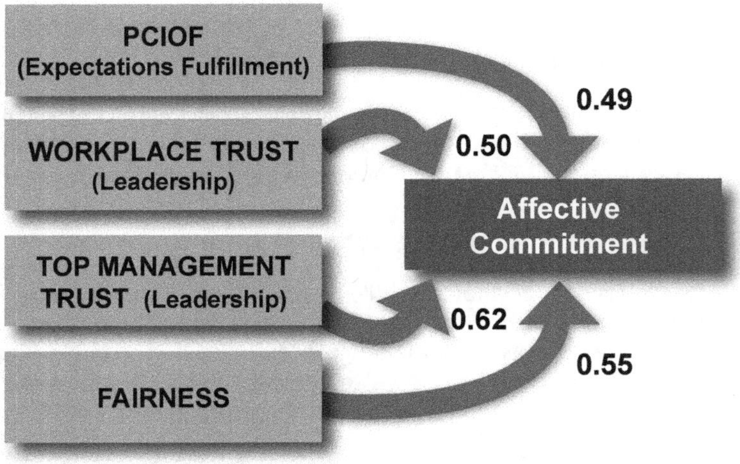

Psychological Contract Health Factors and Job Satisfaction Correlations

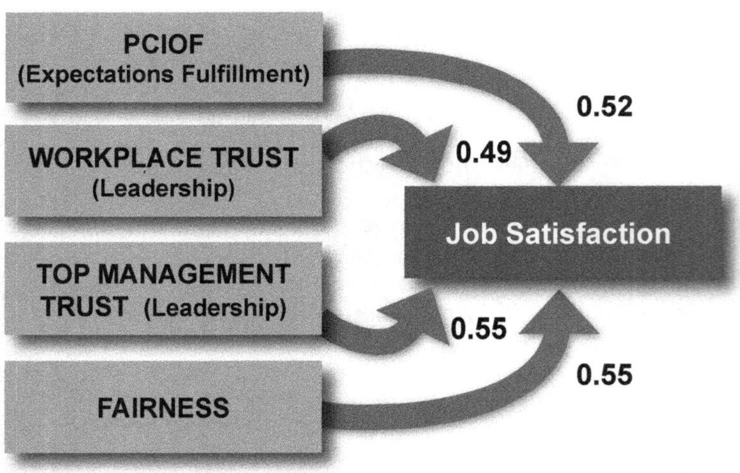

Previously in Chapter 6, we had also presented the relationship between the four "holy grail" workforce measures, but for ease of reference, we have presented these correlations again below.

> Note. PCIOF is defined in the WRDI® Profile C in the coloured pages of this chapter.

Affective Commitment, Job Satisfaction and Job Commitment/ Discretionary Effort Correlations

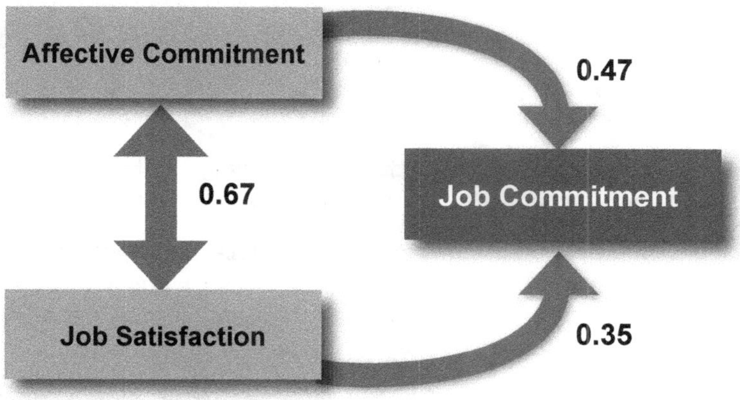

Affective Commitment, Job Satisfaction and Intention to Stay Correlations

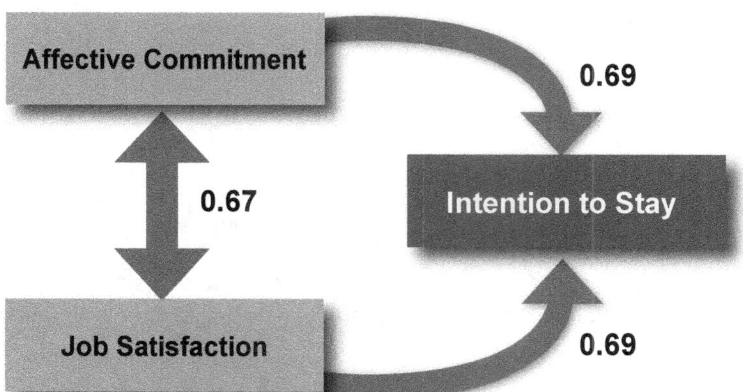

Key questions about your workforce that WRDI® reporting is able to answer

wRDI® reporting is able to answer key questions (see below) for those executives, managers and professionals who are seeking deeper workforce insights into managing their workforce and associated risks.

Acquisition of human capital - attraction:

- Whether your organisation is delivering on the EVP/"deal" (both the tangibles and intangibles)

- The level of new employees' fit to both the organisation (i.e., affective commitment) and to their jobs (i.e., job satisfaction), thus validating recruitment and selection processes
- The data to substantiate Employer of Choice (EOC) claims.

Utilising and engaging human capital - engagement and retention risk (including talent):

- the quantification of employee/talent flight risk (i.e., number of high performers/high potentials at high risk of leaving your organisation)
- The "teasing out" or differentiation of local workplace factors from wider organisational factors, and from selection and recruitment deficits, any of which may be contributing to disengagement, dissatisfaction and retention risk
- The engagement and retention "hot spots" in your organisation (e.g., by demographic group, business unit, job level, length of time in the organisation, etc.)
- "Drilling down" to understand and address individual engagement and retention issues (particularly for key talent and Criticals)
- Retention of the "right" people (i.e., those who indicate higher levels of commitment, satisfaction and intention to stay), as opposed to a workforce that is disengaged, dissatisfied, de-motivated but unlikely to leave
- Numbers of people that are either poor fit to the organisation, or poor fit to the job (i.e., "square pegs in round holes")
- What strategies and targeted interventions should be applied to comprehensively address employee disengagement, dissatisfaction and retention risk.

Refer to an example of this reporting output in the coloured pages of this chapter and also Chapter 9.

Retaining human capital - exit:

- Determining the real reasons why people have left your organisation (i.e., whether due to "Push", "Pull" or "Personal" reasons), including the associated costs

The nine unique features of the WRDI®

The WRDI® incorporates nine unique features:

- Measures and diagnoses employer/employee relationships
- Measures the EVP/"deal", and its delivery
- Quantifies retention risk in terms of numbers of high risk leavers and what this risk represents in $ terms
- Unpacks engagement from retention and differentiates turnover from retention (i.e. selective retention)
- Provides a fine grained assessment of the reasons for leaving according to the "3 P's": "Push", "Pull" or "Personal" reasons
- Captures the dynamic process of leaving
- Measures and diagnoses person–organisational "fit" and person–job "fit"
- Drills down to individual engagement, retention and career issues (particularly for key talent), over the employment life cycle from on-boarding, through to career management, through to exit interviews
- A whole of employment life cycle solution to engagement and retention, with the capacity to track data (with consistent measures) from on-boarding through to exit.

WRDI® endorsement: Australian test "guru", Ian Kendall (KWA Associates)

In our opinion, the WRDI® is not "just another employee opinion survey" cashing in on the growing demand for climate surveys. Having examined the 90 WRDI® survey items and questions, the conceptual framework in which these items and questions are embedded, the instrument's psychometric properties and the various output reports, we believe that the WRDI® offers organisations a truly strategic approach to meeting employment relationship challenges. These challenges are likely to become even more critical if predictions concerning the looming skills and talent shortage are accurate, and to that end, the WRDI® is well positioned to meet these challenges. Moreover, we believe that organisations that are serious about surveying Employee Engagement, Commitment and Retention would be well advised to consider using the WRDI® as one of their primary options.

What appears to be unique about the WRDI® is its ability to address the 'bottom-line' issue of an employee's intention to stay with the organisation within the broader context of their feelings about the psychological contract into which they believe they have entered. The focus on employee expectations and their fulfilment does not seem to be a feature of other surveys currently in the Australian marketplace.

The WRDI® is not simply a collection of items grouped together under arbitrary themes. Items in the WRDI® appear to have been chosen and crafted very carefully to reflect the key issues that provide Management with the kind of information that enables them to manage employee relationships more effectively. The item content has been guided by a conceptual model which incorporates the latest academic thinking about Employee Engagement and Retention. This model draws on British conceptions of the "psychological contract" (i.e., the 'deal' into which employees believe they have entered with their employer) and incorporates overseas advances in understanding the relationships among concepts such as Trust, Fairness, Commitment, Job Satisfaction and Intention to Stay as predictors of Retention/Turnover. This gives the WRDI® an underlying theoretical cohesiveness that is lacking in many other instruments. Moreover, it also links the WRDI® to a model that has been extensively validated by researchers in Britain and America, and which has been capable of demonstrating direct links with organisational performance and profitability.

The WRDI® is one of very few Employee Engagement Surveys in the Australian marketplace that can justifiably live up to its claim to be "new generation" and "leading edge". It is a thoughtfully constructed and rigorously researched tool that rests on a solid conceptual basis. It is a dynamically focused instrument that delivers measurable and predictable outcomes, pointing the way to sensible interventions. The WRDI® offers a sophisticated approach to surveying employee opinions, which yields the kind of diagnostic information that is essential to sound human resource planning, especially in regard to an organisation's ability to retain key talent.

Kendall Want Associates has little hesitation in endorsing the WRDI® as one of the most powerful and effective surveys of its kind in the Australian marketplace. Moreover, this Australian-produced survey boasts several features that are currently unique. Kendall Want Associates regards the WRDI Institute Pty Ltd as a leading specialist in the areas of Employee Engagement and Retention and would defer to their judgment on issues and concerns in these topical and specialised areas.

Ian Kendall, KWA Associates

Kendall Want Associates (KWA) are specialists in using and evaluating psychometric tests, inventories and questionnaires in organisational contexts. KWA endeavour to monitor, through Kendall's Australian Directory and its supplements, all assessment tools in the Australian marketplace in the interests of encouraging users to make informed decisions when choosing an appropriate instrument. As Management Psychologists, KWA has a particular interest in endorsing products that meet high professional standards both in their construction and practical utility.

Other features of the WRDI®

In addition to the above, there are a number of other features of this tool including:

- A sound empirical research underpinning with a strong emphasis on the measurement of key performance and retention related drivers
- Rigorous psychometric properties and high diagnostic capability, with targeted interventions having predictable outcomes
- Generic items that can apply to any organisation, and benchmarks that enable comparisons within and between organisations (i.e., standardised survey)
- Clinical reporting (e.g., by workforce segmentation, business unit, job level, etc.), with graphical profiles that can be easily interpreted
- Efficient on-line administration, with flexible coding procedures for various comparisons.

Applications of the WRDI®

The WRDI® covers all the engagement and retention bases plus more as set out in the diagram below.

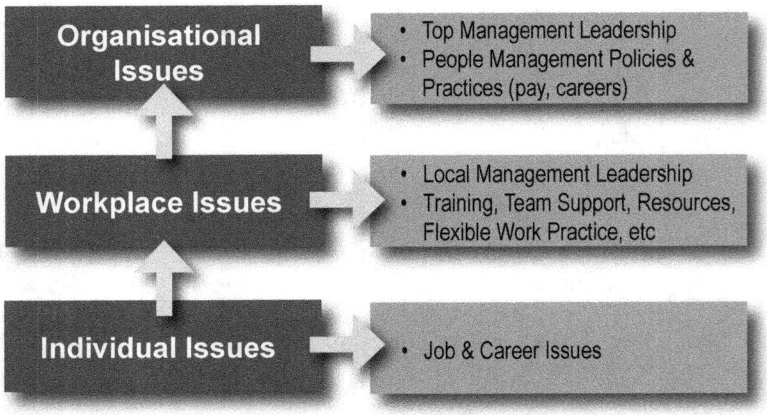

It has application in the following areas:

- A general employee opinion, engagement and retention survey
- Key talent retention risk assessment and succession planning
- Leadership effectiveness
- Mergers and acquisitions risk assessment
- Enterprise Bargaining Agreements
- Career development
- On-boarding
- Coaching
- Exit interviews
- Recruitment effectiveness.

The WRDI® has been used by a number of prominent Australian companies from "blue chips" through to SMEs, across a diversity of industries, and arguably represents the most advanced and comprehensive engagement and retention tool available. WRDI® clients include: AICD, APBC, AWB Ltd, Business Objects, Caroma Industries, CBA, CBHS Friendly Society, Chemtura Industries, Citibank, CS Energy, Cue Clothing Company, Entity Solutions, EDI Downer, Lawcover, Main Roads Department (Qld), NCIG, NEC, Olivier Recruitment, PageUp, Roche Mining, TMP Hudson, Qenos, Vero Insurance, Virax Holdings, Wavelength International, etc.

Examples of the various applications of the WRDI® have been provided throughout this book in various case studies.

7.24 SUMMARY: FOUR KEY STEPS TO ENHANCING EMPLOYEE ENGAGEMENT AND RETENTION – AN ORDERED APPROACH

1. **Maximise fit: Person- Job fit and person –organisational fit**

   - Unless the right foundation is in place, other engagement and retention initiatives likely to be waste of resources
   - It is harder to fix person-organisational fit
   - Person–job fit may be changed through either redeployment or job redesign
   - Selection and recruitment processes should not only focus on people who can do the job, but also on the need to maximise fit

   > Note. As mentioned in Chapter 6, not everyone is suited to co-existing. People and organisations have their values and characteristics, and if these are too diverse (i.e., between the individual and the organisation), no amount of interventions will work.

2. **Address organisational/systemic deficits**

   This may include issues concerning:

   - Top management trust/leadership
   - HR policies and practices (e.g., pay/financial incentives, flexible work practices, career development)

3. **Address local workplace deficits**

   This may include issues concerning:

   - Local management trust/leadership (e.g., recognition, support, supportive work environment)
   - Effective dialogue between managers and employees, including coaching, mentoring

4. **Address individual issues**

   This could include issues concerning:

   - Stress, personal and family matters

- Career development and training needs

The above approach foreshadowed is an ordered or cascading one. It follows that what is required is a tool (i.e., the WRDI®), that is able to measure and serves as a basis for diagnosing the extent to which any of the above deficits are present, in order to systematically and comprehensively address engagement and retention risk deficits. Improving engagement and reducing retention risk is not necessarily expensive. Indeed, many of the things that really matter to the workforce (i.e., the intangibles) don't cost anything at all.

Chapter 8

The Psychological Contract and Human Capital

KEY POINTS

Key questions and issues that we will address in this chapter:

- *How the psychological contract is applied over various stages of the employment life cycle and managing risk*
- *More specifically, how the psychological contract is applied to post recruitment assessment, on-boarding, employee engagement and retention, exit interviews, and talent management*
- *Why the psychological contract is such a pervasive concept in relation to other HR initiatives and aspects of organisational life*
- *How the psychological contract is relevant to individuals and their career.*

What are the consequences of failing to adequately address these questions/issues or ending up with the wrong answers?

- *Ignorance or misunderstanding of the importance and impact of the psychological contract on various organisational activities most probably will result in deficiencies in the management and measurement of human capital*
- *The case studies presented illustrate the application of the psychological contract to a wide range of organisational scenarios – without this information, organisations will be more in the dark concerning where their real people issues lie and therefore unable to take remedial action to address perceived deficits and manage risk*
- *The result of the above ignorance or omissions is lower performance and/or increased turnover, including the loss of key people.*

8. THE PSYCHOLOGICAL CONTRACT AND HUMAN CAPITAL

8.1 HOW IS THE PSYCHOLOGICAL CONTRACT RELEVANT TO THE BUILDING OF HUMAN CAPITAL?

As stated previously, the psychological contract is a pervasive and useful concept that has direct relevance to many aspects of building human capital. In Chapter 4, we looked at a model of the five ways of enhancing human capital. In this chapter, we will show how the psychological contract is relevant to four of these ways:

- Acquiring human capital
- Utilising/engaging and retaining human capital
- Developing human capital
- Mergers/acquisitions

as well as many other associated aspects of organisational development and HR.

8.2 ACQUISITION OF HUMAN CAPITAL AND THE PSYCHOLOGICAL CONTRACT

Recruitment and selection

We have explained how different EVPs or "deals" are related to different types of psychological contracts in Chapter 7. We have also explained how recruitment strategies also vary for different psychological contract types in Chapter 3, including:

- Investment in recruitment
- The intensity of assessment processes
- Whether recruitment may be outsourced or undertaken in-house
- The importance of person-organisational fit and person-job fit.

In the case of the latter, the challenge for organisatons is, in the first instance, to optimise person-job fit and person-organisational fit through recruitment and selection methodologies. If there are initial deficits in fit through flawed recruitment and selection decisions (i.e., a square peg in a round hole), no amount of subsequent interventions are likely to work to improve fit. It's like a couple in a relationship who are unsuited to each other. No amount of counselling is likely to be effective in drawing the two parties together if they are not psychologically compatible in terms of personality, interests, values, etc.

It is therefore important to be able to measure fit for the purposes of validating selection and recruitment processes, and also to be able to measure and diagnose the reasons for poor fit. For example, are the reasons for poor fit due to:

- Flawed selection and recruitment processes?
- Dysfunctional wider organisational factors?
- Dysfunctional local workplace factors?
- Individual factors?

The psychological contract provides a basis for answering these questions. Coupled with its linkage to the EVP, person-job and person-organisational fit and retention risk, the psychological contract is a fundamental concept underpinning the recruitment and selection process.

Post recruitment assessment: New recruits are the highest "at risk" group

Couples are most likely to divorce within the first few years of marriage. Similarly, new recruits are the highest "at risk" group in terms of turnover. Their turnover in their first 12 months of employment is typically around 25% higher than for longer tenure employees. Research by Chandler McLeod (2007) concluded that around half of all new recruits make a decision during the initial three months of employment as to whether they will stay or go, even though they may not go immediately. We have discussed in Chapter 7 the formation of the psychological contract and identified the initial few months of employment as a critical period. Managing new recruits during this period is vitally important to engagement and retention. It is during this time where the possible miss-match of employer/employee expectations, and other issues of adaptation and concern, including the identification of contentious issues (for either party), are likely to emerge. Typically equipment suppliers conduct after sales services as a precautionary check that all is well. If anything, there is a greater potential for things to go wrong with people compared to equipment.

The cost of a wrong selection and recruitment decision

The direct and indirect costs of replacing new recruits who resign prematurely is a "no win" result for all concerned. A significant investment has been made in the acquisition of a new asset. For example, the direct acquisition costs of a professional or senior manager could lie anywhere between $15,000

-$50,000 or even higher, not to mention the indirect costs. The implications of a wrong decision for the three parties involved are as follows:

- For the recruiter, there are issues concerning minimum guarantee periods (and consequent replacement) and loss of reputation
- For the employer, there is the wasted time and effort (not to mention the associated costs), spent in inducting and training the new recruit, plus the additional work load on other employees until another replacement is found and trained
- For the new recruit, there is the potential damage to their reputation and career/job stability, and them having to start again in the job hunting process.

Jobs and work environments are unique, as are people. Selecting the "right" people for the "right" job is crucial to retention, particularly with the shrinking availability of skilled talent. So it makes good sense to validate this initial investment decision, and ensure that it is achieving the purpose intended.

Evaluating selection and recruitment decisions

However very few companies bother to assess the results of their recruitment decisions in a rigorous and quantitative manner. Despite the ramping up of selection and recruitment methodologies and systems, and investment in the same in more recent years, the area of evaluation is spectacularly lacking. Furthermore many firms pay "lip service" to the three month probationary review, largely because there is no objective basis upon which to conduct this review.

Surveying of new employees in this initial three to four month period provides the opportunity to:

- Determine whether the organisation is delivering on the "deal" or the promise
- Assess "fit" with both the job (i.e., measures of job satisfaction), and the organisation (i.e., affective commitment)
- Assess retention risk or intention to stay
- Assess adaptation issues and determine appropriate interventions.

For example, it may be the case that the individual indicates a higher level of affective commitment, but lower levels of job satisfaction. This would point towards either that:

- Their psychological contract is "unhealthy"

- They are in the wrong job (in which case there may be opportunities for redeployment to something more suitable in the future)
- Their job requires some redesign
- It may in retrospect be a wrong selection decision, in which case there needs to be some resolution and amicable parting of the ways.

> Note: The surveying of new recruits is best conducted through a third party. In the case of individuals (as opposed to aggregate survey data), the WRDI Institute has developed an approach to confidentiality and debriefing of the survey findings and report. This approach provides access to a nominated professional representative of the client (typically from HR who agrees to maintain confidentiality), without compromising the integrity of the survey responses and the data.

On-boarding

Given the substantial investment in recruiting new people referred to earlier (particularly key professionals, managers and executives), it is vital that this newly acquired asset be protected and developed. On-boarding is a process which signals to the employee that the company cares about them, and wants them to stay. It assists:

- In the development and adaptation of the new employee, with the process often extending up to the end of the first 12 months of employment
- The new employee to "hit the ground running", and otherwise compresses the initial start-up or break even period of employment (i.e., when the employee begins to become more productive).

On-boarding involves coaching of the new employee, typically by an external specialist, during the initial period of employment. It differs from orientation or induction (which typically occurs over a few days in the initial week or so of employment), in that it represents a full process of engagement and is considerably more comprehensive. Surveying of new employees and debriefing can underpin on-boarding by adding some objective rigour and focus to the process. Organisations spend lots of money wooing new recruits, but as soon as they start, they treat them like strangers. In the new human capital perspective, recruiting is viewed as only half the task of hiring. Orientation and on-boarding is the other half and often ignored element.

Case Study: Global Professional Services Company

I was recently approached by a competitor who was establishing a new leadership development consultancy arm of their business. The newly appointed manager of this consulting arm (Stephen) was interested in a tool that was able to drill down to individuals, thus providing more "fine grained" information for their clients concerning the retention risk of critical employees.

After discussions and the signing a confidentiality agreement, we agreed that Stephen would complete the WRDI® survey and I would then debrief him on his report. This would enable him to become familiar with the tool and the survey administration, reporting and feedback process. Stephen had only been in this new role for a few months, having been recruited from outside of the company.

The survey findings indicated that Stephen was at very high risk of leaving. The explanation for this was as follows:

- He had been oversold the role and he was also probably a little naive, as he was effectively working as a "one man band" (he indicated a lack of recognition, autonomy and resources in terms of delivery of the "deal")
- He also indicated low levels of fairness in terms of the demands of the job and reward for his effort
- He was originally from the U.K. but working for a US based company, and partly because of the above two points (i.e., psychological contract health factors) and the cultural differences, this had contributed to low levels of top management trust and affective commitment (i.e., poor person-organisational fit).

Stephen was a little surprised that the report was so revealing. We then agreed that we would discuss the potential use of the survey tool as part of his consultancy arm in another month as he was off travelling and running courses. When we did link up again a month or so later, Stephen informed me that he had already resigned. This was no great surprise given that it had been a poor selection and recruitment decision, and that under the circumstances, it was probably best for both parties to part company. It was somewhat ironic that Stephen's employer provided services in the territory of employee engagement and retention, yet they didn't have their own act together when it came to managing their people.

Case Study: Business Development Manager, Recruitment Company

A recruitment company had recently appointed Stuart as their new Business Development Manager. They asked us to conduct a post recruitment assessment survey (i.e., the WRDI®) and report. Stuart had been in the role for approximately three months.

The report indicated Stuart was at high risk of leaving the organisation. The explanation for this was as follows:

- He indicated lower levels of workplace and top management trust (i.e., psychological contract health factors)
- This in turn was contributing to lower levels of affective commitment and job satisfaction (i.e., psychological contract consequences).

In the report debriefing process, it transpired that Stuart had been recently retrenched from a senior HR role in a large organisation: an experience from which he had been "burnt" and which he was still carrying the scars (figuratively speaking). As a consequence, he had become generally suspicious of management (which explains his lower levels of trust). This, coupled with the fact that Stuart had made a career move into a more commercial environment to which he was not necessarily suited, had contributed to his high risk leaving status.

After a period of reflection, Stuart was agreeable to meeting with senior management to discuss the above findings in general terms. It was decided that Stuart needed to take some time out and determine what he really wanted to do, and an amicable termination arrangement was reached.

8.3 UTILISATION/ENGAGEMENT AND RETENTION OF HUMAN CAPITAL AND THE PSYCHOLOGICAL CONTRACT: EMPLOYEE SURVEYS

Employee surveys (e.g., engagement, retention) including talent

As we will see in Chapter 9, organisations use employee surveys on a recurring basis as strategic tools for enhancing performance, and to understand and manage the impact of people and organisational systems on business outcomes. To that end, the measurement of the state or health and consequences of the psychological contract can be applied on a regular basis over the employment life cycle for various groups/segments of employees.

The findings can serve as a basis for:

- Giving people a "voice"
- Validating what the organisation is doing well
- Assessing trust/leadership at a local, as well as top management level
- Assessing readiness for change

- Assessing the impacts of change (e.g., restructuring, downsizing for the survivors)
- Determining organisational "hot spots"
- Monitoring the effectiveness of HR interventions, etc.

Case Study: Heavy Manufacturing Company and Industrial Relations Issues

We undertook an employee survey project with the WRDI® for a heavy manufacturing company that had recently experienced some industrial relations problems. The site was heavily unionized with the plant having been recently shut down for a period of three months with a major strike.

The survey findings indicated low levels of top management trust (i.e., psychological contract health deficit) and lower levels of affective commitment and job satisfaction, but above average levels of intention to stay (i.e., psychological contract consequences). In other words, employees (predominantly "blue collar"), were unlikely to leave despite the fact that they were not enamoured with management, the company and their jobs.

The explanation for these findings was that they were effectively "locked in", with dim prospects of them earning an equivalent competitive salary elsewhere in the local area. These findings were hardly a recipe for meeting the challenges of the dynamic workplace and maximising performance.

Management had started making a concerted effort to rebuild trust, but this was going to be a long hard road to recovery, given the past circumstances.

Case Study: Research and Development Company and Retention of Key People

We were approached to conduct a survey by a research and development company that was concerned about staff retention, including some key scientists who were world experts. The WRDI® survey findings indicated that around 40% of key staff was at risk of leaving. Top management trust was low for these key staff.

The company had been experiencing some difficult times in terms of capital raising, and there had been a number of meetings behind closed doors which senior staff had got wind of. However these staff had not been briefed on the position of the company. Furthermore, there were some issues between the CEO and his direct reports over his "hands on" management style (i.e., lack of delegation). The CEO had built the company from scratch and was having difficulty letting go of the reins.

The subsequent activities undertaken were:

- Facilitated feedback of the overall findings with senior staff, with the CEO present
- Individual survey reports generated and debriefs conducted of the key people
- A workshop designed to address issues of concern which had emerged for both parties.
- These issues included the survey findings, together with some concerns of the CEO about staff (specifically the difference between working for a large company versus a SME).

The outcome of the consultancy was that only one person ended up leaving over the ensuing 12 months.

Case Study: National Manufacturing and Sales Company and Local Workplace Issues between a Business Unit Manager and His Direct Reports

We undertook a WRDI® survey assignment for a national sales and manufacturing company, the findings of which indicated lower levels of trust between one of the Business Unit Managers and his direct reports. These survey findings also revealed perceptions (by the direct reports) of a lack of recognition and delegation by this Business Unit Manager.

In the first instance, these findings (which didn't come as a total shock), were discussed with the Business Unit Manager's State Manager. Individual reports were generated for the Business Unit Manager's direct reports and we then conducted debriefs with them. Part of these debrief sessions focused on coaching them as to how to best raise their issues of concern with the Business Unit Manager at an imminent job/ career one-on-one discussion.

At the same time, the Business Unit Manager was provided with training on how to facilitate job and career dialogue with his direct reports. Then both parties were brought together for one-on-one job/career dialogue sessions between the Business Unit Manager and his direct reports. A coaching program was also initiated for the Business Unit Manager with the aim of improving his people skills and management style.

The overall outcome was an improvement in the relationship between the relationship between the Business Unit Manager and his direct reports.

8.4 UTILISATION/ENGAGEMENT AND RETENTION OF HUMAN CAPITAL AND THE PSYCHOLOGICAL CONTRACT: EXIT INTERVIEWS

About exit interviews

Exit interviews provide further valuable information relevant to retention/turnover, and in particular, why people leave organisations (i.e., "Push", "Pull" or "Personal" reasons). They should form part of an organisation's overall retention strategy. Furthermore exit interview information keeps employers in touch with market trends in employment movements and competitor initiatives and practices. Knowing who the competition is, and what they are doing, constitutes key retention information, particularly in respect of "Pull" factors. Exit interviews also give employees the opportunity to vent, gain a sense of closure, and provide information that may help colleagues left behind.

Limitations of exit interviews

Notwithstanding, exit interviews are not a lead indicator and can be unreliable at times if not conducted appropriately. As indicated in Chapter 6, it's a case of "shutting the stable door after the horse has bolted". Also, there are concerns about the honesty or integrity of exit interviews in that some leavers may not want to "burn their bridges", or may be concerned about reference checks. Whilst exit interviews constitute a part of an organisation's retention strategy, they should not represent the lead strategic activity. Trying to solve a retention issue through exit interviews is like trying to drive looking through the rear vision mirror of your motor car!

How to conduct exit interviews

There are certain key guidelines which should underpin the exit interview process. These are as follows:

- They should be conducted through an outsourced provider
- Confidentiality of information should be protected, with only authorised information by the departing employee released back to the nominated person in the organisation
- They should be undertaken around the time of departure, preferably after written references, if any, have been provided.

> Note: As in the case of post recruitment assessment application of the psychological contract and associated surveying, the WRDI Institute has developed an approach to confidentiality and debriefing of the exit interview survey findings and report that provides access to a nominated employee of the client (typically from HR), without compromising the integrity of the survey responses and the data.

The timing of exit interviews

There is debate as to the most appropriate timing to conduct exit interviews, and whether some time should be allowed (e.g., three months), for the "dust to settle". With a delayed interview, there may be less emotionality and more objectivity with the findings. Whilst these reasons may be legitimate, there are other drawbacks with the delayed approach, which are as follows:

- The difficulty of tracking down the ex-employee and gaining their commitment to complete an exit interview, given that life has moved on for them
- If delays occur, then the possibility of re-engagement becomes more remote
- The loss of immediacy and potential for action, be it for example a counter offer, exploration of other possibilities within the organisation, or changes to working arrangements (e.g., part-time rather than full-time role), addressing issues of concern (e.g., harassment, personal issues), which may have wider implications across the organisation.

The diagnostic survey exit interview approach (see below) with administration through a third party, partly offsets concerns about data integrity. Therefore the benefits of having immediate access to information, and being able to act accordingly, go a long way towards overcoming the perceived disadvantages of conducting immediate exit interviews.

A diagnostic approach to exit interviews

Given that the HR metric of the moment is employee engagement, some companies are now starting to place a new emphasis on employee disengagement by reinventing the exit interview. A diagnostic survey approach through an outsourced provider to departing employees offers a superior approach to exit interviewing. Departing employees often offer superficial reasons for leaving that are a "smokescreen" to conceal the deeper reasons. A diagnostic survey approach helps to "flesh out" and classify the real reasons for leaving (i.e., "Push", "Pull" or "Personal"), with comparisons of key measures (e.g., job satisfaction, affective commitment), against benchmarked data.

Case Study: "Push" Reasons for Leaving

We were engaged by a medium size insurance firm to undertake a diagnostic exit interview using the WRDI® on Stan, the HR Manager. Whilst there had been some "chemistry" issues between the CEO and Stan, the CEO wanted to follow due process and determine whether there were any other contributing factors to Stan's resignation decision.

Stan completed the survey and was debriefed on his report findings. These findings indicated that:

- There were indeed some issues of trust between the Stan and the CEO (i.e., psychological contract health factor)
- This then reflected in Stan's lower levels of job satisfaction, notwithstanding that he liked working for the organisation (i.e., higher affective commitment) and was putting in the "hard yards" (i.e., higher discretionary effort) in the role (i.e., psychological contract consequences).

However Stan's situation with the organisation, *vis a vis* his relationship with the CEO, was no longer tenable, unlikely to be recoverable, and as such it was best that he leave under these circumstances. There were no other extenuating circumstances in terms of his reasons for leaving.

Case Study: "Personal" Reasons for Leaving

Victor was a valuable member of the management team and following a recent merger with another engineering company he resigned. The company wanted to determine the real reasons for Victor's departure, and engaged us accordingly.

Victor completed the WRDI® survey and was then debriefed on his WRDI® report findings. These findings indicated that whilst he was not enamoured with the consequences of some aspects of the merger, a personal (family) matter had suddenly arisen which had resulted in his resignation. Up until this personal issue arose, he had not been seriously considering leaving.

Case Study: "Pull" Reasons for Leaving

Andrew worked in an estimating role for a contracting company and had been there for over two years. He had resigned and we were engaged to conduct a diagnostic exit interview using the WRDI® survey.

Andrew completed the survey and was debriefed on his report findings. These findings indicated that he:

- Did not believe that he was being given sufficient recognition in his role and that he was also under resourced
- Was not being treated fairly in respect of his work load and reward for effort
- Was not overly enamoured with the organisation (i.e., lower affective commitment), although he liked the job (i.e., higher job satisfaction)
- Had not been seriously thinking of leaving, but was offered a similar job with better conditions with a company whom he admired.
- Thus, his reasons for leaving were primarily "Pull" related – he opted for the "greener grass" on the other side.

8.5 UTILISATION/ENGAGEMENT AND RETENTION OF HUMAN CAPITAL AND THE PSYCHOLOGICAL CONTRACT: TALENT MANAGEMENT

Talent management and succession planning

Talent management and succession planning have been elevated in many enterprises to the top tier of objectives - on a par with generating revenue and managing costs. As referred to earlier in Chapter 4, experienced, knowledgeable, high-performing and loyal employees are the lifeblood of any organisation. As we move into the knowledge economy, the need to secure and optimise talent becomes extremely crucial. Identifying talent, and then managing them through identifying and then developing various competencies, constitutes a key organisational survival strategy. Succession planning offers an approach to formalising the same.

Succession planning usually implies a broader process for examining a range of senior jobs in which executives relate the supply of senior people and their successors to the future needs of the business. Talent should be developed at multiple levels where the development of a good supply of future leaders from within is a key business issue. This supply will not emerge without a pro-active process of succession planning to ensure that their development takes place. In lean, high-performing organisations, every vacancy needs to be filled by someone who can "hit the ground running". Having the right people ready is crucial.

Furthermore succession planning is also about ensuring appropriate people are available in readiness for contingencies, unexpected events, organisational expansion, entering new markets and handling changes in technology. Succession planning is therefore a key factor in determining business success by ensuring an organisation has capable and trained managers to guide its growth. Ultimately succession planning helps corporations leverage the full value of their human capital.

Against this background, it is clear that a strong motivational argument exists for developing talent from within. Like farming, the quality seed material with growth and potential must be planted in a supportive environment, nurtured and developed. Throwing these seeds at barren ground and hoping some will sprout is hardly likely to produce a quality crop. A more scientific farming approach in which the organisation identifies the seed with the most potential, cultivates the ground, and nurtures and feeds the plants as they grow, is much more likely to bear fruit.

A "grow-your-own" strategy sends a positive message to the workforce and is generally less expensive than searching for the best external candidates. The emphasis is on balancing the career aspirations of individuals, with those of the organisation. Traditionally people would have gained experience by upward moves but nowadays this may not be possible, because organisations are less hierarchical with fewer management layers. A sideways move into a different job may be all that is available. Therefore status and money may not necessarily be such strong motivators.

Looking for external candidates takes time (an executive search can take up to six months or longer), leaving open positions and subsequent lost opportunities. Whilst a "grow-your-own" strategy is the preferred option, the importation of talent can provide new ideas and skills. They may have valuable experience or training not available inside the organisation. Also, imported talent may be unencumbered by traditions and past practices, so they may offer a fresh perspective, be more objective in looking at people and projects, and have a greater readiness to act.

The correct ratio of internal to external recruiting will depend upon the age and growth rate of the organisation, and the degree of volatility in the market. It may be the case that the:

- Need for experienced managers exceeds the capability to develop them internally
- Requirements of the organisation are such that the knowledge of new technology, markets and operating methodologies are not available internally.

In the case of a market downturn, and consequent lack of available positions for successors to be promoted into (i.e., "queing" of talent already developed but nowhere to go), then the investment in their internal training and development may not be recoverable, and they may leave for better opportunities. Hence whilst internal development of talent is the most cost effective option, it is nevertheless desirable to be cautious about over development.

Talent management encompasses resourcing strategy, aggregate analysis of supply and demand, a skills analysis, the job filling process and management development. Given the importance of talent management and succession planning, and the significant and disproportionate investment in the development of those individuals who are part of such a program, it makes sense to adopt a risk management approach, as one would do with any significant investment. Critical questions include:

- *Are these talented individuals likely to remain with the organisation, at least in the medium term?*
- *Are these talented individuals satisfied in their respective jobs?*
- *Do these talented individuals like working for the organisation?*

- *Are there any factors that may be adversely impacting upon answers to any of the above questions, either at a local workplace level, or a wider organisational level?*
- *If so, what interventions should be applied now to mitigate risk and protect the investment in their development?*

Case Study: Large Australian Conglomerate Firm Looking to Expand
A large Australian conglomerate firm was on an expansion path. This firm had recently recruited a number of professionals from outside of the main industries in which this company operated. This firm requested a retention risk assessment be undertaken to check that these relatively new professionals were there for the longer haul, and engaged us accordingly.

The WRDI® survey assessment indicated that some of these more recently recruited professionals (who were one level below the executive team and hence reporting to those executives), were at risk of leaving. The health of their psychological contracts indicated lower levels of top management trust, whilst the consequences of their psychological contract indicated moderate levels of affective commitment and job satisfaction.

As in all case studies, the survey data needs to be considered in the context in which the organisation operates. In this case, the company operated in a political environment with multiple stakeholders to satisfy. This at times resulted in what appeared to be some puzzling decisions from above (i.e., top management). Also partly because of the diversity of operations, a silo mentality had arisen with a lack of communication as to what was happening across the organisation. The combination of these two factors also contributed to trust issues between these professionals and top management.

Interventions included a workshop focused on trust building in the organisation, comprising a group of some executives and professionals. This in turn resulted in a series of initiatives to rebuild trust, together with improved communication from above.

8.6 UTILISATION/ENGAGEMENT AND RETENTION OF HUMAN CAPITAL AND THE PSYCHOLOGICAL CONTRACT: OTHER APPLICATIONS

Performance management and rewards systems

Managing the performance of human resources is a function of at least three systems:

- Goal setting
- Performance appraisal
- Reward systems.

These systems seek to align work behaviours with the business strategy, employee involvement and workplace technology. Goal setting specifies the kinds of performances and outcomes that are desired. Performance appraisals involve:

- Assessing performance data and the achievement of those outcomes
- Facilitating career development, providing information about strengths and development needs.

The feedback aspect of performance appraisals is particularly critical, as it brings both the organisation's and employees' expectations to the surface. Reward systems provide the reinforcers to ensure that outcomes are repeated.

Performance management systems should be effectively integrated with psychological contracts. For example, the emphasis on the performance appraisal system for various types of psychological contracts will be as follows:

- Transactional psychological contracts – results focused with the reward system more directly linked to those results
- Relational psychological contracts – results focused as well as a developmental focus.

Refer to Chapter 3 for a summary of HR policies and practices for the skills' based workforce segmentation model, which accommodates various psychological contract types.

Enterprise bargaining and EBAs

The concept of the psychological contract (which represents the essence of the employer/employee relationship), provides a framework for structuring and managing employer/employee relationships, be it in applications of:

- Industrial disputes
- Strengthening or changing workplace agreements
- Building more productive relations.

Some key questions about employer/employee relations for HR and IR professionals include:

- *What are the key elements of the employment relationship and how do you measure them?*
- *How do you know whether your organisation is meeting its workplace agreement obligations?*
- *How healthy are your workplace agreements?*

- *How do you measure the effectiveness of changes to your employment relationships?*
- *How do you assess the extent of industrial dispute issues and/or employees'/workers' dissatisfaction?*

> Note: A number of the items comprising the "deal" plus measures of trust and fairness incorporated in the WRDI® survey relate closely to typical workplace agreement obligations.

Changes to workplace agreements

Whether one is seeking to implement, change or strengthen a workplace agreement, the concept of the psychological contract should be central to the approach. Two types of change are applicable to the psychological contract - accommodation and transformation (Rousseau, 1995).

Accommodation is about honouring the spirit of the existing agreement. Accommodation occurs when changes are successfully subsumed under existing psychological contract arrangements. Good faith generally prevails and the core terms of the psychological contract remain relatively unaffected, with fewer changes. Participation in the change process can promote accommodation.

Transformation constitutes a more radical or fundamental change, which is built on new frameworks, and can be disruptive and irreversible. Transformation may occur as a result of a violation or breach of the psychological contract. The process of transformation determines whether the change generates into violation, or transforms the basis of the relationships.

The measurement and diagnosis of the state or health of the psychological contract can assist in determining which of the above two types of change might be appropriate in any given situation.

Case Study: Large Australian Heavy Manufacturing Company Following an Industrial Dispute

We were engaged to conduct a survey (WRDI®) for a large Australian heavy manufacturing company shortly after they had emerged from a serious industrial dispute and the renegotiation of a new Enterprise Bargaining Agreement. The findings indicated that at an operator and maintenance level, psychological contracts were somewhat unhealthy as evidenced by:

- Perceptions that the "deal" was not being delivered with a lack of recognition, concerns about job security, deficits in the provision of training, lack of management support and resources (i.e., asked to do more with less)
- Lower levels of trust in management, both at a local as well as top management level
- Only moderate levels of affective commitment, job satisfaction and intention to stay.

The changes that had been implemented had not yet been accepted and this company had some distance to go towards rebuilding trust and restoring healthy and productive relationships. To that end, the company embarked on a more consultative approach to both the unions and the workforce to improve communication and explain its future strategic direction.

Stress and well-being

Stress and its causes

Stress is the reaction that people have to excessive pressure or other types of demands placed on them. It arises when they worry that they cannot cope. Stress at work is influenced by a number of factors including:

- Support from supervisors
- Relationships with colleagues
- Status of the role
- Sense of identity with the organisation
- Work load or demands of the job, including the degree of control over those demands.

There is sometimes confusion between the terms "pressure" and "stress'. While it is healthy and essential that people experience challenges within their lives that cause levels of pressure, too much pressure can be harmful and destructive to health. Up to a certain point, an increase in pressure will improve performance and the quality of life. However if the pressure becomes excessive, it loses its beneficial effects and becomes harmful. This excessive pressure becomes stressful.

The impacts of stress

Stress reduces employee well-being and excessive or sustained work pressure can lead to stress. Occupational stress poses a risk to most businesses and compensation payments for stress-related injuries are rising. Recent research has found that:

- Stress is one of the most important reasons behind sickness at work
- 75% of executives say that stress adversely affects their health, happiness and home life, as well as their performance at work (CIPD, 2004)
- Stress may be experienced as a result of an exposure to a wide range of work demands and in turn, can contribute to an equally wide range of health outcomes (stress is a state, not an illness)
- Where employees are stressed because they have no say on how work is done, or need to do work that involves a fast pace which may involve the need to resolve conflicting priorities, or have lack of recognition, understanding and support from their managers, then there is a higher risk of the employee suffering from a psychiatric disorder.

Stress can manifest itself in absenteeism, reduced productivity and increased staff turnover. Excessive stress can lead to fatigue, impaired judgment and decision making, and the onset of both mental and physical health problems. Examples of long-term or chronic stress are the fear, frustration and anger that may be produced by an unhappy relationship with one's boss or with a difficult customer, or the unhappiness associated with an unsuitable job.

Relationships and identifying sources of stress

The concept of relationships (and hence the psychological contract), is therefore very relevant to stress in the workplace. The application of the dynamic model of the state of the psychological contract enables an identification of the underlying causes of stress. More specifically it enables the pinpointing of dysfunctional organisational factors (either at a local workplace or wider organisational level – refer abovementioned causes of stress) versus poor fit issues, or other individual related causes that may be unrelated to the organisation (e.g., personal reasons). For example, lower scores on trust and fairness, coupled with higher scores on job commitment/ discretionary effort and lower levels of affective commitment and job satisfaction, are most likely to indicate a stressed workforce.

Case Study: Large Australian Bank, Previous Employee now Working as a Consultant

I was in discussions with Jack concerning a turnover problem within customer service of the retail banking arm of a large Australian bank. Jack wanted to evaluate the WRDI® tool and its possible application to addressing this turnover problem, so he undertook the survey. I then debriefed him on his individual report.

Jack had previously been in a higher management role in the bank but was now working as a consultant part-time whilst he pursued other career interests (he was involved in a career transition). His WRDI® report indicated high levels of job commitment/discretionary effort, but low levels of affective commitment and job satisfaction. In other words, Jack was putting in the "hard yards", but was disenchanted with the organisation that he was once employed with, and dissatisfied in his new role as a consultant.

His psychological contract was unhealthy, as evidenced by his:

- Perceptions about the "deal" not being delivered (i.e., recognition, job challenge, autonomy, support)
- Low levels of trust, both at a local and top management level.

In short, Jack was not suited to the role of a consultant and he was having difficulties adjusting to a scenario where he once was in a higher status role compared to the current one. His relationships with management within the organisation were somewhat strained. Upon questioning, Jack indicated that he was stressed and I suggested that he seek some career counselling and assistance while in transition.

Note: Career transition can be a stressful time when one goes from a state of higher competence to one of lower competence and having to start again, and acquire new learnings. Often there is the loss of self-esteem in this transition process.

Employee Assistance Programs (EAPs)

Research has shown that the availability of support is a factor in turnover reduction. The successful use of EAPs has been linked with decreased turnover and absenteeism. Furthermore the tracking of counselling issues (e.g., management issues, conflicts at work, stress or burnout, etc.), provides an early warning system in respect of potential turnover issues. Burnout has been implicated as a factor in high turnover rates.

Absenteeism

Lateness represents the mildest form of withdrawal from the workplace, with turnover representing the most extreme from, and with absenteeism lying somewhere in the middle. Lower levels of affective commitment and job satisfaction are weakly related to higher levels of absenteeism.

8.7 DEVELOPMENT OF HUMAN CAPITAL AND THE PSYCHOLOGICAL CONTRACT: CAREERS

Heriot (1992) wrote "only those organisations that negotiate careers will survive into the next century". He linked careers and psychological contracts by defining an organisational career as "the sequence of renegotiations of the psychological contract, which the individual and the organisation conduct during his/her period of employment". Focusing on the psychological contract emphasises the importance of balancing both the individual and organisational concerns about careers.

Career development as a retention strategy

We have seen in Chapter 6 that career development, or the lack thereof, is a major reason why people leave organisation. Career development now forms an important part of organisational development in the contemporary workplace. Today's world of work requires that people be constantly growing and increasing their value to the organisation. The development of organisations through development of their employees is an intuitively appealing concept. As individuals are provided with the opportunities to develop their careers (consistent with the needs of the business), their levels of commitment to the organisation and job satisfaction will most likely be enhanced, leading to higher levels of workforce alignment, retention and performance.

Career development should not be seen as a stand-alone activity. Rather it should support the growth of individuals in ways needed by the organisation. It can constitute an agent of change for creating a development culture: develop the employee and you develop the organisation! Hence there are both organisational and individual benefits accruing from an integrated approach to career development.

While for some, career development may be viewed as a retention strategy which appears "counter intuitive" in that it may encourage some employees to leave, the upside for organisations is that they end up with a more independently minded and empowered workforce. The reality is that most people prefer to stay with their current organisations: better the devil you know!

The psychological contract offers a starting point to achieving dual organisational and individual benefits. It is consistent with the "new deal", providing a methodology for satisfying the needs of both parties. It provides a baseline for assessing the status of employees' careers, and can underpin a career management/development and workforce alignment program.

Career development therefore constitutes a vital retention strategy by:

- Stimulating healthy dialogue between management and employees to pro-actively address the career concerns of employees
- Unearthing "hidden" career possibilities that can be accommodated within the organisation for a "win–win" outcome

- Otherwise preventing needless resignations.

Case Study: Global IT Company, Key Management and Technical Role

We referred to a case study in Chapter 3 concerning a global IT company that was experiencing high turnover among their 40 technical professional staff.

Apart from making recommendations concerning the wider systemic deficit issues in the organisation, we also debriefed Ivan, the manager of these IT technical staff, on his individual WRDI® survey report. This report indicated that whilst Ivan's psychological contract was reasonably healthy, and his affective commitment was average, his job satisfaction was low. In discussing this profile, Ivan indicated that he would prefer a more strategic role in the organisation, divorced from day-to-day management responsibilities.

Ivan was one of the top 10 most valued employees in the company (globally) because of his technical knowledge, but he was a "square peg in a round hole" in terms of the job (i.e., not suited to a management role). Ivan had been promoted more for his technical expertise rather than his management skills. He was agreeable to sharing his report findings with top management, which resulted in him being redeployed to his preferred role, with a suitable replacement recruited to replace him.

This was a win-win-win outcome for Ivan, the company, and the technical staff who were previously reporting to him.

Person – organisational fit, person – job fit and careers

The level of satisfaction in the job and affective commitment or emotional attachment with the organisation, would seem to be an appropriate starting point to assess the status of an individual's career. As stated earlier in Chapter 6:

- Job satisfaction may also be viewed as an indication of person – job "fit"
- Affective commitment may also be viewed as an indication of person – organisational "fit".

Critical Measures for Assessing an Individual's Career Status

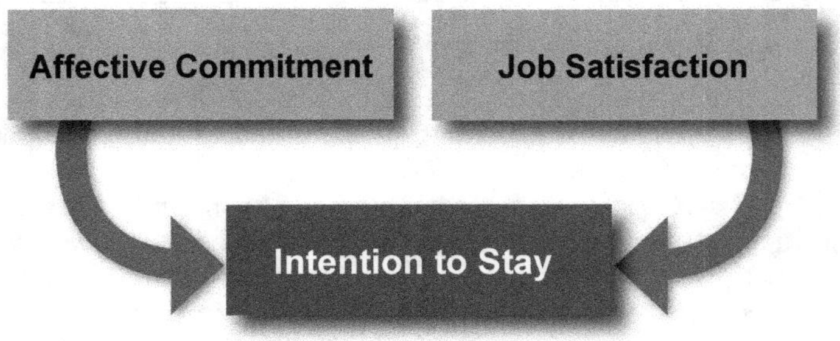

These two measures provide answers to the two vital questions:

- *Is this individual happy/satisfied in their job?*
- *Is this individual happy/committed in working for the organisation?*

The answers to these questions provide an indication of the individual's work life quality and status of career management. However beyond the above two vital questions, lies a third question:

- *Is this individual intending to stay with the organisation?*

The answer to this third question has obvious implications for both the individual and the organisation, as we have already discussed in Chapter 6, in a typology which classifies various types of "Stayers" and "Leavers" and the associated career and organisational implications.

Diagnosing reasons for poor fit

Refer to the model of the Psychological Contract (PC): Causes, "Health" and Consequences, in the Introduction Chapter coloured pages and also Chapter 6. In the case of either lower levels of job satisfaction and/or affective commitment, the concept of the psychological contract is useful. An examination of an individual's psychological contract provides answers as to whether any fit issues are due to:

- Poor selection and recruitment decisions as evidenced by relatively healthy psychological contract but lower levels of job satisfaction and/or affective commitment (i.e., square peg in a round hole)
- "Unhealthy" psychological contract, either due to dysfunctionality at a local workplace level, or at a wider organisational level (e.g., the "deal" not being met, lower levels of trust and/or fairness), any of which may be depressing levels of job satisfaction and/or affective commitment

If it's a case of a square peg in a round hole, then this poses some career implications for the individual concerned (i.e., possible career or job change), as well as the organisation in maximising performance.

Case Study: Talent Retention Risk Assessment for a Large Australian Firm

We were undertaking a talent risk assessment for a large Australian firm. Within one of the Business Units, there were two out of seven key talent who were at high risk of leaving the organisation. Following individual debriefs, it transpired that both of these employees had been redeployed in the organisation. Their original jobs had disappeared as a consequence of some rationalisation of the organisation's activities and being valuable employees, the company wanted to keep them. They were offered other roles within the organisation without any selection process in place or subsequent training.

The result was that their job satisfaction and hence intention to stay were low – they were a poorer fit to the job, and as a consequence, had started to look outside of the organisation.

Apart from initiating career discussions between these individuals and the organisation to determine what other opportunities might be available, one of our other recommendations was that the organisation strengthen its internal selection and recruitment processes. Even though their initiative of redeployment was an admirable one (i.e., to retain keep these two talented employees), this needed to be executed more scientifically.

The benefits to both organisations and individuals

Higher alignment (i.e., employees' affective commitment and job satisfaction), together with higher job commitment/discretionary effort, will result in:

- Higher levels of performance
- More satisfied customers
- A higher intention to stay, and therefore enhanced retention
- Enhanced workforce-well being (i.e., less workplace stress).

Hence there are both organisational and individual benefits in achieving enhanced alignment. This is also consistent with the "new deal" philosophy of meeting (or attempting to meet), the needs of both the organisation and the individual.

Workforce Remodelling, Career Status and Performance Enhancement

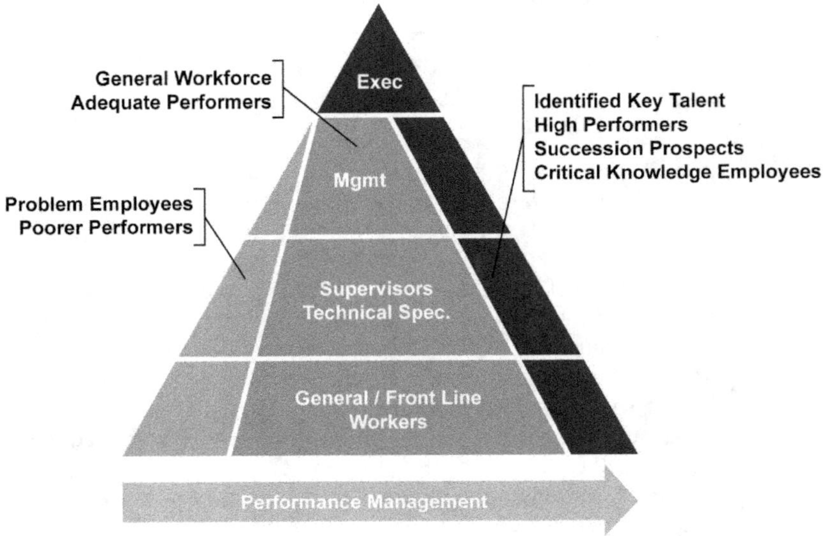

Where an organisation has an effective performance management system in place, a more "fine grained" approach can be adopted towards career management/development, workforce alignment, performance enhancement and associated interventions. Career development should link to performance management systems, since opportunities on the job or in the organisation should be based on strong current performance. Ultimately the aim should be to enhance alignment and performance of various workforce segments or layers of the organisation.

8.8 DEVELOPMENT OF HUMAN CAPITAL AND THE PSYCHOLOGICAL CONTRACT: OTHER TOPICS AND THEMES

Leadership development

Much has been written about the importance of leadership. Research findings confirm a strong link between leadership effectiveness and employee engagement and retention. The success of any leadership development program should therefore be reflected in higher levels of trust and affective commitment, job satisfaction and retention of:

- Leaders' direct reports
- General employees.

Despite the enormous investment in leadership development programs over recent years, the jury is still out on evaluating the effectiveness of these programs. A recent study by PWC (2005) found very little difference in organisational performance between those companies that had invested heavily in leadership development programs, compared to those that hadn't. This raises a number of questions:

- *Are good leaders either born or made?*
- *Is sound leadership more of a reflection of character and personal proficiency?*
- *Does self-interest, self-preservation and politics inhibit couragess leadership and the making the hard decisions when required?*
- *Has the disproportionate reward systems and bonuses paid to top executives, based on short-term results, corrupted sound longer-term leadership decisions?*

Coaching

The recent explosion of coaching indicates:

- A recognition of the importance of "soft skills", particularly concerning people management
- A need to enhance or maximise performance
- The importance of career development in the contemporary workplace
- A recognition of the stresses of coping with the increased demands, complexity and challenges of the modern world.

Coaching is about improving skills and performance, usually for the current job, but also to support career transitions. The goal of retaining employees through coaching and feedback is a secondary one to performance enhancement.

The psychological contract interfaces with coaching in respect of:

- Addressing any issues of concern with the health of the psychological contract (delivery of the "deal", trust/leadership or fairness)
- Affective commitment (fit to the organisation), job satisfaction (fit to the job) and job commitment/discretionary effort
- Retention, given that coaching represents a significant investment with the implicit understanding that individuals undergoing coaching are more likely to stay with the organisation).

The direction of coaching will be influenced by any issues of concern that emerge in relation to the above.

Training and development

In Chapter 3 we summarized approaches to investment in training and development and associated strategies according to the skills' based segmentation model, which in turn is related to the nature of psychological contracts. For example:

- Transactional psychological contracts – lower investment in training
- Relational psychological contracts – higher investment with development of organisational specific skills and competencies, coaching and mentoring for more senior roles.

Knowledge management

> Knowledge is generated through organisational dialogue that results in reciprocal exchange of messages in a specific context (Harvey, Novicevic, Buckley, & Ferris, 2001).
>
> Since about 70% of learning occurs informally (Evans, 2003), employees need to discover that it is in their best interest to share knowledge (Stevens, 2000).

In today's dynamic global economy, knowledge is viewed as a key competitive resource by organisations, and the effective management of individual knowledge within the workplace has become critical to business success. With the prevalence of knowledge workers and knowledge-intensive firms, management of individual knowledge and organisational memory is critical to business success. There are two factors which often hamper knowledge sharing in organisations:

- Turnover
- An unwillingness to share knowledge.

We have seen that turnover is directly relevant to the health and consequences of the psychological contract and that turnover of knowledge workers can be significantly higher than that of other workers. It is argued below that knowledge sharing is also related to the health of the psychological contract.

Whilst technology typically constitutes the first step towards promoting knowledge sharing, such infrastructure, whilst essential to knowledge capture and exchange, is only effective to the extent that it is used in a continuous manner. To achieve sustained knowledge sharing that improves organisational profitability and enhances employee morale, management practices that motivate employees to share knowledge on a continuous basis must complement technological investments (Davenport & Prusak, 2000; Hislop, 2003).

Knowledge workers are probably more committed to their careers than the organisation, and therefore must be encouraged to share knowledge. Efforts to mandate such knowledge sharing behavior are likely to be unsuccessful, as knowledge workers are more autonomous people who resist a command and control culture. It is reasonable to assume that knowledge worker's willingness to share knowledge may be contingent on, amongst other things, the health of their psychological contracts. More specifically, this willingness to share will depend on the quality of relationships and connections that they form within the workplace (i.e., their relationship with their boss, other team members), all of which form part of the health of the psychological contract.

8.9 DEVELOPMENT OF HUMAN CAPITAL AND THE PSYCHOLOGICAL CONTRACT: MERGERS/ ACQUISITIONS

> Note: Mergers/Acquisitions constitute one of the five ways of building human capital as per the model in the coloured pages of the Introduction Chapter.

Merger/Acquisition (M/A) research findings

Published statistics show that just 23% of all acquisitions earn their cost of capital, and 47% of executives leave within the first year in acquired companies, with people problems typically heading the top of the list in failed integrations (McNiece, 2004). More specifically, research findings confirm that people factors are critical to M/A success:

- Statistics show that 50-75% of key mangers from acquired organisations voluntarily leave the new organisation within a few years following the union, and this may well be regarded in the longer term as a failure of the M/A (Buchholtz, Ribbens, & Houle, 2003)
- The attrition of top performers often undermines the achievement of M/A goals
- High levels of employee identification (i.e., affective commitment) with organisation's identity (the new or acquiring) is beneficial and results in increased work motivation, performance and organisational citizenship behaviours and reduced labour turnover (Haslam, 2001)

> Note: Most writers use the term merger to imply a marriage of equals, and the term acquisition to involve the purchase of one organisation by another, with the purchaser in the dominant role. In this sense, the

occurrence of mergers is rare, although many acquisitions are described as mergers to avoid the appearance of dominance by one firm.

Subjective measures of Merger/Acquisition (M/A) success

People factors are often overlooked in the M/A process, yet the alignment and retention of staff (particularly key talent), is critical to the success of the process. Based on the above research findings, it would seem to make good sense to subjectively assess M/A success in terms of the psychological contract, including in particular, employees' job satisfaction, commitment and intention to stay/leave. More specifically, executives should want to know the following key employee information:

- Their reactions and how they view leadership (both locally in the workplace and at a top management level, communication, etc.)
- To what extent they are committed to and identify with the new organisation
- To what extent they are satisfied in their roles
- To what extent they are likely to remain with the organisation in the medium term.

Note: Bias can be an issue depending on whether staff originate from the present or target firm, or whether individuals stand to gain or lose from the M/A, either financially or status wise.

8.10 OTHER ASPECTS OF ORGANISATIONAL DEVELOPMENT AND HR AND THE PSYCHOLOGICAL CONTRACT

People management policies and management standards

Most organisations have a suite of people management policies or management standards. These documents represent a written description of rights and responsibilities of managers and staff and reflect a desire to formalise arrangements in the area of people management and development. They:

- Should be designed to support general management strategy
- Are crucial to effective people and development
- Assist employers to develop fair and consistent approaches and can protect the organisation against legal claims

- Provide guidance for managers and others when deciding what to do in a particular circumstance
- Provide staff with guidance about their own responsibilities, as well as those of the organisation.

The important aspect of these policies is that they:

- Should be differentiated for different workforce groups and segments (i.e., not everybody will be equal)
- Should include some flexibility to cater for different needs
- Must be transparent and clearly communicated to all employees/ workers.

Research indicates that by adopting bundles of HR practices, employers are likely to improve business performance. The suite of policy/management standards should include, but will not necessarily be limited to, the following topics:

- Position descriptions
- Salary administration and rewards
- Recruitment and selection
- Performance management
- Managing diminished performance
- Education, training and development
- Handling grievances (i.e., procedural and distributive fairness)
- Managing diversity
- Flexible work practices.

Many of the above topics directly relate to the psychological contract. To a large extent, what is contained in these documents constitute the specifics or expression of most of the items that comprise the psychological contract (refer to Chapter 7). Consequently these documents imply the nature of various psychological contracts that may exist in an organisation (i.e., from relational to transactional). They are also relevant to the relationship constructs that comprise the state or health of the psychological contract (i.e., trust and fairness).

Workforce planning

Workforce Planning is a process that takes input from a multitude of directions and translates it into a forecast of supply and demand for numbers of people with appropriate skills. Recruitment should be driven by forecasts from the workforce planning process. Recruitment departments or HR is then responsible for filling new talent needs that cannot be mitigated though internal redeployment or development.

Two areas where the psychological contract intersects with workforce planning are:

- Performance
- Retention.

Given the relationship between healthy psychological contracts and performance, productivity will influence labour demand and specifically employee numbers. Similarly high or low turnover estimates (and hence consequent labour replacement), will be influenced by the psychological contract and retention risk data. Workforce planning should therefore accommodate consideration of both of these issues.

Employer of choice

Employer of Choice: What does it mean?

Successful companies will be those that can attract, develop and retain skilled and talented employees. To that end, many companies are arbitrarily claiming "Employer of Choice" status as they seek to enhance their reputation. Some key questions arise:

- *What does this term mean?*
- *On what basis does an organisation claim to be an Employer of Choice (many claiming this status are delusional)?*
- *How can these claims be validated?*
- *How do organisations, both large and small, enhance their Employer of Choice status?*

As mentioned in Chapter 5, the term "Employer of Choice" has become a hackneyed phrase in today's corporate environment. It can mean different things to different people. For some, their interpretation of this term refers to corporate peripheral benefits such as provision of gym memberships, fresh fruit for staff, dry cleaning services, etc. However it is contended that becoming an employer of choice is not fundamentally about providing such "superficial" or peripheral employee benefits and services - they do not differentiate Employers of Choice.

There are many Employers of Choice, each for different reasons. Employers of Choice compete with each other on the basis of their distinctiveness. They create attractive EVPs or "deals", tailoring the company's/organisation's "brand" and "products" (i.e., the jobs it has to offer), to appeal to the specific people it wants to find and keep, and then they deliver on those "deals". Refer to Chapter 5 for a further discussion on EVPs.

Putting substance to the rhetoric

> Organisations that desire to become "employers of choice" must devise strategies and innovative programs which will satisfy a spectrum of both work and personal needs, including tangible and intangible rewards. They need to develop a competitive advantage in recruiting and retaining staff. They need to develop positive psychological contracts with their employees (Anderson & Pulich, 2000).

It is contended that the concept of the psychological contract lies at the heart of Employer of Choice claims and validation. An Employer of Choice, by inference, will have:

- Healthy psychological contracts with their workforce segments (including the delivery of the "deal")
- Higher levels of employee job satisfaction (i.e., person – job "fit")
- Higher levels of employee affective commitment (i.e., emotional attachment/engagement or person - organisational "fit")
- Higher levels of employee intention to stay with the organisation, which should be reflected in lower turnover rates.

Hence the psychological contract model provides a basis from which Employer of Choice claims can be validated, from structuring EVPs through to the measurement and validation of Employer of Choice claims.

Organisational change

The impacts of organisational change and restructuring

A number of studies have highlighted the fact that major organisational change and restructuring results in increased stress, confusion and loss of productivity, and that it takes a significant period of time before satisfaction and trust is regained and stress levels decrease. Some research suggests that restructuring undermines employee attachments, and makes recruiting and retaining employees more difficult (Reilly, Brett & Stroh, 1993).

However on the positive side, restructuring makes employees focus on their careers. In some cases, the process of restructuring seems to have made the remaining jobs more satisfying, despite employee perceptions of greater workloads, insecurity and reduced commitment. With many companies introducing work redesign measures with flatter structures, increased teamwork, employee empowerment and participation, greater decision making authority and problem solving discretion - this has helped them to become more productive.

Change management programs and the psychological contract

The human factor in many change management programs (e.g., restructuring, downsizing), is often inadequately addressed, and in particular, the changing nature of the psychological contract and the consequent implications. This neglect may provide an explanation, in part, of the failure of many such programs to achieve their stated intent. Often these programs are akin to putting a "positive icing on a negative cake"! The glue which binds organisations is their people and knowledge. The consequences of people not accepting change, including the loss of their cooperation, motivation and knowledge, constitute a decline in the competitiveness of the organisation.

Employees are more likely to accept breaking or changing of the psychological contract:

- If it is due to outside pressures, and beyond the control of employer
- If existing psychological contracts are healthy, such that there are "brownie relationship points" in the bank for people to tolerate change in the reconfiguring of the organisation.

Corporate fraud

Recent incidents of organisational betrayal have had a devastating effect on companies' reputations and share prices. This is an area of workforce risk that has potentially catastrophic consequences. According to a recent joint report by the Australian Institute of Criminology and PricewaterhouseCoopers, corporate fraud costs Australia about $3.5 billion a year (Furnham & Taylor, 2004). PricewaterhouseCoopers (2003) in its report on economic crime, identified seven different forms of fraud:

- Asset misappropriation
- Financial misrepresentation
- Corruption and bribery
- Money laundering
- Cyber crime
- Industrial espionage
- Product piracy.

Pearce and Henderson (2000) put breaching of the psychological contract as central to their analysis of organisational betrayal. Furnham and

Taylor (2004) highlight the importance of organisational factors contributing to acts of betrayal, citing lack of trust, fairness and unmet expectations as being critical. Even in the case of Nick Leeson and Barings Bank, where the perception may have been that one rogue trader single handedly brought down one of the U.K.'s most respected banks, the reality was that most commentators were generally agreed that Baring's senior management contributed significantly to its own demise. Laying the blame on the workplace deviant (i.e., individual personality factors), typically represents a simplistic and convenient explanation for corporate fraud.

Chapter 9

Measuring and Reporting Human Capital

KEY POINTS

Key questions and issues that we will address in this chapter:

- *What are the key human capital measures?*
- *What are the key characteristics of a human capital measurement system?*
- *What are the differences between, and the relative importance of, lag (autopsy) and predictive (physician) human capital measures?*
- *What are the three categories of human capital data?*
- *What are the main reasons why many surveys don't work?*
- *What are the four critical questions to ask in selecting an employee survey?*
- *What HR metrics should be collected concerning the acquisition of human capital (i.e., new recruits)?*
- *What is workforce analytics?*
- *How to unlock the hidden value from your HR data bases to provide the essential workforce intelligence leading to better people decisions*
- *How the reporting of human capital data links to the skills' based workforce segmentation model*

What are the consequences of failing to adequately address these questions/issues or ending up with the wrong answers?

- *You can't manage what you don't measure – it is essential to have the right data for people investment tracking, continuous improvement monitoring and managing risk*
- *Unless the reporting of human capital data is presented in a compelling, correctly structured format, management "buy-in" will be compromised, with desired workforce insights unable to be achieved*
- *You may be "in the dark", unaware of the "hot spots" in your organisation, be they local workplace or wider organisational hot spots, and therefore unaware of what targeted interventions to apply to address these hot spots*
- *You may be throwing dollars at ineffective interventions or treating symptoms rather than causes*
- *You may not have adequate data to present a compelling business case for proposed HR initiatives.*

9. MEASURING AND REPORTING OF HUMAN CAPITAL

9.1 DEVELOPING A HUMAN CAPITAL MEASUREMENT FRAMEWORK

Human capital reporting in need of a revamp

As mentioned earlier, companies have revamped practically every business process in their search for competitive advantage, apart from the area of human capital. It is one of the least measured and analysed investments – a weak link in the chain of corporate investments. Ideally information about the workforce should be provided at the same level of sophistication as a basis for decision making, as would be the case for decisions about technology, money, products and services.

The same level of rigour and surgical precision as that which applies to managing and reporting on financial processes, should be applied to human capital. However many HR and people management measurement systems are weak or non-existent. Without valid and reliable people measures, politics fills the gap! The quality of measurement and reporting on human capital generally lags well behind that of other key assets of the business. This measurement and reporting deficiency has been instrumental in keeping HR Directors or Managers from their legitimate "seat at the table".

> Note: As referred to in the Introduction Chapter, the measurement of people is not as precise as perhaps in some other areas of business. However this doesn't excuse the lack of scientific principles, precision and methodologies being applied to this area.

What gets measured gets managed!

What gets measured gets managed! Human capital systems and measures should be used by management to optimise the value they create through effective investments in the management of employees. Without the right data, executives have a less than adequate basis for informed decision making in managing their most vital intangible asset. The phrase that "people are our greatest asset" becomes empty rhetoric!

Executives are data hungry and data needy. Furthermore measurement drives behavior. Opportunity now beckons for HR professionals to "step up to the plate" by providing better human capital measures and reporting.

9.2 KEY CHARACTERISTICS OF A HUMAN CAPITAL MEASUREMENT SYSTEM

In an era of talent and skills shortages, measuring, diagnosing and reporting on key drivers of performance and retention are essential for:

- People investment tracking
- Continuous improvement monitoring
- Managing risk.

This measurement system should incorporate the following characteristics:

- A well established empirical research underpinning
- Standardisation*
- Reliability*
- Validity*
- Forward-looking and predictive (of performance and retention)
- Diagnostic (where appropriate).

*these terms are explained later on in this chapter.

The measurement system must be simple yet powerful, with the reporting component able to "speak the language of business", or show a clear linkage to the "bottom line".

"Coroner"/autopsy (lag) and "physician" (predictive) measures

Many human capital measures are "lag" indicators (e.g., turnover). They constitute "coroner" measures or autopsy results by capturing the outcomes of what has been produced in the past. Focusing exclusively on such measures is akin to trying to win a game of football by watching the scoreboard! Past history doesn't always predict future outcomes. Whilst not denying the need to monitor and track continual improvement and outcomes, what is more critical is knowing the drivers or "levers to pull" to produce those outcomes. These are called "physician" or predictive measures.

9.3 KEY HUMAN CAPITAL MEASURES

There is no universal agreement on the measurement and evaluation of human capital. Notwithstanding this lack of agreement, factors that consistently emerge from the empirical literature include employees':

- Knowledge and experience
- Affective commitment (which is related to both performance and retention)
- Job satisfaction (which is related to both performance and retention)
- Discretionary effort (which is related to motivation and performance)
- Intention to stay (which is the main predictor of turnover)
- Turnover
- Skills/competencies (including both technical, leadership and "soft skills")
- Performance ratings.

These factors relate to both the performance and retention of human capital. Also from our previous discussion of human capital, we know that the performance of human capital resides in the following definition:

Human Capital = Knowledge + Skills + Experience + Initiative

> Note: Discretionary effort relates to initiative. It is reasonable to assume that the summation of knowledge, skills, experience and initiative equates to performance. Put another way, the higher the value of human capital, the higher the performance, notwithstanding that there are also a range of other factors that contribute to or impact on performance (e.g., systems, processes, environment, etc.).

Non-financial performance measures

These above human capital factors and their measures are continual drivers of organisations' non-financial performance, which in turn drive organisational results. They may be viewed as "lead" indicators – non financial performance measures - which are the key drivers of future organisational performance. However collecting information on these performance measures is an important, but not sufficient, step in developing measurement systems that are forward-looking and predictive. Being able to identify and diagnose those factors that influence these measures, and hence applying appropriate interventions which have predictable outcomes in addressing perceived deficits, is equally, if not more important. Diagnosis is addressed more comprehensively later on in this chapter.

9.4 THREE CATEGORIES OF HUMAN CAPITAL DATA

We shall categorise data relating to the human capital measures referred to in the previous section, according to the following:

1. Demographic data
2. Organisational process data (coroner data)
3. Predictive or attitudinal data (physician data).

Demographic data

Demographic data includes data relating to the workforce composition and structure. More specifically, it includes both:

- An employee focus (e.g., age, gender, length of time with organisation, length of time in job, education level)
- And a role focus (e.g., job level, workforce segment, business unit, location).

Demographic data relates to knowledge and experience referred to in the previous section. However the latter are difficult to measure, but can be assessed (somewhat imprecisely) through age, qualifications, length of time in the job, length of time in various roles, length of time in the organisation and in the industry.

Organisational process data

organisational process data is typically drawn from pay roll and human resource information systems (HRIS), and may include performance ratings, turnover, potential ratings, salary increases, investment in training and development, absenteeism, sick leave, etc. Performance is typically measured by managers' ratings as part of a performance management system. Potential may be assessed by managers, or assessed independently though various assessment procedures (e.g., assessment centres, psychometric testing).

Additionally specific business metrics can be added to this type of data (e.g., sales revenue or volume per person). These business metrics then form a basis for an analysis and identification of whether there are any particular characteristics of people that result in superior performance (refer later section in this chapter on workforce analytics).

Predictive or attitudinal (subjective) data

Predictive or attitudinal (subjective) data, which is the most important data, is typically gathered through a combination of surveys, questionnaires, managers' ratings or 360º feedback. This data should include measures of employees':

- Levels affective commitment and job satisfaction
- Levels of discretionary effort
- Intention to stay/leave (i.e., retention risk)
- Competencies/capabilities, including leadership.

These subjective measures are not necessarily less accurate than more objective measures, provided they are valid, reliable and standardised.

9.5 HUMAN CAPITAL DATA: PUTTING IT ALL TOGETHER

The three categories of human capital data are represented in the following Human Capital Data Matrix. This (1) demographic, (2) organisational process and (3) predictive/attitudinal data, when combined together, form the basis of a practical framework of key workforce measures. This matrix transforms *ad hoc* or disjointed data into a more integrated platform for effective human capital reporting and analysis.

A Typical Human Capital Data Matrix

Demographic Data		Employee Focused					Role Focused			
		Age	Gender	Length of Time in Organisation	Length of Time in Job	Salary Level	Workforce Skills Segment	Job Level	Business Unit	Location
Organisational Process Data (from client)	Performance Rating#									
	Turnover#									
	Salary Increases#									
	Investment ($) in Training & Development*									
	Potential Rating*									
Predictive / Attitudinal Data (self report) — Survey Data#	Discretionary Effort									
	Affective Commitment									
	Job Satisfaction									
	Intention to Stay									
Predictive / Attitudinal Data (self report) — "Soft Skill" Competencies*	Leadership									
	Other									

relates to the utilisation and retention of human capital;

* relates to the development of human capital

This Human Capital Data Matrix can then be applied to three of the ways of increasing human capital:

- Acquiring
- Utilising/engaging
- Developing.

Refer later in this chapter to workforce analytics, which provides for the analysis of different combinations of the three categories of data and the People Data Cube – a model for human capital data analysis. Additional HR metrics relating to acquisition (i.e., selection and recruitment) are also provided later in this chapter.

9.6 UNDERSTANDING SOME OF THE BASICS: PSYCHOMETRIC PROPERTIES OF A MEASUREMENT INSTRUMENT

> Note: An instrument includes a test, inventory, survey, 360 degree feedback tool, etc.

Many HR professionals are in the dark!

As mentioned earlier, HR professionals are typically not trained in measurement or psychometrics. Many consumers of human capital measurement tools are therefore in the dark, unable to differentiate between a quality instrument (i.e., which incorporates rigorous psychometric properties based on empirical research findings), and a questionnaire which has been dreamed up or derived on an intuitive basis. To that end, the following brief explanatory overview is provided concerning psychometrics.

About psychometrics

Psychometrics refers to the statistical qualities of an instrument's questions (i.e., items) and scales, including issues such as reliability, validity, factor structure, diagnostic capability. We shall briefly explain what is meant by these terms.

Standardisation ensures that the procedures used to measure performance are uniformly applied, and that the measures can be compared against established norms or benchmarks.

Reliability is concerned with the dependability or consistency of the measure (i.e., whether the measure has a minimum of error). Without reliability there can be no validity.

Validity (which is the most important psychometric property), refers to how well a measure captures what it is intended to capture.

Factor structure relates to the dimensionality of a scale (i.e., whether the items for each scale load on one scale or are sufficiently closely related to each other as opposed to being disparate).

The **diagnostic capability** of an instrument refers to the extent to which an independent variable (e.g., trust in management), predicts a dependent variable (e.g., job satisfaction).

There are various accepted statistical tests to confirm the above psychometric properties. More specifically, certain statistical techniques (e.g., multiple regression analysis, structural equation modelling), can indicate which practices drive important organisational outcomes (i.e., which practices drive performance and retention). Hence targeted interventions can then be implemented, knowing the "cause and effect" relationship, with outcomes able to be confidently predicted.

The above psychometric properties constitute the fundamental make up or DNA of the tool or instrument. It's akin to asking for a specification on the performance of a new motor vehicle or appliance that you may be considering purchasing (e.g., the energy rating, power, speed, fuel consumption, etc.). Knowing what questions to ask is vital, and unless complete and satisfactory answers are forthcoming from the provider, then caveat emptor – buyer beware!

> The minimum information that consumers of human capital measurement tools should request:
>
> - A summary of the psychometric properties of the tool, according to the above criteria
> - Empirical research references
> - Details of the norm base that has been established for the tool and associated benchmarks.

9.7 ENGAGING AND RETAINING HUMAN CAPITAL: EMPLOYEE SURVEYS

Why surveys are important

Organisations use employee opinion surveys, culture surveys, engagement surveys and climate surveys on a recurring basis as strategic tools:

- For enhancing performance
- To understand and manage the impact of people and organisational systems on business outcomes.

Their use underscores a growing recognition that people drive long-term competitive success. Selection of a survey design and provider constitutes an important strategic and operational decision for any organisation and its future. It is critical to effective workforce management. As indicated previously, what gets measured gets managed!

Survey imperatives

The survey objectives should be clearly defined, with a regular and formal survey process, and with the findings used to:

- Enhance employees' engagement/performance and retention
- Manage, measure and reshape the organisation's strategic HR priorities, including people management policies and practices
- Play a role in the promotion, retention and compensation of those in a leadership capacity.

A diagnostic approach to survey design

Employee surveys have now grown to become far more sophisticated, having evolved beyond basic tools to appease employees or provide general feedback to management. Survey design has become more of a science with recent advancements having seen the emergence of diagnostic survey tools (i.e., that have cause and effect capability). These tools are based on models (which should have an empirical research underpinning), and corresponding measures that link to either performance and/or retention. Such tools typically provide more meaningful data beyond measuring climate, hygiene or "feel good" factors. Not only do these surveys identify a problem, but they then uncover the reasons why people feel the way they do.

Survey design: Shorter may not be better!

Whilst surveys of around 20 or less items are intuitively appealing from the perspective of simplicity and convenience, they are hardly likely to produce the comprehensive key measures and diagnosis required. Shorter surveys do not provide a basis for confidently and comprehensively identifying and addressing a range of possible causes or deficits (i.e., disengagement or retention risk), and then confidently applying targeted interventions accordingly.

Those survey providers with models which:

- Are not diagnostic
- Include relatively few items
- Do not separate out and provide comprehensive measures of the key drivers of performance and retention offer an incomplete engagement and retention solution, as illustrated in the following example.

Example: Causes of high turnover not identified because of survey limitations

My daughter (who is now a registered psychologist), was previously working in the recruitment section for one of the large banks. One of the managers complained that people were leaving the organisation, despite the fact that their department was recording reasonably high Engagement Index scores. The particular engagement survey, which only included a handful of items, didn't measure retention risk (i.e., intention to stay), nor did it directly measure job satisfaction, which is one of the key drivers of intention to stay.

Furthermore this survey only addressed some of the key drivers of job satisfaction at a local management or workplace level, and had no diagnostic capability. As such, the bank's measurement system was unable to detect to what extent:

- Selection and recruitment deficits (e.g., poor fit to either the job or the organisation)
- Wider systemic issues (e.g., people policies and practices, including rewards) may have been contributing to high turnover.

Without a comprehensive measurement system in place, there were significant gaps that did not enable the pin-pointing of the cause of the turnover problem.

Note: If only some of the antecedents or predictors of job satisfaction are being measured, without any corresponding direct measure of job satisfaction itself, then such an approach excludes the identification of other causes of lower job satisfaction (as in the above example referred to).

It may be the case that selection and recruitment practices are poor (i.e., an individual or group of individuals are poor "fit" to the job and therefore indicate lower levels of job satisfaction), or alternatively, there is a need for job redesign. Under such circumstances, without the right survey model and the right measures, attempts to enhance job satisfaction by targeting only predictors of job satisfaction, may well prove to be relatively fruitless. Such attempts or interventions would constitute a wasteful use of human resources expenditure. It's akin to putting a positive icing on a negative cake!

9.8 SURVEY DIFFERENCES AND LIMITATIONS

Oils ain't oils with surveys

"Oils ain't oils" when it comes to surveys (i.e., not all surveys are the same). They can differ quite significantly in terms of their orientation, models, measures or scales, items, psychometric properties, rigor, empirical research underpinning, diagnostic capability, etc. There are a plethora of survey tools available in the market, and these vary considerably in their design and quality. Even some of the more popular engagement survey tools fall short of the minimum survey design requirements. Their popularity is perhaps more of a testament to the marketing prowess (i.e., "spin") of their suppliers, and a lack of sophistication of the market, as opposed to the substance and rigor of their tools.

Engagement and retention surveys

Reference has been made earlier to the term "employee engagement" and the somewhat dubious reporting practice of Engagement Indices. Engagement surveys (of which there are a wide variety from which to choose), now assume much greater prominence in the market. Typically these surveys fall into the diagnostic category, with measures linked to both performance and retention, and hence the "bottom line". As such, engagement surveys have a stronger appeal to executives and managers, which accounts for their emerging popularity.

Engagement surveys typically include:

- Some of the four "holy grail" workforce measures as their key predictors of performance and retention (see below)
- Antecedents or drivers of job satisfaction, and/or affective commitment, and/or discretionary effort, and/or intention to stay (depending upon the survey model).

The Four Holy Grail Workforce Measures

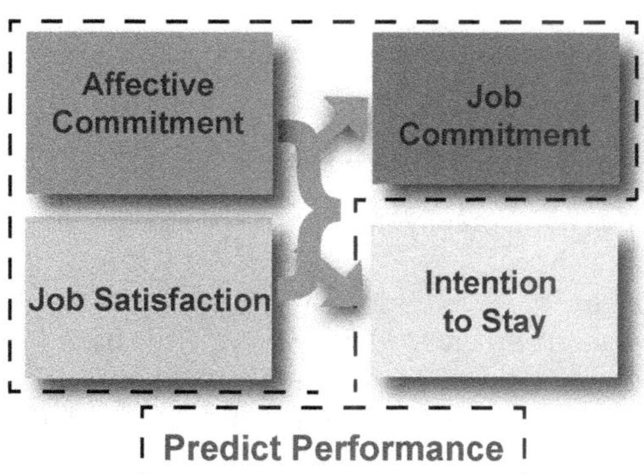

Given that performance and retention are multi-faceted phenomena (i.e., there is no "silver bullet" solution), these antecedents or drivers should therefore include a range of:

- Job related factors (e.g., job challenge, training)

- Workplace related factors (e.g., local management leadership, support, recognition)
- Organisational related factors (e.g., top management leadership/trust, remuneration).

It's then a case of positively impacting upon those antecedents to in turn influence affective commitment and job satisfaction. It is within these antecedents that the diagnostic capability and real value of the survey lies. These antecedents provide the basis for discerning the cause and extent of issues that may be contributing to disengagement, dissatisfaction and retention risk.

Key Antecedents of Affective Commitment and Job Satisfaction

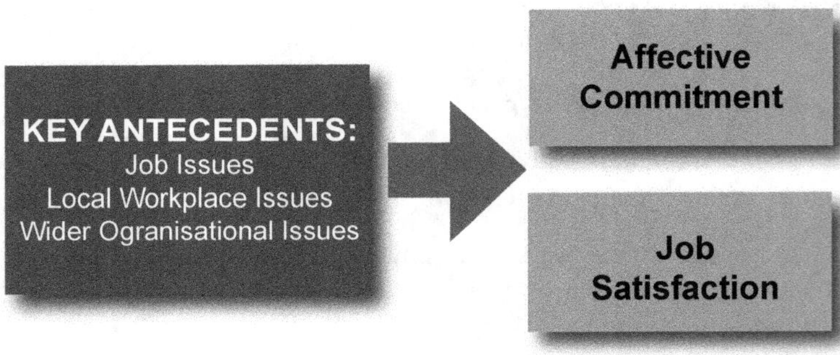

For example, it may be the case that:

- The "deal" or promise isn't being delivered (e.g., lack of training, lack of resources)
- Local management is deficient (e.g., lower levels of management trust)
- Leadership at a top management level is deficient (i.e., top management trust low).

Any of the above perceived deficits provide the basis for the selection and implementation of targeted interventions (that have predictable outcomes), in enhancing affective commitment and job satisfaction. Refer to Chapter 7 for an indication of the diagnostic capability of the WRDI® relating to the above key antecedents.

Culture surveys

Culture is an elusive and deeper concept, which is difficult to measure and change. Cultural surveys typically assess the behavioural practices in place within an organisation, which is only one aspect of culture (refer to Chapter

5). Some so called culture surveys are in fact more like climate surveys. It's like the ice berg analogy – what is above the water line is climate, whereas what is below the water line is culture, which is less visible and more difficult to measure. Whilst the same scientific principles should apply in culture survey design (i.e., should be researched based, sound psychometric properties, etc.), and there may well be a relationship between behavioural measures and performance, these linkages are invariably weaker compared with engagement surveys.

Furthermore there is no one ultimate preferred culture. The culture of an organisation involved in say the defence or security industries, will vary significantly from the culture of, for example, a professional services company or a start up ICT company. However with engagement surveys, the key performance and retention measures are universally important and consistent – they apply across various organisations and contexts. Whilst the data collected from a culture survey may be useful, if it's not the right data, then desired outcomes regarding enhanced performance and retention are unlikely to be achieved.

High performance cultures must inevitably be underpinned by workforce alignment. Get employee alignment "right" (refer to the four holy grail workforce measures), and this provides the basis for further culture change!

Climate surveys or employee opinion surveys

Organisational climate is like the weather – what is out there in the ether, and what it feels like to work in a particular organisation. Typically climate surveys provide more surface measures without addressing underlying issues. They:

- Measure hygiene factors (e.g., morale), with the link between these hygiene factors and the "bottom line" unclear
- Are not diagnostic, so the causes of climate are unclear, in so far as to whether climate is the property of the organisation or the perceivers.

Climate surveys, whilst popular a decade or so previously, have lost favour in more recent times because of the above limitations.

Designing surveys: Why "growing your own" is a waste of time

"Growing your own" survey is likely to fall into the futile category. Even if the survey scales meet the necessary reliability and validity criteria (which requires considerable effort, including the collection and assembly of a large data base), any norms or benchmarks, if established, will only suffice for internal comparisons (i.e., within the organisation). Hence an internally designed survey is hardly likely to provide an accurate indication as to how well that organisation compares with other similar organisations.

Whilst every organisation will claim that they are different (and therefore need customised items), there are some universals that apply. The research regarding the four "holy grail" workforce measures and their key drivers has been conducted across a wide range of industries and populations – it is robust, stable and compelling. Unless the "do-it-yourself" model version has an empirical research based underpinning, it will most likely be deficient in its design and comprehensiveness. Notwithstanding, it may be appropriate to collect additional information on particular areas of interest and suspected concern within an organisation, and also to provide an opportunity for free text responses (i.e., employees' comments), as part of the survey.

Of course the other significant issue with the do-it-yourself survey version is that of confidentiality. Unless survey participants can be assured that their responses will be kept in strictest confidence (i.e., with aggregated data fed back to management in such a way that no individuals are able to be identified), then serious doubts will exist concerning the honesty of the responses, and therefore the integrity of the data. A third party survey provider can largely overcome this confidentiality concern, and so maximise the data integrity accordingly.

Questionnaires versus surveys

There is a vast difference between questionnaires and a quality survey tool. A questionnaire typically does not boast any of the following desirable qualities:

- Is based on a model which is underpinned by theory and research
- Has rigorous psychometric properties
- Is diagnostic (i.e., has cause and effect capability)
- Has key measures which are strongly linked to "bottom line" considerations
- Has a well developed norm base.

Questionnaire information is hardly likely to provide the quality data which serves as a sound platform for management decisions and HR interventions.

9.9 PROBLEMS WITH SURVEYS

Corruption of the survey process

There is considerable anecdotal evidence that when Engagement Indices are incorporated into managers' KPIs (Key Performance Indicators), the survey process can become corrupted. For example, some survey items ask questions about managers'/supervisors' behaviour towards their subordinates in very recent times (e.g., over the past few weeks has your manager/supervisor...). Then just prior to the time that the survey is due to be administered, some managers/supervisors, knowing the survey questions that will be asked, ensure that they hold discussions with their people, or provide recognition of their performance, in order to achieve a higher Engagement Index score.

Furthermore when manager's KPIs are linked to survey results and performance based pay, the survey process can become a mutual "back scratching" exercise. The manager is seeking positive survey findings from his or her direct reports, and in return, that manager provides favourable performance assessments on those direct reports. The end result is that the real issues may not be adequately dealt with.

Why many surveys don't work

Many organisations expend a significant amount of time and energy on employee surveys that are unsatisfactory, and are an exercise in futility. Nothing much happens beyond the information collection stage, in so far as actions and targeted interventions that have effective outcomes. One of the reasons why surveys fail to help organisations is a lack of a clear understanding of the link between the survey findings and the "bottom line" business results (i.e., the link to performance and retention). If the wrong survey model and measures are selected, then the follow up management of the findings and management "buy in" becomes somewhat problematic.

Effective survey application

Apart from the selection of the survey tool itself (see later), in order for the application of a survey to be effective, it should:

- Have a clear, strategic rationale that can be justified on a cost benefit basis
- Provide compelling data in order to obtain management "buy-in" and commitment
- Provide actionable insights that directly link to enhanced performance and retention.

Big isn't always beautiful: International benchmarks may be a myth!

some survey providers promote their international benchmarks as a key selling point. However there is little point in having such benchmarks if they based on inadequate or incomplete measures. The purported benefits of masses of data may well be illusory. As referred to earlier, there is a significant gap between the empirical research and some of the customs and practices in survey design and application, even amongst some of the more popular survey tools. A provider with global presence doesn't necessarily mean that their survey tool has the necessary substance, rigour and empirical research underpinning.

Choosing a survey: The four essential questions to ask

There are four essential questions to ask when evaluating a diagnostic engagement/retention survey. The effectiveness of interventions (i.e., based on outcomes from the survey findings), will be largely dependent upon satisfactory answers to these questions.

Four essential questions to ask when evaluating a survey:

1. *Are the measures based on empirical research and do they provide for a comprehensive assessment of performance and retention (i.e., the four "holy grail" workforce measures), as opposed to a piecemeal solution?*
2. *Is there psychometric rigour associated with the tool, and what are its psychometric properties (e.g., reliability, validity, factor structure)?*
3. *What is the diagnostic capability and predictability of the tool (or for the more technically minded, what % of variance is accounted for by the model between the drivers or antecedents and the key measures or consequences)?*
4. *Are there established norms and benchmarks, and do these norms differentiate between various job levels (e.g., higher level jobs intrinsically have higher levels of job satisfaction, and typically attract higher levels of effort and commitment), so that desired comparisons are appropriate?*

> Note: Norms provide a basis for comparisons (i.e., how does a particular score on say job satisfaction for a group of employees compare or rate with other employees). Furthermore these norms should be differentiated by job level. For example, higher level jobs have intrinsically higher levels of job satisfaction. Therefore it is not appropriate to compare the job satisfaction of a CEO with that of a janitor (without wishing to demean the latter). The CEO may well have a higher level of job satisfaction compared to the janitor, but the CEO's job satisfaction may be low compared with that of other CEOs.

A rating guide for survey selection

Refer to the "Ready Reckoner" (see coloured page) as a guide to selecting an employee survey.

Rate your employee survey on a scale of 1 to 10

Your Survey Rating

Design

Ad Hoc Construction → Research-based Construction

- ►Collection of ad hoc scales
- ►No psychometric properties
- ►No norms

Based on a research validated model
Rigorous psychometric properties
Developed norms

1 2 3 4 5 6 7 8 9 10

Stakeholders

Low Stakeholder Buy-in → High Stakeholder Buy-in

- ►Management ignore survey findings
- ►Not linked to management performance
- ►Poor participation rates (<70%)
- ►No meaningful output for participants

Data quality impacts management
Basis for management KPI
High participation rates (>85%)
Meaningful career focused individual report

1 2 3 4 5 6 7 8 9 10

Administration

High HR Workload → Low HR Workload

- ►"Paper & pencil" survey admin
- ►Cumbersome and disruptive
- ►Inflexible administration process

Online 15 minute survey admin
Minimal work disruption
Flexible administration options

1 2 3 4 5 6 7 8 9 10

Reporting

Limited Report Outputs → Multiple Levels of Reporting

- ►No individual participant outputs
- ►1 type of organisational report
- ►Reporting on general workforce
- ►Reports take weeks to compile

Choice to produce individual reports
2 types of organisational report
Reporting by segment and job level
Rapid report turnaround

1 2 3 4 5 6 7 8 9 10

Applications

Single-purpose Application → Multi-purpose Applications

- ►Organisational "health"

Retention — Alignment — Career Development
Performance enhancement
Organisational development

1 2 3 4 5 6 7 8 9 10

Outcomes

Unclear Outcomes → Predictable Outcomes

- ►No cause and effect relationship
- ►Right interventions are unclear
- ►Uncertain outcomes from interventions

Validated diagnostic capability
Targeted interventions
Predictable intervention outcomes
Key measures relate directly to bottom line

1 2 3 4 5 6 7 8 9 10

Total Rating

Total Rating:	*Likely Outcomes of Survey:*	*Recommendation:*
55 to 60	Highly effective, significant benefits	Preserve best practice
50 to 55	Effective, a number of benefits	Consider upgrading survey
40 to 50	Marginal, unlikely to make a difference	Upgrade existing survey
Below 40	Ineffective, a waste of resources	Abandon or upgrade existing survey

Summary of Key Human Capital Data

KEY ISSUE	SKILLS QUADRANT				TOTAL
	1. Criticals	2. Professionals, Skilled & Semi Skilled	3. Doers	4. Specialists	
No. of full-time employees	20	59	156	6	241
PERFORMANCE PREDICTORS					
Discretionary Effort	65%	52%	61%	58%	
Affective Commitment	62%	58%	57%	48%	
Job Satisfaction	58%	38%	50%	52%	
RETENTION RISK					
Intention to Stay (retention risk)	**59%**	**39%**	**50%**	**69%**	
No. of high risk leavers	3	11	24	1	39
Estimated contingent employee turnover costs (next 12 months)	$260,000	$374,000	$182,000	$36,000	$852,000
No. of high performers at high risk of leaving	1	2	N/A	N/A	3
No. of low performers at high risk of leaving	0	1	N/A	N/A	1
No. of high potentials at high risk of leaving	1	3	N/A	N/A	4
ROI FOR PEOPLE INITIATIVES / INVESTMENTS					
Effectiveness of salary increases on reducing retention risk	ITS increased from 52% to 56%	ITS increased from 52% to 56%	N/A	N/A	
Effectiveness of leadership development	AC and JS of direct reports increased by 6% and 4%	N/A	N/A	N/A	
EXPERIENCE					
Average age	51 years	35 years	38 years	42 years	38.4 years
Average length of time in organisation	7.3 years	3.2 years	3.6 years	5.1 years	3.9 years
Average length of time in job	3.3 years	2.5 years	2.4 years	6.3 years	2.6 years
TURNOVER					
No. who left & % turnover past 12 months	2 (10%)	9 (15%)	22 (14%)	0 (0%)	13%
No. & % of high performers who left	1 (5%)	2 (3%)	2 (1%)	0	5

KEY ISSUE	SKILLS QUADRANT				TOTAL
	1. Criticals	2. Professionals, Skilled & Semi Skilled	3. Doers	4. Specialists	
No. & % of low performers who left	0	2 (3%)	5 (3%)	0	7
No. & % turnover in initial 12months	0 (0%)	1 (18%)	1 (14%)	0 (0%)	2 (6%)
Cost of turnover in past 12 months	$720,000	$910,000	$680,000	0	$2,310,000
INVESTMENT IN PEOPLE					
Total $ investment in salaries	$3,600,000	$7,830,000	$12,640,000	$500,000	$24.57m
Total $ investment in training and development	$88,000	$50,000	$46,000	$3,000	$187,000
PERFORMANCE					
Average overall performance rating	3.8	3.6	N/A	N/A	
For the overall performance ratings: 5 = Outstanding; 4 = More than satisfactory; 3 = Satisfactory; 2 = Moderate; and 1 =Low.					
RECRUITMENT NEEDS					
No. of estimated new recruits over next 12 months	2	14	62	0	78
No. of successor positions not covered	5	N/A	N/A	1	6

Notes: AC = Affective commitment; JS = Job satisfaction; ITS = Intention to stay.

The % scores for discretionary effort, affective commitment, job satisfaction and intention to stay have been standardised whereby: 0-20% = Low Range, 20-40% = Below Average Range, 40-60% = Average Range, 60-80% = Above Average Range, and 80-100% = High Range

Different norms or benchmarks apply to different level jobs, so for example, the absolute discretionary effort of Criticals may be higher than for Doers, but the standardised score for Criticals based on a comparison with their norm group may be lower.

The above table excludes the reporting of competencies.

9.10 DEVELOPING HUMAN CAPITAL: MEASURING COMPETENCIES

Various measurement approaches

Leadership and "soft skills" (e.g., resilience, relationship building, drive, conscientiousness), can be measured through various methodologies including:

- Self-report questionnaires
- Interviews (including behavioural based interviews)
- Personality type questionnaires
- Managers' ratings
- 360 degree feedback (which may include subordinates, peers, colleagues, etc.).

Personality type questionnaires and some 360 degree feedback tools typically have more rigorous psychometric properties and established benchmarks for accurate comparisons.

> Note: Technical competencies are best measured from a menu that has been developed and tailored to the needs of the organisation organisation and the role in question.

About 360 degree feedback

360 degree feedback is a somewhat controversial methodology in the eyes of soome. Different sources of feedback almost always disagree. Typically managers tend to rate themselves higher than what their direct reports do, which raises the question as to which source is the more accurate. Furthermore, increasing the number of sources (i.e., people providing feedback), increases the likelihood of negative feedback. It is also sometimes the case that various sources are not in a position to accurately assess certain competencies or behaviours because of a lack of exposure to the individual whom they are rating. Negative and discrepant feedback is perceived as less useful, less accurate and leads to more negative reactions.

Four essential questions to ask when selecting a competency instrument

The selection of skills to be measured will vary according to the nature of the role. However the same rules still apply concerning psychometric properties of the instrument. To that end, there are the same four essential questions to ask when evaluating a soft skills and leadership instrument.

Four essential questions to ask when selecting a competency instrument:

1. *Are the measures based on empirical research and do they provide for a comprehensive assessment of the skills or competencies?*
2. *Is there psychometric rigour associated with the instrument, and what are its psychometric properties (e.g., reliability, validity, factor structure)?*
3. *Are there established norms and benchmarks, and do these norms differentiate between various job levels or job types so that comparisons are appropriate?*
4. *What is the relationship between the competencies being measured and performance outcomes in the role?*

9.11 ACQUIRING HUMAN CAPITAL: RECRUITMENT METRICS

Typical metrics collected

Typical information collected by organisations concerning the acquisition of human capital (i.e., selection and recruitment), includes:

- % of vacancies filled within a given time frame
- Ratio of acceptances to offers
- Cost per hire
- Ratio of candidates tested to those hired
- Manager's satisfaction with the new hire
- Average time to proficiency in the job
- Retention rate of new hires in the initial 12 months.

This information collectively, is an indication of the quantity, quality and efficiency of the hire.

> Note: A dynamic among these measures is that ease of entry (i.e., % of vacancies filled within a given time frame), may come at the cost of higher turnover.

Additionally, the following workforce information is also typically of interest to management and HR:

- Projected recruitment needs (i.e., number of estimated new recruits for the next 12 months)
- Number of successor positions not covered in key roles (i.e., with suitable potential replacements).

Recruitment metrics omissions

Notwithstanding the above, some critical omissions from this list of recruitment metrics include:

- The extent to which expectations have been met (i.e., whether the EVP or the promise or "deal" has been delivered)
- The new hire's fit to both the organisation (i.e., affective commitment) and fit to the job (i.e., job satisfaction).

The new hire's intention to stay/leave

These measures, as we have seen previously (refer to Chapter 6 for further details), are vital to new recruit engagement, performance and retention. The omission of these measures highlights the:

- Disconnect or "black hole" between recruitment and retention in many organisations
- Lack of rigorous evaluation of the effectiveness of selection and recruitment methodologies, including branding, delivery of EVPs or fulfilling the promise.

We have previously commented on various HR activities being disparate. Typically recruiters have no KPIs or budget relating to engagement and retention. One of the consequences of this deficiency is that in tight labour markets, jobs have been oversold to attract candidates, with the subsequent fall out passed on to others in the organisation.

9.12 THE PEOPLE DATA CUBE MODEL AND WORKFORCE ANALYTICS: UNLOCKING THE HIDDEN VALUE OF HUMAN CAPITAL DATA

Many organisations have a loose conglomeration of HR initiatives, with little connection to each other or alignment with the business goals by way of measurement and reporting of "bottom line" impacts.

One of the difficulties in human capital reporting is the challenge of drawing together relevant information from multiple data bases (e.g., HRIS, finance). Workforce analytics brings together such data from various sources, which then enables various analyses and comparisons to be made.

The three categories of human capital data referred to earlier can be represented in the form of a People Data Cube. This cube model provides a conceptual platform for three levels of data analysis and reporting outputs (see model in the coloured pages in this chapter).

Three levels of analysis and reporting

The three levels of human capital analysis and reporting are as follows.

1. **Basic analysis and reporting.**
   This is demographic data reported against either organisational process or predictive data (e.g., intention to stay by workforce segment), which identifies organisational "hot spots".

2. **More complex analysis and reporting.**
   This is either organisational process data or predictive data, reported against either organisational process or predictive data. For example:

   - performance rating by intention to stay, which indicates the extent to which high or low performers may be intending to stay/leave

   - salary increases by intention to stay, which indicates the extent to which recent salary increases may have reduced retention risk

   - competency ratings against performance ratings, which indicates those competencies which differentiate higher performers.

3. **Trend reporting.**
   This is either data from (1) or (2) reported or tracked over time (e.g., intention to stay over time), which serves as a basis for determining the effectiveness of previous interventions and initiatives.

Developing powerful new insights

Typically organisations report on some of (1) and (3), but not (2). Type (2) analysis above enables organisations to analyse a multitude of inter-related factors, drilling down into places that couldn't previously be reached. Meaningful correlations can then be provided that help predict future behaviour and human capital investment demands.

Type (3) analysis provides a basis for tracking the results of previous decisions by measuring outcomes. By developing an integrated data capability, this workforce analytics approach takes human capital reporting to the next level of sophistication, enabling the development of new and powerful insights into the workforce, and creating business value. This integrated data platform unlocks the hidden value of HR data silos and exploits the full potential of all of the data, thus creating business value. It provides the workforce intelligence to make more informed people decisions leading to better outcomes.

Typical key workforce questions that can be answered with workforce analytics

Using this People Data Cube model, typical workforce questions that can be answered include the following.

Acquisition:

- *What is the fit of new recruits to both the job and to the organisation?*
- *Are your new recruits at risk of leaving and if so why?*

Engagement and retention:

- *Are your people (and in particular key talent and high performers), likely to stay with your organisation in the medium term?*
- *Is the retention risk of your high performers/potentials decreasing over time?*
- *Where are the engagement, retention and performance "hot spots" in your organisation (e.g., by business unit, job level, workforce segment, gender, generation Y, X or baby boomers)?*

Performance:

- *Do you have the right people in the right jobs (i.e., high person-job "fit" and high person–organisational "fit")?*
- *Which competencies are linked to higher performers for various roles, and are you recruiting against and rewarding these competencies?*

Return on $ investment of HR initiatives:

- *Are investments in your people yielding satisfactory returns, e.g.,:*
- *Have your recent salary increases or investments in training and development reduced retention risk?*
- *Have recent investments in training, career development, or coaching, increased levels of engagement of your people?*
- *Has your leadership development program increased employees' trust in management and their engagement, and reduced their retention risk?*
- *Is increased pay or improved rewards resulting in increased effort?*
- *Where should you be focusing your future investments in people (which workforce segments), to optimise their performance and retention?*

Workforce analytics: Reporting of human capital data according to the skills' based workforce segmentation model

We have previously indicated that the skills' based segmentation model provides a rational basis for differentiated HR policies and practices in the management of human capital. It therefore follows that the reporting of human capital should be based on this segmentation model. To that end, the summary of Key Human Capital Data sample reporting output (see coloured pages in this chapter) is an example of human capital data reported for a Small Medium Sized Enterprise (SME), according to the skills' based workforce segmentation model. This form of reporting output, which is included in an organisation's Human Capital Strategic Plan, provides a basis for identifying where the "hot spots" or issues are including risk, what their consequences might be (in terms of the imminent cost of turnover), and a basis for best directing interventions and investment in people initiatives.

Epilogue

E1. RECAPPING ON THE CHALLENGES IDENTIFIED IN CHAPTER 1

We said at the beginning of this book that relationships are important. We shall now return to this theme and revisit or recap on how the concept of relationships (or more specifically the psychological contract), along with the four other human capital models, apply to many of the key challenges facing organisations that were indentified at the end of Chapter 1. These implications and challenges, together with our responses, have been summarised below.

The need for the workforce to be flexible and to adapt in a volatile environment

We have presented a workforce segmentation model and tool (i.e., the Skills Segmentation Questionnaire), together with a range of other considerations, on how organisations can and should best configure their workforces to respond to this challenge (i.e., to maximise flexibility and minimise risk). We have outlined how a variety of HR policies and practices (including different "deals"), should apply to different workforce segments in acquiring, utilising/ engaging and retaining, and developing human capital. Furthermore we have integrated this segmentation model with another model and tool (i.e., that of the psychological contract and the WRDI®). This latter model links the concept of the EVP or "deal" with employee engagement/performance and retention. Amongst other things, it serves as a basis for measuring, diagnosing and then addressing employee commitment, satisfaction and retention risk, which are *de facto* measures of employee adaptation. This diagnostic model then provides a scientific basis for addressing perceived deficits. We have also said that healthier psychological contracts and higher levels of employee job satisfaction and affective commitment, can act as a buffer to discourage employees from leaving and otherwise assist in them accommodating and adapting to change.

Greater workforce diversity with organisations having to reckon more with the needs of various demographic groups (e.g., Gen Y, Gen X and Baby Boomers, Sandwich Generation, etc.)

Our model of the psychological contract provides a framework for different "deals" to be provided to different workforce segments and groups, together with a rationale as to the willingness or preparedness of organisations to address their respective needs. Although mindful of the need to treat people as individuals (see later), we have nevertheless provided examples of "deals" which incorporate the common preferences of various demographic groups.

Structuring and managing a variety of employer/worker relationships in an increasingly complex workplace, consistent with the needs of the business

Again, our skills' based workforce segmentation model and our model of the psychological contract, provide a framework for achieving the above, with its flexibility to cater for a variety or employer/employee relationships from relational to hybrid, through to transactional psychological contracts. We have also explained how these various types of psychological contracts are inextricably linked to the business strategy, and have provided some examples of the adverse consequences for organisations when this is not the case. We have provided a methodology for identifying critical roles and linking roles to the business strategy. Given the adage that you can't manage what you don't measure, the WRDI® tool provides a scientific basis for structuring, measuring and diagnosing the health and consequences of these relationships/psychological contracts.

Fostering of citizenship commitment amongst employees/ workers and a sense of community

We would contend that healthy psychological contracts, together with sound recruitment and selection methodologies, will go a long way to achieving this objective.

> Note: The original version of the WRDI® tool included a measure of citizenship commitment. We were able to demonstrate the linkage between citizenship commitment and healthy psychological contracts, affective commitment and citizenship commitment. However we also decided that citizenship commitment was less important to performance and retention than the four "holy grail" workforce measures. For the sake of simplifying the WRDI® model, we then deleted this construct.

Maintaining organisational coherence and some semblance of internal equity, given the polarisation between skilled and unskilled jobs, and the different workforce strategies applicable to these two groups (e.g., reward mechanisms, flexible work practices, etc.)

We do not claim this to be an easy objective to pursue or outcome to achieve. However from a measurement perspective, the psychological contract model and the WRDI® tool includes a scale of fairness. This scale comprises a number of items relating to both distributive (i.e., outcomes) as well as procedural fairness. The psychological contract model also incorporates the concept of the "deal" which includes various HR policies and practices (e.g., rewards, flexible work practices). Thus a measurement and reporting system is available to monitor employees' perceptions concerning equity/ fairness and affective commitment (i.e., their emotional attachment to the organisation). Furthermore we have offered a scientific basis for diagnosing perceived deficits and determining targeted interventions to address them.

Building commitment in new ways and enhancing performance (i.e., doing more with less)

In the skills' based workforce segmentation model, we have indicated how different performance management approaches apply to different workforce segments. We have advocated that the quickest route to improving organisational performance is to focus on those in critical roles. Then we have explained how the psychological contract model and the WRDI® tool include scales directly relating to key predictors of performance and retention. We have also demonstrated the cause and effect relationship between psychological contract health factors and building commitment (which we have interpreted as performance and retention in this context). These health factors include the impacts of both local and top management practices and behaviours, as well as organisational wide HR policies and practices. Thus we have presented a performance enhancement framework, together with a comprehensive measurement and reporting system to monitor employees' perceptions concerning their commitment and aspects of performance.

Maintaining trust with their workforce, against a background of uncertainty, rapid change, greater demands, and flatter structures (i.e., "walking the talk" with organisational rhetoric)

The psychological contract model and the WRDI® tool include scales of local workplace trust as well as top management trust, which are also *de facto* measures of leadership. We have the capability to "drill down" to individual items to identify any sources of miss-trust (e.g., failure to follow through on previous commitments, failure to consult with and communicate with employees). Thus we are able to measure and diagnose trust at various levels of the organisation. Furthermore as part of the WRDI® tool, we have developed a "cook book" of interventions to address perceived trust deficits.

Greater vulnerability in terms of the labour market (i.e., not just competing locally), with opportunities to import labour

One of the reporting outputs of the WRDI® tool includes a quantification of retention risk. This risk data can be acted upon before the "horse bolts from the stable". We have explained how healthier psychological contracts and higher levels of employee commitment and satisfaction can provide a salary buffer of up to 20% before employees seriously consider leaving. Furthermore the generation of individual reports enables a more "fine grained" assessment of this risk according to the three P's why people leave organisations (i.e., "Push", "Pull" or "Personal" reasons). We have explained strategies to minimize the impacts of these three reasons or causes of turnover.

Greater demands on managers, employees/workers, some of whom need to be accessible 24/7, given customer service standards constantly increasing

We don't claim to have a magic wand solution to overcome this challenge. However the psychological contract model and the WRDI® tool include a variety of measures concerning the above (e.g., workloads, flexible work practices, rewards, etc., including fairness). Thus a measurement and reporting system is available to monitor employees' perceptions concerning these above demands. We have also stressed the need for managers to better connect with their people and the need to provide time off or relief after periods of heavy work loads.

Accommodation of a variety of needs of their employees/ workers and connecting better with individuals

We have explained how the concept of the psychological contract can serve as a framework for addressing the various needs of employees/workers (where prudent or appropriate to do so). Furthermore we have explained how the individual reporting capability of the WRDI® tool provides a structured basis for the promotion and facilitation of healthy dialogue between managers and their people, and for individual needs to be discussed and addressed where appropriate.

Providing for the changing work/career needs of people over the employment life cycle, and assisting/supporting employees in their career development, ongoing education and transitions

We have explained the relationship between the psychological contract model and careers (or more precisely, job/career status). The WRDI® individual reporting output provides a basis for career discussions between managers and their people. It also provides a measurement system for answering some key job/career related questions concerning employees' commitment, satisfaction and intentions to stay/leave.

> Note. The WRDI Institute has produced a career development and assistance document for employees entitled "A Guide to Refreshing Your Career" which comprehensively addresses typical career issues and challenges over the employment life cycle, including career transitions.

Continuously competing for talent (i.e., attraction, development and retention of talent), with "poaching" of talent on the increase (with the growth of search firms)

We have explained how the concept of the EVP is important initially to employee attraction, and then subsequently to performance and retention. We have also provided defensive retention strategies including a retention risk assessment methodology and measurement system to assess and address the "Pull" factor. We have explained the need to build trust such that individuals are more inclined to discuss alternative job offers with their current employer before acting on any of them. As referred to above, we have also pointed out that those organisations with healthy psychological contracts can be buffered by up to 20% in terms of salary premiums or increases before their people seriously start to think about alternative offers.

Balancing autonomy with control, particularly with flexible work practices and managing a remote workforce

One of the reporting outputs of the WRDI® tool includes measures of autonomy and flexible work practices (i.e., part of the "deal"). Trust is also a critical factor in achieving the above balance given the lack of face-to-face contact. The WRDI® tool provides for a comprehensive assessment of trust –

both at a local workplace level (which in this instance is the more important), as well as at a top management level. Obviously there are other issues that are relevant and which need to be dealt with in achieving the above balance, including technology and reporting systems.

Responding to increased community sensitivities concerning the environmental and social impacts of their business activities.

Whilst this is a much broader issue than the scope of this book, we have identified the construct of affective commitment (i.e., the level of emotional attachment between employees and the organisation), as being important to both performance and retention. For example, the scale of affective commitment includes an item relating to the match of values between employees and the organisation. It follows that if employees perceive that organisations are more in tune with environmental and social issues, and if they themselves are that way inclined, then this preference should be reflected in their higher levels of affective commitment. Thus there is an organisational benefit relating to attraction, performance and retention of employees/workers in maximising their affective commitment.

E2. RECAPPING ON THE DEFINING ISSUES IN THE WORKPLACE OF THE FUTURE IDENTIFIED IN CHAPTER 2

We shall now briefly revisit or recap on how the concept of relationships (or more specifically the psychological contract), along with the skills' based workforce segmentation model and other human capital models presented, apply to some of the defining issues indentified in Chapter 2. These issues or themes (some of which have been grouped together for the sake of convenience), together with our responses, have been summarised below.

The rise of market influences, the potential for a vicious cycle of skill deterioration and the (possible) death of employment

These trends have the potential to seriously impact on the success and sustainability of organisations. What is required are better frameworks and models to enable organisations to configure and manage their workforces more effectively. Whilst there are no simple answers to complex questions, we have offered selective investment and risk mitigation approaches to minimize these impacts.

A legacy of the Global Financial Crisis (including more authentic leadership)

We have provided a measurement system to monitor and identify issues concerning the above, with the WRDI® scales of trust in management (at a local as well as at a top management level), a *de facto* measure of leadership.

The optimisation of human resources, including better measurement systems, and the continued focus on talent and careers

This book is concerned with transforming human capital in organisations. It is underpinned by a "3M" approach – developing the right Mindsets, Models and Measures. To that end, it is contended that what has been presented herein, will assist organisations towards achieving enhanced optimisation of their human resources. We have stressed the importance of organisations moving beyond workforce planning and developing a Human Capital Strategic Plan and have presented an example of better measurement systems and reporting. We have also provided an approach to identifying critical roles and investing disproportionally on those in such roles.

The proliferation of flexible work practices, the virtual workplace and working from home

We have provided a measurement framework (i.e., the WRDI®) which includes flexible work practices. More specifically, flexible work practices, sufficient power and autonomy, and supportive management form part of the "deal" as measured in the WRDI®. Also the WRDI® scales of trust at a workplace level and job satisfaction, when combined with these "deal" items, provide a reasonably comprehensive basis from which the ongoing management and effectiveness of flexible work practices can be monitored and interpreted.

The need to overcome the anti-age bias

The WRDI® includes a measure of fairness, including an item relating to whether some employees are favoured over others (i.e., equitable treatment). If the anti-age bias is alive and well, one would expect lower scores on the fairness construct from more mature employees compared to other demographic groups. Thus we have provided a measurement framework from which to monitor this bias. We have also suggested strategies for addressing this bias.

Retention of later Baby Boomers and earlier Gen X

We have provided a measurement system to monitor the retention risk of the above, with the individual WRDI® reporting providing a basis for the career issues of these cohorts to be discussed.

> Note: The other defining issue not included in the above summary is the new role of managers. This issue has been dealt with in part, but does not fall directly within the scope of this book, notwithstanding its importance.

Appendices

APPENDIX A: STAGES OF LIFE

A.1 ERIKSON'S STAGES OF LIFE

The American psychoanalyst Erik Erikson (1969), felt that the social problems encountered in the course of development were more important than the biological ones. He described a progression of psychological stages in which the child faces a wide range of human relations as he/she grows up. According to Erikson, all human beings pass through a series of major crisis with each stage as they progress through the life cycle. At each stage there is a critical confrontation between the self the individual has achieved thus far, and the various demands posed by his/her social and personal setting. A failure to resolve a particular stage crisis means that "baggage" may be carried through until perhaps a later resolution.

If we look at Erikson's proposed stages from adolescence, through to early adulthood, to middle age and then later years, he sets out these development tasks appropriate to that stage and the psychosocial crisis of that stage.

Erikson's Eight Stages Of Man

Approximate Age	Development Task at that Stage	Psychosocial Crisis of that Stage
0 - 11/2 years	Attachment to mother, which lays foundations for later trust in others	Trust versus mistrust
11/2 - 3 years	Gaining some basic control of self and environment (e.g., toilet training, exploration, tying shoe laces)	Autonomy versus shame and doubt
3 - 6 years	Becoming purposeful and directive	Initiative versus guilt

6 years - puberty	Developing social, physical and school skills	Competence versus inferiority
Adolescence	Making transition from childhood to adulthood; developing a sense of identity	Identity versus role confusion
Early Adulthood	Establishing intimate bonds of love and friendship	Intimacy versus isolation
Middle Age	Fulfilling life goals that involve family, career and society; developing concerns that embrace future generations	Productivity versus stagnation/self-absorption
Later Years	Looking back over one's life and accepting its meaning	Integrity versus despair

In particular for middle age, the development task proposed is "fulfilling life goals that involve family, career and society: developing concerns that embrace future generations". The psychosocial crisis of that stage is "productivity versus stagnation" (i.e. there is an absence of a sense of growth and the alternative is stagnation and decay). Now Erikson talks about the "mid-life transition" in adult development in which the individual reappraises what he/she has done with her life thus far (i.e. what is happening in relationships with partners, relatives and friends, including a re-evaluation of his/her marriage, career, lifestyle etc.).

This is also a period when the individual begins to see physical changes as the biological clock ticks away; changes that show "the summer of life is over and the autumn of life has begun" (Jung, as in Jaffre, 1963). There is a shift in the way one thinks from "How long have I lived?" to "How much time do I have left?" One starts to become aware of one's own mortality!

A.2 JUNG'S THEORY OF INDIVIDUATION

Carl Jung (Jaffre, 1963), was a Swiss physician, whose theory of human development is based on the process of moving towards fulfillment of the unique potential within each of us - hence the term "individuation". Jung had a view of life which emphasised growth and change over the lifespan. Now the first half of life, according to Jung, is one of accommodation - we adapt to the world. For instance, we identify with individuals, groups and organisations, and our roles amplify who we are. We develop a persona or mask that enables us to develop stable and reliable ways to interact with others.

However our persona can also hide who we are. We can become over identified with certain roles. For example, stereotypes of the pinstripe suited lawyer or the staid accountant are examples of occupational roles which come to mind. During this first half of life, we are preoccupied with our career and possibilities, and perhaps have lost touch with the important hidden properties of our nature. According to Jung, our goals up until this stage have been mastery and achievement of the outside world.

So having an "external" orientation in the first half of life, Jung contends that the second half of life has a more internal orientation, concerned with the search for:

- Individual identity
- Self-authenticity
- Self-actualisation
- Achieving a sense of integration or wholeness.

At mid-life we begin the transition of turning inwards, which for some people may mean a "crisis". So in a sense, this crisis represents a compensatory mechanism, which enables us to develop neglected aspects of ourselves. An imposed loss such as the experience of organisational change, redundancy or job loss, may act as an external trigger precipitating such a crisis. Alternatively there may be internal triggers to do with the personal circumstances of the individual which precipitate such a crisis, for example:

- Divorce
- Death of a friend or family member
- Loss of youth/health
- Unfulfilled dreams, hopes and ambitions.

In summary, we have seen that adulthood or mid-life can be viewed as a stage of our growth and development as a person. As in the case of other stages of life (refer the Erikson model presented earlier), there are certain challenges which need to be faced, and changes or adjustments which need to be made, which for many may constitute a crisis. Erikson talks about developing concerns for others and fulfilling goals in terms of family, career and society, whilst Jung talks about finding ourselves.

APPENDIX B: CAREERS IN THE CONTEMPORARY WORKPLACE

B.1 THE TRADITIONAL CAREER MODEL

> Career is the evolving sequence of a person's work experience over time (Arthur, Hall & Lawrence, 1989).

Careers are an important part of who we are. An individual's career has a major impact on their life. As referred to earlier in Chapter 1, under the "old deal" employment relationship between employer and employees (which operated up to the mid to late 1980s), employers virtually guaranteed job security and assumed the major responsibility for an individual's career. In return, employees provided loyalty and service to the employer. The traditional or old career model was characterised by:

- A series of upward moves with steadily increasing power, status and income, where organisations were structured like pyramids
- Employees staying in one career with 40 years uninterrupted work, sometimes with the one organisation (which was typically rewarded with a presentation of a gold watch on retirement at 65 years of age)
- Employees moving through one cycle of discrete career stages (e.g., exploration, establishment, maintenance, and decline)
- A continuous and relatively stable process where people had a single career identity
- Career development being more the responsibility of the organisation.

However the paternalism and dependency which characterised the industrial age is no longer applicable. Under the "new deal" employment relationship, which is more "exchange based" (i.e., what's in it for the employee as well as what's in it for the organisation), career management has now become much more the employee's responsibility. The rungs on the corporate ladder have become broken or obsolete! The career ladder has been replaced by a career lattice.

In today's turbulent workplace, some jobs/occupations have almost disappeared, whilst new ones have emerged. New career possibilities with seemingly previously unrelated combinations of disciplines, now constitute viable career paths (e.g., law and information technology).

The ability of organisations to compete is predominantly vested in their people. Organisations therefore need to energise and retain their key talent and valued employees, who are critical to the success of the enterprise. Some critical career management questions include:

- *What does the concept of a career mean in the contemporary workplace, given flatter organisational structures and no long-term guarantees?*
- *How much responsibility should the organisation take for the career development of their employees?*
- *What are some of the key career challenges which employees are facing in the contemporary workplace?*

B.2 NEW CAREER MODELS

> The shift from a traditional career model to a new model confronts us with a problem outside our experience! No norms exist to tell us how to evaluate, plan, review, analyse, promote or otherwise live out the new career. The largely static, restrictive assumptions of the old view of careers and organsations, needs to be replaced by a more dynamic, knowledge driven model (Arthur & Rousseau, 1996).

On average, an individual will have between two to three career changes, and seven to nine jobs over their working life. Given that the old career model is relatively obsolete:

- *What has replaced it?*
- *What is the new career model?*

The answer to these questions is not straightforward. There is no one single new career model, but a number of models that include:

- **The spiral career** - a combination of vertical and lateral career moves and life experiences
- **The boundary-less or portfolio career** - a series of interwoven projects, patchwork of contracts/activities, where a person's career is not "bounded" by an organisation

- **The protean career** - the adaptable career (Proteus was a Greek god who could re-invent himself and adapt to any situation)
- **The hyphenated career** - where a person's work life may be interrupted by periods of unemployment or "time out" for family or other personal reasons
- **The internal career** - a person's perceptions and self-constructing of their career, where the importance of career script and psychological success (pursuing one's own purpose, goals and values and a search for inner meaning and connectedness), is emphasised.

All of the above models involve a more holistic concept of careers - looking at the whole person and their career within their total life: not just in terms of their occupation.

B.3 IMPLICATIONS OF NEW CAREER MODELS FOR EMPLOYEES

The implications of new career models for employees typically include the following:

- Assuming greater responsibility for their career management and development (we are all self-employed!)
- Coming to terms with issues of self-definition (who am I?) and normlessness (what are the rules?) - particularly for older workers who have grown up under the old career paradigm
- The need for personal identity development and strengthening (one's identity is no longer so closely tied to the organisation)
- Development of career sub-identities (with dual qualifications and/or multiple occupational identities and/or industry associations)
- The possible need for frequent reinvention.

In short, employees need to take more responsibility for their career, develop new "career mindsets" and develop more of an inner focus. Career growth is now one of self-actualisation or self-fulfillment of:

- Doing one's own thing and following one's own destiny
- Developing one's own "personal compass"!

> Your only sustainable competitive advantage is your ability to learn (Hakim, 1994).

Career development now requires a commitment to lifelong learning given the rapid explosion of new knowledge. However it may be difficult to balance time for learning against the demands of the job and/or the family or other responsibilities. Careers may need to be built both across and within organisations - staying too long may erode employment value! Career diversity is now much more valued in the contemporary workplace, and "employability" has now become much more important than employment! Job security:

- Now lies more within the individual
- Is not so dependent upon the organisation
- Is a readiness and willingness to adapt!

Thus these changes in meaning and emphasis to the terms "careers" and "career development" pose significant personal development challenges and demands for many employees. Career development is no longer a "one off" event following completion of secondary education (which involved making a choice and the completion of initial training or education), but rather a life-long process.

B.4 THE NEW WORKER AND CAREERS

Surviving and thriving

Just as organisations have been reinventing themselves in order to "survive and thrive", employees/workers have been undergoing a similar process of reappraisal. This process has involved:

- A questioning of traditional beliefs and values
- The shift to a more internal focus
- A reappraisal of abilities, interests and attributes
- Development of new understandings and adoption of contemporary career models (including associated career expectations and attitudes)
- Enhanced self-awareness and understanding
- A strengthening of self-identity and purpose.

The demands of the contemporary workplace require a "new kind of worker": one who is better equipped to manage a complexity of career and workplace issues, and deal more effectively with psychological pressures (whether their origin is from inside or outside of the workplace).

However development is a two-way responsibility. Some workers may decline or be unable to take up the challenges of the contemporary workplace. They risk being left riding in the "white water turbulence"!

How organisations can assist

Organisations can play a part in assisting their employees to make sense of what is happening in the contemporary workplace. Implicit in this approach is an understanding of the drivers of recent workplace change, the dynamics of the contemporary workplace, and effective adaptation and coping strategies. The development of "soft skills" needs to be reinforced, including:

- Self-responsibility
- Proactivity
- Perseverance
- Relationship building
- Resilience or hardiness
- Flexibility and adaptability
- Innovation
- Continuous learning
- Self-marketing skills.

Studies have shown that one of the key reasons for employee dissatisfaction is a lack of career options and self development (refer to Chapter 5). Organisations can partly combat this by offering career self-development programs, so that individual career success and performance are optimised. Such an arrangement constitutes a learning partnership between the organisation and the employee.

Benefits for organisations

Apart from the need for employment relationship alignment, there are other organisational benefits in addressing the "deeper" or "soft skills" development needs of employees, including:

- The increased requirement for self-discipline and self-sufficiency with the delocalisation of work
- The need for self-regulation in the workplace, given the prevalence of flatter structures without formal hierarchy
- A required emotional display and self-management of feelings, particularly in customer service roles.

Personal development includes an emphasis on:

- Interpersonal and relationship building skills

- Developing resilience
- Handling change and ambiguity
- Enhancing general life skills, all of which are transferable to any job/ career (i.e., development of "soft skills").

The development of self-management and self-reliance skills reduces management load. Converging theories of work motivation emphasise the critical influence of volition and self-influences on performance. A person with a strong sense of mastery and high level of optimism is likely to approach change in a positive way, and is likely to exhibit a high level of work commitment, even in the face of uncertainty.

B.5 IMPLICATIONS OF NEW CAREER MODELS FOR ORGANISATIONS

The role for organisations in the career development of their people has now become one of more support and assistance. This may typically involve:

- Providing access to career development knowledge, resources and techniques (including, where appropriate, online services, independent professional career guidance and coaching, etc.)
- Training and development on themes such as resilience, transitions, etc.
- Encouraging continual learning in the form of training and development (including recognition of external studies)
- Fostering a career management and development ethos in the organisation (which may involve typical career pathing prospects, regular career development discussions where the continually changing needs of both parties can be reviewed, etc.)
- The accommodation of a variety of career needs of employees (consistent with the needs of the business).

However in the era of flatter structures, management is sometimes unsure as to what they are able to offer their employees by way of career development. Some employees are also unsure of what the concept of a career means in the contemporary workplace, given that the traditional career model is dead! Consistent with this approach is the need for organisations to:

- Develop career paths within the organisation
- Provide cross functional learning opportunities
- Have a clearly defined training and development policy.

B.6 IMPLICATIONS OF NEW CAREER MODELS FOR MANAGERS

Most managers have a responsibility to develop their people. Furthermore, career management and development constitutes the central theme of individual development. It therefore follows that basic career dialogue/counselling skills should form an essential or core management competency. However for managers to assist and develop their people, they need to be confident about their own career management and development. A manager, who is unsure about his or her career direction, training and development needs, challenges, etc., is hardly in a position to assist his or her subordinates. Managers therefore need to:

- Have a deeper appreciation/understanding of what constitutes a career in the contemporary workplace, the issues and challenges facing employees, and the attributes required to "survive and thrive"
- Have worked through their own career management and development issues
- Demonstrated the personal qualities that contribute to a climate of trust and openness with their subordinates
- Manage change and transitions effectively (given the constantly changing workplace)
- Manage a variety of relationships with their people
- Have developed some basic skills towards engaging and assisting others in their careers.

One of the outcomes of the above support, assistance and relationship building, is a more engaged and satisfied workforce.

> Note: The WRDI Institute has developed a Total Career Management package comprising the following:
>
> - A Career and Talent Development Policy
> - A Managers Guide to having Constructive Career Conversations
> - A Guide to Refreshing your Career (for employees)
>
> Refer to the WRDI Institute web site for further details.

APPENDIX C: THE SKILLS SEGMENTATION QUESTIONNAIRE (SSQ)

C1 PLOTTING OF ROLES: DEVELOPMENT OF THE SKILLS SEGMENTATION QUESTIONNAIRE (SSQ)

As referred to in Chapter 3, the WRDI Institute has developed a 49 item questionnaire called the Skills Segmentation Questionnaire (SSQ). This questionnaire enables roles to be analysed and categorized according to the four quadrant skills' based workforce segmentation model. Depending upon in which quadrant a role lies, this will impact on the HR policies and practices applicable to that role, including the reporting of human capital data.

The questionnaire accommodates the eight ways in which roles can contribute to skills value (i.e., roles can be scored according to these skills value elements), together with the degree of impact of those skills on the provision of products and services to clients (i.e., local or concentrated versus widespread impact).

These eight skills elements include skills that contribute to:

- Revenue and sales
- Stakeholder relations
- Costs and efficiency
- Quality
- Innovation
- Organisational capability
- Reputation and risk management
- Financial performance.

> Note. Example plots have been provided in the coloured pages of the Introduction Chapter, but it is stressed that the positioning of these plots is dependent upon particular organisational considerations.

C2 LINKING THE SKILLS SEGMENATION QUESTIONNAIRE (SSQ) TO THE BUSINESS STRATEGY

The Skills Segmentation Questionnaire (SSQ) can be further extended to include a weighting factor applied to each of the eight skills value elements, according to the business strategy.

The purpose of the application of these weightings is therefore to link the relative importance of roles to the business strategy.

Unique and valuable skills are relevant to differentiating capabilities and core competencies (refer to Chapter 5 including examples of firms, their critical capabilities and their drivers, and core competencies), and establishing a competitive advantage. It is therefore important to identify those skills value elements which are the drivers of these differentiating capabilities and core competencies. Thereafter it is important to focus on developing those drivers (or skills value elements), and the roles which incorporate those drivers, in order to maximise that differentiating capability or core competency. .

We shall see in an example in C3, how the various skills value elements or drivers are able to be weighted or prioritized, according to the business strategy, with these weightings applied to various roles. We shall now look at how the plotting of critical roles can be "adjusted" with the application of these weightings.

> Note. Either a firm performs different activities from its rivals (which require unique skills), or it performs or executes similar activities to rivals in more efficient and effective ways (which relates more to valuable skills). A "me to" strategy may keep a firm in the game but it isn't the basis for long-term above average performance.

C3 AN EXAMPLE: ADJUSTMENT AND COMPARISON BETWEEN DIVERSE ROLES

> People in the future will be paid based more for on the importance of role to the business rather than their professional affiliation. (Beames, 2009)

To illustrate the adjustment of roles approach foreshadowed, consider four senior management/executive roles in ACME Pharmaceuticals:

- The Research and Development Manager
- The HR Director
- The CFO (Chief Financial Officer)
- The Marketing Manager.

Of these roles, which is the more critical? Which role adds more value? Which role is more important to the execution of the business strategy? This initial job analysis approach, based on the SSQ, includes three key considerations:

1) The relevance of the eight skills value elements that contribute to the overall skills value of the role (refer C1)
2) The impact of the role on the provision of products and services to external clients (e.g., local versus widespread)
3) The extent to which the role requires the acquisition of unique skills.

Relevance of Skills Value Elements to the Four Roles

	SKILLS VALUE ELEMENT	R & D MGR	HR DIR	CFO	MKT MGR
1	Revenue	+			+++
2	Customer satisfaction	++			++
3	Costs	+			
4	Quality	++			
5	Innovation	++			+
6	Organisational capability		++		
7	Reputation	+	+	+	+
8	Financial performance	+		+++	

Note. The above table is in a simplified or summary form. There are a number of items in the SSQ relating to each of the eight skills value elements.

A greater number of + indicates a high skills value element associated with the role.

Roles that include more than one skills value element have the potential to have a synergistic impact on a firm's performance.

From the initial plot, without adjusting for the business strategy, the Marketing Manager and the R & D Manager's roles are slightly more valuable and critical compared to the HR Manager and the CFO roles.

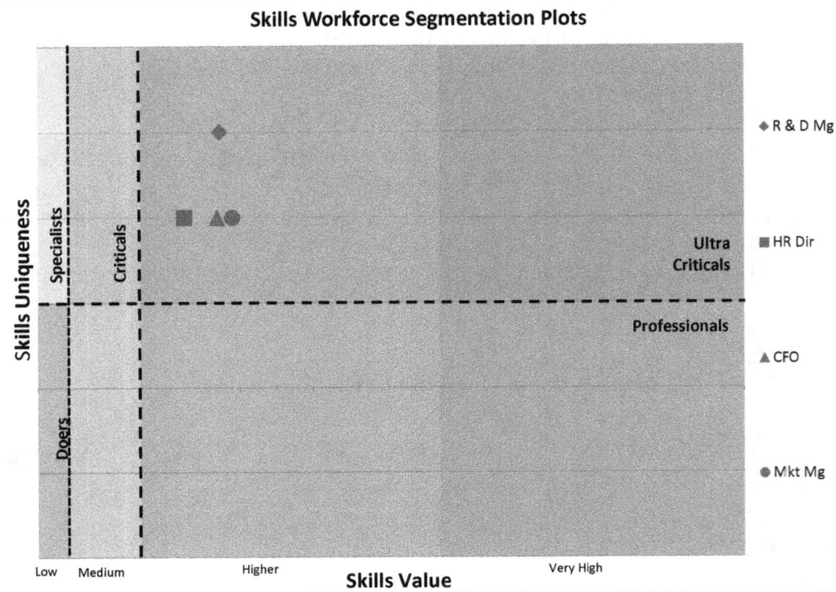

But let's assume that the firm has been developing a new drug of which there is projected high sales demand. Based on the above business strategy, the eight skills value elements have been allocated the following weightings.

	SKILLS VALUE ELEMENT	IMPORTANCE OF SKILLS ELEMENT TO THE BUSINESS STRATEGY
1	Revenue	Extremely Important
2	Customer satisfaction	Extremely Important
3	Costs	Less Important
4	Quality	More Important
5	Innovation	Extremely Important
6	Organisational capability	More Important
7	Reputation, brand	More Important
8	Financial performance	Less Important

As referred to earlier, some of the eight skills value elements will be more important to the execution of the business strategy. Accordingly, in adjusting skills value scores for critical roles, weightings have then been applied to the four roles. The selection of this weighting is a strategic decision.

Then each these four roles have been adjusted based on these weightings. Further adjustments are then made based on the risk of making a mistake in the role (which impacts on skills value) and the difficulty of replacement (which impacts on skills uniqueness). What is just as important as the positioning of the final role plot is the process of working through and considering these relevant concepts.

	ROLE	RISK OF MAKING A MISTAKE	DIFFICULTY IN ATTRACTION OF REPLACEMENT
1	R & D Manager	Reasonably High	Moderate
2	HR Director	Moderate	Moderate
3	CFO	Moderate	Moderate
4	Marketing Manager	Moderate	Moderate

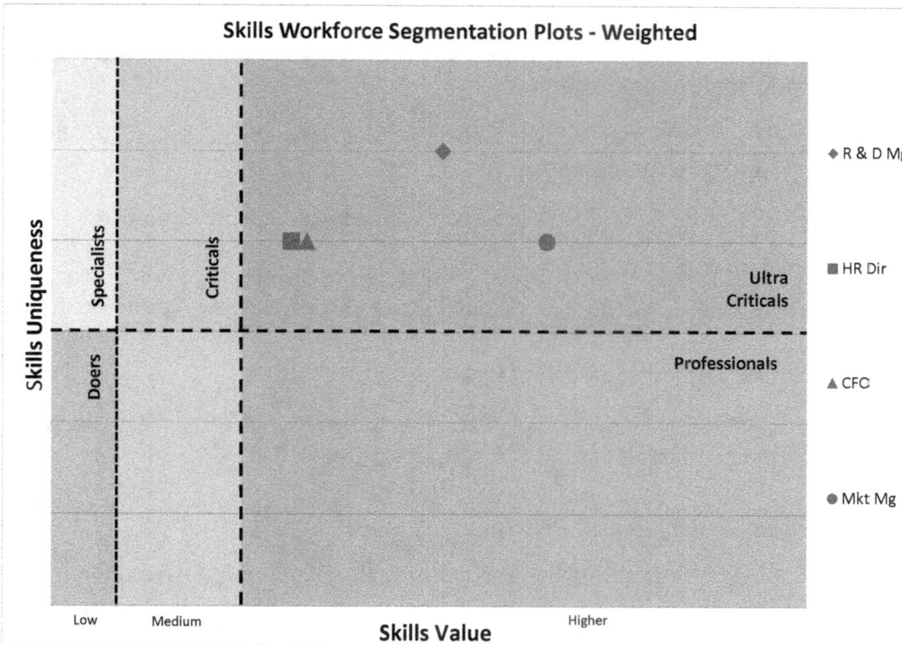

Compared to the initial plot:

- The Marketing Manager's role and the R & D Manager's role becomes even more valuable and critical;
- The CFO the HR Director's roles become a little less valuable and critical.

Resources should therefore be directed to ensuring maximum performance in the above two more critical roles.

One of the outcomes of the approach foreshadowed is that people in the future will more likely be paid based more for on the importance of role to the business, rather than on their professional affiliation. In other words, the role of a HR Director may be assessed as being more critical to business outcomes in a professional services firm (and paid accordingly), compared to say a manufacturing company.

C4 THREE STEPS TO QUICKLY INCREASING BUSINESS PERFORMANCE: FOCUS ON CRITICAL ROLES

> **The quickest route to increasing shareholder wealth is to increase employee performance in critical positions.** (Becker, Huselid & Beatty, 2009)

Following the identification of more critical roles, the focus should then be on maximizing the performance of people in these roles to increase business performance. To that end:

- The people occupying these roles should have the necessary capabilities and core competencies
- Rewards should be structured to encourage high performance.

People investments should be targeted at developing people occupying these roles. Without a compelling strategic logic as to where people investments should be directed, personal influence, politics and traditional levers of power carry the day.

> Note: These more critical roles or jobs may not necessarily always be those roles in the top few rungs of the organisational

Step 1: Identify Critical Roles

- The identification of critical roles should be based on the following five key considerations:
  - The extent to which the skills are valuable (i.e., enhance revenue, customer satisfaction, and quality, reduce costs, contribute to innovation, protect the firm's reputation, etc), and unique
  - The impact of the role on the provision of products and services to clients
  - The importance of the skills (associated with the role) to the business strategy
  - The risk associated with the role i.e., the consequences of making a mistake in the role)
  - The difficulty of finding a replacement in the role.

Step 2: Assess capability of those in Critical/Ultra-Critical roles

- Using a combination of methodologies (e.g., performance ratings, 360 degree feedback, psych assessment), assess current performance and future potential of those in more critical roles
- Determine whether incumbent(s) are capable or potentially capable, and if not recruit replacement(s).

Step 3: Enhance performance and develop those in Critical/Ultra-Critical roles

- Prepare an individual development and performance improvement plan and implement the same
- Conduct an engagement and retention risk assessment and implement interventions that may be adversely impacting on performance and retention
- Review the remuneration and benefits package attached to the role, including the performance based component
- Provide coaching (including on-boarding in the case of a new incumbent), to assist in this development and performance improvement plan.

C5 ADDRESSING SOME KEY QUESTIONS ABOUT THE SSQ METHODOLOGY

What is the orientation of the SSQ

The SSQ has both an internal (i.e., internal efficiency, effectiveness and sustainability), as well as an external (i.e., impact of the skills on the provision of products and services to customers), orientation.

How are the skills value elements, impacts and weightings determined for the SSQ?

The construction of the questionnaire has been determined on the basis of:

- Its adaptation from the Lepakk and Snell model
- Focus groups with managers and professionals
- Interviews with academics
- The judgment of the developer of the tool.

The questionnaire is typically completed with involvement from the following personnel:

- An internal HR person who has been trained in the SSQ methodology
- The senior or immediate manager of the role in question
- Executives in the case of the application of weightings of the eight skills value elements and their link to the business strategy, and risk factors.

Can the weightings be applied on a functional basis (i.e., different weightings to say the HR Department roles versus the Marketing Department roles) in the SSQ?

Not under normal circumstances (see reference to a conglomerate organisation below). The purpose of the SSQ is to assess the relative importance of roles to the business, divorced from organisational structural considerations.

> Note. It may be the case that from time to time, a role or some roles become very important because of short term business imperatives (e.g., completion of a project to meet agreed deadlines). However these are short term rather than medium term concerns. As such, short term concerns are not typically taken into account in the SSQ, as ultimately the intent of the SSQ is more strategic, linking the importance of roles to the business strategy – not short term deadlines.

How should the weightings be applied in a conglomerate organisation?

In a conglomerate organisation (i.e., where there are diverse functions), the weightings can be applied to each Business Unit Profit Centre (which implies that each of these Business Units will need to develop their own Human Capital Strategic Plan), mindful that the strategies of these profit centers will link to the overall strategy of the business. For high level positions or shared services roles, then the weightings should reflect the overall business strategy (i.e., for the organisation as a whole).

In a more vertically integrated organisation, the weightings would typically be applied to the whole organisation.

How should the weightings be applied in a global organisation?

In a global organisation, the weightings can be applied to each region, mindful that the strategies of these regions will vary, but also presumably will link to the overall strategy of the business. For high level positions or shared services roles, then the weightings should reflect the overall business strategy (i.e., for the organisation as a whole).

How are systems and technology considerations accommodated in the SSQ?

Technology and systems are not considered to be a separate skills value element or category in their own right. A role which encompasses the development or implementation of technology or systems may be contributing to innovation, organisational capability, costs, etc., and will be scored accordingly in the SSQ.

How is the management of people accommodated in the SSQ?

People management is accommodated in the skills value element of Organisational Capability. More specifically, a role that involves managing people impacts on developing employees, and engaging and retaining them (and may also impact on recruitment). Such a role will therefore score on this skills value element of the questionnaire and contribute to the overall skills value score for the role.

How is the ability of the role to substantially impact on cost savings or generate substantial revenues taken into account in the SSQ?

The SSQ takes into account the skills value of the job, together with the impact of those skills in the delivery of products and services to clients or customers. This impact could be local or more widespread, or it could be on part or all of the range of products and services. If this impact is assessed as being disproportional in either reducing costs or increasing revenues (i.e., over and above what would normally be the case), then there is provision in the impact assessment part of the questionnaire to accommodate this (i.e., to increase the impact assessment rating over and above what would normally be the case).

How are the skills value weightings determined and applied for the SSQ?

The weightings for the eight skills elements in relation to the business strategy are determined by the executives in the organisation. Hence the tool can be customized to suit particular organisational circumstances (e.g., increasing sales revenue and customer satisfaction may be much more important than reducing costs, and as such, the former skills element can be weighted more heavily). These weightings should be reviewed on a regular basis, consistent with a review of the business strategy.

What is the process for determining and applying these skills value weightings for the SSQ?

Workshop (with the executives) to explain the SSQ concept and agree on the weightings, consistent with the business strategy.

Should the SSQ be used as a basis for setting salary levels?

This tool lies somewhere in between a qualitative and quantitative approach to job evaluation and it should be used as a guide only. The process of working through the business strategy, weightings of the various skills elements, assessing risk, difficulty of replacement and scoring of the roles, is equally as valuable as the final plot of various roles and associated report. Ultimately judgments need to be applied to assessing role importance, including any subsequent interventions.

The aim of the tool is to provide a deeper appreciation and understanding of the importance of roles and then to allocate resources where they will have maximum impact. This process will invariably involve reviewing where an organisation wishes to position itself in the salary range established for particular jobs. Does it want to position itself in the mid-range or towards the top or bottom.

Should traditional methodologies for job evaluation and salary level determination be abandoned?

Traditional methodologies still have their place and as such should be preserved. However they don't provide a basis for the most effective allocation of resources. Rather they represent a starting point - not a finishing point, in ultimately determining investments in people occupying various roles, including rewards and benefits, training and development, etc.

How can the SSQ be applied in terms of job redesign to increase skills value and hence the competitive advantage of the firm?

The skills value of a job can be increases in two ways:

1) Either increase the relevance of the various eight skills elements to the role (a form of up-skilling or multi-skilling)
2) Increase the impact of the various skills elements of the role.

By way of illustration, in Disneyland comparing the roles of the people in the Mickey Mouse outfit and the role of the Cleaners, which one is more important?

By training the Cleaners in customer service, and then the Cleaners providing advice and assistance to visitors, this role becomes more important because it encompasses two skills elements:

1) The cost of products and services (i.e., maintaining the facilities)
2) Contributing to customer service/satisfaction.

Whereas the Mickey Mouse role encompasses only one skills element – it contributes to customer service/satisfaction.

In the case of the Cleaner, organisational efficiency was enhanced by combining diverse tasks into a single role, rather than employ additional staff to provide direction and advice and assistance to visitors. Most likely it also increased the job satisfaction of Cleaners, providing a benefit to both the individuals and the organisation.

Therefore the SSQ provides a framework from which to analyse how the skills value of the role can be increased, which in turn provides increased customer benefits and organisational efficiency, and/or reduces costs.

Aren't all roles important in an organisation?

Yes. Obviously organisations cannot function efficiently if some roles are not filled, or the people occupying those roles are poor performers. Every link in the chain is important in producing an overall result. In the same way, a football team would not be competitive it if did not have all its full complement of players on the field, or some of those players were playing injured.

However as in the case of the football team, some roles/positions are more important than others, and this importance can fluctuate over the length of the game. For example, if the team is defending at a particular stage in the game (i.e., adopting a defensive strategy), then defensive positions become more important than attacking positions. And so it is the same in the workplace, where some roles are more important than others in contributing to the business strategy and successful outcomes.

In summary roles can vary dramatically in the extent to which they contribute strategically and add value.

> Note. The SSQ and associated plotting tool forms part of the Human Capital Strategic Plan package and the Recruitment Strategic Plan package (Advanced Versions) which are able to be purchased from the WRDI Institute.

APPENDIX D: AN INTERVIEW WITH COLIN BEAMES

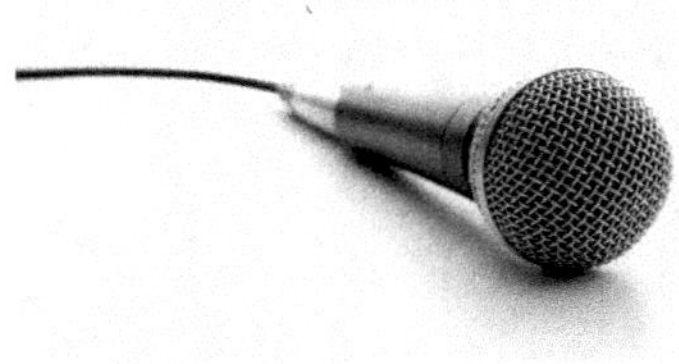

What is your background?

My first career was as a civil engineer where I worked in a number of roles from technical, through to management and consultancy, predominantly in the concrete and quarrying, civil construction and mining industries. I wasn't exactly clear on a specific career path, and I didn't have a burning desire to be an engineer. However having done reasonably well in the maths and sciences at school, it was a case of choosing either a science or engineering course at university. I chose engineering, and more specifically civil engineering, because it kept my options open with wider choices and greater flexibility.

So having qualified as an engineer, I worked as a design engineer for a consulting firm for a couple of years. At the end of this period, I was keen to gain some exposure to the commercial world, so I joined a national pre-mix concrete and quarrying company as a quality control engineer. I worked in the company's concrete and raw materials testing laboratories for three years. Then quite fortuitously (although I do believe to a certain extent in fate and destiny provided one does the "hard yards"), I was selected to join a small group of internal consultants or advisors, working with an external consultant, implementing Management by Objectives (MBO) throughout the company's Australian operations.

This was a fantastic opportunity for me in my late 20's, travelling around the country and being exposed to the world of management and organisational consultancy for 12 months. It was a position that I revelled in. However at the time, I was too interested in climbing the management tree, and it was only later in life that I returned to consultancy – a role to which I consider that I am better suited to. Following this 12 month MBO consultancy stint, I then worked in various senior line management and consulting roles in the resources sector up until my mid 40's.

What made you study psychology?

My wife had started her own counselling business in my early 40's – she had a background in social work. At that time, I had become involved in some human resources and internal management consulting activities with the firm I was working with (i.e., the Training Guarantee Scheme, business and strategic planning, recruitment and selection). I found this to be more interesting than some of the other engineering activities which I was also engaged in at that time. My wife's business started to flourish and I had always been interested in psychology, having had a strong interest in people and "what made them tick" (including myself), as well as an interest in organisations and how they worked. So I decided to "dip my toe in the water" and enrol part-time at university in the early 90's in a Bachelor of Arts degree to study psychology. I worked full-time and studied part-time, with the interest and conviction in my new career path growing progressively.

The topic which I selected for my 4th year psychology honours thesis was mid-life career change. Given that I was experiencing this phenomena, I thought that I had better develop some understanding of it! I remember at that time (i.e., in the early 90's), that people who changed careers at a more mature age were regarded with some level of suspicion - as being somewhat unstable and occupying university places that should be the domain of school leavers. How attitudes have since changed dramatically in a relatively short space of time with the advent of life-long learning and career changers now being regarded as having transferable skills!

Following my graduation with a BA (majoring in psychology), I started work as a psychologist, with a focus on career transition and general counselling. I wanted to be independent and "do my own thing", whatever that might turn out to be, having had enough of the politics of working for larger organisations. I was required to undergo supervision for a two year period (which I found invaluable), as part of the registration requirements for practicing as a psychologist. During my psychology studies, I had undertaken a counselling orientation in my choice of subjects, partly because of the timing and availability of those subjects, which fitted in better with my work schedule. However after a period of time, I gravitated back towards working with organisations in HR and management consulting, so I decided to "top up" my knowledge in organisational psychology by completing a Graduate Certificate in this field.

During that period, I undertook a number of consulting assignments both in Australia and Papua New Guinea (PNG) involving business and strategic planning, organisational development and change, human resources services, training and development, psychological assessment and selection, and career guidance. I then decided to articulate my Graduate Certificate into a Masters of Business Administration (MBA), as my consulting activities were spreading wider than a strictly organisational psychology focus. I felt that I needed to be across such matters in terms of latest thinking, concepts, trends, research, etc. Working in PNG enabled me to complete part of these studies as a remote student. Being somewhat confined at weekends, because of security reasons, provided me with the free time to do so.

I also supervised some conditionally registered psychologists (as I had also been supervised), mentored to some 4th year psychology students at Griffith University, and lectured to 3rd year psychology students at the Queensland University of Technology. During this time, I was appointed an adjunct lecturer at the University of Queensland with two master's organisational psychology students undertaking practicums for me, and assisting me in some initial development work associated with the WRDI®.

How did you become interested in developing the WRDI®?

I was counselling three males in their mid 40's in the late 1990's who had opted for job security, hoping their employers would look after them. However they had been outplaced, having become victims of rationalisation in their industry sectors. These three males had failed to take adequate responsibility for their own career development. They were operating under the outdated "old deal" or more paternalistic employment relationship, where the employer promised job security, took more responsibility for the carer development of their employees, and the employees would offer loyalty and service in return.

This was the irritant or catalyst for the birth of the WRDI®, although I didn't know it at the time. I started to think that a more proactive approach was needed by individuals in managing their careers and charting their own destiny, particularly as I noted some considerable stress and uncertainty in the workforce with changes that were occurring. So I commenced developing some materials around new career models, given that the old career model of one career with say two or three jobs and 40 years of continuous work with the handshake and gold watch at 65 years of age had become somewhat obsolete.

At that time I was reading some material on the characteristics and dynamics of the contemporary workplace, and the changing workplace relationship or the new psychological contract between employer and employee. I talked to a number of colleagues and bounced ideas off them and so my ideas and a conceptual framework of understanding progressively developed. Then to put this in an organisational context, I came to the view that fundamentally the traditional employer/employee or workplace relationship had changed. The powerful cocktail of technological change and globalisation was responsible for this shift. Job security could no longer be guaranteed by organisations (even if they promised it), and individuals had to become more responsible for their own career development. The "old deal" or more paternalistic workplace relationship was dead!

I thought that relationships were important in personal life so they must be important in the workplace. So I reasoned that it would be interesting to examine and measure the workplace or employer/employee relationship with a survey. This could then serve as a front-end diagnostic tool from which interventions might follow. During my reading around these matters, I spotted a model of the psychological contract in a journal article by David Guest, who is regarded as a world "guru" on the psychological contract. The light bulb went on - I immediately saw how this model could be adapted into a generic, commercial tool.

Hence the WRDI® - Workplace Relationship Development Indicator - was born! At that stage of my MBA, I had three units to complete, so I decided to undertake these units with a dissertation (25,000 word thesis), on the development of the WRDI®. This dissertation was supervised by two psychologists, one of whom was an expert statistician. I figured that this undertaking would impose additional discipline on me and add rigor and credibility to the development of the tool.

I incorporated a number of enhancements into Guest's model, including a model of turnover and performance, and a greater emphasis on specifying the "deal" (both the tangibles and intangibles). Initially the WRDI® started life as a mass survey tool, but then the concept of optional individual survey reports emerged, which provided employees with a print out of their own psychological contract or relationship with the organisation. This individual report generation capability was consistent with the philosophy of the "new deal" employment relationship – one which is more exchanged based and more arms length – providing a framework where both the individual's needs as well as the organisation's needs could be discussed and addressed.

This individual report generation option also served as a basis for a career management/development discussions, which tied in neatly with my earlier work on contemporary career models. From my own experience, as well as that of WRDI® licensees, individual report debriefing can be a significant transforming and empowering experience. The individual report and associated debrief addresses the fundamental questions as to whether individuals are committed to the organisation, satisfied in their jobs, motivated to exert effort and likely to stay with the organisation in the medium term. Importantly, it provides a forum for individuals to "tell their story", to bring issues to the surface, and for empowering them to take appropriate action concerning job and career related issues. This action may, under some circumstances, include assisting individuals to leave the organisation where they may be "square pegs in round holes". One of the criticisms of surveys is that the findings are not always acted upon. However in the case of individual reports, transformation can occur from the "bottom up", and if nothing else happens with the aggregate report findings and recommendations, at least the individual gets something valuable out of the process.

Other progressive developments that emerged with the WRDI® included its applications over the employment life cycle, from post recruitment assessment or audit through to exit interviews. Aggregate survey reporting was also developed to include a quantification of retention risk and alignment, including a calculation of imminent employee turnover risk in dollar terms, all of which has been patented. A further reporting refinement included a classification of leavers according to the three Ps: "Push", "Pull" and "Personal" reasons, to provide a more fine grained assessment of retention risk quantification (i.e., numbers of leavers in each of these three categories).

One of the unique features of the WRDI® is the comprehensiveness of the approach in that we are able to differentiate and address systemic organisational issues (i.e., "top down" approach with aggregate measurement or reporting and diagnosis), local workplace issues, as well as individual issues (i.e., "bottom up" approach), providing a more complete and powerful solution. Because the psychological contract is such a fundamental concept, the flexibility and utility of the WRDI® is truly unique, with its application extending well beyond that of other survey models of engagement and retention.

I also realised that a "one size fits all" approach to engagement and retention would not suffice in the contemporary workplace, given the diversity and complexity of the various employer/employee relationships that had emerged. I came across a skills' based workforce segmentation model which was developed by USA academics David Lepak and Scott Snell. Like Guest's model of the psychological contract, I then adapted their model from a research orientation to a more practical application. This model, which takes into account both the value and uniqueness of skills relative to the role, classifies employees according to four quadrants. I then developed a questionnaire which enables roles within an organisation to be analysed and plotted according to this four quadrant model. With this adapted skills' based workforce segmentation model, the WRDI® was then able to be embedded in a more strategic workforce framework – a framework for developing employment strategies, differentiated "deals", and approaches to engagement and retention. Furthermore, this model forms the basis for developing a human capital strategic plan including the reporting of human capital data.

What is involved in developing a survey tool?

There is a vast difference between developing a questionnaire, as opposed to a quality survey tool that:

- Is based on a model which is underpinned by theory and research
- Has rigorous psychometric properties
- Is diagnostic (i.e., has cause and effect capability), including high levels of predictability
- Has key measures which are strongly linked to "bottom line" consideration
- Has a well developed norm base.

The survey development process involves firstly being across the relevant research. Then there are a series of questions to be addressed concerning:

- *What other survey tools are out there in the market place?*

- *To what extent the new tool is different or offers a potential competitive advantage?*
- *What the perceived need may be in the market place (as opposed to interest)?*
- *To what extent prospective purchasers may be predisposed to adopting or embracing a new survey tool?*
- *What business model should be adopted to get traction in the market place?*
- *What Information Technology platform is appropriate, consistent with the above?*

The development process looks something like this:

- Select the survey model
- Develop items and scales based on previous research and focus groups
- Trial the survey, ensuring sufficient participants for an adequate sample size
- Evaluate the survey instructions and process, and confirm that those items comprising scales have psychometric properties that fall within acceptable criteria (i.e., reliability, validity and factor analysis)
- Determine the predictability of the model by statistical analysis (i.e., multiple regression analysis or structural equation modeling)
- Substitute new items for those that don't work and repeat the process regarding the analysis of psychometric properties
- Develop the norm base so that appropriate comparisons can be made, both within and across organisations and industries
- Develop reporting outputs and templates, explanation of meaning and interpretation of the findings, and possible interventions
- Develop a comprehensive Technical Manual, including a full description and analysis of psychometric properties
- Develop online hosting and reporting capability, with functionality consistent with the business model
- Collect case studies and testimonials
- Seek endorsements from expert third parties and develop a profile and brand awareness

- Develop marketing collateral including brochures, white papers, power point presentations, proposal templates, advertising materials
- Develop other documents (e.g., policy documents) and workshops and processes which wrap around the survey tool and its application
- In the case of a licensing model, develop licensing agreements and training/accreditation materials
- Continue to fine tune all of the above through ongoing iterations.

In short, the conceptual and technical development through to the commercialisation of a new quality survey tool is not a five minute exercise! The evolvement of the WRDI® has been a journey over a number of years, and what may appear as a linear and ordered process in retrospect, was not necessarily experienced to be so at the time.

What have been some of the difficulties in developing and commercialising a new HR product?

Doing something for the first time can be a steep learning curve, but notwithstanding, the exploration, investigation and conceptual development constitutes an integral part of the creative process. It's a matter of balance between learning from others and seeking their advice, whilst at the same time, approaching things with a relatively blank slate, and not being contaminated by past experiences. To that end, I liaised frequently with colleagues and sought their advice and assistance, and read and absorbed everything I could about the psychological contract and related themes. In particular, I liaised with a colleague Jim Bowden who was undertaking a similar development activity to me (can you believe that we met through tennis and were playing in the same tennis team), although Jim was further advanced along the track than what I was.

Obviously one makes mistakes, goes up "dry gullies" and can get diverted. The problem is that a good deal of your efforts don't lead to anything, and whilst you become more savvy and directed in respect of these efforts, you don't always know what will work in advance. People get enthusiastic and make promises, but fall by the wayside and fail to follow through, either because of other priorities, or lack of resources, commitment or capacity. What has been an eye opener for me is that what some firms claim to do (and I am talking global organisations in the HR space), and what they actually do, can be quite different. A number of these firms provide services to clients (e.g., leadership development), which are totally inconsistent with how those firms operate internally (i.e., they don't walk the talk).

Another trap is that you think that you are more advanced in the development process than what is actually the case. Things take longer to be accomplished than what was planned. One creates expectations and then gets frustrated when these things are not achieved. Furthermore there is a significant gap or time delay between effort and reward, which creates tension and contributes to financial pressures. Obviously a strong sense of conviction and vision is important in being able to sustain oneself and persevere. It's a bit like being on a moving train – difficult to jump off until one arrives at an appropriate station or interim point. It can be challenging enough establishing one's own business with an existing product, let alone developing and commercialising a new product.

I also underestimated the inherent conservatism of people, and their preoccupation with the more immediate, rather than their concern for longer term, more strategic considerations and systemic solutions. People get trapped in obsolete mindsets and the pressures of dealing with immediate issues, and often lack a conceptual framework and depth of understanding or appreciation of some of the changes, trends and fundamental challenges facing organisations and their people. Furthermore I have been surprised at the general lack of knowledge and unenlightenment around people management and measurement issues, and the tendency to *ad hoc* rather than strategic initiatives and approaches. In the book, I have lamented the state of the HR profession and its lack of influence at a time when people issues with the skills shortages (particularly key talent), are likely to dominate the business landscape over the next decade and beyond.

How do you view your career looking back?

What may have been viewed as a somewhat erratic career, at various stages of its unfolding, has ultimately come together to make sense. At the time of my career change from engineering to psychology, I was regarded with a degree of curiosity, and certainly this decision represented somewhat of a "leap in the dark". It was very much a case of following my inner voice, my intuition, and taking one step at a time. I used to worry about a lack of clarity around the outcome of my foray into psychology, but after discussing this with other mature aged career changers during my university studies, I realised they were less clear than me, so I stopped fretting about it.

My experience in counselling people about mid-life career change is that the answers invariably lie within the individual. The role of the career advisor is to assist in unlocking the solution – bringing it from the back of the brain to the front. Often this answer is more "grey" rather than "crystal clear". It's a case of being prepared to take risks, trust in the process, and most importantly, having the support of others. To that end, I have been extremely fortunate in having a wife whose support has been unfailing, even through more difficult times when I lost focus and wondered what in the name of goodness I was doing.

Looking back on my career, a diversity of experiences in a range of job/occupational settings are certainly very much to the fore, although at the time, my career development didn't make the same sense as what it now does in retrospect. It was only on subsequent reflection and readings that it became clearer that I was following the new career model, and embracing the attributes of lifelong learning and development. The elements of the WRDI® concept together with the skills' based segmentation model and human capital strategic plan concept (see later) coalesce into an ideal fit for me. It brings together my interests in relationships, organisations, careers and personal development, commercial/consulting activities and the development of my business, and the provision of an overarching and scientific approach to addressing some of the key challenges of the contemporary workplace, both for organisations and their people. Additionally, there is an altruistic, and dare I say it, spiritual aspect to the WRDI® in that through relationships, we grow and develop. Given the amount of time people spend at work; their relationship with their employer (or psychological contract) is a key relationship in their lives.

More recently you have created a Human Capital Strategic Plan package and a Recruitment Strategic Plan package. What are these packages and how did this come about?

I designed these packages because of the perceived need for HR Professionals to become more strategic and exert greater influence in their organisations, and otherwise address some of the key workforce management and human capital challenges ahead. These packages constitutes the practical application of much of this book, incorporating the various human capital models therein

You have also adapted the concept of the psychological contract to other applications. What are they?

With a colleague, I have developed a diagnostic tool called the Alliance Benchmark (ABTM) survey tool for application in multi-disciplinary project and program alliances in the construction industry. This tool which has extensive benchmarking, also has application for high performance teams (refer www. alliancebenchmark.com).

A related version of this diagnostic tool has also been developed called the Client/Stakeholder Relationship survey (based on the same psychological contract model), which measures and diagnoses the relationship between the client or stakeholders and the contact/alliance.

Also I have developed another tool called the Safety Commitment (SCTM) survey which is based on the concept of the safety psychological contract between employers and their workers (refer www.safetycompliance.biz). Most organisations have a safety charter which sets oout what they consider their obligations to be, and what they in turn expect from their workers, but they have no means of measuring adherence to the same.

Both of these tools combine my first life as an engineer, with my second life as a corporate psychologist, in so far as the nature of the industries to which they are applicable.

APPENDIX E: ABOUT THE WRDI INSTITUTE

The WRDI Institute is an Australian consulting firm which specialises in human capital solutions, providing business focused human capital metrics that link people with results. The Institute provides products and services in the following areas:

- Human capital measurement and reporting
- Employment/people management strategies and psychological contracts
- Workforce segmentation based on skills
- Human capital strategic plans and recruitment strategic plans
- Workforce analytics
- Employee engagement and retention surveys
- Talent flight risk assessment
- On-boarding metrics
- Exit interview metrics
- Career development
- Stimulating workshops on the above themes.

With a national network accredited consultants, the Institute's clients include blue chips through to SMEs, across a variety of industries. For further information to: www.wrdi-institute.com.

Bibliography

BIBLIOGRAPHY

INTRODUCTION

CIPD (2003). Voices from the boardroom. *CIPD Press Release, 18 January, 2003.*

DelCampo, R. (2007). Psychological contract violation: An individual difference perspective. *International Journal of Management, 24*(1), 43-52.

Erikson, E. (1969). *Childhood and society*. Middlesex UK: Pelican.

Guest, D. E. (1998). Is the psychological contract worth taking seriously? *Journal of Organisational Behavior, 19*, 649-64.

Hall, B. W. (2008). *The new human capital strategy: Improving the value of your most important investment - year after year*. New York: Amacon.

Lepak, D. P., & Snell, S. A. (1999). The human resource architecture: Toward a theory of human capital allocation and development. *Academy of Management Review, 24*(1), 31-48.

Lepak, D. P., & Snell, S. A. (2002). Examining the human resource architecture: The relationships among human capital, employment, and human resource configurations. *Journal of Management, 28*(4), 517-543.

Schein, E. H. (1978). *Career dynamics: Matching individuals and organisational needs.* Reading, MA: Addison-Wesley.

CHAPTER 1: LOOKING BACK AND EMERGING TRENDS IN THE EMPLOYMENT LANDSCAPE

Bronson, P. (2005). *What should I do with the rest of my life? The true story of people who answered the ultimate question.* New York: Random House.

Dytchwald, K., Erikson, T. J., & Morison, R. (2006). *Workforce crisis: How to beat the coming shortage of skills and talent.* Boston: Harvard Business School Press.

Cascio, W. (2009). *HR lessons from the global financial crisis-building sustainable organisation*. AHRI/Wayne Cascio Masterclass 17th February: Melbourne.

CEDA (2005). *Transitions in Australian labour markets: Initial perspectives.* CEDA Information Paper 8: Melbourne.

Covey, S. (1994). *First things first.* New York: Simon & Schuster.

Evans, C. (2003). *Managing for knowledge: HR's strategic role.* Oxford: Butterworth-Heinemann.

Farr, J. L., & Ringseis, E. L. (2002). The older worker in organisational context: Beyond the individual. In G. P. Hodgkinson & J. K. Ford (Eds.), *International Review of Industrial and Organisational Psychology*, 17 (pp. 31-76). Chichester: Wiley.

Harvey, M. G., Novicevic, M. M., Buckley, M. R., & Ferris, G. R. (2001). A historic perspective on organisational ignorance. *Journal of Managerial Psychology, 16*(5/6), 449-469.

Levinson, D. (1977). The mid-life transition: A period of adult psychosocial development. *Psychiatry, 40*, 99-112.

Levy, L., Carroll, B., Francoeur, J., & Logue, M. (2006). 'The generational mirage? A pilot study into the perceptions of leadership by generation X and Y'. http://au.hudson.com/documents/emp_au_whitepaper_generation_mirage.pdf

Millward, L. J., & Brewerton, P. M. (2000). Psychological contracts: Employee relations for the twenty-first century? In C. L. Cooper & I. Robertson (Eds.), *International Review of Industrial and Organisational Psychology,* 15 (pp. 1-61). Chichester: Wiley.

Nicholson, J., & Nairn, A. (2006). 'The manager of the 21st century: 2020 vision'. www.bcg.com.

Parker, V. A. (1996). Growth-enhancing relationships outside work (GROWS). In D.T. Hall and Associates (Eds.), *The career is dead: Long live the career* (pp. 180-195). San Francisco: Josey-Bass.

Stevens, L. (2000). Incentives for sharing. *Knowledge Management, 3*(10), 54-60.

CHAPTER 2: A LOOK INTO THE WORKPLACE OF THE FUTURE

Buch, K. (1992). Quality circles and employee withdrawl behaviours: A cross functional organisational study. *Journal of Applied Behavioural Science, 28*(1), 62-73.

Dytchwald, K., Erikson, T. J., & Morison, R. (2006). *Workforce crisis: How to beat the coming shortage of skills and talent.* Boston: Harvard Business School Press.

Farr, J. L., & Ringseis, E. L. (2002). The older worker in organisational context: Beyond the individual. In G. P. Hodgkinson & J. K. Ford (Eds.), *International Review of Industrial and Organisational Psychology*, 17 (pp. 31-76). Chichester: Wiley.

Langford, P., H., & Parkes, L., P. (2008). Work-life balance or work-life alignment? A test of the importance of work-life balance for employee engagement and intention to stay in organisations. *Journal of Management and Organisation,* 14, 267-284.

Levinson, D. (1977). The mid-life transition: A period of adult psychosocial development. *Psychiatry, 40*, 99-112.

CHAPTER 3: WORKFORCE SEGMENTATION – DETERMINING EMPLOYMENT STRATEGIES

Beatty, R. W., Becker, B. E., & Huselid, M. A. (2009). *The differentiated workforce: Transforming talent into strategic impact*. Boston: Harvard Business Press.

IBISworld (2008). *Economic outlook & growth industries: 2008 & beyond*. NPA Asia Pacific Conference, 22nd May: Sydney.

Lepak, D. P., & Snell, S. A. (1999). The human resource architecture: Toward a theory of human capital allocation and development. *Academy of Management Review*, *24*(1), 31-48.

Lepak, D. P., & Snell, S. A. (2002). Examining the human resource architecture: The relationships among human capital, employment, and human resource configurations. *Journal of Management*, *28*(4), 517-543.

Cascio, W. F. (1991). *Costing human resources: The financial impact of behavior in organisations*. Boston: PWS-Kent.

Schein, E. H. (1990). *Career anchors: Discovering your real values*. San Francisco: Josey-Bass/Pfeiffer.

CHAPTER 4: ALL YOU EVER WANTED TO KNOW ABOUT HUMAN CAPITAL

Axelrod, E. L., Handfield-Jones, H., & Welsh, T. A. (2001). 'The war for talent part two'. http://www.mckinseyquarterly.com/ab_g.asp?ar=1035&L2=9 -17k

Bassi, L., McGraw, K, & McMurrer, D. (2003). *Beyond quarterly earnings: Using measurement to create sustainable growth*. Human Capital Capability, Inc.

Cascio, W. F. (1991). *Costing human resources: The financial impact of behavior in organisations*. Boston: PWS-Kent.

Cascio, W. F., Young, C. E., & Morris, J. R. (1997). Financial consequences of employment-change decisions in major U.S. corporations. *Academy of Management Journal*, *40* (5), 1175-1189.

CFO Research Services. (2003). *Human capital management: the CFO's perspective*. Boston: CFO Publishing Corp.

Chandler McLeod (2007). 'Employer of choice: A reality check'. http://www.workplacebarometer.com.au/LinkClick.aspx?fileticket=L15jJEdZENM%3d&tabid=987&mid=2175

Chandler McLeod (2008). 'Avoid distressed purchasing with recruitment strategy'. http://www.workplacebarometer.com.au/LinkClick.aspx?fileticket=vgaMCrxB5fI%3d&tabid=987&mid=2184.

CIPD (2003). Voices from the boardroom. *CIPD Press Release, 18 January, 2003.*

Drucker, P. F. (1999). *Management challenges for the 21st century.* New York: Harper Business.

Fitz-enz, J. (2002). Knowledge Capital. *Drake Business Review, 1*(1).

Griffeth, R. W., Hom, P. W., & Gaertner, S. (2000). A meta-analysis of antecedents and correlates of employee turnover: Update, moderator tests, and research implications for the next millennium. *Journal of Management, 26*(3), 463-488.

Jones, T. O, & Sasser, E, (1995). Why satisfied Customers Defect. *Harvard Business Review,* Nov-Dec, 88-99.

Kaplan, R.S., & Norton, D. P. (1996). *The balanced scorecard.* Boston: Harvard Business School Press.

Lavelle, L. (2003). After the jobless recovery, a war for talent. *Business Week,* 3851, 92.

Lee, T. W., Mitchell, T. R., Sablynski, C. J., Burton, J. P., & Holtom, B. C. (2004). The effects on job embeddedness on organisational citizenship, job performance, volitional absences, and voluntary turnover. *Academy of Management Journal, 39,* 5-36.

Patterson, M., West, M., Lawthom, R., & Nickell, S. (1997). Impact of people management practices on business performance. *Issues In People Management No. 22,* IPD: London.

Philpott, J. (2003). CIPD urges Porter to tackle the "Implementation Gap" in UK management. *CIPD Press Release, 22 January.*

Rodgers, K., & Howlett, D. (2002). People, performance, process and profit: A new approach to customer relationship management and human capital. www.websterb.com

Rynes, S. L., Colbert, A. E., & Brown, K. G. 2002. HR professional's beliefs about effective human resource practices: Correspondence between research and practice. *Human Resource Management, 41,* 149-174.

TMP Worldwide Employee Retention Survey, June 2005. htpp://www.tmp.worldwide

Sturman, M. C., Trevor, C. O., Boudreau, J. W., & Gerhart, B. (2003). Is it worth to win the talent war? Evaluating the utility of performance pay. *Personnel Psychology, 56,* 997-1035.

Welch, J. (2005). *Winning.* London: Harper Collins Publishers.

CHAPTER 5: HOW TO DEVELOP AND DISPOSE OF HUMAN CAPITAL

Appelbaum, S. H., Everard, A. & Hung, L. T. S. (1999). Strategic downsizing: Critical success factors. *Management Decision, 37*(7), 535-552.

Cascio, W. F. (2002). *Responsible restructuring: Creative and profitable alternatives to Layoffs*. San Francisco: Berrett-Koehler Publishers.

Chandler McLeod (2007). 'Employer of choice: A reality check'. http://www.workplacebarometer.com.au/LinkClick.aspx?fileticket=L15jJEdZENM%3d&tabid=987&mid=2175

Krueger, A. B., & Mas, A. (2002). 'Strikes, scabs, and tread separations: Labor strife and the production of defective Bridgestone/Firestone Tires'. www.irs.princeton.edu

Meglino, B. M., Ravlin, E. C., & DeNiši, A. S. (1997). When does it hurt to tell the truth? The effect of realistic job reviews on employee recruiting. *Public Personnel Management Volume, 26*(3), 423-422.

Reilly, R. R., Brown, B., Blood, M. R. & Malatesta, C. Z. (1981). The effects of realistic job previews: A study and discussion of the literature. *Personnel Psychology*, 34, 823-834.

Rousseau, D. M. (1995). *Psychological contracts in organisations; Understanding written and unwritten agreements.* California: Sage Publications.

Trevor, C. O., & Nyberg, A. N. (2008). Keeping your headcount when all about you are losing theirs: Downsizing, voluntary turnover rates, and the moderating role of HR practices. *Academy of Management Journal, 51*(2), 259-276.

U.S. Department of Labor, Office of the American Workplace (1995). 'Guide to responsible restructuring'. www.dol.gov/dol/oaw/public/nonregs/publications/respres.htmabout.

CHAPTER 6: ABOUT ENGAGEMENT AND RETENTION: EVERYTHING YOU EVER WANTED TO KNOW

ARHI (2003). *HR: Creating business solutions: A positioning paper*. Joint ARHI & CEDA Publication: Melbourne.

Axelrod, E. L., Handfield-Jones, H., & Welsh, T. A. (2001). 'The war for talent part two'. http://www.mckinseyquarterly.com/ab_g.asp?ar=1035&L2=9-17k

Branham, L. (2005). *The 7 hidden reasons employees leave.* New York: Amacon.

Cappelli, P. (1999). *The new deal at work: Managing the market-driven workforce.* Boston: Harvard Business School Press.

Cascio, W. F. (1991). *Costing human resources: The financial impact of behavior in organisations*. Boston: PWS-Kent.

Chandler McLeod (2008). 'Avoid distressed purchasing with recruitment strategy'.

http://www.workplacebarometer.com.au/LinkClick.aspx?fileticket=vgaMCrxB5fI%3d&tabid=987&mid=2184.

CIPD (2005). 'Recruitment, retention and turnover: Annual survey report (2005)' http://www.cipd.co.uk/surveys

Davidson, B, & Fitz-enz, J. (1997). *Retention management, study released by The Saratoga Institute.* New York: American Management Association.

Glebbeek, A. C., & Bax, E. H. (2004). Is high employee turnover really harmful? An empirical test using company records. *Academy of Management Journal, 47*, 277-286.

Griffeth, R. W., Hom, P. W., & Gaertner, S. (2000). A meta-analysis of antecedents and correlates of employee turnover: Update, moderator tests, and research implications for the next millennium. *Journal of Management*, 26(3), 463-488.

Hackett Best Practices Study (2002). 'Best practices in strategic decision-making'. http://www.tgc.com/dsstar/02/0326/104057.html

Heskett, J., Jones, T, Loveman, G., Sasser, W. E., & Schelesinger, L. (1994). Putting the service –profit chain to work. *Harvard Business Review*, March-April.

Irvine, D. M., & Evans, M. G. (1995). Job satisfaction and turnover among nurses: Integrating research findings across studies. *Nursing Research, 44* (4), 246-253.

Judge, T. A., Thoresen, C. J., Bono, J. E., & Patton, G. K. 2001. The job satisfaction-job performance relationship: A qualitative and quantitative review. *Psychological Bulletin, 127*(3), 376-407.

Kacmar, K. M., Andrews, M. C., Rooy, D. L., Steilberg, R. C., & Cerrone, S. (2006). Sure everyone can be replaced....but at what cost? Turnover as a predictor of unit-level performance. *Academy of Management Journal*, 73, 265-283.

Lee, T., & Mitchell, T. (1994). An alternative approach: The unfolding model of voluntary employee turnover. *Academy of Management Review, 19*, 51-89.

Mercer Delta, (2006). Executive Onboarding Research Summary of Effective Practices.

Meyer, J. P., Paunonen, S. V., Gellatly, I. R., Goffin, R. D., & Jackson, D. N. (1989). Organisational commitment and job performance: It's the nature of the commitment that counts. *Journal of Applied Psychology, 74*(1), 152-156.

Noer, D. M. (1995). *Healing the wounds: Overcoming the trauma of layoffs and revitalizing downsized organisations*. U.K.: John Wiley & Sons.

Patterson, M., West, M., Lawthom, R., & Nickell, S. (1997). Impact of people management practices on business performance. *Issues In People Management No. 22*, IPD: London.

Pryor, L. (2008). *The pin striped prison: How over achievers get trapped in corporate jobs they hate*. Sydney: Pan Macmillan.

Reichheld, F. E. (1996). *The loyalty effect: the hidden force behind growth, profits, and lasting value.* Boston: Harvard Business School Press.

Rynes, S. L., Gerhart, B., & Parks, L. 2005. Personnel psychology: Performance evaluation and pay-for-performance. In Kasdin (Eds.), *Annual Review of Psychology, 56* (571-600). Palo Alto, CA: Annual Reviews.

Shaw, J. D., Gupta, N., & Delery, J. E. (2005). Alternative conceptualizations of the relationship between voluntary turnover and organisational performance. *Academy of Management Journal, 48*, 50-68.

Sullivan, J. (7th May 2004). *Make HR a profit centre – Metrics for the new HR*. Seminar: Melbourne.

Tett, R. P., & Meyer, J. P. (1993). Job satisfaction, organizational commitment, turnover intention, and turnover: Path analyses based on meta-analytical findings. *Personnel Psychology, 46*, 259-293.

CHAPTER 7: ABOUT THE PSYCHOLOGICAL CONTRACT

Anderson, N., & Schalk, R. (1998). The psychological contract in retrospect and prospect. *Journal of Organizational Behavior, 19*, 637-647.

Anderson, N., & Thomas, H. D. (1996). Work group socialization. In M. A. West (Ed.), *Handbook of work group psychology* (pp. 443-450). Chichester: John Wiley & Sons.

Armstrong-Stassen, M. (2002). Designated redundant but escapoing lay-off: A special group of lay-off survivors. *Journal of Occupational and Organisational Psychology, 75*, 1-13.

Batt, R. (2002). Managing customer services: Human resource practices, and quit rates, and sales growth. *Academy of Management Journal, 45*, 587-597.

Berg, T. R. (1991). The importance of equity perception and job satisfaction in predicting employee intent to stay at television stations. *Group and Organisation Studies, 16*(3), 268-284.

Branham, L. (2005). *The 7 hidden reasons employees leave.* New York: Amacon.

Cascio,W. F. (1991). *Costing human resources:The financial impact of behavior in organisations.* Boston: PWS-Kent.

CIPD (2005). 'Recruitment, retention and turnover: Annual survey report (2005)'. http://www.cipd.co.uk/surveys

Cohen-Charash, Y., & Spector, P. E. (2001). The role of justics in organisations: A meta-analysis. *Organisational Behaviour and Human Decision Processes, 89*, 1-44.

Colquitt, J. A., Conlon, D. E., Wesson, M. J., Porter, C. O. L. H., & Ng, K. Y. (2001). Justice at the millenium: A Meta-analytical review of 25 years of organisational justice researc. *Journal of Applied Psychology, 86*, 425-445.

Dahlgaard, J. J., Kristensen, K., & Kanji, G. K. (1998). *Fundamentals of total quality management.* London: Chapman & Hall.

Dansereau, F., Graen, G., & Haga, W. J. (1975). A vertical dyad linkage approach to leadership within formal organisations. *Organisational Behaviour and Human Performance, 13*, 45-78.

Davenport, T. H., & Prusak, L. (2000). *Working knowledge: How organisations manage what they know.* Boston: Harvard Business School Press.

DelCampo, R. (2007). Psychological contract violation: An individual difference perspective. *International Journal of Management, 24*(1), pp. 43-52.

Eisenberger, R., Faolo, P., & David-LaMastro, V. (1990). Perceived organisational support and employee diligence, commitment and motivation. *Journal of Applied Psychology, 75*(1), 51-59.

Freese, C. & Schalk, R. (1996). Implications of differences in psychological contracts for Human Resources Management. *European Journal of Work and Organizational Psychology, 5* (4), 501-509.

Gladwell, M. (2008). *Outliers: The story of success.* Maryborough: Allen Lane.

Guest, D. E. (1998). Is the psychological contract worth taking seriously? *Journal of Organisational Behavior, 19*, 649-64.

Guest, D. E., & Conway, N. (1997). Motivation and the psychological contract. *Issues In People Management No. 2,* IPD: London.

Guzzo, R. A., Noonan, K. A., & Elron, E. (1994). Expatriate managers and the psychological contract. *Journal of Applied Psychology, 79*, 673-677.

Hislop, D. (2003). Linking human resource management and knowledge management via commitment: A review and research agenda. *Employee Relations, 25*(2), 182-202.

Irvine, D. M., & Evans, M. G. (1995). Job satisfaction and turnover among nurses: Integrating research findings across studies. *Nursing Research, 44*(4), 246-253.

Judge, T. A., Thoresen, C. J., Bono, J. E., & Patton, G. K. 2001. The job satisfaction-job performance relationship: A qualitative and quantitative review. *Psychological Bulletin, 127*(3), 376-407.

Kalleberg, A. L., & Reve, T. (1992). Contracts and commitment: Economic and Sociological perspectives on employment relationships. *Human Relations, 45*(9), 1103-1132.

Knudsen, H. K., Johnson, J. A., Martin, J. K., & Roman, P. M. (2003). Downsizing survival: The experience of work and organisational commitment. *Sociological Inquiry, 73*, 265-283.

Mathieu, J. E., & Zajac, D. M. (1990). A review and meta-analysis of the antecedents, correlates, and consequences of organisational commitment. *Psychological Bulletin, 108*, 171-194.

Makin, P., Cooper, G., & Cox, C. (1996). *Organisations and the psychological contract: Managing people at work.* Manchester: The British Psychological Society.

McNiece, D. (2004). Company Director, 21(11).

Meyer, J. P., Paunonen, S. V., Gellatly, I. R., Goffin, R. D., & Jackson, D. N. (1989). Organisational commitment and job performance: It's the nature of the commitment that counts. *Journal of Applied Psychology, 74*(1), 152-56.

Millward, L. J., & Hopkins, L. J. (1998). Psychological contracts, organisational and job commitment. *Journal of Applied Social Psychology, 28*, 1530-1556.

Morris, J., & Steers, R. (1980). Structural influences on organisational commitment. *Journal of Vocational Behaviour, 17*, 50-57.

Mowday, R. T., Porter, L. W., & Steers, R. M. (1982). *Employee – organisational linkages*. New York: Academic Press.

Muchinsky, P. M. (2000). *Psychology applied to work (sixth edition)*. California: Wadsworth Thomson Learning.

Murphy, K. R. (2005). *I/O Psychology's Greatest Hits and Misses*. Keynote address at the I/O Conference, Gold Coast.

O'Reilly, C., & Chatman, J. (1986). Organisational commitment and psychological attachment: The effects of compliance, identification, and internalization on prosocial behavior. *Journal of Applied Psychology, 71*, 492-499.

Robinson, S. L., Kraatz, M. S., & Rousseau, D. M. (1994). Changing obligations and the psychological contract: A longitudinal study. *Academy of Management Journal, 37*(1), 137-52.

Robinson, S. L., & Morrison, E. W. (1995). Psychological contracts and OCB: The effect of unfulfilled obligations on civic virtue behavior. *Journal of Organisational Behavior, 16*, 289-298.

Robinson, S. L., & Rousseau, D. M. (1994). Violating the psychological contract: Not the exception but the norm. *Journal of Organisational Behavior, 15*, 245-259.

Rotondi, T. (1975). Organisational identification and group involvement. *Academy of Management Journal, 18*, 892-897.

Schalk, R., Freeze, C., & Van den Bosch, J. (1995). Het psychologisch contract van part-timers en full-timers, *Gedrag en Organisatic*, *8*, 307-317.

Schein, E. H. (1978). *Career dynamics: Matching individuals and organizational needs*. Reading, MA: Addison-Wesley.

Shankar, G., & Weitz, B. A. (1996). The impact of staffing policies on retail buyer job attitudes and behaviors. *Journal of Retailing*, *72*(1), 31-56.

Steel, R. P., & Ovalle, N. K. (1984). A review and meta-analysis of research on the relationship between behavioral intentions and employee turnover. *Journal of Applied Psychology*, *69*, 673-86.

Stevens, J. M., Beyer, J., & Trice, H. M. (1978). Assessing personal, role, and organisational predictors of managerial commitment. *Academy of Management Journal*, *2*, 380-396.

Tett, R. P., & Meyer, J. P. (1993). Job satisfaction, organisational commitment, turnover intention, and turnover: Path analyses based on meta-analytical findings. *Personnel Psychology, 46*, 259-293.

Trevor, C. O., & Nyberg, A. N. (2008). Keeping your headcount when all about you are losing theirs: Downsizing, voluntary turnover rates, and the moderating role of HR practices. *Academy of Management Journal*, *51*(2), 259-276.

CHAPTER 8: THE PSYCHOLOGICAL CONTRACT AND HUMAN CAPITAL

Anderson, P., & Pulich, M. (2000). Retaining good employees in tough times. *The Health Care Manager*, *19* (1), 50-58.

Buchholtz, A. K., Ribbens, B. A., & Houle I, T. (2003). The role of human capital in post acquisition CEO departure. *Academy of Management Journal*, *46*(4), 506-514.

Chandler McLeod (2007). 'Employer of Choice: A reality cheque'. http://www.workplacebarometer.com.au/LinkClick.aspx?fileticket=L15jJEdZENM%3d&tabid=987&mid=2175

Chartered Institute of Personnel Development (2004). 'Employee absence 2004: A survey of management policy and practice'. http://www.cipd. co.uk/surveys

Furnham, A., & Taylor, J. (2004). *The dark side of behaviour at work.* New York: Palgrave Macmillan.

Haslam, S. A. (2001). *Psychology in organisations: The social identity approach.* London: Sage.

Heriot, P. (1992). *The career management challenge.* London: Sage.

Pearce, J., & Henderson, G. (2000). Understanding acts of betrayal. In C. Cooper and I. Roberston (Eds.) *International Review of Industrial and Organisational Psychology, 15* (pp. 163-87). New York: Wiley.

PricewaterhoursCoopers (2003). *Economic crime survey*. London: PricewaterhouseCoopers

Reilly, A. H., Brett, J. M., & Stroh, L. K. (1993). The impact of corporate turbulence on manager's attitudes. *Strategic Management Journal, 14*, 167-179.

Rousseau, D. M. (1995). *Psychological contracts in organisations; Understanding written and unwritten agreements.* California: Sage Publications.

Trevor, C. O., & Nyberg, A. N. (2008). Keeping your headcount when all about you are losing theirs: Downsizing, voluntary turnover rates, and the moderating role of HR practices. *Academy of Management Journal, 51*(2), 259-276.

CHAPTER 9: MEASURING AND REPORTING HUMAN CAPITAL

Nicholson, J., & Nairn, A. (2006). 'The manager of the 21st century: 2020 vision'. www.bcg.com

APPENDIX A

Erikson, E. (1969). *Childhood and Society*. Middlesex UK: Pelican.

Jaffre, A. (1963). *Memories, dreams, reflections of Carl Jung*. Toronto: Random House.

APPENDIX B

Arthur, M. B. & Rousseau, D. M. (1996). A career lexicon for the 21st century. *Academy of Management Executive, 10*(4), 28-39.

Hakim, C. (1994). *We are all self-employed: The new contract in a changing world of work*. San Francisco: Berrett-Koehler Publishers.

APPENDIX C

Beatty, R. W., Becker, B. E., & Huselid, M. A. (2009). *The differentiated workforce: Transforming talent into strategic impact.* Boston: Harvard Business Press.

APPENDIX E

Guest, D. E. (1998). Is the psychological contract worth taking seriously? *Journal of Organisational Behavior, 19*, 649-64.

INDEX

A

B

C

D

E

I

J

K

L

M

N

O

U

V

W

Colin Beames

BA (Hons) Qld, BEng (Hons), MBA, MAPS,
Corporate Psychologist

Colin Beames is a thought leader in the measurement and reporting of human capital, workplace trends, employee engagement and retention and careers, with a deep and expansive knowledge of these subjects. He is the Director of the WRDI Institute, an Australian boutique consultancy firm which specialises in the development, commercialisation and provision of a range of innovative human capital products, tools, services and resources.

Colin's organisational consultancy experience includes assignments in Australia and overseas, both in the private and public sectors. Industries in which Colin has worked include the: agricultural distribution and export, agricultural research, banking and finance, biotechnology research, building and construction, information technology, insurance, health, manufacturing, retail, resources, and tourism industries.